THE INTERNATIONAL HANDBOOK OF LABOUR UNIONS

T0319549

The International Handbook of Labour Unions

Responses to Neo-Liberalism

Edited by

Gregor Gall
University of Hertfordshire, UK

Adrian Wilkinson
Griffith University, Australia

Richard Hurd
Cornell University, USA

Edward Elgar
Cheltenham, UK • Northampton, MA, USA

Published by
Edward Elgar Publishing Limited
The Lypiatts
15 Lansdown Road
Cheltenham
Glos GL50 2JA
UK

Edward Elgar Publishing, Inc.
William Pratt House
9 Dewey Court
Northampton
Massachusetts 01060
USA

This book has been printed on demand to keep the title in print.

A catalogue record for this book is available from the British Library

Library of Congress Control Number: 2011928596

ISBN   978 1 84844 862 9 (cased)
        978 0 85793 882 4 (paperback)

Typeset by Cambrian Typesetters, Camberley, Surrey

Printed and bound in Great Britain by
Marston Book Services Limited, Didcot

Contents

Contributors

Sarah Ashwin is Professor of Industrial Relations in the Employment Relations and Organisational Behaviour group of the Management Department at the London School of Economics. She has been studying the Russian workers' movement and trade unions since 1991. Her publications on the subject include *Russian Workers: The Anatomy of Patience* (Manchester University Press, 1999) and *Russian Trade Unions and Industrial Relations in Transition* (co-authored with Simon Clarke, Palgrave, 2003).

Dr Maurizio Atzeni is Lecturer in Labour and Industrial Relations, Loughborough University, and Research Fellow at the Centre for Industrial Relations, University of Cagliari, Italy, and at the Centre for Labour Investigation (CEIL-Piette/Conicet), Buenos Aires, Argentina. He coordinates with Pablo Ghigliani the research network Labouragain at the International Institute of Social History, Amsterdam, the Netherlands. His recent publications include a research monograph on labour conflict in Argentina (Palgrave, 2010), an edited collection on alternative work organisations (Palgrave, 2011), several book chapters on unionism in Argentina and journal articles on workers' collective action for the *Industrial Relations Journal* and on workers' self-management for *Work, Employment and Society*.

Janis Bailey is Associate Professor in the Department of Employment Relations and Human Resources, Griffith University, Gold Coast, Australia. Her recent publications include articles on school-aged workers published and forthcoming in *Journal of Industrial Relations*, *Australian Bulletin of Labour*, *Industrial Relations Journal* and *Work, Employment and Society*, and articles on the intersection of labour and environmental history published in *Labour History*. She is co-editor of a forthcoming book on young people at work (Ashgate, 2011) with co-authors Robin Price, Paula McDonald and Barbara Pini. In 2009, she carried out research for the Liquor, Hospitality and Miscellaneous Workers' Union regarding a pay claim for ambulance officers, and was an expert witness in the subsequent Industrial Commission hearing, and in 2007 co-authored major commissioned reports on the effects of Australia's WorkChoices legislation on low-paid women workers.

David Beale is a Visiting Research Fellow and was formerly a Lecturer in Employment Studies at Manchester Business School, University of

Manchester. His work on union responses to new management practices and restructuring has been published in the *British Journal of Industrial Relations*, *Industrial Relations Journal* and *Employee Relations*. He was awarded a PhD from the University of Manchester Institute of Science and Technology in 2000 on this subject and is currently working with Ernesto Noronha on a project about public sector trade unions and the challenges they face in two Indian states. He has considerable experience as a workplace union representative and branch officer, as well as in wider labour movement organisations and campaigns, and worked for ten years as a union education tutor. Another – and at times overlapping – research interest of his is workplace harassment and bullying, with his work with Helge Hoel published in the *British Journal of Industrial Relations*, *European Journal of Industrial Relations* and *Work, Employment and Society*.

Bob Bruno is Professor of Labor and Employment Relations and Director of Labor Education Program School of Labor and Employment Relations, University of Illinois, Urbana–Champaign, IL, US. He is author of *Justified by Work: Identity and the Meaning of Faith in Chicago's Working-Class Churches* (Ohio State University Press, 2008), *Reforming the Chicago Teamsters: The Local 705 Story* (Northern Illinois University Press, 2003) and *Steelworker Alley: How Class Works in Youngstown* (Cornell University Press, 1999). He has published in *Labor History*, *Labor Studies Journal*, *Advances in Industrial and Labor Relations*, *Journal of Labor Research*, *Working USA: The Journal of Labor and Society* and is co-editor of *Labor Studies Journal*.

Dae-oup Chang is a Senior Lecturer in Development Studies in the Department of Development Studies, School of Oriental and African Studies (SOAS), London. His research interests include labour relations in East Asia, political economy of East Asian development and critique of the developmental state. His current research aims to investigate East Asia's place in global capitalist development by analysing changing capital-labour relations in East Asian countries, regional integration of East Asia and its implication for the globalising circuit of capital. In so doing, he has been working with a wide range of labour organisations including Asia Monitor Resource Centre, Asian TNCs Monitoring Network, Building and Wood Workers International, and other national union federations and grass-root labour NGOs in Asia. His recent publications include *Capitalist Development in Korea: Labour, Capital and the Myth of the Developmental State* (Routledge, 2009) and 'Informalising labour in Asia's global factory' in *Journal of Contemporary Asia* (2009, 39/2).

Sylvie Contrepois is Senior European Researcher at London Metropolitan

University's Working Lives Research Institute, and a member of the CRESPPA CNRS Institute in Paris, France. She is a specialist in French industrial relations. In 2003, she published her PhD on the practices and strategies of French unions as 'Syndicats, la nouvelle donne. Enquête au cœur d'un bassin industriel'. She recently co-edited *Globalising Employment Relations: Multinational Firms and Central and Eastern Europe Transitions* (Palgrave, 2010) and *Changing Work and Community Identities* (Palgrave, 2011).

Dr Fang Lee Cooke is Professor of Human Resource Management and Chinese Studies at the Department of Management, Faculty of Business and Economics, Monash University, Australia. Previously, she was Professor at Manchester Business School, University of Manchester. Her research interests are in the areas of employment relations, gender and employment, diversity management, strategic HRM, knowledge management and innovation, outsourcing, Chinese outward FDI and employment of Chinese migrants. Fang is the author of *HRM, Work and Employment in China* (Routledge, 2005), *Competition, Strategy and Management in China* (Palgrave Macmillan, 2008), and *Human Resource Management in China: New Trends and Practices* (Routledge, 2011). Cooke is also the co-editor (with Chris Rowley) of *The Changing Face of Management in China* (Routledge, 2010). She has a developing interest in HRM and employment relations issues in India and in Asia more broadly. Her studies on diversity management, innovation and HRM in India have been published in *Human Resource Management* (with Debi Saini, 2010).

Dr Pauline Dibben is a Senior Lecturer at the University of Sheffield. Published volumes include a co-authored textbook *Employment Relations: A Critical and International Approach* (CIPD, 2011) and two co-edited collections, *Contesting Public Sector Reforms: Critical Perspectives: International Debates* (Palgrave, 2004) and *Modernising Work in Public Services: Redefining Roles and Relationships in Britain's Changing Workplace* (Palgrave, 2007). Dibben has also published in the field of employment relations, job security and public sector reform in journals such as *Work, Employment and Society*, *Journal of World Business*, *British Journal of Management* and *Public Administration*.

Dr Heiner Dribbusch is a Senior Researcher with the Institute of Economic and Social Research (WSI) within the Hans-Boeckler-Stiftung in Düsseldorf, Germany. His major research areas are industrial relations and trade unionism with a special focus on union organising, collective bargaining and industrial action. His major publications in English are 'German trade unions between neoliberal restructuring, social partnership and internationalism' in *Labour* *and the Challenges of Globalization: What Prospect for International Solidarity?* (Pluto Press, 2008) and 'The end of an era: structural changes in German public sector collective bargaining' in *Industrial Relations in the New Europe: Enlargement, Integration and Reform* (Edward Elgar, 2007), both of which are co-authored with Thorsten Schulten. He is co-editor of *Strikes Around the World, 1968–2005: Case Studies of 15 Countries* (Aksant, 2007).

Bill Fletcher Jr is a Senior Scholar with the Institute for Policy Studies, the immediate past President of TransAfrica Forum, and the co-founder of the Center for Labor Renewal. He served as the Belle Zeller Visiting Professor at Brooklyn College-City University of New York from 2005–2007. He is co-author (with Dr Fernando Gapasin) of *Solidarity Divided* which analyses the crisis in organised labour in the US. He is co-author (with Peter Agard) of *The Indispensible Ally: Black Workers and the Formation of the Congress of Industrial Organizations, 1934–1941*, a pictorial examination. Fletcher has served in the union movement as a grassroots activist, organiser/representative, and as a senior staff person.

Dr Gregor Gall is Research Professor of Industrial Relations and Director of the Work and Employment Research Unit at the University of Hertfordshire. He was previously Professor of Industrial Relations at the University of Stirling. Gall is the author of *The Meaning of Militancy? Postal Workers and Industrial Relations* (Ashgate, 2003), *The Political Economy of Scotland: Red Scotland? Radical Scotland?* (University of Wales Press, 2005), *Sex Worker Union Organising* (Palgrave, 2006), *Labour Unionism in the Financial Services Sector: Fighting for Rights and Representation* (Ashgate, 2008) and *Tommy Sheridan: From Hero to Zero? A Political Biography* (Welsh Academic Press, 2011). He is also the editor of four volumes on union organising (Routledge 2003, 2005, Palgrave 2009, 2009) and editor of forthcoming volumes on anti-unionism, and new forms of workplace conflict. He has written a fortnightly column in the *Morning Star*, the daily newspaper of the labour movement in Britain, since 2005, and has carried out commissioned research for a number of unions like Connect, FBU and PCS.

Pablo Ghigliani is a full-time Researcher at the Consejo Nacional de Investigaciones Científicas y Técnicas (CONICET) and Professor of Social History in the Universidad Nacional de La Plata, Argentina. He is author of *The Politics of Privatisation and Trade Union Mobilisation: The Electricity Industry in the UK and Argentina* (Peter Lang, 2010).

Richard Hurd is Professor of Labor Studies and ILR Associate Dean for External Relations, Cornell University, Ithaca, NY, US. He has worked closely with labour organisations, developing training programmes and offering technical assistance on strategic issues, including trade union management, organisational change, internal and external organising, strategic planning, and leadership development. He has co-edited three volumes published by Cornell University Press, *Rekindling the Movement* (2001), *Beyond the Organizing Model* (1998) and *Restoring the Promise of American Labor Law* (1994) as well as publishing extensively in journals like *Industrial and Labor Relation Review* and the *Labor Studies Journal* and those with a practitioner orientation like *New Labor Forum*, *Perspectives on Work* and *Working USA*.

John Kelly is Professor of Industrial Relations, Department of Management, Birkbeck College, University of London and previously worked at the London School of Economics. His main areas of research are comparative labour relations, unions and industrial relations theory and recent publications include *Ethical Socialism and the Trade Unions: Allan Flanders and the Reform of British Industrial Relations* (Routledge 2010), *Rethinking Industrial Relations* (Routledge, 1998) and the co-authored *Parties, Elections and Policy Reforms in Western Europe: Voting for Social Pacts* (Routledge, 2011), *Varieties of Unionism* (OUP, 2004) and *Union Organization and Activity* (Routledge, 2004). In addition, he has published in a wide range of journals including the *British Journal of Industrial Relations, Comparative Political Studies, European Journal of Industrial Relations* and *Industrial Relations.*

John McIlroy is Professor of Employment Relations at Middlesex University Business School. He was formerly Reader in Sociology at The University of Manchester and Professor of Industrial Relations at Keele University. He has recently co-edited *Histories of Labour: National and International Perspectives* (Merlin Press, 2010), *Trade Unions in a Neoliberal World* (Routledge (paperback), 2010), *Making History: Organisations of Labour Historians in Britain* (Maney Publishing, 2010) and *Industrial Politics and the 1926 Mining Lockout* (University of Wales Press, second edition, 2009). His articles have appeared in periodicals from *Past and Present* and the *Journal of Contemporary History* to the *British Journal of Industrial Relations, Industrial Relations Journal, Industrial Law Journal*, the *New Statesman* and *Marxism Today*. For 25 years, he organised and taught classes for trade unionists and published extensively on educational issues. He is Secretary of the Society for the Study of Labour History.

Ronaldo Munck is Head of Civic and Global Engagement, Dublin City University, Ireland, and visiting Professor of Sociology at the University of Liverpool. He has written widely on international labour issues from a critically engaged perspective from *The New International Labour Studies* (Zed, 1988) to *Globalisation and Labour: The New 'Great Transformation'* (Zed, 2002) as well as on Latin America in for example *Argentina: From Anarchism to Peronism – Workers, Unions and Politics, 1855–1985* (Zed, 1987). More recently his work has focused on labour migration issues with publications including *Globalisation and Migration: New Issue, New Politics* (Routledge, 2009) and a special issue of *Globalizations* (2011) on globalisation, informal labour and migration. Currently, he is working on a major transnational project on the way unions have responded to the new migrant 'precariat'. He is editor of an open access e-journal on migration in Ireland, www.translocations.ie.

Ernesto Noronha has a PhD from the Tata Institute of Social Sciences, Mumbai, India, and is currently a Professor at the Indian Institute of Management, Ahmedabad, Gujarat, India. His academic interests include technology and work, labour and globalisation, organisation control, unionisation, ethnicity and diversity at the workplace and research methodology. Besides being a contributor to various international journals he has published two books, *Employee Identity in Indian Call Centres: The Notion of Professionalism* (Sage, 2009, co-authored with Premilla D'Cruz) and *Ethnicity in Industrial Organisations: Case of Two Organisations in Mumbai* (Rawat, 2005). He contributed to research on the Indian ITES-BPO sector with the current work examining the experiences of lawyers and engineers working in the knowledge process outsourcing organisation in India. Given his interest in the issues of informal labour, he has been photographing the working lives of people in the brick kilns of Ahmedabad.

David Peetz is Professor of Employment Relations, Griffith University, Gold Coast, Australia. He previously worked at the Australian National University and in the then Commonwealth Department of Industrial Relations. He has been a consultant for the International Labour Organization in Thailand, Malaysia and China, and undertaken work for unions, employers and governments. He is author of *Brave New Workplace: How Individual Contracts are Changing Our Jobs* (Allen and Unwin, 2006) and *Unions in a Contrary World: The Future Of The Australian Trade Union Movement* (Cambridge University Press, 1998).

Dr Thorsten Schulten is Senior Researcher with the Institute of Economic and Social Research (WSI) within the Hans-Boeckler-Stiftung in Düsseldorf, Germany. His major research areas are international political economy, industrial relations, wage policy and collective bargaining, and European integration. His major publications in English are 'Towards a European minimum wage policy? Fair wages and Social Europe' in the *European Journal of Industrial Relations* (14(4): 421–39), and 'Liberalisation and Privatisation of Public Services and Strategic Options for European Trade Unions' in *Transfer – European Review of Labour and Research* (14(2): 295–312, with Torsten Brandt and Christoph Hermann).

Richard L. Trumka was elected President of the American Federation of Labour and Congress of Industrial Organizations (AFl–CIO) in 2009 after serving for 14 years as its Secretary Treasurer. A member of its Executive Council since 1989, Trumka chaired the Strategic Approaches and Capital Stewardship Committees and was instrumental in developing tactics to rally the support of international labour on behalf of US workers struggling for workplace justice against multinational conglomerates. When first elected to the AFL-CIO, Trumka was serving his third term as President of the United Mine Workers of America (UMWA). A third generation coal miner from Pennsylvania, Trumka began working in the mines at age 19 and soon became an activist in the Miners for Democracy reform movement. As UMWA president, he led the union in one of the most successful strikes in recent American history against the Pittston Coal Company resulting in significant advances in enhanced mine workers' job security, pensions and benefits. While working in the mines, Trumka attended Pennsylvania State University where he received his BS degree. In 1974, he earned a law degree from Villanova University.

Lowell Turner is Professor of International and Comparative Labor in the School of Industrial and Labor Relations, at Cornell University, Ithaca, NY, US. His most recent book, co-edited with Daniel Cornfield, is *Labor in the New Urban Battlegrounds: Local Solidarity in a Global Economy* (ILR, 2007). He is also the author of *Democracy at Work: Changing World Markets and the Future of Labor Unions* (ILR, 1991) and *Fighting for Partnership: Labor and Politics in Unified Germany* (Cornell, 1998); and co-editor with Richard Hurd and Harry Katz of *Rekindling the Movement: Labor's Quest for Relevance in the 21st Century* (ILR, 2001). His article 'Institutions and activism: crisis and opportunity for a German labor movement in decline' in *Industrial and Labor Relations Review* in 2009 won the James Scoville Best International/Comparative Paper Award from the Labor and Employment Relations Association in 2010. Prior to entering academia, he was shop steward, chief steward and branch editor for the National Association of Letter Carriers in San Francisco.

Adrian Wilkinson is Professor of Employment Relations, Griffith University, Gold Coast, Australia, and Director of its Centre for Work, Organisation and Wellbeing. He has written nine books and over 100 articles in refereed journals, as well as numerous book chapters and other papers. His books (with co-authors) include *Making Quality Critic*al (Routledge, 1995), *Managing Quality and Human Resources* (Blackwell, 1997), *Managing with TQM: Theory and Practice* (Macmillan, 1998), *Understanding Work and Employment: Industrial Relations in Transition* (Oxford University Press, 2003), *Human Resource Management at Work* (Chartered Institute of Personnel and Development, 2008), *Contemporary Human Resource Management* (3rd edn, Pearson, 2009), *The Sage Handbook of Human Resource Management* (Sage, 2009) and *The Oxford Handbook of Organisational Participation* (OUP, 2010).

Geoffrey Wood is Professor in Human Resource Management at the University of Sheffield. Previously, he was Professor and Director of Research at Middlesex University Business School. He has also held visiting fellowships at Cranfield University, Victoria University of Wellington, New Zealand, the American University in Cairo, Egypt, Cornell University, Ithaca, NY and Rhodes University, Grahamstown, South Africa. He has served as Commissioned Researcher for the South African Truth and Reconciliation Commission. He is also Visiting Professor, Nelson Mandela University. He is co-editor of *Modernising Work in Public Services* (Palgrave, 2007), *Industrial Relations in Africa* (Palgrave, 2007), *Institutions, Production and Working Life* (Oxford University Press, 2006) and *Trade Unions and Democracy* (Manchester University Press, 2004).

1 Labour unionism and neo-liberalism

Gregor Gall, Richard Hurd and Adrian Wilkinson

INTRODUCTION

The widely televised and subsequently reported upon 'Battle of Seattle', a large scale conflagration at the scene of the World Trade Organization meeting in 1999, has become known for the 'unity of the Teamsters and the turtles' in opposing neo-liberalism. This epithet signified the hitherto unknown alliance of organised labour – labour unions[1] – with the environmental protection movement. To the wider public throughout the world, this must have seemed like the first major, visible act by organised labour against not just the effects (or symptoms) of neo-liberalism but also in a sense their cause too (in terms of the global institutions associated with neo-liberalism). However, there are a number of paradoxes involved here. First, while organised labour's policy and ensuing behaviour towards neo-liberalism have developed and expanded since 1999, the 'Battle of Seattle' was not organised labour's first foray into this arena. Rather, the 'Battle of Seattle' has a pre-history as well as a post-history and this is what we intend to explore and analyse in the chapters of this handbook. Second, and just as importantly, what is also vital to demonstrate and then explore is that such a high profile event as the 'Battle of Seattle' does not adequately portray the diversity of the range of labour union responses to neo-liberalism. For example, in the United States many major labour unions have willingly cooperated with the drive towards neo-liberalism, and within this context have sought to safeguard US workers' interests to the detriment of other workers elsewhere – even though or alongside the AFL-CIO rhetorically opposing neo-liberalism since the mid-1990s. To the extent that other labour unions in the United States have opposed free trade and the Bush (2001–2009) administration's economic policies did not necessarily imply opposition to neo-liberalism *per se* but rather a certain type of neo-liberalism and its effects at a certain point in time. In other words, most US unions have operated within the confines of neo-liberalism without mounting an ideological or political challenge to it, effective or otherwise. Thus, this handbook will not just examine labour union opposition and resistance to neo-liberalism but also labour support for and acquiescence with neo-liberalism.

The term neo-liberalism is a relatively recent arrival to the lexicon of popular discourse, and is not an appellation which neo-liberals use to describe

themselves. So our first task in this introductory chapter is to lay out a definition of neo-liberalism and to present an overview as to what the implications
of this are for workers and for their labour unions. From here, we make an
appraisal of their relative effectiveness. Then, we outline a schema for cate-
gorising and understanding the responses of labour unions to neo-liberalism.
This is an aid to identifying and accounting for the variation in their responses,
responses which are derived from an interaction of constituency of interests
and ideology (forming the basis of intention to act or react) and played out
through processes and outcomes with other actors (employers, states, NGOs
and so on). Finally, we give an overview of the structure and content of the
handbook, not so much by summarising what they do as individual chapters
but rather what the sums of their parts represent.

NEO-LIBERALISM

Neo-liberalism is a contemporary ideology based on historical economic liberalism which favours a minimised role for the state and a maximised role for the
market (the private business sector) in the belief that the market is: (a) the most
efficient and equitable distributor of resources and rewards; (b) the best guar-
antor of economic growth; and (c) the most able protector of individual liberty.
In other words, anything that 'crowds out the market' is an impediment to the
realisation of these outcomes. In this vein, economic growth and higher living
standards for citizens are seen as directly linked to neo-liberalism because
economic liberty and freedom would lead to more capital investment and
greater output. Equally important, economic freedom is viewed as a precursor
to political democracy. Thus, the attainment of anything approximating to
social justice or decent, civilised and humane living standards for the majority
of citizens in each society is argued to be bound up with this process. In this
sense, neo-liberalism is not the open repudiation of the pursuit of social justice
and redistribution of wealth and resources for it is posed as the great leveller
for all citizens, even if the spoils of growth are distributed on a very uneven
basis as per the process of *de facto* trickledown economics.

Neo-liberalism is thus bound up in a language and discourse of markets,
market efficiency, labour market flexibility, and consumer choice where risk
is shifted from governments and corporations onto individuals. Therefore, its
principal means of operation are privatisation, marketisation, liberalisation,
deregulation, and reductions in state spending. Where it differs critically from
classical economic liberalism of the era of Adam Smith and David Riccardo is
that it no longer holds that price is determined by the labour theory of value,
whereby price is to be constructed by the amount of labour time used to
produce a good or service. Rather, price is determined by what the market will

bear and what individuals are prepared to pay in terms of the laws of human desire and supply and demand. This change in value theory arose in the 1880s with the rise of the Austrian school and the development of utility theory.

There is a sense that neo-liberalism, for good or for ill, has increasingly swept away all pre-existing forms of economic activity. While an exaggeration, part of this perspective is an erroneous conflation of neo-liberalism with globalisation, not least because globalisation arguably predates neo-liberalism even though neo-liberalism has a pedigree extending back before the establishment of the post-war settlement – and because there are many different types of globalisation (Guillen 2001), of which the neo-liberal version is only one, albeit now the dominant one. Indeed, one could think of better appellations such as globalised neo-liberalism or neo-liberal globalisation for the phenomenon with which this handbook is concerned. Nonetheless, an overview of the literature by Guillen (2001) stressed that such globalised forces like neo-liberalism should neither be regarded as omnipotent nor as omnipresent, not least because of the counter-pressures and trajectories led by nation states. Obvious examples would include Cuba, Venezuela, contra Argentina and Brazil in Latin America.

The wider point that also emerges here is that neo-liberalism is not predicated upon the decline of the power and authority of the nation state, but rather the use of the nation state by internal and external forces to promote and implement neo-liberalism for international institutions like the World Bank, the International Monetary Fund, the World Trade Organization *et al.*, dating from the Bretton Woods era, as advocates and agents for neo-liberalism are insufficient in themselves to effectively promulgate neo-liberalism. Given the centrality of the nation state to the neo-liberal project, different outcomes should be expected because there are different traditions and the sociopolitical and economic geography of nation states vary. Contrasting Britain, France and Germany with each other or the United States with Canada in this regard underlines the point. However, whether such differences in the guise of a 'varieties of capitalism' perspective necessarily implies that there is greater similarity or dissimilarity, divergence or convergence between and among the nation states is a moot point. While there are clearly differences in methods of implementation and outcomes *vis-à-vis* neo-liberalism, it can also be the case that these are but variations on a (grand) theme. Thus, what is common to the economic and societal change across the nation states of the last few decades may outweigh in importance inter- and intra-nation state differences that have emerged and developed. Here, critical analysts, such as Callinicos (2009), Castells (1996) and Harvey (2005), have argued that not to recognise this kind of meta-picture perspective is not to see the proverbial wood for the trees. In other words, the whole is greater than the sum of the parts.

That said, the ascendency and now hegemony of neo-liberalism has its roots in the post-war economic and political crisis that dates from the late 1960s. Initially, this crisis was one of rising political resistance to the capitalist *status quo* often led by unions. By the mid-1970s, the crisis had become far more of an economic one with the end of the long boom, whereupon the post-war settlement was decided by the progenitors of what we now call neo-liberalism to have been the cause of the problem rather than the workings of capitalism itself. Therein followed a battle between the forces of the right and the left to determine how best to respond to the crisis. Suffice it to say that the forces of the right – the neo-liberals – won to the extent that they colonised such a large part of the political spectrum that the centre of gravity of politics *in toto* shifted towards them. Social democracy and Keynesianism were cast in the role of guilty parties. So it was not just that right-wing neo-liberal governments gained power and implemented their agenda throughout many countries. Britain under Thatcher and the United States under Reagan and Bush are only the most obvious examples of this. It was also that social democracy – defined as the regulation of the market and its outcomes for the purposes of attaining social justice – was undermined to such an extent that even where (formerly) social democratic parties were elected to office, often as a reaction to openly neo-liberal governments, they too pursued neo-liberal policies. This was because social democracy had transmogrified into (contemporary) social liberalism which in the Anglo–American world was denoted as the 'third way' (Giddens 1998) between unregulated capitalism and socialism. Thus, many commentators felt that no matter the professed belief of social liberalism in social justice, the bowing down to the market meant that social justice came a very poor second to the primary goals of economic growth and market efficiency, and that in effect, what came to pass was only a slightly restrained form of neo-liberalism.

Putting together its hegemony – in its two guises of outright neo-liberalism and social liberalism – at the level of the nation state also allowed neo-liberalism to mould the policy and work of the international regulatory institutions of the word economy, namely the International Monetary Fund, the World Bank and the World Trade Organization, and their many regional counterparts. The consequences of this were the erosion and elimination of barriers to the movement of capital and goods (and sometimes labour) between nation states, as well as absolute and relative reductions in social welfare spending. Such influence at international, regional and national levels was cemented by the implosion of the state capitalist[2] regimes of the Soviet Union and eastern Europe by 1990, and the endorsement and expansion of the market in China from the 1990s. Around this time, the term 'globalisation' entered the popular lexicon. In a further show of the influence of neo-liberalism, globalisation meant neo-liberal globalisation as opposed to globalisation imbued with social justice or (progressive) social revolution. Among the most obvious experiments in nation-state based neo-liberalism have been Australia, Britain, Canada, Chile, Japan, Mexico, New Zealand, Russia, Sweden, South Africa and the United States. This brief list indicates that neo-liberalism has captured the political high ground in an array of economies which have different historically dominant values and paths.

Harvey (2005) argued that neo-liberalism is a global capitalist class *power* restoration project. This line of argument stipulates that the political resistance of the 1960s and 1970s heightened the awareness of the ruling elites that a relative transferral of wealth and power from the employers to workers had taken place during the long boom, and that a resuscitation of profit levels in a period of economic contraction required the reduction of the workers' share of national wealth through the intensification and extensification of the wage-effort bargain. In other words, the rate of exploitation of workers was required to increase through intensifying their productivity and output within their existing hours of work, and extending their hours of work and thus their overall productivity and output. The ability to do this necessarily also required – indeed, comprised – the restoration of the economic and political power of the ruling class on a global basis. Put more simply, neo-liberalism was the response of the ruling elites to the economic and political crisis. Before moving on to examine the implications of the enforced advance of neo-liberalism upon workers and their organs of collective representation, it is worth noting that the economic and political crisis of neo-liberalism of the early part of the twenty-first century has not witnessed the resurgence of Keynesianism, the regulation of markets or of social democracy. State intervention has been used to support and reinforce market mechanisms (at the expense of cutbacks in public expenditure to service the national debts incurred to do so) rather than reduce or expunge the extent of market mechanisms. Economically and politically, neo-liberalism has emerged relatively unscathed from this crisis because of the palpable inability of the left to challenge the dominant ideological narrative. The only part of the global economy where neo-liberalism has been successfully and effectively challenged to date, albeit still within a global framework of neo-liberalism, has been in a number of economies in Latin America. Venezuela is the most obvious example here (Gott 2001, 2005). The case of South Africa, it seems, is one where the potential to realise such opposition to neo-liberalism under the ANC-COSATU-CPSA alliance since the ending of apartheid in 1994 has not come to fruition, as the ANC has marginalised its former leftist allies and become a home for advocates of a version of African neo-liberalism. In regard of China, the state still maintains a considerable role in organising, directing and constituting the economy so that the impact of neo-liberalism is significantly blunted. The issue of which groups in Chinese society benefit from this maintained state role and to what degree is a point of considerable debate.

The import of this brief discussion has been to emphasise the encompassing, if not quite all encompassing, nature and strength of neo-liberalism as a political force. For workers and labour unions, outright neo-liberalism and its social liberal variant have been equally important. Neo-liberalism here can be viewed as dangerous and pernicious. This is either because it is a deliberate and conscious subterfuge for the project of the transferral of wealth and power to existing political and economic ruling elites, where there is a redistribution of wealth away from the poor and towards the rich, or because despite the intentions, the processes and results of actual neo-liberalism serve to lead to this outcome as existing economic elites seize the opportunities to achieve such an outcome. However, social liberalism has in one sense been even more pernicious for it has colonised the main organs of political representation upon which labour unions have traditionally relied, in the process not only robbing unions of that political representation but also disorientating them. This has made the task of attempting to resist neo-liberalism more challenging and difficult.

WHAT NEO-LIBERALISM MEANS FOR WORKERS

At base, when implemented neo-liberalism means the greater direct exposure of workers to vagaries of the market and to the ability of employers to intensify and extensify the wage-effort bargain in their own favour. Furthermore, neo-liberalism is associated with reduced protection for workers in the form of state actions to regulate and modify market outcomes, and thus there is a reduced ability for workers to act collectively in defence of their interests through legal and quasi-legal means. Moreover, human resource management, whether in its hard or soft versions, can be viewed as the application of neo-liberalism in the workplace. Of course, there is an array of forms which this collective scenario can take, varying across time and space. Flexible work organisation and working-time and employment practices where the flexibility is tilted towards the employer are some of the most obvious means. Examples are deskilling, zero-hour contracts, and self-employment respectively. It is not the case that there is a single way in which neo-liberalism has operated and been implemented whether at the level of the workplace or the enterprise. In Britain and the United States, for example, leveraged buyouts (including the use of private equity) seem more common than elsewhere – possibly reflecting the relatively less regulated financial and economic regimes within these economies which facilitate this phenomenon – whereby massive debt is run up to take over another company by the acquisitor. This, over and above the search for profits, increases the pressure to slash and burn in order to service and pay off the incurred debt. The most obvious targets are the jobs and terms and conditions of workers. Labour costs not only represent a large proportion of operating costs, they can also be used as shock absorbers when other costs are outside the control of employers.

The greater exposure of workers to the vagaries of the market and the interests and power of employers is the direct result of the reduction in state intervention in the market – whether in terms of social wages funded, in part, through corporate taxation, the terms of minimum wages and pension provision through enforced obligations upon employers, or other forms of regulation of the employment relationship. Indeed, in many cases states have gone further by not only allowing labour and capital to self-regulate their relationship – which almost always means allowing capital to dominate – but also intervening on the side of capital to restrict the ability of organised labour to aggregate its forces. This is most evident in the regulation of industrial action and strikes.

The battle cry of neo-liberalism has been to tear down any barriers that impede labour market flexibility and that constitute so-called 'labour market rigidities'. Reduced labour market regulation and reduced regulation of the employment relationship have increased freedom for employers to act, but also has reduced regulation over capital movements and financial forms of capital. The two come together particularly sharply in the so-called 'race to bottom' where unionised workers are faced with the prospects either of ceding concessions from their hard won gains of collective bargaining, of moving to non-unionised workplaces working under worse conditions than before, or of seeing their jobs transferred to an area of lower labour costs (normally in another country but also possibly within countries). And the drive for profits means that capital will search for areas of lower labour costs than those which were previously the lowest, so creating the downward spiral.

However, greater exposure of workers to the vagaries of the market can also come about as the result of employers off-loading previous commitments to employees in terms of pensions, employment security and employability among others. For example, many employers have cut back on the worth and existence of pensions which are conventionally conceived as deferred wages, while outsourcing, particularly through using previously employed workers as self-employed contractors, divests employers of many financial responsibilities. The rise of the notion of employability heralds a new era where it is the responsibility of already employed workers, not employers, to make sure that they are trained and skilled in the requisite needs for the employer's business demands.

Some may view neo-liberalism as just capitalism 'plain and simple' – or just another form of capitalism with its underlying dynamics unchanged. And, in this regard, the impact upon workers would be viewed as neither new nor surprising. (Indeed, every technique deployed in the service of the greater exploitation of workers under neo-liberalism can be found to have an antecedent in pre-neo-liberal times of the late 1970s onwards or a prior parallel.) And while there is some truth in this, such a perspective would, nonetheless, downplay the specific

importance of the neo-liberal project as a means of refashioning and reconfig-
uring capitalism through a persuasive ideology and at a key point in human
history as per the crisis of contemporary capitalism after the long boom.

The implications for unions as collective organisations of workers in the
workplace are equally grave. In the industrial arena, the rights to associate, to
organise and to take industrial action have come under attack not only as
lawful rights but also as effective rights through a combination of *de jure* and
de facto restrictions. Consequently, in most, though not all, economies this has
been one of the key factors – along with unemployment and associated job
insecurity – in demobilising the ability of labour unions to respond effectively
to the challenges from employers. Furthermore, as neo-liberal globalisation
has marched on apace, the ability of unions to act internationally has been
impeded by instances like those within the European Union where the right to
take industrial action has been struck down by the judiciary because it is
deemed to interfere with a higher right, namely that of companies to trade (see
the Viking, Laval, Ruffert and Luxembourg judgments of European Court of
Justice). Of course, it would be wholly wrong to give the impression that it is
only external factors and processes that prevent a more robust response from
labour unionism. That is clearly not the case and is testified to by the inability
to develop effective forms on international labour unionism. Yet, it remains
the case that this environment in which unions operate is a critical impediment
to the success of achieving their goals.

LABOUR UNION RESPONSES

It can be judged from both the content and tone of the prior discussions of neo-
liberalism and its implications that labour union responses have been inadequate and ineffectual in the realms of ideas and actions. Whether that is to
presuppose that different responses could be wholly adequate and effective
given the scale of the challenge neo-liberalism represents is another matter.
Nonetheless, and notwithstanding a few individual and small scale 'bright
sparks' like organising immigrant workers in Los Angeles (Milkman 2006),
the rebuilding of the RMT union as a militant body (Darlington 2009) or the
effectiveness of the International Transport Workers Federation (Anner *et al.*
2006), labour and organised labour have suffered the blows of neo-liberalism
and have been unable to construct an effective industrial or political counter-
response to turn back the tide. The proportion of enterprise operating costs
accounted for by workers' labour costs has fallen leading to relative immiseration and degradation as, thus, has their share of the wealth generated through
enterprises. Meanwhile in most western economies the influence of workers
per se and through their unions within the enterprises has been diminished.

The flipsides to these are that the proportion of wealth taken by managers, employers and shareholders has increased and dramatically so, while the right of management to (unilaterally) manage has been considerably reinforced and extended. This trajectory of ineffective forms and action of labour unionism is all the more noticeable on the international stage where international labour unionism is still woefully underdeveloped despite over one hundred and fifty years since the International Workingmen's Association was established (with the participation of Marx and Engels) and which recognised the need for this.

Setting aside the problems and issues of union developing and applying strategies, much less effective ones (see Gall 2011), and based on observation of existing practice, there are many broad categories of responses and reactions that labour unions could take towards neo-liberalism. Whether they are of the unions' own genuine volition, a result of extremely limited choices or grudgingly and reluctantly enforced upon unions is of some importance as well. The same is true of whether these are implicit or explicit assessments and whether unions make these at higher levels of abstraction such as the nation-state and world economy levels. Nonetheless, a rough categorisation would include the following.

The first could be termed *agreement and support*. Here, neo-liberal globalisation is viewed as benign or progressive, and unions and their members can benefit from it where the relevant companies, sectors or economies can successfully compete. This would be a mutual gains agenda and is the territory of some business-type labour unionisms in a number of advanced economies.

The second could be termed *qualified and conditional support*, where unions advocate that workers require sympathetic strategic state and supra-state action to provide protection for themselves and for their employers/sectors/industries in order to compete fairly and successfully, as well as to protect themselves from the worst effects of globalisation and 'the race to the bottom'. Here, the language of simply wanting 'a level playing field' and the 'equality of opportunity' to compete are common, including state provision of educational and technological services to allow fair competition.

The third could be termed *social democratic opposition*, where unions believe in the policy and practice of opposition to corporate globalisation and advocate social democracy as an alternative in order to socialise, not abolish, the capitalist economy. Here, market processes and outcomes are moderated to ensure some semblance of equality of outcome in terms of attaining social justice whereby not all considerations are reducible to the single issue of enhancing profitability. One example of the pursuit of this approach at the global level is that of establishing international labour standards.

The fourth could be termed *socialist resistance* where unions believe in opposition and resistance in word and deed to capitalist globalisation, and advocate socialism on a national and global basis as the alternative. In this instance, the operation and role of the market would be greatly diminished or abolished so that need rather than profit became the guiding light of society.

In summary, the four positions could be labelled neo-liberalism, social liberalism, social democracy and socialism. In order to operationalise such categorisation, it is more helpful to see these four positions as poles of attraction on a spectrum ranging from right to left. Within this conceptualisation, unions, peak union organisations and union movements would be capable of shifting over time from one position to another in response to internal and external dynamics, as well as creating hybrids of those positions. Their respective positions would comprise ideologies, policies and actions primarily in the industrial and political arenas. The relative balance of power between unions, employers and the state, and the interplay of this in regard to how they perceive their interests, would be a major explanatory variable in unions deciding which of the four positions to adopt and their ability to prosecute this.

CONTENT OF THE HANDBOOK

The aim of this handbook is to provide an overview and assessment of union responses to neo-liberalism over the last thirty or so years. It will use the aforementioned four-fold framework to examine the key issues and important emerging trends within and across national union movements in an array of different countries. In this way, we hope that some fairly explicit threads can be seen to be running through this handbook. While there are other books in this field, they tend to focus on a single country, or a limited number of countries, or they may cover only a limited number of issues. There are also comparative books that examine one important issue, for example, the role, behaviour, influence and recent decline of unions within a particular trading region or across trading regions. We seek to combine these various facets but on a deeper and broader scale with regard to neo-liberalism and using the framework establish a common means for doing so. The handbook comprises introductory and reflective essays which are the outer coating and foundation stones for a larger number of country-based studies where contributors examine labour union responses. We are delighted to have contributions from Richard Trumka of the AFL-CIO and Bill Fletcher Jr of Center for Labor Renewal in the US. The handbook is primarily designed for academics and for students taking advanced courses in comparative employment relations. But the book is also intended to appeal to practitioners, interest groups and policy makers who have an interest in examining approaches to employment relations problems and issues that differ from their own national context. Inevitably, there are gaps in terms of the country studies, such that there are no chapters on Brazil, Canada, Japan and Mexico, for example. This is always the case where space is limited. Nonetheless, we hope that the range and scope of the chapters is sufficient to provide a basic foundation in understanding the 'how', 'when', 'why' and 'where' of union responses to neo-liberalism. Unfortunately, no chapter has been able to identify the magic panacea with which unions can turn back the tide of neo-liberalism and return to some progressive form, at least, of fundamental market regulation. That book is still waiting to be written but it would be a sweet point if the emerging battles in Wisconsin, Ohio and Indiana in early 2011 played a role in allowing this.

ACKNOWLEDGEMENTS

We thank all our contributors for their acceptance to write their chapters. Much of the editing of this handbook was carried out while Gregor Gall was in receipt of a Sir Allan Sewell Fellowship at Griffith University, Australia. He is grateful for the opportunity afforded by this.

NOTES

1. Most unions are no longer either *trade* unions or unions of *trades* despite the continued widespread usage of the term by writers. Rather, they are – certainly by membership coverage – increasingly general and industrial unions. Thus, we use the terms 'labour unions' and 'labour unionism' because this more appropriately and accurately focuses upon the fundamental aspect of unions as collective bodies of labourers whose organisational *raison d'être* is, at the very least, regulating the wage-effort bargain. To the extent that unions remain as specialist unions, these are more commonly occupational unions, occupation being a wider construct than 'trade'.
2. These regimes of 'actually existing socialism' are better approximated to by the concept of state capitalism, whereby an elite controlled – and benefited from – the extraction of surplus labour from the majority of the populaces.

REFERENCES

Anner, M., I. Greer, M. Hauptmeier, N. Lillie and N. Winchester (2006), 'The industrial determinants of transnational solidarity: global inter-union politics in three sectors', *European Journal of Industrial Relations*, **12**(1) 7–27.
Callinicos, A. (2009), *Imperialism and Global Political Economy*, Cambridge: Polity Press.
Castells, M. (1996), *The Rise of the Network Society – The Information Age: Economy, Society and Culture, Vol. 1*, Oxford: Blackwell.
Darlington, R. (2009), 'Leadership and union militancy: the case of the RMT', *Capital and Class*, **98**, 3–32.
Gall, G. (2011), 'Union strategy and circumstance: back to the future and forward to the past?', in K. Townsend and A. Wilkinson (eds), *Research Handbook on Work and Employment Relations*, Cheltenham, UK and Northampton, MA, USA: Edward Elgar.
Giddens, A. (1998), *The Third Way: the renewal of social democracy*, Cambridge: Polity Press.

Gott, R. (2001), *In the Shadow of the Liberator: the Impact of Hugo Chávez on Venezuela and Latin America*, Verso: London.

Gott, R. (2005), *Hugo Chávez and the Bolivarian Revolution*, Verso: London.

Guillen, M. (2001), 'Is globalization civilizing, destructive or feeble? A critique of five debates in the social science literature', *Annual Review of Sociology*, **27**, 235–40.

Harvey, D. (2005), *A Brief History of Neo-liberalism*, Oxford: Oxford University Press.

Milkman, R. (2006), *LA Story: Immigrant workers and the future of the US labor movement*, New York: Russell Sage Foundation.

2 Theories of collective action and union power

John Kelly

'Power is almost certainly the most contentious and the most elusive concept in social analysis.'

(Hyman, 1994: 127)

INTRODUCTION

The 'austerity' policies proposed by many West European governments from 2008 onwards posed major threats to wages and conditions of employment, to welfare and pension benefits and to the degree of protection enjoyed by workers against dismissal and redundancy (EIRO 2009, 2010). Many union confederations opposed many of these policies but mobilising effective opposition raises important questions about trade union capacity, strategy and power, not least because of the economic and political context. Unions have had to face an increasingly adverse labour market as unemployment levels rose throughout the advanced capitalist world from summer 2008, with particularly sharp increases in Ireland, Spain and the USA (Hyman 2010: 2). Unions have also found the political arena to be fairly inhospitable because the Socialist governments in Greece, Portugal and Spain for example have proved to be just as committed to public spending cuts as their Conservative and Christian Democratic counterparts elsewhere. Nonetheless unions have responded to government policies with a wave of protests and general strikes, most notably in France, Greece, Italy and Spain (Kelly *et al.* 2010). Popular discussions of these contemporary events are rooted in assumptions about trade union power which often go unexamined and that is a problem precisely because of the 'contentious' and 'elusive' nature of the concept.

In the social theory literature, Steven Lukes' short monograph *Power: A Radical View* has proved to be one of the most influential essays on this subject. First published in 1974 but reissued in 2005 with almost 100 pages of additional material, the book has received over 4400 citations and has become a modern classic (Google Scholar, 1 October 2010). In brief, Lukes' argument was that power could be analysed along three separate dimensions: the first dimension involved conflicts between two or more groups (such as a union and an employer) and the balance of power could be deduced from the outcome of any conflict between them, such as a strike settlement. However by concentrating on issues that comprise the agenda of negotiations between unions and employers, this approach overlooks those issues that are simply prevented by the employer from entering the negotiation process: agenda control is therefore the second dimension of power. Yet there is a third, and deeper dimension of power, based on the hegemony of ruling class ideas (or pro-business) ideas. For example, the idea that economic success requires wage reductions and longer work hours may go unchallenged because substantial numbers of union members endorse and legitimate, however vaguely and incoherently, the paramount importance of business interests.

A number of authors (including Hardy and Leiba-O'Sullivan 1998) have argued for a fourth dimension of power, based on the ideas of Foucault. In particular, they have rejected the idea of a concentration of power in the hands of particular agents, arguing instead that power is dispersed among networks of relationships; and have asserted that social actors are so deeply implicated in these networks of power that resistance simply ends up reinforcing, not overthrowing, existing power relations (Hardy and Leiba-O'Sullivan 1998: 458–60). There are so many examples of collective protests that *have* 'overthrown' existing power relations, from the New Unionism in Britain in the 1890s, the labour unrest in the USA in the 1930s and the civil rights movement in the Southern states of the USA in the 1960s, that it is hard to take seriously the Marcusian bleakness of Foucauldian analysis (see Thompson and McHugh (2009: 133–6).

Yet despite frequent reference to, and discussion of, union power and its apparent decline over recent years, Lukes' work is rarely mentioned in contemporary industrial relations literature (Edwards and Wajcman 2005 is an exception) although it has enjoyed greater impact in the adjacent field of labour process studies (such as Thompson and McHugh 2009). Industrial relations scholars have developed few explicit frameworks for studying power, but it is possible to discern five principal models in the literature. Some of these are general models of union power while others have also been applied to the more specific, power-related subject of strike activity, understood as the exercise of power. The factors identified in the literature on power overlap to some degree with the factors identified in the literature on strikes. This is hardly surprising given that the former is centred on the determinants of power and the latter on the exercise of power. Different strike theories address different facets of strike activity – frequency, workers involved, days lost – although days lost per 1000 workers is the most widely used measure in the comparative literature (Barratt 2009; Edwards and Hyman 1994). Moreover these different theories are not logically exclusive: they have sometimes been combined in models of strike activity and elements of some or all of them can be traced in many industrial relations texts (such as Franzosi 1995; Scheuer 2006).

First, we can distinguish a market theory of union power that draws on the ideas of the economist Alfred Marshall and assigns substantial weight to the impact of competition in product and labour markets on union bargaining power (see Brown 2008; Brown *et al.* 2009; Simms and Charlwood 2010, and for details of the 'Marshallian rules' see King 1990: 25–27). Second, we can discern a resource mobilisation perspective in which union power is thought to be strongly influenced by personnel and material resources, notably union membership. Within this approach the decline of union membership and density in Western Europe since the early 1980s represents a decline in union power, as indicated for example in data on moderate wage settlements in recent years and on the widespread decline in days lost through strike action (Dribbusch and Vandaele 2007; Keune 2008; and on resource mobilisation theory see Edwards and McCarthy 2004). Third, we can also find strong traces of an institutionalist perspective in which union power is influenced by the structures of both unions themselves and collective bargaining, in particular by the existence of employer-supported 'extension clauses' that maintain levels of bargaining coverage often well in excess of union density (Brandl and Traxler 2010; Hamann and Kelly 2008; Simms and Charlwood 2010). Fourth, there exists a labour process perspective in which union power is seen to be influenced by the organisation of the production process, either nationally or internationally, and the degree to which this creates strategic groups of workers with high levels of disruptive capacity (Silver 2003: 13ff). Finally, mobilisation theory argues for the importance of ideas about injustice – 'collective action frames' – as the essential foundation for worker engagement in collective organisation and action (Kelly 1998). While mobilisation theory has much to say about union power resources – the traditional focus of much industrial relations research – it also contains ideas about the willingness and capacity of union leaders at all levels to exercise power through various forms of collective action. In that sense the theory forms a bridge into the literature on strikes.

As will become clear, each of these perspectives offers useful insights into the patterns and outcomes of union responses to neo-liberalism. While there are some affinities between these first four approaches and the first two dimensions of Lukes' framework, mobilisation theory arguably comes closest to the Lukesian emphasis on ideas and hegemony. The next section of this chapter (part two) explores the concept of power itself in the light of Lukes' framework; part three then works through the five approaches to power in the industrial relations literature and shows how each of them might contribute to our understanding of union power in general and strike activity in particular; part four builds on the preceding sections through a consideration of union mobilisation and part five concludes.

THE CONCEPT OF POWER

Power has many different facets but at its core is the capacity of agents (whether individuals or groups) 'to bring about significant effects, specifically by furthering their own interests and/or affecting the interests of others, whether positively or negatively' (Lukes 2005: 65). The exercise of power can therefore be seen in conflicts between unions and employers and the balance of power between them may be gauged from the outcomes of strikes or other forms of collective action. On this view, the National Union of Mineworkers (NUM) was more powerful than the National Coal Board and the British government in 1972 and again in 1974 when it secured significant strike victories, but the balance of power had shifted by the mid-1980s, culminating in the NUM defeat in 1985. Critics of this approach – including Lukes – argued that a deeper level of power can be discerned in agenda control, so that potentially contentious issues are removed from the normal channels of debate and cannot therefore be contested. In the realm of industrial relations, the fact that core issues of business strategy – what to produce; how to produce; where to produce – are subjects of managerial prerogative that simply do not appear on the agendas of collective bargaining committees would constitute *prima facie* evidence for the second dimension of power. Quite why such agenda control mostly goes unchallenged however is an interesting problem that takes us to the limit of work on the second dimension of power. That is because it raises questions about the ideas held by various actors on power and authority and on the rights of various groups to make decisions (see below).

Lukes' general definition of power also hints at the distinction between 'power to' and 'power over'. An employee who has the motivation and time to enrol in a union training programme on learning and skills and eventually become a union learning representative has the 'power to' pursue her interests. An employer who declares that his factory can only remain in production if workers accept a pay freeze is exercising 'power over' the interests of others, forcing workers to choose between more pay and continued employment. 'Power over' is the capacity to induce or coerce others to act in accordance with your interests rather than their own interests, or what Simms and Charlwood (2010: 128) refer to as 'coercive power'. In analysing interests, Lukes notes that the power of different agents may vary from one issue to another. For example an industrial union may have power on the issue of workloads or size of work teams within a factory but have virtually no power on the issue of factory closure and relocation. Moreover agents' power may be more or less dependent on context. For example, the employer's power to dismiss an employee is likely to vary with the content of employment protection laws that prevail within different countries: some legal regimes impose significant constraints on dismissal, whereas others impose very few constraints so that in examining employer power, legal context matters (Hamann and Kelly 2008: 140). Finally, it is inherent in the general definition of power given above that power is relational: the capacity of an employer to secure their interests at the expense of their employees depends in part on the reactions of employees. Under the anti-union laws prevailing in the UK, unofficial wildcat strikes – not sanctioned by a union's national executive committee and not preceded by a majority vote in a secret ballot – are unlawful. Such strikes can expose the union to crippling damages claims by employers and the virtual absence of such strikes since the early 1980s appears to constitute strong evidence of overwhelming employer power (Dickens and Hall 2010). Yet in spring 2009 an unofficial strike at the Lindsey oil refinery, backed by (unlawful) solidarity action elsewhere in the UK, forced the employer to make significant concessions to workers on the issue of hiring foreign employees on inferior terms and conditions of employment (Gall 2010). One of the important issues raised by this case turns on the means by which powerful groups maintain their domination over subordinate groups and secure their compliance with legal regulations. Why have so many workers accepted the constraints imposed by anti-union laws and why did the Lindsey workers refuse to accept those constraints?

Addressing questions of this type led to what is perhaps the major innovation in Lukes' original work, namely the introduction of what he called the third dimension of power, complementing the two dimensions that had already been identified in the literature. For Lukes, power is manifest not only in the outcomes of conflicts and in the control of the agendas of decision-making bodies, but in the capacity of ruling groups to shape the ideas and values of subordinate groups:

> ... the most effective and insidious use of power is to prevent such conflict from arising in the first place.... Indeed, is it not the supreme exercise of power to get another or others to have the desires you want them to have – that is, to secure their compliance by controlling their thoughts and desires? (Lukes 2005: 27)

By way of illustration, one strand of the recent literature on globalisation has explored the ways in which politicians and policy makers have sought to construct a discourse in which processes such as factory relocation, welfare retrenchment and labour market flexibility are portrayed as inexorable, and positive, developments (see Schmidt 2002 among others). Insofar as this particular view of globalisation becomes internalised among workers and union leaders it is likely to have the effect of framing resistance to such processes as both futile and irrational.

APPROACHES TO THE ANALYSIS OF POWER

Markets

Turning now from the concept of power to the different ways of analysing power, it was noted earlier that the industrial relations literature contains five different approaches, the first of which (and the most familiar) turns on the role of markets. According to this argument both labour and product market competition have significant effects on unions: it has long been recognised that high and rising unemployment tends to be associated with falling levels of union membership, lower wage expectations and hence a decline in the number of days lost through strikes (*cf.* Ashenfelter and Johnson 1969, Cronin 1979).

More recently the role of product market competition has come to the fore in analyses of declining union membership and bargaining coverage (including Brown *et al.* 2009). According to this argument, downward pressure on costs in markets with more intense competition and greater capital mobility has weakened the capacity of workers to protect terms and conditions of employment or even to protect collective bargaining itself. In recent years the growth in size and numbers of multinational corporations, coupled with the deregulation of capital markets by neo-liberal inspired governments has significantly increased the international dimension of product market competition. This combination of developments has exposed growing numbers of workers in the advanced capitalist world to the prospect of job loss. Import penetration of domestic markets by foreign producers, most recently from China, has resulted in declining manufacturing employment throughout Western Europe and the USA. In 1950, foreign manufactured goods accounted for just 6 per cent of market share in Western Europe but by 2001 this had risen dramatically to 39 per cent (Glyn 2006: 97). At the same time, the USA and the UK continue to supply approximately one third of the world's ever-expanding stock of foreign direct investment, a growing proportion of which is in developing countries, notably Hong Kong, China and Mexico (Dicken 2007: 61). It is argued that this increased mobility of capital has significantly undercut union bargaining power in manufacturing and in some parts of the service sector. This is because worker resistance to wage reductions, hours' increases or work intensification can be met with the threat of closure and relocation to countries where labour is substantially cheaper. Piazza's (2005) study of 15 OECD countries 1952–2001 found that two measures of globalisation – increased international trade and reduced controls on capital mobility – are significantly associated with a decline in days lost to strikes. The effect holds up even with controls for bargaining centralisation, union density and the degree of left party presence in government and is especially pronounced in countries with low (below-median) union density. While this approach rightly identifies the role of markets, and to a lesser degree of union resources, it is not clear how it would account for the shifting patterns of strike action within countries.

The theoretical models of unions and the bargaining process that underlie some of these labour and product market studies often assume that strike demands centre on wages or monetary benefits without taking into account other, non-wage demands that might also motivate strikes (Tsebclis and Lange 1995: 103–107). A related problem is the tendency to equate union density with union power but, as mobilisation theory suggests (see below), union power is also highly dependent on the capacity of unions to mobilise their members in collective action (Sullivan 2010). Finally, it is important to note that as much as 60 per cent of the OECD workforce is 'largely insulated from international trade competition' (Glyn 2006: 99). This is because many organisations in social and personal services and wholesale and retail trade necessarily supply immediate services to consumers in spatially circumscribed local markets: local bars, restaurants, schools and hospitals simply cannot relocate overseas and continue to service domestic markets. This degree of shelter from international product market competition helps explain why a large and growing proportion of strikes in Western Europe now occur in the service sector, especially among heavily unionised public sector workers (Bordogna and Cella 2002: 601 see also Silver 2003: 103–22).

Union Resources

It has also been argued that union bargaining power has been eroded in recent years by declining resources, most obviously membership and density and political influence over social democratic governments (Kelly 1998: 37; Korpi and Shalev 1979; Scheuer 2006: 155). Between 1970 and 1980, union density rose in almost all advanced capitalist countries (Austria and the Netherlands were the exceptions). In contrast union density declined in 17 out of 21 OECD countries between 1980 and 2000 (the exceptions were Belgium, Finland, Spain and Sweden); and between 2000 and 2007 decline occurred in 19 of these 21 countries (the two exceptions were France and Norway where density remained unchanged) (Barratt 2009; Hamann and Kelly 2008). Consistent with this trend, union wage bargaining successfully increased the share of national income going to wages and salaries between 1970 and 1980 but the past 30 years of density decline has witnessed a continuous redistribution of income from labour to capital (Glyn 2006: 7). If we disaggregate union density decline by sector, it is clear that density levels are generally much higher in the public sector compared to the private sector. This fact is consistent with the recent shift in the locus of strikes across much of the advanced capitalist world. For example, public sector strikes accounted for 20.8 per cent of all working days lost in Canada 1960–94 but 44.1 per cent of days lost between 1995 and 2004 (Briskin 2007: 101).

The power resource argument of Korpi and Shalev (1979) suggests strong unions that are able to influence pro-labour governments will have less need to strike against employers. Brandl and Traxler's (2010) data confirm the predicted link between social democratic dominance of government and low levels of strike action although the mechanisms connecting the variables are somewhat unclear. In the classical corporatist literature governments traded concessions to unions in exchange for wage moderation and labour peace. Yet in recent years many West European social democratic governments have enacted neo-liberal reforms, to labour markets and to welfare systems (in Germany for example) and to wages and pensions (in Greece, Portugal and Spain for instance). While there remains significant cross-national variation in the types of policies enacted by such governments and in their willingness to include unions in policy formation, it is also true that unions have found it harder to extract concessions from their social democratic allies in government in recent years compared to the 1970s (Hamann and Kelly 2011; Upchurch *et al.* 2009).

Yet the resource mobilisation approach to the analysis of power is also problematic because it implies that union resources are largely synonymous with union density: a decline in one automatically represents a decline in the other. However, it is clear from the positive outcomes of some of the recent general strikes in France (January 2009) and Spain (June 2002) that there is only a weak correlation between union power and union density and this is for three reasons: first, unions may be able to mobilise non-dues paying workers in collective action (Kelly *et al.* 2013); second, unions may be able to mobilise support from other social movements, increasing their own power through coalition building (Tattersall 2010); third, given that power is a relational concept (see above), unions may be powerful because of divisions or resource depletion among their governmental opponents (Tarrow 1994).

Institutions

In contrast with the decline in union density discussed by resource mobilisation theorists, it appears that institutional supports for union power are still widespread throughout Western Europe. Bargaining coverage as of 2004 for instance remains high at approximately 80 per cent despite evidence of widespread fragmentation of bargaining structures since the 1980s (Flanagan 2008). The number and size of strikes continues to be influenced by industrial relations institutions, especially the degrees of centralisation and coordination of collective bargaining (Clegg 1976 and others). The centralised bargaining structures that facilitated corporatist policymaking in the 1970s used to be associated with fewer but larger strikes. Those countries with highly decentralised bargaining structures do appear to have somewhat higher levels of strike activity than more centralised structures, notwithstanding the generalised decline in strike activity since the early 1980s (Brandl and Traxler 2010). However, there is no robust link between cross-national variations in union density and strike activity: the most strike-prone countries in Europe (2002–06) include high-density Finland, modest-density Italy and low-density Greece and Spain (Hale 2008). In addition the focus on bargaining institutions alone cannot tell us about the outcomes of those institutions for the different actors or tell us how far the institutions have become a 'hollow shell', concealing the reality of seriously weakened unionism and dominant employers (Millward *et al.* 2000: 138ff).

Labour Process

The fourth approach to the analysis of power stems from the tradition of labour process analysis but it is difficult to discuss because of the absence of systematic cross-industry evidence on the structure of international production chains, the degree of surplus capacity built into those chains, the availability of alternative suppliers of raw parts, materials, labour and transportation and the degree of union organisation in the less developed economies (Dicken 2007: 137–71). It was argued many years ago that lean production systems, built on 'just in time' principles, are highly vulnerable to disruption by strategic groups of workers (Turnbull 1988; and for more recent discussion see Silver 2003). The parallel growth of international trade since the early 1980s has contributed to an enormous expansion in the volume of freight transport, by air, sea and land (Dicken 2007: 410 ff). In certain countries organised dockworkers have therefore been able to exert bargaining leverage, both over national employers and, acting through the International Transport Workers' Federation, over multinational employers (Lillie 2006).

Before we turn to mobilisation theory, we should briefly consider the implications of these four different perspectives for the capacity of unions to respond to neo-liberalism. Labour and product market pressures, declining membership and density and the power of multinational firms to reshape the labour process would all portray a sombre, if not depressing picture of the prospects for organised labour. On the other hand, the partial insulation from international competition of workers in public services and some private services, suggests that resistance to neo-liberalism is likely to be concentrated among the unions representing such employees. In many countries, even the USA and Canada, such workers have retained relatively high rates of union density and bargaining coverage and both factors would therefore reinforce the likelihood that they could play a central role in campaigns against neo-liberal policies. However, it is one thing to suggest some workers may have the capacity to resist government austerity policies, but under what conditions is that capacity likely to be activated and turned into collective action in some form?

Mobilisation Theory

Mobilisation theory tries to identify the conditions under which collective organisation and action are most likely to occur. As summed up in an earlier essay on union growth:

> [I]t is not simply dissatisfaction at work which triggers unionization, but a sense of injustice, a breach of legal or collective agreement rights or widely shared social values. ... In order to generate support for unionism ... such grievances must be felt by substantial numbers of workers. Workers with a shared sense of grievance are more likely to feel their grievance is legitimate and are more likely to develop a shared sense of group identity ... workers must either attribute blame for their problems to an agency, normally the employer or the government, or must feel the employer or government is liable for solving them. ... Finally people must have a sense of agency (or efficacy), that is the belief that collective organisation and action can make a difference. (Kelly 2005: 66)

These sets of beliefs, or 'collective action frames', are developed and disseminated through collective organisations, in this case unions, by leaders at different levels. The most wide ranging collective action frames provide an alternative world view, sometimes constituting an ideology, in which all of the main components of prevailing orthodoxy are challenged. Within the world's union movements varieties of Marxism have historically constituted one influential ideology shared by groups of communist and Trotskyist militants. In Britain for example, Marxist ideas were deployed in the 1960s and 1970s to challenge government calls for wage moderation (Callaghan 2003: 226ff). The decline of the European communist parties that began in the late 1970s and the partial adoption of neo-liberal ideas by many social democratic parties were not matched by a corresponding growth of other leftist parties (Callaghan 2000; Gallagher *et al.* 2006: 235–38; Moschonas 2002). The number of Marxist-inspired activists within Europe's unions has almost certainly diminished over this period although reliable data is very hard to locate. For all their problems, Marxist ideas constituted a coherent narrative that could be deployed by union activists to legitimate opposition to neo-liberal reforms. The details of particular reforms, whether it was an increase in the retirement age or a reduction in the duration of unemployment benefits, could be related to a wider set of propositions about the fundamental properties of market economies and the behaviour of firms and governments. In the terms of Lukes' perspectives on power, Marxist ideas enable union militants not only to contest employer and government actions and the agendas surrounding reform policies, but to challenge the ideas and values routinely used by such agencies to make sense of the world.

If we look at recent union-organised protests against austerity, in Ireland 2009–10 or Greece 2010 for example, these actions appear to have been framed in terms of a diffuse notion of 'fairness' that does not necessarily challenge the underlying logic of neo-liberal-inspired austerity. The Irish Congress of Trade Unions mounted a series of demonstrations and strikes in late 2009 under the slogans 'Get Up, Stand Up' and 'For a Fairer, Better Way'. The programme of proposed government spending cuts was not rejected in its entirety, or in principle, but was challenged because the distribution of cuts across the social classes was unfair. Insofar as the unions drew on an alternative world view, it was perhaps that of Keynesian economics: government should increase, not reduce spending in recession even at the price of higher borrowing and a short term and substantial rise in government debt. Nonetheless, the reported levels of participation in the November 2009 protests suggest that even these vague and ill-defined slogans may have been sufficient to capture, or generate, a sense of injustice and facilitate mobilisation for collective action.

The types of 'collective action frames' that are developed within unions depend partly on the structure of union organisation and in particular on the degree of democracy: 'the forms of membership participation and relationships among and within leadership, activists, and the membership more generally' (Hyman 1994: 122). In addition the mobilising capacity of union leaders and activists will also depend on the power resources of their opponents and on the capacity of those opponents to impose, or to raise, the costs of collective action. For example, participation in general strikes against government policy is lawful in several Southern European countries but such strikes are unlawful in Germany and the UK (Jacobs 2007).

One aim of mobilisation theory is to account for participation in various forms of collective action, including but not confined to, strikes. However the theory is less adequate in accounting for the choices made by actors among different forms of collective action. The variety of actions, at different times and in different countries, includes workplace occupations in Britain in the 1970s and 2000s and the abduction of senior managers in France in the 2000s ('bossnappings') (Gall 2010; Gall and Hebdon 2008). Some literature in mobilisation theory refers to 'repertoires of collective action', the sets of readily available ideas about various forms of protest that are in circulation in a particular country at a particular time (Tarrow 1994). So, the general strike is arguably part of the 'repertoire of contention' of French, Greek and Italian unions but does not comprise part of the repertoire of British unions. Yet this line of argument does beg the question how repertoires of action are constructed in the first place and under what conditions and through what mechanisms they can be changed.

EXERCISING POWER: COLLECTIVE ACTION AGAINST NEO-LIBERAL REFORMS

Despite their conceptual and empirical problems, market, institutional and resource mobilisation theories, alone or in combination, have been used more or less successfully to explain the widespread decline in economic strike activity in the advanced capitalist world since the early 1980s. However they appear unable to account for the simultaneous resurgence of general strikes across Western Europe since 1980. Between 1980 and 1989, unions in Western Europe (EU15 plus Norway) staged 19 general strikes (including credible strike threats) against government policies, a number that almost doubled to 34 in the following decade; between 2000 and 2009 the number of general strikes grew again to 39; and in the first nine months of 2010 there had already been 11 general strikes with more threatened (Kelly *et al.* 2013). While Greece certainly contributed significantly to the large number of general strikes and to the upward trend since the early 1980s, the rising number of general strikes is still apparent even if we exclude Greece. Although several countries with a relatively high level of general strikes also tend to have relatively high levels of economic strike activity (such as Greece, Italy and Spain), general strikes have also been called in countries with below-EU average levels of strike activity, such as Austria, Luxembourg and the Netherlands (Kelly *et al.* 2013). Preliminary evidence suggests some of these strikes have led to the partial or wholesale abandonment of government reforms, as in Finland (2009), France (1995), Greece (2009) and Spain (2002), although further research is required to establish the pattern of outcomes across all of these strikes.

Nonetheless, it is plausible to argue that while union power in relation to employers may have declined in recent years, especially in the manufacturing industry, this may not be true of union power in relation to governments. After all, general strikes are fundamentally different from economic strikes against employers: they are not normally linked to collective bargaining processes or structures; they attempt to mobilise the workforce at the national level rather than at the company or sectoral level; and they target the government and planned policy changes rather than the employer and workplace-related issues. Now a substantial component of the neo-liberal agenda has centred on flexible labour markets and welfare reform, most recently in the form of debates around the concept of 'flexicurity' (European Commission 2007). Insofar as these measures require government intervention, often in the form of legislation, they provide a focus for union protest and resistance. The data on general strikes suggests that union movements in many parts of Western Europe have demonstrated a remarkable capacity and willingness to mobilise people in protest against these reforms and to seek concessions from governments.

But given that power is a relational concept, why have governments sometimes responded to general strikes by offering concessions to unions and their allies? One clue to their behaviour comes from evidence on social pacts which has shown governments that are themselves weak, either because they are minority administrations or because they comprise a coalition of heterogeneous parties (an unconnected coalition), are far more willing to include unions in negotiations on contentious policy reforms compared to majority and single party administrations (Hamann and Kelly 2011). Governmental weakness in turn is underpinned by the phenomena of electoral volatility and party weakness: compared to the 1960s contemporary voters are less attached to a single political party, more willing to switch parties from one election to the next and more willing to vote for new parties (Greens, far right and so on) if they vote at all. Political party membership has declined dramatically in many European countries since the 1960s so the personnel resources available to parties have also declined at the same time as their electorates have become more volatile (Gallagher *et al.* 2006). The net effect of these trends has been to weaken some mainstream parties in their relations with key social actors, both business and unions. This weakening of parties and governments could form part of the explanation for the success of some union organised anti-government protests and strikes in recent years.

CONCLUSIONS

If unions are viewed as representative organisations of workers that seek to protect terms and conditions of employment through collective bargaining, then the prospects of effective resistance to neo-liberal policies would have to be considered very poor. A combination of product and labour market pressures and dwindling organisational resources has led to a decline in levels of collective action and a steady fall in wage shares in national income. However, if we turn our attention to the political arena and use the concepts provided by mobilisation theory, then the prospects for union action look rather different. Since 1980 union movements in a variety of Western European countries have demonstrated a remarkable capacity to mobilise substantial numbers of people in general strikes, called to protest government policies. We need more research to establish the effectiveness of such action and the conditions under which different types of government are more or less responsive to union pressure.

Nonetheless the neo-liberal austerity packages being pursued by a wide range of governments through 2009–10 appear to be generating a sense of injustice among sufficiently large numbers of people to provide the raw material for continued collective action and protests.

If we return to the Lukesian perspectives on power, we can raise a different set of questions and issues. In terms of the first and second dimensions of power – conflict outcomes and agenda control – we can ask to what extent union protests have succeeded in their stated objectives and to what degree unions have been able to shape the agenda of debates around austerity policies and the alternatives to austerity. Perhaps the most telling contribution from the Lukesian perspective emerges from the third facet of power: how far have unions been able to change the ways in which people think about the economy, about the role of governments and markets and about their own interests, as employees, consumers and citizens. At this juncture the Lukesian approach to power intersects with the concept of collective action frames, derived from mobilisation theory. While acknowledging the role of markets, institutions and actors, the literatures on power and on mobilisation have highlighted the importance of ideas in shaping people's behaviour and in particular their willingness to participate in collective action.

REFERENCES

Ashenfelter, O. and G. Johnson (1969), 'Bargaining theory, trade unions and industrial strike activity', *American Economic Review*, **59**(1), 35–49.

Barratt, C. (2009), *Trade Union Membership 2008*, London: Department for Business, Enterprise and Regulatory Reform.

Bordogna, L. and G. Cella (2002), 'Decline or transformation? Change in industrial conflict and its challenges', *Transfer*, **8**(4), 585–607.

Brandl, B. and F. Traxler (2010), 'Labour conflicts: a cross-national analysis of economic and institutional determinants, 1970–2002', *European Sociological Review*, **26**(5), 519–40.

Briskin, L. (2007), 'Public sector militancy, feminisation, and employer aggression: trends in strikes, lockouts, and wildcats in Canada from 1960 to 2004', in S. van der Velden, H. Dribbusch, D. Lyddon and K. Vandaele (eds), *Strikes Around the World, 1968–2005: Case Studies of 15 Countries*, Amsterdam: Aksant, pp. 86–113.

Brown, W. (2008), 'The influence of product markets on industrial relations', in P. Blyton, N. Bacon, J. Fiorito and E. Heery (eds), *The Sage Handbook of Industrial Relations*, London: Sage, pp. 113–28.

Brown, W., A. Bryson and J. Forth (2009), 'Competition and the retreat from collective bargaining', in W. Brown, A. Bryson, J. Forth and K. Whitfield (eds), *The Evolution of the Modern Workplace*, Cambridge: Cambridge University Press, pp. 22–47.

Callaghan, J. (2003), *Cold War, Crisis and Conflict: The History of the Communist Party of Great Britain 1951–68*, London: Lawrence and Wishart.

Callaghan, J. (2000), *The Retreat of Social Democracy*, Manchester: Manchester University Press.

Clegg, H. (1976), *Trade Unionism Under Collective Bargaining*, Oxford: Blackwell.

Cronin, J. (1979), *Industrial Conflict in Modern Britain*, London: Croom Helm.

Dicken, P. (2007), *Global Shift: Mapping the Changing Contours of the World Economy*, London: Sage.

Dickens, L. and M. Hall (2010), 'The changing legal framework of employment relations', in T. Colling and M. Terry (eds), *Industrial Relations: Theory and Practice*, 3rd edn, Chichester: Wiley, pp. 298–322.

Dribbusch, H. and K. Vandaele (2007), 'Comprehending divergence in strike activity: employers' offensives, government interventions and union responses', in S. van der Velden, H. Dribbusch, D. Lyddon and K. Vandaele (eds), *Strikes Around the World, 1968–2005: Case Studies of 15 Countries*, Amsterdam: Aksant, pp. 366–81.

Edwards, B. and J. McCarthy (2004), 'Resources and social movement mobilization', in D. Snow, S. Soule and H. Kriesi (eds), *The Blackwell Companion to Social Movements*, Oxford: Blackwell, pp. 116–52.

Edwards, P. and R. Hyman (1994), 'Strikes and industrial conflict: peace in Europe?', in R. Hyman and A. Ferner (eds), *New Frontiers in European Industrial Relations*, Oxford: Blackwell, pp. 250–80.

Edwards, P. and J. Wajcman (2005), *The Politics of Working Life*, Oxford: Oxford University Press.

European Commission (2007), *Towards Common Principles of Flexicurity: More and Better Jobs Through Flexibility and Security*, Luxembourg: Office for Official Publications of the European Communities.

European Industrial Relations Observatory (EIRO) (2010), *Industrial Relations Developments in Europe 2009*, accessed 10 November 2010 at www.eurofound.europa.eu/eiro/studies/tn1004019s/tn1004019s.htm.

EIRO (2009), *Industrial Relations Developments in Europe 2008*, accessed 10 November 2010 at www.eurofound.europa.eu/eiro/studies/tn0903029s/tn0903029s.htm.

Flanagan, R. (2008), 'The changing structure of collective bargaining', in P. Blyton, N. Bacon, J. Fiorito, J. and E. Heery (eds), *The Sage Handbook of Industrial Relations*, London: Sage, pp. 406–19.

Franzosi, R. (1995), *The Puzzle of Strikes*, Cambridge: Cambridge University Press.

Gall, G. (2010), 'Resisting recession and redundancy: contemporary worker occupations in Britain', *Working USA: The Journal of Labor and Society*, **13**(1),107–32.

Gall, G. and R. Hebdon (2008), 'Conflict at work' in P. Blyton, N. Bacon, J. Fiorito and E. Heery (eds), *The Sage Handbook of Industrial Relations*, London: Sage, pp. 588–605.

Gallagher, M., M. Laver and P. Mair (2006), *Representative Government in Western Europe: Institutions, Parties, and Governments*, New York: McGraw Hill.

Glyn, A. (2006), *Capitalism Unleashed: Finance, Globalization, and Welfare*, Oxford: Oxford University Press.

Hale, D. (2008), 'International Comparisons of Labour Disputes in 2006', *Economic and Labour Market Review*, **2**(4), 32–9.

Hamann, K. and J. Kelly (2011), *Parties, Elections and Policy Reforms in Western Europe: Voting for Social Pacts*, Abingdon: Routledge.

Hamann, K. and J. Kelly (2008) 'Varieties of capitalism and industrial relations', in P. Blyton, N. Bacon, J. Fiorito and E. Heery (eds), *The Sage Handbook of Industrial Relations*, London: Sage, pp. 129–49.

Hardy, C. and S. Leiba-O'Sullivan (1998), 'The power behind empowerment: implications for research and practice', *Human Relations*, **51**(4), 451–83.

Hyman, R. (2010), 'Social dialogue and industrial relations during the economic crisis: innovative practices or business as usual?', International Labour Office working paper 11, Geneva.

Hyman, R. (1994), 'Changing trade union identities and strategies' in R. Hyman and A. Ferner (eds), *New Frontiers in European Industrial Relations*, Oxford: Blackwell, pp. 108–39.

Jacobs, A. (2007), 'The law of strikes and lockouts', in R. Blanpain (ed), *Comparative Labour Law and Industrial Relations in Industrialised Market Economies*, The Hague: Kluwer, pp. 633–87.

Kelly, J. (2005), 'Social movement theory and union revitalization in Britain', in S. Fernie and M. Metcalf (eds), *Trade Unions: Resurgence or Demise?*, London: Routledge, pp. 62–82.

Kelly, J. (1998), *Rethinking Industrial Relations: Mobilization, Collectivism and Long Waves*, London: Routledge.

Kelly, J., K. Hamann and A. Johnston (2010), 'Unions against governments: explaining general strikes in Western Europe 1980–2008', unpublished manuscript.

Keune, M. (2008), 'Introduction: wage moderation, decentralisation of collective bargaining and low pay', in M. Keune and B. Galgóczi (eds), *Wages and Wage Bargaining in Europe*: *Developments Since the 1990s*, Brussels: European Trade Union Institute, pp. 7–27.

King, J. (1990), *Labour Economics*, Basingstoke: Macmillan.

Korpi, W. and M. Shalev (1979), 'Strikes, industrial relations and class conflict in capitalist societies', *British Journal of Sociology*, **30**(2), 164–87.

Lillie, N. (2006), *A Global Union for Global Workers*: *Collective Bargaining and Regulatory Politics in Maritime Shipping*, New York: Routledge.

Lukes, S. (1974), *Power: A Radical View*, London: Macmillan.

Lukes, S. (2005), *Power: A Radical View*, Basingstoke: Palgrave Macmillan.

Millward, N., A. Bryson and A. Forth (2000), *All Change at Work? British Employment Relations 1980–1998, As Portrayed by the Workplace Employment Relations Survey Series*, London: Routledge.

Moschonas, G. (2002), *In the Name of Social Democracy: The Great Transformation: 1945 to the Present*, London: Verso.

Piazza, J. (2005), 'Globalising quiescence: globalisation, union density and strikes in 15 industrialised countries', *Economic and Industrial Democracy*, **26**(2), 289–314.

Scheuer, S. (2006), 'A novel calculus? Institutional change, globalisation and industrial conflict in Europe', *European Journal of Industrial Relations*, **12**(2), 143–64.

Schmidt, V. (2002), *The Futures of European Capitalism*, New York: Oxford University Press.

Silver, B. (2003), *Forces of Labor: Workers' Movements and Globalization since 1870*, New York: Cambridge University Press.

Simms, M. and A. Charlwood (2010), 'Trade unions: power and influence in a changed context', in T. Colling and M. Terry (eds), *Industrial Relations: Theory and Practice*, Chichester: Wiley, pp. 125–48.

Sullivan, R. (2010), 'Labour market or labour movement? The union density bias as a barrier to labour renewal', *Work, Employment and Society*, **24**(1), 145–56.

Tarrow, S. (1994), *Power in Movement: Social Movements, Collective Action and Politics*, New York: Cambridge University Press.

Tattersall, A. (2010), *Power in Coalition: Strategies for Strong Unions and Social Change*, Ithaca, NY: ILR Press.

Thompson, P. and D. McHugh (2009), *Work Organizations: A Critical Approach*, Basingstoke: Palgrave Macmillan.

Tsebelis, G. and P. Lange (1995), 'Strikes around the world: a game theoretic approach', in S. Jacoby (ed), *The Workers of Nations*, New York: Oxford University Press, pp. 101–26.

Turnbull, P. (1988), 'The limits to Japanisation: just-in-time, labour relations and the UK automotive industry', *New Technology, Work and Employment*, **3**(1), 7–20.

Upchurch, M., G. Taylor and A. Mathers (2009), *The Crisis of Social Democratic Trade Unionism in Western Europe: The Search for Alternatives*, Farnham: Ashgate.

3 Union renewal: objective circumstances and social action

Pauline Dibben and Geoffrey Wood

INTRODUCTION

This chapter locates the problems and prospects of union renewal within contemporary theoretical debates. The first section critically appraises accounts that see the position of unions primarily as a product of objective circumstances that are not easily changed, including institutionalist accounts and approaches that locate the fortunes of unions in terms of economic long waves. The second section reevaluates approaches that see the fortunes of unions as linked to subjective interpretations and actions, and reviews the strategic alternatives promoted. Finally, we bring together recent thinking on the interrelationship between social action and structure, and the extent to which the former may remake the latter. We conclude that the wholesale destruction of 'good' jobs that provide decent terms and conditions of working and the resurgence of temporary, part time and contingent working poses great challenges for unions, and indeed, the idea of trade unionism itself. On the other hand, the visible failings of neo-liberalism open up a space for alternative, new and better ideas and practices.

CONVERGENCE APPROACHES

There are two strands of the literature that link union decline (or at least, constraints on the possibilities for union revival) to economic circumstances and which see the position of unions worldwide converging on a common outcome. The first is the broad area of globalisation. Conventional neo-liberal approaches within the literature on globalisation suggest that, in their imaginary reality composed of rational profit maximising individuals, firms are in the business of making money, and anything that distracts them from it will have negative consequences for their individual viability and the well being of an economy as a whole (Friedman 1997). This suggests that over time, inefficient systems will be driven out by efficient ones, closer to the market ideal (Fukuyama 2000).

A cautionary note is in order here. While neo-liberalism is often depicted as a coherent phenomenon, there is considerable difference between the purer ideological form (*cf.* Fukuyama 2000; Friedman 1997) and its supposed practice. The latter departs considerably from the neo-liberal ideal. Many supposed proclaimed proponents of neo-liberalism in the political and the policy arena are at the same time greatly in favour of big government when it comes to a wide range of areas. These include defence and security, in the direction of resources towards the mass incarceration of the criminal poor, in the restriction of the movement of labour across national boundaries, and indeed, in large scale bailouts of failed investment banks (MacEwan 2000; Standing 2011; Wood 2004). Again, highly competitive industries in countries that are upheld as beacons of neo-liberalism are often reliant on indirect state subsidies and support from the non-profit sector: a good example of this would be the reliance of the pharmaceutical industry and Silicon Valley in the US on research and development conducted within the universities. Hence, the term neo-liberalism needs to be deployed with a great deal of caution. For the purposes of this chapter, it is taken to refer to the loose set of policy prescriptions and practices promoted by international financial institutions and right wing (even if, in some instances, ostensibly socially democratic) governments, which, in practice, are often profoundly statist. This would include, inter alia, a commitment to labour market deregulation, cutbacks in non-defence related government spending, a withdrawal from active industrial policy outside of support for the banking and financial services industry and a reduction of social security and welfare provision. At the same time, it is recognised that much of what takes place under the banner of neo-liberalism is far removed from the ideal.

As unions – by challenging the allocation of resources within the firm, and the amount that can be returned as profits – weaken market efficiency, they will be gradually marginalised: those firms that entertain union demands will become visibly unviable, incentivising employers elsewhere to get rid of them. Such thinking still remains highly influential within both the conservative media and international financial institutions; ironically, while the 2008 financial crisis was about poor regulation and market failure, the bank bailouts seem only to have emboldened financial elites and the neo-liberal policy establishment. However, union decline has remained uneven, and many large firms with pluralist industrial relations have performed better than those without. A good example of the former is Volkswagen, while a firm illustrating the latter is General Motors. Moreover, at the national level, even in the late 1990s and early 2000s neo-liberal heyday, developed liberal market economies did little better than coordinated ones (the European social democracies), with countries such as Sweden generally performing better across a range of measures (OECD 2007).

Although the second area of literature is ideologically the antithesis of neo-liberal theories of convergence, it does make similar conclusions regarding ultimate uniformity. From this perspective, it is argued that intensive global competition has triggered a 'race to the bottom'; the corrosive effects of light regulation have resulted in countries and firms seizing short term competitive advantages through labour repression, only to find their position rapidly undermined by the emergence of new, even cheaper and more repressive alternatives (Sklair 1995; *cf.* Guest 2001). On the one hand, there is indeed an element of truth to this argument: for example, established manufacturing firms in East Africa with broadly pluralist industrial relations policies have battled to compete with new competitors from the Far East that have demonstrated lower wages and reduced terms and conditions (Wood and Brewster 2007). On the other hand, in the light of such circumstances the fortunes of unions remain uneven. Unions need a sizeable pool of potential members in jobs: if jobs are absent, union organisation simply is not possible. However, when ejected from the formal labour market many seek livelihoods in the informal sector, where alternative forms of collective organisation may be possible. This is an issue that we return to in a subsequent section of this chapter. Finally, the attitudes of right wing governments in parts of Europe towards unions, as exemplified by the Thatcher government's behaviour during the 1984 miners strike (Collings and Wood 2009) can be contrasted with the emergence of a large number of progressive governments in Latin America that have challenged the positions of old oligarchies, opening up new opportunities for improving workers' rights and representation. This is not to suggest that the Thatcher government coherently and consistently promoted neo-liberalism; it can be argued that subsequent UK governments have been even bolder in promoting neo-liberal reforms. And, across continental north western Europe, even right wing governments have shied away from the scale and scope of neo-liberal reforms experienced in the UK and the US; in such contexts, the environment in which unions operate remains far more hospitable.

Finally, there is more to globalisation than simply neo-liberalism. An important social change has been the increasing urbanisation of the world's population, reflecting not just the dislocation brought about by neo-liberal reforms but also climate change, war and demographic shifts. Most of the world's population are now slum dwellers, and some two out of five of the world's people today are in the process of migrating both within and between nations (Davies 2006; Standing 2011). One of the many contradictions of neo-liberalism is that despite a depiction of labour as simply another commodity, proponents of the doctrine are generally very hostile to migration across national boundaries (MacEwan 2000); indeed, one area where state intervention has increased in the developed world has been in terms of increased barriers to such mobility.

These developments open up new challenges and opportunities for organised labour. Existing constituents may fear being undercut through the influx of large numbers of ultra-cheap workers. At the same time, large urban concentrations of the poor may facilitate political mobilisation and the forging of new community based solidarities (Standing 2011).

PERSISTENT DIFFERENCE IN UNION FORTUNES

The persistence of national developmental paths – which include considerable variations in worker rights and representation – underlines the limitations of assumptions of inevitable convergence. However, regardless of these obvious limitations, there has still been an increasing influence of fundamentally neo-liberal rational hierarchical approaches to institutions. Such approaches suggest that national institutions are embedded (that is to say, they are not easily changed) and that persistent differences account for the uneven fortunes of nations (North 1990). Of fundamental importance to this line of argument is the right to private property: certain institutional environments accord greater protection to private property than others. Where property rights are stronger, individuals have greater incentives to maximise profits, making for better macro-economic outcomes (North 1990). An influential strand of this literature has highlighted the defining effect of legal systems: in civil law countries, property rights are weaker and in common law ones they are stronger (La Porta *et al.* 1999). While undeniably more sophisticated than some other theories of convergence, such approaches still assume that employee and owner rights represent a 'zero sum game' (Goergen *et al.* 2009). If workers are stronger, they will divert resources in their direction, thus decreasing profits, and making firms and economies ultimately less viable (La Porta *et al.* 1999).

In practical terms, what does this mean for union renewal? In the common law tradition, a defining feature is the importance of individual property (La Porta *et al.* 1999), and anything that is done to challenge this has historically been circumscribed. And, under common law, the courts play a central role in fleshing out and developing the law, but employers are likely to have greater legal resources at their disposal than that held by unions. In contrast, a key feature of the civil law tradition has been the promotion of social solidarity (La Porta *et al.* 1999). This has meant that the rights of property owners are offset against the rights of others in society. Botero *et al.* (2004) argue that this has meant that union rights under the law are much stronger in civil law countries than common law ones; in other words, the legal strength of unions is in inverse proportion to property rights.

On the one hand, there is some merit to this basic argument. Unions are generally weaker in developed common law countries than in civil law ones, and this does, at least in part, reflect their position under the law (*cf.* Godard 2004). And successful litigation, even if having a collective dimension, will invariably depend on individual employees – removed from the anonymity of collective and union protection – opening themselves up to future victimisation (Psychogios and Wood 2009). Given that legal traditions are not subject to change, this limits what unions can do in common law systems; the best prospects for unions therefore appear to be within civil law contexts.

On the other hand, there are clear limitations to such approaches. First, a closer scrutiny reveals that owner and worker rights are not mutually exclusive. In Scandinavian countries, which fall under a tradition of civil law where property rights are not quite as weak as in French civil law ones (Botero *et al.* 2004), unions are nonetheless stronger (Goergen *et al.* 2009). This suggests that there are situations of complementarity, where both sides in the employment relationship may be better off than they would be if one side had disproportionate power (Goergen *et al.* 2009). Moreover, there is considerable diversity within each category. For example, Canadian unions remain stronger than US ones, despite the fact that both have common law legal systems. Second, irrespective of legal origin, there are contexts where the law has limited effects. In much of the developing world, the enforcement of labour law is very uneven, and in some areas nearly completely absent (*cf.* Webster and Wood 2005; Wood and Frynas 2005). The same situation is apparent even in the case of many southern European countries (Wood and Psychogios 2009). This is true for both civil law countries (for example Francophone and Lusophone Africa) and common law ones (for example Anglophone Africa). While property rights may also be weaker, a lack of law enforcement favours those who have more resources at their disposal, with the poor worse off. In civil law contexts with extreme right wing governments, such as Columbia, the role of quasi official paramilitaries and death squads against those who threaten the social order makes union organisation extremely dangerous. In others, such as across most of Africa, extremely high unemployment rates make it difficult for workers to challenge owner agendas. Yet, in such contexts, union organisation is difficult, but not impossible: the courage of individuals has challenged what appear to be objective circumstances, even if the latter appear stubbornly immune to change.

VARIETIES OF CAPITALISM AND UNION RENEWAL

Variations in the fortunes of unions may be the result of institutional configurations. An influential strand of contemporary institutionalist thinking is the Varieties of Capitalism literature. This literature holds that what firms do is the product of webs of relationships (rather than hierarchical features, with a particular set of institutions, such as the law, impacting on all others) (Hall and Soskice 2001). As many sets of viable combinations are possible, this means that more than one institutional framework may be viable at any time; this sets such approaches apart from rational hierarchical approaches such as that of La Porta *et al.* (1999). Within much of this literature, a key distinction has been made between liberal market economies, and coordinated market ones (Hall and Soskice 2001; *cf.* Dore 2000). Within the former, shareholder rights enjoy primacy, while in the latter, this is diluted through the embedded rights of other stakeholder groupings (Hall and Soskice 2001). The latter include workers and their collectives. Examples of liberal markets are the United States, Britain and Australia, while coordinated ones include the continental European social democracies and Japan.

Such approaches hold that national institutions do make a difference (Kelly and Frege 2004: 182), but that institutional environments are not just the construct of abstract market forces, but social interactions as well. What the firm does reflects relationships, ties and choices in a wide range of different spheres (Kelly and Frege 2004: 183). While central to this literature is an implicit assumption as to the continued viability of coordinated market economies, this literature is not explicitly progressive; it assumes that a range of different institutional configurations are possible at any time, with each being viable to at least some key players (Hall and Soskice 2001); one institutional configuration is not assumed to be necessarily superior to another. However, from a union perspective, certain institutional environments are certainly 'better' for them than others; these are the situations where shareholder power is not dominant, but is mitigated by the role of other associations in society and related rules (Dore 2000). This raises the question of how institutional configurations that are not only 'good' for owners but a range of other stakeholders, including unions, emerge, and the role and potential of unions in institutional redesign.

UNIONS RENEWAL AND LONG WAVES

An alternative approach has been to see variations in the fortunes of unions in terms of economic long waves. A feature of the global economy that apparently predates capitalism is of long periods of growth, interspersed by periods of stagnation, recession and transition phases (Kelly 1998). During long periods of growth, workers are in a stronger bargaining position owing to low unemployment and competition among firms for skills. As long upswings draw to a close, rates of profit fall. Employers try to restore profits through wage freezes or cuts, or by raising prices, which places pressure on worker standards of living (Kelly 1998: 98). Price rises across an economy heighten pressures on workers, and hence feelings of injustice (Kelly 1998: 98). In turn, this fuels mobilisation, leading to waves of resistance. This then leads to counter-attacks by employers; as recession nears, the bargaining position of workers declines, leading to the weakening of unions and demobilisation, and ultimately, through the downswing, a long period of employer ascendancy (Kelly 1998: 102).

There is considerable empirical evidence to support such arguments. The end of the postwar long upswing was marked by waves of strikes, employer counter-offensives and global declines in union membership. The fragility of many firms, and a decline in the proportion of 'good' – as adverse to deskilled and contingent – jobs placed workers in a very poor position to resist. A weakness of Varieties of Capitalism theories is that they discount the effects of general trends – unions have declined even in the more conducive environment of coordinated markets. However, by equal measure any approach that focuses on broad changes in global economies discounts the effects of national institutions; union decline may be global but it is also uneven (*cf.* Kelly and Frege 2004).

A broader problem with long wave approaches is that they are short on predictive power. Long waves are by no means of uniform length. And the transition prior to the long boom of the 1950s was long, bitter and contested: it was marked by the rise and fall of fascism and global war. Only when reactionary politics were totally (although only temporarily) discredited was it possible to reach meaningful social compromises and for worker power to recover. Disturbingly, our current position vis-à-vis a future long wave may not be the late 1940s, but rather the late 1920s or early 1930s, with the possibility of resurgences in reactionary and fascist politics, founded on coalitions between segments of capital and the fearful downwardly mobile, who blame systemic failings on the weakest in society (coalitions such as already encountered in right wing US politics, and those actively promoted by conservative British tabloids) (*cf.* Standing 2011).

A further concern for the current time is that unions are better equipped to expand in sectors where they have a historic presence (Kelly and Frege 2004: 191). For example, in the postwar period in the UK, unions were well placed to capitalise on the growth in the engineering industry; there are fewer strategically placed union enclaves in the UK in the 2000s from which to springboard a recovery. While a new long boom will definitely enhance the bargaining position of workers, it is by no means certain that traditional style unions will be the primary vehicle used to pursue their demands.

A final challenge to long wave theories is what can be termed the 'black plague problem'. Broader environmental catastrophes or epidemics can depress the global economy for centuries (Casti 2010). In medieval Europe, there is evidence of the existence of Kondratieff Waves, but there is also evidence that at times, these waves represented steps in a descending staircase. The rise of the modern world from the 1600s onwards led to exponential increases in the size of the economy in specific parts of the globe, even if this very long trend was an irregular, metaphorical ascending staircase. But the onset of peak oil (and peak coal) challenges the basis of hydrocarbon based economies; global warming undermines the basis of human existence across large parts of the planet. And, as Giddens (2009) notes, it is likely that political elites will not do much about it until it is too late: only when the negative consequences become clearly and irrefutably visible will there be sufficient political will to tackle the underlying issues. What does this mean for workers? Quite simply, if we are embarking on a downward trajectory, then large components of society – and indeed, whole nations, regions and continents – are likely to become much poorer. As Diamond (2003) notes, there is little evidence to suggest that our society will be any more immune than its predecessors from eventual decline. What can unions do? Impoverishment for all of society, with the exception of a small global elite, means that workers worldwide will be in a very poor bargaining position. There is little doubt that as the cake shrinks, elites will bitterly defend their existing slices; and as their position weakens, an increasing proportion of the world's population (as indeed most already are) will be locked into ongoing equally bitterly competitive horizontal struggles for survival, with diminishing opportunities for collective action. As Breman (2009) notes, the most vulnerable are locked in constant inter-competition for resources and opportunities, resulting in alliances on caste, ethnic, religion or other 'primordial identities'.

Global warming and sustainable energy alternatives are union issues; if nothing is done, then the lot of a sizeable component of the world's population will become ever more fragile. Standing (2011) refers to this process as precariatisation; there has been a global shift towards increasingly insecure and contingent working. The danger is that, in the face of day to day struggles over livelihoods, these issues will be placed on the back burner: not only political elites, but also the union leadership are not likely to accord such issues central priority until it is too late (*cf.* Giddens 2009).

UNION RENEWAL AND STRATEGIC CHOICE

The more progressive of the approaches that depict unions largely as subjects of external forces may provide some comfort to unions in hard times (the bargaining position of workers *will* change, and there are some contexts where unions will *always* be more secure), but they do not solve the day to day problems of leadership, of making the best of, or bettering bad situations, nor can they explain isolated incidences of union resurgence on apparently infertile ground.

Within the developed world, a strategy aimed at recapturing some of the social movement role has been the organising model (Roberts 1999: 38). Originating in California, this model seeks to mobilise workers via communities, through being relevant to community issues and questions of social justice, as well as to day-to-day struggles at the workplace (Roberts 1999: 38). In practice, this model places a strong emphasis on recruitment, and working through local activists (Frege 1999: 279). Successful organising among immigrant cleaners in Los Angeles encouraged the emulation of this model across a number of liberal market economies (Gall 2003). While many unions from Britain to New Zealand experimented with the organising model, the results were often mixed. Indeed, Hurd (2004) notes that across much of the US the model failed to deliver. And, as Gall (2003: 234) observes, 'organising came to encompass many different meanings'; there was no ideal type template that could be successfully transposed across a variety of settings. Fulfilling a genuine social movement role is itself very difficult, given inevitable contestations over legitimacy and representivity, and the problems of accommodating inevitable compromises (von Holdt 2002).

In emerging economies, the social movement role has had more success, as demonstrated by the COSATU federation in South Africa helping to bring to an end to the apartheid system that created racial divisions between workers and within broader society. It was here that the notion of 'social movement unionism' was arguably most clearly apparent. Unions took a proactive role as central player, in the transformation of society. In this sense, they may have been closer to a traditional social movement role (Touraine 1981), but also exhibited certain characteristics that have since been regarded as central to 'social movement unionism'. They developed internal democratic structures, effectively dealt with political opportunities and constraints, and reached out to marginalised communities (Dibben 2004; Moody 1997; Webster 1991). These strategies have also been evident in other countries, including Brazil and South Korea, although the historical contexts, political landscape, and economic situations have created different conditions.

The term 'social movement unionism' has also been used to describe union behaviour in more recent times, but questions have been raised about the extent to which unions have been able to take a truly transformative role, particularly given their lack of ability to represent the growing numbers of workers in atypical or contingent work (Webster 2004). In Southern Africa and India, informal sector workers form the majority of the workforce, yet often remain outside unions. In South Africa, individual unions in industries as diverse as retail and domestic work have attempted to reach out to such workers, but have had limited success; in countries such as Mozambique and

Ghana they have sought to represent informal sector workers through affili-ated organisations (Dibben, 2010).

Therefore, unions appear not to have taken a transformative role, as origi-nally envisaged by the concept 'social movement unionism'. At the same time, they have attempted to build their membership and influence their political and economic context. A variety of adaptations have therefore been developed to capture the way in which union strategies have evolved. Some have used the term 'Social Unionism' or 'New Social Unionism' to capture the chal-lenges inherent in globalisation and to emphasise the need for unions to develop international networks in order to defend members against interna-tional corporations (Waterman 2001). Meanwhile, the term 'Social Justice Unionism' encapsulates the need for unions to proactively address the diverse needs of marginalised groupings and to embrace concerns about poverty (Scipes 2003; Tattersall 2006). As with social movement unionism, these terms have been used for both prescriptive and descriptive purposes, and applied to a range of contexts.

In short, while a social movement role may be desirable, and the organis-ing model may be one way (in very specific contexts) of regaining it, union revitalisation cannot flow from a single strategic framework. First, there is the problem of transferability to different contexts: specific institutional frame-works and relationships may facilitate some interventions and thwart others. And, while unions worldwide have much to learn from each other, there is also a need for further innovation. This is particularly so given the decline of regu-lar, relatively secure jobs worldwide, and the resurgence of contingent, in-secure and informal working. Organising in the latter areas is extremely difficult given debilitating daily struggles for survival and inevitable horizon-tal conflicts for resources among the dispossessed.

INSTITUTIONS AND ACTION: THEORIES AND PRACTICES

There are many approaches to understanding the relationship between action and social structure. Simmel (1980) highlighted the interaction between subjective interpretations and actions and objective circumstances, and the extent to which they impact on each other. Such themes were developed in Elias's works in the 1960s. More recently, Giddens (1984) has outlined what he has termed 'structuration theory'. Simply understood, this implies that through a process of structuration, practices impact and remake social struc-ture, and in return are remade (Giddens 1984). Thus social action cannot be independent of objective circumstances. In practical terms, this means that when implemented, strategies for union renewal may indeed remake embedded social structures, but in turn, social structures will impact back on practices. In other words, when transposed into a different setting, strategies will inevitably (even if unconsciously) be adapted. In turn, all actions, even if slight, will have an impact on social structures: what appears to be 'failure' may indeed have positive long term effects, while successes may spark off negative feedback loops (Sztompka 1991), worsening the situation.

There has been a range of critiques of structuration theory. Of particular relevance here arc two fundamental weaknesses that are important to take into consideration in theorising union renewal. First, the theory retraces well trodden ground on the inevitable interface between social structure and action; it is worth noting that writers such as Parsons pointed to this possibility many years ago (Cohen 1984). Second, in concentrating on the interface between social action and structure, it pays insufficient attention to effects at horizontal level; the extent to which structures will not just be remoulded through action, but may be substituted, hybridised and remade through both innovation and serendipity (Boyer 2006).

More recent attempts at exploring the relationship between action and structure include the proposition put forward by Sorge (2005: 240) that institutional development reflects the recombination of different elements coexisting in close proximity: societies have a capacity to decouple and combine institutional domains. In simple terms, this means that some institutional features may cease to work, others may be eliminated, and new ones may arise. The rise of new institutional features may reflect regional dynamics, historical legacies and new complementarities, following on from experimentation (Lane and Wood 2009). What does this mean in practice for union renewal? First, unions are not an inevitable feature of modernity. The place of unions and what they do in societies represents the product of constant contestation and innovation. Unions cannot count on survival just because they have always been there; but, as with any other social collective, they may reinvent themselves in such a way as to secure and expand their role and invent new ones.

Second, any set of social institutions that provides the basis for growth is, as regulation theorists remind us, always temporarily and spatially confined (Jessop 2001). Neo-liberalism (or financialisation for that matter) has never brought about enough stability or secured enough sustained growth to constitute a coherent growth regime (Wolfson 2003; Wood and Wright 2010). At the time of writing, we remain in a long period of experimentation, with policy solutions that often seem to be more concerned with inflating new speculative bubbles than providing the basis for sustainable new growth. But, although neo-liberalism may not work, it remains the dominant policy framework across much of the world: as Wood and Frynas (2006) suggest, objectively dysfunctional sets of rules and practices may persist when they suit the short term interests of powerful elites. However, each new bubble has become more fragile (Brenner 2003) which suggests that neo-liberalism's lack of viability will ultimately result in a new or reconfigured institutional basis for stable economic activity and growth.

This does not mean that neo-liberalism will vanish quietly in the night. First, there are powerful vested interests in the present order, who have gradually refined the politics of 'astro-turfing', the creation of essentially fraudulent mass movements that successfully tap into popular anger at increasing insecurity, while blaming governments and the even more vulnerable for the crisis. Second, the violent dimensions of neo-liberalism should not be underestimated. From a neo-liberal perspective, if markets operate properly the poor have themselves to blame for their plight. This may lead to divisions between the poorest, and horizontal disputes over the proverbial crumbs makes progressive counter-mobilisation more difficult. With much to be angry about, and lacking a coherent voice, the precariat are likely to fall victim to reactionary extremism (Standing 2011).

CONCLUSION

Existing research evidence suggests that there is no 'magic bullet' for union revival. Much touted strategies for renewal, such as organising unionism, have yielded very mixed results when rolled out in social circumstances significantly different to those where it was originally conceived. The economic crisis that began in 2008 has, in many contexts, resulted in further rounds of job losses in traditional union strongholds. Yet, while it is vital for unions to seek to reach out to those in highly insecure jobs and in the informal sector, mobilising workers in such areas is highly difficult, given the smaller average sizes of workplaces and the problems of enforcing labour law in such areas. However, while the global downturn may have created new challenges for unions, it has also opened up new opportunities. The contemporary heterodox institutional literature highlights the temporary nature of any period of growth, and the need for institutional redesign following on from crisis. This both poses challenges and opens opportunities for organised labour; unions have to defend members whose relative position has weakened and, at the same time, actively seek to promote policy alternatives. Central to this is the challenge of promoting ties and solidarities with the objective of reengaging the precariat, those in contingent, poorly rewarded and insecure work (Standing 2011).

As Walter Benjamin (1979) noted, 'the angel of history' moves on, leaving rubble behind. Unions cannot return to the models of the past. In countries where deindustrialisation is most advanced, regular secure employment has become increasingly scarce; the prospects of reversing this trend in the foreseeable future appear remote. Quite simply, a large component of the traditional constituency of unions has vanished. At the same time, resurgent global poverty and injustice give unions much to do: this may mean a return to the bitter and unequal struggles of the nineteenth and early twentieth centuries that more often than not led to defeat, but ultimately forced meaningful social compromises. We are cautious regarding the possibilities for a Polanyian 'double movement': we may be entering a long period of global economic decline as a result of environmental changes and increased scarcity in primary resources, with uncertain consequences. At the same time, the process of change is always uneven, episodic and non-linear, opening up the possibility for new accommodations, compromises and ways of doing things. Unions may not currently be, nor be in the future, a force for societal and economic transformation, but they should continue to seek opportunities to play a central role in representing both their core workers and those in more vulnerable, insecure jobs, and to challenge governments and powerful international institutions where their policies lead to increased inequality.

REFERENCES

Benjamin, W. (1979), *One-way Street and Other Writings*, London: New Left Books.

Botero, J., S. Djankov, R. La Porta and F. Lopez-de-Silanes (2004), 'The Regulation of Labor', *The Quarterly Journal of Economics*, **119**, 1339–82.

Boyer, R. (2006), 'How do Institutions Cohere and Change?', in G. Wood and P. James (eds), *Institutions and Working Life*, Oxford: Oxford University Press, pp. 13–61.

Breman, J. (2009), 'Myth of the global safety net', *New Left Review*, **59**.

Brenner, R. (2003), *The Boom and the Bubble*, London: Verso.

Casti, J. (2010), *Mood Matters*, Berlin: Springer.

Cohen, I. (1984), *Anthony Giddens and the Constitution of Social Life*, London: Macmillan.

Collings, D. and G. Wood (2009), 'Human resource management: a critical approach', in D. Collings and G. Wood (eds), *Human Resource Management: A Critical Approach*, London: Routledge.

Davies, M. (2006), *Planet of the Slums*, London: Verso.

Diamond, J. (2003), *Guns, Germs and Steel*, New York: Vintage.

Dibben, P. (2004), 'Social movement unionism', in G. Wood and M. Harcourt (eds), *Trade Unions and Democracy*, Manchester: Manchester University Press.

Dibben, P. (2010), 'Trade union change, development and renewal in emerging economies: the case of Mozambique', *Work, Employment and Society*, **24**(3), 468–86.

Dore, R. (2000), *Stock Market Capitalism: Welfare Capitalism*, Cambridge: Cambridge University Press.

Frege, C. (1999), 'The challenges to trade unions in Europe', *Work and Occupations*, **26**(2), 279–81.

Friedman, M. (1997), 'The social responsibility of business is to increase its profits', in T. Beauchamp and N. Bowie (eds), *Ethical Theory and Business*, Upper Saddle River, NJ: Prentice Hall.

Fukuyama, F. (2000), 'The End of History', in R. Burns and H. Rayment-Pickard (eds), *Philosophies of History*, Oxford: Blackwell.

Gall, G. (2003), 'Conclusion' in G. Gall (ed), *Union Organising*, London: Routledge.

Giddens, A. (1984), *The Constitution of Society*, Cambridge: Polity.

Giddens, A. (2009), *The Politics of Climate Change*, Cambridge: Polity.

Godard, J. (2004), 'The U.S. and Canadian Labour movements: markets vs. states and societies', in G. Wood and M. Harcourt (eds), *Trade Unions and Democracy*, Manchester: Manchester University Press.

Goergen, M., C. Brewster and G. Wood (2009), 'Corporate Governance regimes and employment relations in Europe', *Industrial Relations/Relations Industrielles*, **64**(6), 620–40.

Guest, D. (2001), 'Industrial relations and human resource management', in J. Storey (ed), *Human Resource Management*, London: Thomson Learning.

Hall, P. and D. Soskice (2001), 'An Introduction to varieties of capitalism', in P. Hall and D. Soskice (eds), *Varieties of Capitalism: The Institutional Foundations of Competitive Advantage*, Oxford: Oxford University Press, pp. 1–68.

Hurd, R. (2004), 'The rise and fall of the organising model in the US', in G. Wood and M. Harcourt (eds), *Trade Unions and Democracy*, Manchester: Manchester University Press.

Jessop, B. (2001), 'Series preface' in B. Jessop (ed), *Regulation Theory and the Crisis of Capitalism – Volume 4: Country Studies*, Cheltenham, UK and Northampton, MA, USA: Edward Elgar.

Kelly, J. (1998), *Rethinking Industrial Relations: Mobilisation, Collectivism and Long Waves*, London: Routledge.

Kelly, J. and C. Frege (2004), 'Conclusions', in C. Frege and J. Kelly (eds), *Varieties of Unionism*, Oxford: Oxford University Press.

Lane, C. and G. Wood (2009), 'Introducing diversity in capitalism and capitalist diversity', *Economy and Society*, **38**(4), 531–51.

La Porta, R., F. Lopez-de-Silanes and A. Shleifer (1999), 'Corporate ownership around the world', *The Journal of Finance*, **54**(2), 471–517.

MacEwan, A. (2000), *Neo-Liberalism or Democracy?*, London: Zed.

Moody, K. (1997), *Workers in a Lean World*, London: Verso.

North, D. C. (1990), *Institutions, Institutional Change and Economic Performance*, Cambridge: Cambridge University Press.

Organisation for Economic Cooperation and Development (OECD) (2007), *Country Statistical Profiles*, Paris: OECD.

Psychogios, A. and G. Wood (2009), 'Human resource management in comparative perspective: alternative institutionalist perspectives and empirical realities – the case of Greece', University of Sheffield: unpublished working paper.

Roberts, M. (1999), 'The future of labor unions: a review', *Monthly Labor Review*, **122**(10), 38–9.

Scipes, K. (2003), 'Social movement unionism: can we apply the theoretical conceptualisation to the new unions in South Africa – and beyond?', LabourNet Germany, accessed at www.labournet.de/diskussion/gewerkshaft/smuandsa.html.

Simmel, G. (1980), *Essays on Interpretation in Social Science*, Manchester: Manchester University Press.

Sklair, L. (1995), *Sociology of the Global System*, Hemel Hempstead: Harvester-Wheatsheaf.

Sorge, A. (2005), *The Global and the Local: Understanding the Dialectics of Business Systems*, Oxford: Oxford University Press.

Standing, G. (2011), *The Precariat: The New Dangerous Class*, New York: Bloomsbury.

Sztompka, P. (1991), *Society in Action: The Theory of Social Becoming*, Cambridge: Polity.

Tattersall, A. (2009), *Power in Coalition – Strategies for Strong Unions and Social Change*, Crows Nest, NSW: Allen and Unwin.

Touraine, A. (1981), *The Voice and the Eye: An Analysis of Social Movements*, Cambridge: Cambridge University Press.

Von Holdt, K. (2002), 'Social movement unionism: the case of South Africa', *Work Employment and Society*, **16**(2), 283–304.

Waterman, P. (2001), 'Trade union internationalism in the age of Seattle', *Antipode*, **29**(1), 312–36.

Webster, E. (1991), 'Taking labour seriously: sociology and labour in South Africa', *South African Sociological Review*, **4**(1), 50–72.

Webster, E. (2004), 'New forms of work and the representational gap: a Durban case study', in G.

Wood and M. Harcourt (eds), *Trade Unions and Democracy*, Manchester: Manchester University Press.

Webster, E. and G. Wood (2005), 'Human resource management practice and institutional constraints', *Employee Relations*, **27**(4), 369–85.

Wolfson, M. (2003), 'Neoliberalism and the social structure of accumulation', *Review of Radical Political Economics*, **35**(3), 255–63.

Wood, N. (2004), *Tyranny in America*, London: Verso.

Wood, G. and C. Brewster (2007), 'Introduction: comprehending industrial relations in Africa', in G. Wood and C. Brewster (eds), *Industrial Relations in Africa*, London: Palgrave.

Wood, G. and G. Frynas (2006), 'The institutional basis of economic failure: anatomy of the segmented business system', *Socio-Economic Review*, **4**(2), 239–77.

Wood, G., M. Harcourt and S. Harcourt 2004), 'The effects of age discrimination legislation on workplace practice', *Industrial Relations Journal*, **35**(4), 359–71.

Wood, G. and M. Wright (2010), 'Wayward agents, dominant elite, or reflection of internal diversity? A critique of Folkman, Froud, Johal and Williams on financialisation and financial intermediaries', *Business History*, **52**(7), 1048–67.

4 Pragmatism, ideology or politics? Unions' and workers' responses to the imposition of neo-liberalism in Argentina

Maurizio Atzeni and Pablo Ghigliani

INTRODUCTION

Neo-liberalism has imposed itself as a paradigm of the world economy through geographically and historically uneven processes, producing changes in the social milieu and institutional frameworks of nations in different forms and at different times. These variations in national contexts, important as they are to explain differences for instance in terms of trade unions' opposition or accommodation to the system, cannot be grasped without considering both the economic and political aspects of neo-liberalism. The generalised implementation of market oriented economic policies, the liberalisation of labour markets, the commodification of the former public sector through privatisation, and the financialisation of the economy, should not be seen then as just changes in the economic sphere but as parts of a more general political project. As Harvey (2005) has argued, this project, starting as a reaction to 1970s economic and social turmoil, aimed to re-establish conditions for capital accumulation and restoration of class power and involved both the creative destruction of institutions, social relations, work organisations and welfare systems and an hegemonic discourse, which legitimised market reforms as natural and common-sense.

Harvey's analysis of neo-liberalism as a worldwide project aimed at rebalancing the class relationship and thus comprehending economic, political and ideological dimensions, seems particularly relevant in the case of Argentina, where since 1976 a combination of all these dimensions has appeared, responding to macroeconomic international variables, local political struggles and social conflicts. Three main neo-liberal phases can be identified. The liberalisation of the economy introduced by the military dictatorship of the period 1976–1983 the structural and fiscal adjustment policies that characterised the return to democracy in 1983–1989 and the massive programme of privatisations, public sector reform and labour flexibility implemented during the 1990s but opened by the economic terror of the hyperinflation of 1989–1990. Since the 2001 economic and political crisis, a neo-developmental and agricultural commodities export oriented scheme has moved away from crude neo-liberalism, though not reversing the structural changes brought about by the previous decades (Basualdo 2006; Kosacoff 2010).

These phases have, in turn, differently affected workers and unions, which have alternated themselves between full and partial rejection, forced and pragmatic acceptance, complicit and explicit consensus, reflecting not just – within each of these phases – a variety of political and ideological approaches, but occasionally important differences between institutional and grassroot based responses (Atzeni and Ghigliani 2007, 2009). However, as the chapter will show, this diversity does not allow for a clear cut distinction between different unions' ideological stances towards neo-liberalism. These tactical oscillations and more in general unions' politics in Argentina cannot, however, be fully comprehended without considering some distinctive institutional, political and organisational features, around which the activity of unions has been structured. In this respect a crucial aspect is represented by the history of Peronism, a union based political movement, which has marked the political landscape of the country since the mid-1940s.

Thus, in the following sections, the chapter will describe first what makes unionism peculiar in Argentina to show how each different phase of globally imposed neo-liberal reforms produced a series of responses from unions which, mixing pragmatism, ideology and politics, have allowed organisational survival when facing 35 years of neo-liberal policies as well as a renewed political role. However, looking at the devastating effectsof neo-liberalism on the Argentinean working class, it is questionable the extent to which this success in the defence of the institutional role of trade unions really corresponded to better conditions for workers.

PERONISM, THE STATE AND THE UNION STRUCTURE

The rise of Colonel Juan Perón to power (1946–1955) represented a turning point in the history of Argentinean trade unionism, which as a result, became a major political actor with enough institutional power to mobilise workers at a political and industrial level. This new role was rooted in a political alliance based on redistributive policies, to reinforce the process of import substitution industrialisation and framed ideologically by the notion of social justice. By this alliance, the government was expected to favour workers' economic and social demands and empower their unions; whereas the latter had to play a key role guaranteeing the social peace necessary for the country's industrial development. Since that moment, the state played a central role in the system of industrial relations as the transformation of trade unions into the political constituency and structure of the Peronist movement was parallelled by legislation regulating workers' organisations and collective bargaining. This industrial relations context created periodic struggles to defend trade unions' institutional autonomy from attempts to subordinate it to state regulations, political interference and party loyalties (Doyon 2006; James 1990).

First and foremost, the Peronist government regulated workers' representation by giving legal recognition for the negotiation of collective agreements and representation of workers at the workplace or in courts (the so-called *personería gremial*) to just one organisation per industrial sector or economic activity. While generally strengthening trade unionism, this legislation conditioned workers' freedom of association to decisions of the executive power, often putting unions at risk of losing their *personería gremial*. Besides this, legislation also regulated the arbitration and participation of public authorities, making this compulsory, as with the formal approval by the Ministry of Labour of new collective agreements or by enforcing mediation to conflicting parts (*conciliación obligatoria*) (Atzeni and Ghigliani 2009).

This rigid and politically dominated system of industrial relations has been historically supported by most, mainly Peronist, union leaders, as it was thought to be functional to reinforce the union bargaining position. Strategic coincidence about the advantages offered by such legislation has not precluded different views among Peronist unions in the face of changing circumstances. Thus informal and highly volatile alliances, known as *nucleamientos sindicales*, have often been formed, gathering trade unions according to political and tactical aims regarding industrial and governmental issues as well as leadership rivalries (Fernández 1998).

The legislative framework that empowered unions' structures at national level however also corresponded to the expansion of shop steward structures (*cuerpos de delegados* and *comisiones internas*). These have historically challenged both managerial control over the labour process and working conditions and decisions taken by established leadership at central level, expressing workers' concerns over the impact of economic and political reforms upon the workplace. Thus, in the history of labour unionism in Argentina, a threefold dynamic can be identified. On the one hand, the juridification of the system of industrial relations and the relationships between unions and the Peronist political movement have maintained a powerful and centralised union oligarchy, which often looks for government support and political exchange as means to its ends. On the other hand, scattered but vibrant grassroots' worker mobilisations came to the fore time and again, often through the revitalisation of the *comisiones internas*, and frequently, in open confrontation with national or regional trade union leaderships (Basualdo 2009). Finally, unions' power in Argentina rests also on the *obras sociales*, institutions under union management, which provide workers with health care and general social welfare schemes. *Obras sociales* have been a crucial source of financial and political resources for unions since the 1970s, and an axis of union political exchange with the state (Atzeni and Ghigliani 2009).

In sum, every attack to workers' organisations during the three aforementioned neo-liberal phases entailed an attack to their legal and financial underpinnings and, until 1989, an attack to Peronism as well as an assault of *comisiones internas*, the grassroots sources of workers' power (Atzeni and Ghigliani 2007, 2009). This institutional and structural background should be kept in mind to explain the variety of trade unions reactions to neo-liberalism in Argentina.

NEO-LIBERALISM THROUGH REPRESSION: UNION OPPOSITION TO THE MILITARY REGIME

There is common agreement that the military putsch on 24 March 1976 was a turning point in the country's economic and social history (Basualdo 2006). The climate of violence, terror and persecution brought about by the military regime in Argentina during the years 1976–1983 is well known, although much less, it is the price paid by workers' delegates and unions' activists (which represented 30 per cent of the disappeared). The physical repression of workers' resistance, the control of unions, the anti-labour legislation and the overall attempt to increase productivity by imposing discipline and silencing dissent in the workplace, was the most visibly brutal side of a project that, by dissolving unions' political and social power, wanted to entirely restructure the model of capital accumulation in Argentina (Palomino 2005). Indeed, the first historical encounter of Argentina with a fully fledged programme of neo-liberal economic reforms cannot be understood without linking the restructuring of the economy to the physical and associational destruction of the labour movement power (Peralta Ramos 2007). In consequence, in considering this period, unions' response to neo-liberalism should be seen as an attempt to defend workers' historic conquests, their own organisational survival and the ideals of wealth redistribution as embodied in the Peronist ideology of social justice, within a more generalised struggle for democracy. This main response, however, did not avert that a small group of union leaders collaborated with the military rulers (Pozzi 1988).

On the economic front, pressured and justified by growing inflation, the military government introduced a series of fiscal, monetary and financial reforms, all made possible by the expansion of external debt, to liberalise the market, attract foreign investments and increase external competition. This meant the abandonment of the model of import substitution based on the development and protection of local industries that dominated the country's economy for over 30 years. These policies caused de-industrialisation and boosted capital concentration, determining an overall reduction in real salaries and worsening working conditions (Schvarzer 1996). On the legislative front, a series of decrees and acts suspended collective bargaining; changed the labour contract favouring employers; widened wage differentials; facilitated redundancies and layoffs; prohibited the right of strike (and other forms of workers' direct action along with union activities in the workplaces); and paralysed the normal functioning of national and regional trade unions' confederations (by controlling their finances and *obras sociales*) (Pozzi 1988). This legal contraction of workers' rights, disarticulation of trade unions' organisational power, state repression and the use of this apparatus by employers to eliminate any form of dissent in the workplace, thus, went together with the contraction of employment in the industrial sector and the corresponding increase of outsourced, underpaid, informal work in the growing service sector (Chitarroni and Cimillo 2007). These economic and legislative factors, far from being mutually unintended consequences, represented a concerted attack on established workers' rights and on the political power of the unions' movement, which was seen as the cause of both the political revolutionary and economic turbulence that preceded the putsch.

How did workers react to the changes in employment conditions produced by the neo-liberal economic reforms? What sort of reaction was possible in a legally restrictive and repressive environment? At the level of national union coordination, with the Confederacion General del Trabajo (CGT) banned and most important unions under military control, their leaders jailed and in a context of extreme organisational difficulties, divisions emerged between confrontation and participation approaches. The former was more prone to actively oppose the regime and to give voice to the scattered but continuous local struggles, while the latter was more open to dialogue and negotiation. These two approaches operated in parallel over the course of the period through diverse *nucleamientos sindicales*. The Comisión de los 25 favoured a more confrontationist approach and led the call for general strikes in 1979 and 1981. These ended with hundreds of union officials and activists in jail but showed publicly their opposition to the government's economic policy while at the same time claiming the enforcement of civil and political rights for detainee and missing union activists. On these occasions, the Comisión Nacional de Trabajo (CNT), which endorsed an apolitical and servicing unionism, was against the industrial action and in favour of promoting dialogue with military authorities. In 1981, both *nucleamientos* converged within the CGT but the internal struggles caused its division. The confrontationist CGT increased its mobilising capacity and organised two massive demonstrations. Then, with the military forces in retreat, there would be three more general strikes, with the involvement, in the last two, of the 'participation' wing of the union movement (Iñigo Carrera 2007). These mobilisations framed the opposition to neo-liberalism together with the struggle for democracy.

Notwithstanding the importance of the national level in coordinating opposition, in evaluating union responses to neo-liberalism under the dictatorship, it is essential to take into account the level of militancy and grassroots activism (Pozzi 1988). *Comisiones internas*, union locals or simply informal, often clandestine, groups of workers, by defending their salaries and rights to work, constantly challenged the regime and its economic policies, contributing to the return of democracy. The legal prohibition of any forms of dissent, employers' despotism and often their acceptance of military repression, left workers alone and at risk in their struggles against employers. Nevertheless, representing a recurrent trend in the history of Argentine unionism – that of the contradictory interaction between grass-roots mobilisations and central leaderships – workers scattered but continuous opposition strengthened coordination and representation at national level.

There is no doubt that the last military dictatorship has been very effective in reducing what was perceived as a too powerful labour movement. Systematic use of repression, physical elimination of militants and introduction of anti-labour legislation were all used to break worker and union resistance as these were seen as the main obstacle to the introduction of neo-liberal market reforms. By the end of the dictatorship, unions regained political freedom, but not power over employers. Without the support of a Peronist government and in an employment context that had changed consistently since 1976, unions remained divided, at least initially, on their approach to neo-liberalism. However, government attempts to use these divisions to reform their structure and the increasing influence of international financial institutions in defining the economic agenda of the country helped to characterise the first period after the return of democracy as one of intense labour conflict.

UNION REACTIONS TO STRUCTURAL ADJUSTMENTS

Worker and union experiences of, and responses to, neo-liberalism during the 1980s are still under-researched compared to those of the 1990s and this is despite their distinctive character, which stemmed from the contradictions arising from unions' broad opposition to neo-liberalism and their corporate and organisational interests (Pozzi and Schneider 1994). It was within this context that a few influential unions, grouped in the *nucleamiento sindical* Gestión y Trabajo, a continuation of the collaborationist CNT, began to advocate the need to accept change in industrial relations and accommodate their agendas to neo-liberalism, whereas most unions pursued a traditional path and advocated import substitution industrialisation policies. Thus the years between 1983 and 1989, notwithstanding the apparently shared political rejection of neo-liberalism, witnessed the seeds of unions' likely transformation in the face of changing circumstances. The return to democracy did not reverse the structural changes brought about by eight years of neo-liberal policies and military rule (Peralta Ramos 2007). After a short attempt to reintroduce distributive policies, the government of Raúl Alfonsín (Partido Radical – PR) adopted, first, IMF recipes to stabilise the economy; and then, since the Baker Plan (1987), those of the World Bank to promote structural reforms. This meant the privatisation of public firms, free trade and deregulation. According to the government, the idea was to promote primary exports while restructuring the industry towards an export oriented model through market liberalisation (Basualdo 2006). Nevertheless, the development of neo-liberal reforms was uneven and piecemeal during the 1980s; in fact, most of them failed, partly due to inter-bourgeois conflicts, partly due to popular, and increasingly, trade unions' resistance (Palomino 2005).

In the midst of recession, conflicts between agrarian and industrial interests and between local economic groups and external creditors doomed official economic initiatives to failure, making it difficult to deepen neo-liberal reforms. The only shared understanding of the ruling classes was the need to increase productivity (Peralta Ramos 2007). Meanwhile, real wages and the labour income component of the GDP fell steadily. The worsening of the reproductive conditions of the labour force manifested itself in labour market indicators too, with the unemployment rate doubling in the first five years of the democratic government. In brief, the recovering of political and organisational rights for unions was parallelled by the continuing deterioration of the economic situation, which prevented workers from achieving meaningful changes in the relative balance of power with employers (Basualdo 2006).

The electoral defeat of Peronist Partido Justicialista (PJ) in 1983 further complicated the recovery of unions after the ending of military rule. Union leaders had played a central role in the presidential campaign and were blamed for the electoral failure of Peronism. As a result, many politicians within the party began to advocate its de-unionisation (Levitsky 2003). Divisions within the union movement exacerbated the problem; at the end of the dictatorship there were two CGTs and four *nucleamientos sindicales*, clear indicators of disorganisation and lack of strategic perspective. The PR attempted to take advantage of this situation and just a week after Raúl Alfonsín took office, the government sent a bill to reform unions' organisational structures. While this was justified as an attempt to introduce a more democratic system of workers' representation it aimed at the same time to undermine the historical support of trade unions for Peronism. The outcome would be, however, the opposite. Unions reorganised the CGT to face this new threat and to advocate the recovery of the institutions and legal basis of the industrial relations abolished by the dictatorship. This regained unity strengthened the CGT, which by beginning to campaign against neo-liberal recipes gradually ended up leading the social opposition to the overall governmental policies. Between 1983 and 1989, the CGT called 13 general strikes. Most of them had as their main goal the rejection of government economic and social policies and wage increases. Indeed, some of these general strikes held explicitly anti-imperialist slogans and included mass demonstrations (Iñigo Carrera 2007). This widespread union opposition rested, however, on the defence of an inward-looking import-substitution industrialisation model, based on state intervention and distributive policies. This standpoint was majoritarian but, as usual, not unanimous among unions; moreover, within this orientation there were also tactical and strategic differences. A minority of unions, gathered in Gestión y Trabajo, even presented an alternative plan inspired by neo-liberal principles. This *nucleamiento* argued for the need to participate in the political system as an interest group subordinating union policies to the strategic definition of the ruling elites.

However, during this period of return to democracy, more important than some of the unions' arguments in favour of a new, neo-liberal oriented system of industrial relations, was the reactivation of collective bargaining. While this certainly represented a gain in terms of contributing to re-balance power in favour of trade unions, it also opened the door to exchange wage increases for flexibility and productivity. Important unions like those representing the metal and automotive workers who were campaigning at that time against the market reforms as part of the CGT, left the space open for a *de facto* acceptance of neo-liberalism at the workplace by signing these sorts of agreements. At a different level, another sign of opposition to neo-liberal policies, which would gradually develop up to the point of division of the labour movement at the start of the 1990s, was the increasing militancy of public workers caused by the external debt-driven fiscal crisis which led to IMF and World Bank imposed adjustment policies for the public sector. Public sector workers were the prime victims and actively opposed the state reform and its consequences, with health workers, civil servants and teachers being the most active strikers (Pozzi and Schneider 1994; Villanueva 1994).

Finally, it is necessary to underline the ideological and political consequences of the hyperinflation processes that hit the economy between 1989 and 1990. Their disciplining effects prepared the terrain for making the population accept the need for a radical change in economic policy; indeed, this crisis helped too to overcome the resistance of the union movement. Thus, these events brought forward change at the political level and paved the way for a wide programme of reforms in which privatisation was decisive (Thwaites Rey 2003). It was in this critical context that the new Menem's government, despite advocating industrialisation, distributive policies, and the support of unions in the electoral campaign, passed the state reforms and the economic emergency laws which launched the political process of market reforms.

MASSIVE NEO-LIBERAL REFORMS OF THE 1990s

The period of 1989–1993 is crucial in the history of neo-liberalism in Argentina (Bonnet 2007). During these years, the agenda of the New Right was finally put into practice in full through furthering deregulation and market liberalisation, and a set of specific policies: fiscal bonuses to attract multinational investments, anti-inflationary monetary policies, reduction of public employees, cutting public expenditures, privatisation of social security services and labour flexibility. One of the pillars of the programme was the Convertibility Plan introduced in 1991. By fixing the peso to the US dollar, this policy stopped hyperinflation, produced stability and market confidence and created consensus among bourgeois parties and state bureaucracies. However, the decisive policy was the privatisation of public companies. Between 1990 and 1993 the Peronist government launched a fast and massive privatisation programme, technically and financially assisted by the IMF and World Bank. In four years, the government sold 34 companies and let concessions for 19 services and 86 areas for petroleum development. It was one of the broadest and most rapid privatisation programmes in the Western hemisphere (Ghigliani 2010).

The programme was accompanied by an ideological campaign against public sector unions. They were blamed for maximising salaries and benefits for themselves, at the cost of service quality and economic efficiency, and generally at a cost to consumers. Indeed, the need to curb the power of public unions was a topic included in the agenda of public debates of that time. Accordingly, public enterprises underwent significant change prior to privatisation to modify their collective agreements and systems of industrial relations and to break unions' capacity to obstruct the managerial decisions of the future private owners. To that aim, a horde of consultants paid with the World Bank loans were personally involved in negotiations with managers, union officers, and authorities. Negotiations soon gave way to imposition as the government suspended 718 clauses from the collective agreements previously reached by unions with 13 public enterprises. By 1993, there had already been 280 509 job losses in the public sector, with a cost to the state of $2035m in voluntary redundancy packages, again financially supported by the World Bank (Ghigliani 2010).

So, how did unions respond to this attack? To begin with, as the Partido Justicialista (PJ) was the historical channel by which the government was accessed and its favour gained by unions, the implementation of these policies required to keep the redefinition of the relation between the state, the party and unions. In this sense, unions continued to lose influence within the PJ and, therefore, the Parliament (Levitsky 2003). Nevertheless, direct confrontation of a Peronist government implied the risk of political isolation and, more importantly, breakage of the historical alliance that had provided unions with political resources and had served their corporatist interests well so far. Once again, strategic differences led to a new division between those union leaders wanting to confront this departure from the classic legacy of Peronism (the CGT-Azopardo) and those who supported the government (the CGT-San Martín). In turn, the government repressed by force every attempt to oppose privatisation, such as the resistance by telephone (1990–1991) and railway workers (1991–1992), and restricted by decree the right to strike in public services and utilities (Pozzi and Schneider 1994). Moreover, it decided to cut off wage increases to prevent a new inflationary crisis, and issued in 1991 a decree linking rises in wages to productivity growth. Unions opposed this decision, arguing that it limited actors' autonomy in collective bargaining, but its consequences were much deeper. The decrees impacted on the whole structure of collective bargaining by forcing unions to negotiate wages at firm level and to take into account differentials in productivity between companies. They also constrained corporative strategies by precluding demands for governmental wage polices. Thus unions were obliged to discuss with employers how to increase productivity and concede changes in the labour process that they had previously resisted. In 1993, another decree would formalise bargaining at enterprise level and during 1995–2000, 90 per cent of collective agreements of this kind facilitated labour flexibility (Ghigliani 2010).

In the face of governmental determination to further the neo-liberal turn, hesitative unions declined to form part of the opposition, and the CGT once more unified its ranks in 1992 and aligned itself with the Government. The subordination of the CGT to Menemism, and hence, to neo-liberalism ended up, however, in a new and more serious division of the labour movement. In 1992 the Congreso de los Trabajadores Argentinos (CTA) was created, mainly by public workers' unions, and two years later declared itself as an alternative workers' central. Also, in 1994 another split in the CGT led to the creation of the Movimiento de los Trabajadores Argentinos (MTA) with the aim of recovering the tradition of Peronism to oppose the neo-liberal agenda. These three workers' organisations corresponded, broadly, to three different responses to neo-liberalism over the 1990s (Fernández 1997).

The CGT gathered those unions (or union leaders) supporting Menem's reforms in return for business concessions. However, during this Peronist government's first term in office (1989–1995), only eight out of 20 legislative projects to reform labour laws were passed in the parliament. In order to introduce change, the government was forced to give exchange protection and financial support to the *obras sociales*, and permit unions to invest in the new business opportunities brought about by the privatisation of public enterprises and deregulation of social services. This entrepreneurial unionism was discursively legitimised as a strategy to maintain union structures and services to members in an economic and political context in which modernisation of union politics was deemed to be inevitable (Murillo 2001). Thus these unions collaborated actively in the introduction of neo-liberalism.

In turn, the CTA intended to depart from the traditional model embodied by the CGT, advocating independence from the state and from the PJ. The organisation has demanded *personería gremial* since its conception (which has been denied by the Ministry of Labour so far), while promoting a pluralist model of representation. Organisationally, the CTA has developed new forms such as a territorial body for the unemployed, individual affiliation of workers, direct ballots for all union posts, membership among workers from cooperatives and promotion of the organisation of disadvantaged groups. In this way, the CTA became a main actor in the mobilisation against the neo-liberal agenda during the 1990s, seeking coalition building with social movements and political organisations, and enriched the traditional repertoire of the labour movement (Armelino 2004). The formation of the MTA was more a tactic following the traditional divisions of the union movement in *nucleamientos sindicales*, than a proper project to build an alternative to the CGT. Its rationale can be found in the internal struggle of the CGT regarding how to react in the face of Menemism. The MTA advocated the opposition to governmental policies based on the national and popular traditions of Peronism (Fernández 1997). This internal struggle ended in 2000 after the electoral defeat of the PJ, with the effective division, once more, of the CGT into a dialogue-oriented CGT (CGT Dialoguista) and a more combative CGT (CGT Rebelde); the latter built upon the MTA faction.

Despite a general union retreat, if measured by number of conflicts, this period witnessed bitter and active popular resistance. In the privatised public industries, the processes of rationalisation and the closure of production sites led to job loss and strong workforce opposition. When company restructuring impacted areas of the country dependent on one productive sector (metallurgy, oil extraction, sugar cane plantations, among others), resistance translated into broader mobilisations involving rebellions of civil society as a whole, as in the case of the communities of Villa Constitución (Santa Fe), Cutral Có and Plaza Huincul (Neuquén), and Tartagal and General Mosconi (Salta). In all these conflicts, unions played a secondary role. The leading force, instead, were the *piqueteros*, whose organisations gradually occupied the centre stage of the social mobilisation against neo-liberalism. By the end of Menem's second presidency, however, union opposition grew, with four general strikes called by all components of the labour movement in an attempt to block government efforts to further undermine unions' position in collective bargaining. Yet the success of these demonstrations, while it saved union prerogatives, neither changed flexibility at workplace level, already recognised by the Acuerdo Marco agreement, nor negated the thrust of neo-liberal reforms.

REVITALISATION OF UNIONISM AFTER THE 2001 CRISIS?

The popular upheaval of December 2001 led to changes to the neo-liberal model dominating in the country. Angered by the consequences of a downward spiral of economic recession that started in 1998 and that further worsened the unemployment and precariousness generated by the neo-liberal reforms of the 1990s, ordinary people and social movements occupied the streets of Buenos Aires and other major cities demanding political and economic changes. In the space of a few days, different presidents alternated in power and important reforms were finally made to rescue the country from financial default. The end of convertibility and currency devaluation, together with positive conditions in the global agro-commodities market, gave room for a recovery of the economy (Atzeni and Ghigliani 2007). Since 2003, the average annual growth rate has oscillated between eight and 95 per cent, except for 2009 when the GDP shrunk to 0.9% due to the global crisis. This positive context and governmental policies towards a more traditional, consensual system of industrial relations, functional to social stability, have certainly contributed to the revitalisation of unions' politics and mobilisation. However, in order to evaluate unions' politics in the current period, it is important to re-emphasise how more than 30 years of market reforms have profoundly changed the structure of employment in Argentina. On one hand, following international patterns, this has now shifted from industry to services and from big to small enterprises. On the other hand, precariousness, outsourcing, flexibility and informality have become structural components of the employment system (Chitarroni and Cimillo 2007). This situation has objectively weakened the numerical and social basis of unionism, widening the gap between protected and unprotected workers.

Yet, the current positive economic trend manifested in the corresponding growth of employment, particularly in the private industrial sector (Kosacoff 2010). This has been important for unions first to keep control of labour intensive and historically strategic sectors of the economy (automotive, foods, transport, telecommunication, energy) and, second, to use this renewed strength to obtain concessions and wage increases taking advantage of growing capitalist profitability. Thus, through collective bargaining and industrial conflict, workers, particularly those employed in the private sector, have been able to partly recover the value of their real salaries. The other aspect that explains the recently renewed political importance of unions in influencing the employment relations agenda is represented by the explicit government's support and alliance with the more traditionally Peronist sections of the labour movement. This has been expressed in various ways since the election of the Peronist Néstor Kirchner. First, by encouraging collective bargaining at national and plant level and by summoning after ten years of inactivity the Consejo del Salario Mínimo, Vital y Móvil, a tripartite body that aims to spread social dialogue among different actors and to fix the minimum wage. Second, by an initial tolerance to social protests, particularly labour conflicts, although this approach has gradually changed since 2005. Since then, in the face of intense labour conflicts or grassroots defiance to the power of either or both employers and conservative union leaderships, repression and criminalisation of workers' protests have been commonplace in several services and industries, public or private (undergrounds, teachers, health workers, fishing, wood, textile industry, food, railways, among others). Third, by favouring reunification of the CGT in 2004. By this time, the new leadership of the CGT, composed of those opposing neo-liberalism over the 1990s through the MTA, backed the government's departure from neo-liberalism, advocating a return to the traditional Peronist project of industrialisation with social justice and wealth redistribution. Governmental support in turn empowered traditional Peronist union leaders against the unemployed led social mobilisation and the mounting rank and file pressure for wage recovery after the crisis of 2001–2002. In parallel with the reunification of the CGT, the governments of Néstor Kirchner and then Cristina Fernández de Kirchner denied the *personería gremial* to the rival CTA. Thus, the CGT has sided with the government against the bitter opposition from landowners, economic corporations and political parties advocating a return to more liberal policies (Atzeni and Ghigliani 2007).

Whether one considers the combination of these economic and political factors as part of an explicit neo-corporatist project that sees the institutional insertion of unions from strategic sectors of the economy a condition for stability (Etchemendy and Collier 2007), or as a part of the government's attempt to gain hegemonic control over the broader process of social mobilisation launched by the crisis of 2001–2002 (Atzeni and Ghigliani 2007), the concrete result has been a widespread increase of union-led mobilisations. However, these have differed in scope, nature and duration, with workers alternatively contesting or accepting, in exchange for wage increases, the neo-liberal changes imposed in the structure and conditions of employment over the last 30 years. Thus, the case of unions' resistance to neo-liberalism should once again be seen in the light of the distinction between unions as institutions and as movement (Cohen 2006).

Many would point to the fact that the Argentinean union movement has recently recovered strength, especially if compared with those in countries like Chile that went through similar processes of market reforms and liberalisation (Atzeni *et al.* 2011). While this is certainly true for the aforementioned reasons, questions arise about the true nature of this strength and its prospects. In this sense, it is important to underline that so far, the more radical breaks with neo-liberal imposed flexibility and precariousness in the workplace came from the renewed activity of *comisiones internas* and not from the top-down corporatist approach. Even though scant, these cases have been important for setting a precedent not just in terms of their concrete demands but also for re-opening in Argentina the debate about democracy in organising workers and representativeness, an issue crucial to any union movement future. For instance, struggles against temporary contracts in the telecommunication companies and railways, outsourcing of services in the Buenos Aires under-ground, the implementation of the 12-hour shift in Kraft Foods and many other conflicts mainly driven by wage increases and working conditions like those of Fate rubber tyre plant, Maffisa (textile), Stani and Pepsico (food), Parmalat (milk), Paty and Tango Meat (meat), Praxair (chemistry), among others, are just some of the most well-known examples of episodes in which workplace based organisations have been able to lead important industrial action built on democratic principles of representation and participation (Atzeni and Ghigliani 2007). While there have also been cases of struggles for union recognition in previously union-free sectors, as with SIMECA (an indepen-dent union affiliated to the CTA that organises workers in the delivery sector) or UTC (that represents Bolivians in the *maquila* type textile small workshop of Buenos Aires), the main processes of mobilisation were driven by *comi-siones internas*, often in tension, and sometimes in open confrontation, with central union leaderships.

All these grassroot movements share some basic features. To begin with, most of them took advantage of the rise in collective bargaining to organise their workplaces. The majority of their leaders are young and without previ-ous union involvement, though many have passed through experiences of high turnover. In all these conflicts, leftwing activists have played a leading role through grassroots mechanisms of decision-making and intense participation and when conflicts turned bitter, workers resorted to direct action and violence. A few of these conflicts ended up changing workers' representatives at the workplace and even unions' local structures (Ghigliani and Schneider 2010). The salient case being underground workers, whose conflicts with the leadership of the national union forced the shop steward structure to lead a breakaway, which ended up successfully gaining partial official recognition to their new union after acute struggles. Although many of these experiences failed to maintain the organisation in the face of the concerted attack from employers, union oligarchies and public authorities, they have constituted the main workers' attempt to reverse some of the most devastating aspects of the neo-liberal agenda. At the same time, they contributed to open a public, though fleeting, debate about unions' organisational models and democracy.

Notwithstanding the importance of these bottom-up movements, traditional union leaderships have ended up conducting the majority of conflicts in the recent context of economic growth. This contributed to the partial recovery of real wages but did not threaten neo-liberal established standards in the employment relationship as shown by the contents of collective agreements, which have not seriously challenged flexibility. At the same time, this process of collective bargaining reinforced the legitimacy and the economic resources of national leaderships, which obtained the re-introduction of the employers' financial contributions and benefited from a percentage of the wage increases reached in negotiations. In turn, the CTA has insisted in his mobilising tactics to get recognition and broaden its presence in manufacturing and services but with little success, as shown by the failure to obtain the *personería gremial*. In this sense, the CTA has not been able to replicate its successful mobilising policies of the 1990s, which played an important role in the popular resistance to market reforms and translated in a sustained organisational growth. On the contrary, the emergence of the so-called *kirchnerismo*, whose human right, economic and social policies have gradually gained popular support, put the organisation into crisis as an internal faction began to claim a closer relationship to the Peronist national government leading the workers central to virtual rupture. Similarly, the *kirchnerismo* also impacted on the CGT, where a breakaway of former supporters of market reforms ended up in a third, though smaller organisation, the CGT Azul y Blanca, which has sided with those Peronist politicians, who have decided to break with the government adding their support to the opposition parties.

In sum, the main challenges to neo-liberalism from trade unions since the crisis of 2001 have found two different sources in Argentina. On the one side, an institutional revision of the traditional tactics of Peronist unions in alliance to the Peronist Government of Néstor Kirchner and Cristina Fernández de Kirchner, which partially contested the heritage of the market reforms of the 1990s. On the other side, a more fundamental and frontal opposition arisen from those scarce but important events of grassroots activism, which are still too weak to anticipate a real alternative to traditional unionism in the near future.

CONCLUSIONS

The history of the last 35 years of union and worker responses to the implementation of neo-liberal reforms in Argentina cannot be univocally interpreted nor easily framed within pre-defined categories. This is partly a problem related to the inner nature of unions, intermediary organisations trapped within class, market and societies (Hyman 2001), and it is also a matter of the particular history of Argentinean unionism. Moreover, unions' responses have changed over time according to different phases, methods and political conditions through which neo-liberalism developed and consolidated in the country. In conservative environments, neo-liberalism has often been associated with progressive ideas about globalisation and the potential benefits that this can produce for unions willing to support and invest in companies' competitiveness. This ideological mutual gain agenda, however, has never been assumed by unions in Argentina. Even when the accommodation to globalisation and market reforms prevailed, political pragmatism seems to have informed the actions of the bigger unions more than ideologies. During the 1990s, the CGT continued to launch strong criticisms of the worst effects of market reforms and liberalisation, claiming the need for state protection. Meanwhile the CTA, breaking away from the CGT, built its distinctive character on an open opposition to neo-liberalism, advocating redistributive policies and social movement strategies. But despite the CGT's connivance with neo-liberal reforms, unions have generally opposed corporate globalisation and the structural adjustments imposed by local ruling classes and international financial institutions. This has been particularly evident in the 1980s but resumed its strength at the end of the 1990s and in coincidence with the 2001 crisis, and has been based on wide popular support.

However, this opposition has not been framed in social democracy as an alternative but, mainly, in the Peronist ideology of social justice, redistribution and national sovereignty. This, more specifically, implied not just state protection against the unbalances produced by a liberalised market but also the building of institutional forms of exchange with the state. The Peronist identity of most union leaderships, their close association with the fate of Peronist governments and, thus, the power they can exert on state structure to gain advantages might then be considered as one of the main axes of analysis of unions' reaction to neo-liberalism in Argentina. Yet, opposition to neo-liberalism has been the product of grassroots as much as top down workers' mobilisations and of open resistance to capitalist globalisation as much as of institutional forms of exchange with the state. *Comisiones internas*, local union branches and other workplace based organisations have led some of the most radical actions against some of the most severe effects of neo-liberalism on employment security and income. This opposition has also counteracted opportunistic tendencies within unions, encouraging more democratic forms of representation and leadership accountability. It is in these grassroots actions and organisations that the seeds of a more fundamental opposition and anti-capitalist ideology can be found.

The unions' responses, then, have not been uniform, and have produced groupings and temporary alliances more than unity within the labour movement. Indeed, they have heavily depended on the more pragmatic, ideological or politically driven motivations leading the strategy of each union. This lack of unity should not be a surprise, however, if neo-liberalism is seen as both a political and economic project directed to rebalance class relations. Neo-liberalism has destroyed many workers' economic lives by creating unemployment, flexibility and precariousness, and its inception in Argentina as in many other countries has also been associated with the physical destruction of the labour movement power and its institutions. The imposed consensus of the military government was later to be substituted by the financial imposition dominating the structural adjustments of the 1980s and the massive reforms of the 1990s. Following global trends, the imposition of neo-liberal orthodoxy has produced de-industrialisation, de-centralisation of collective bargaining, reduction of the formal sector and labour market flexibility, which have undermined not just the role of unions as progressive social forces but also their own institutional survival. Judging from these outcomes, and notwithstanding workers' resistance and oppositions to neo-liberal policies, the conclusion is that 35 years of market reforms have brought seriously into question the ability of unions as institutions to resist change and channel effectively the bottom-up grievances and collective mobilisations that the model of accumulation associated with global neo-liberalism constantly reproduces. As recent developments seem to suggest, the reconstruction of a political dimension in unions' activity, which is fundamental to any future resistance of the labour movement to changes associated with globalisation, parallels processes of democratic participation, decision making and accountability of the unions to their members. Whether or not traditional unions in Argentina will be able to move in this direction will strongly depend on abandoning a reformist and corporatist approach in the defence of workers' interests.

REFERENCES

Armelino, M. (2004), 'La protesta laboral en los años 90. El caso de la CTA', *Estudios del Trabajo*, 28, Buenos Aires: ASET.

Atzeni, M. and P. Ghigliani (2007), 'The resilience of traditional trade union practices in the revitalisation of the Argentine labour movement', in C. Phelan (ed.), *Trade Union Revitalisation: Trends and Prospects in 34 Nations*, Düsseldorf: Peter Lang.

Atzeni, M. and P. Ghigliani (2009), 'Trade unionism in Argentina since 1945: the limits of trade union reformism', in C. Phelan (ed.), *Trade Unionism since 1945: Towards a Global History*, Düsseldorf: Peter Lang.

Atzeni, M., F. Durán-Palma and P. Ghigliani (2001), 'Employment relations in Chile and Argentina', in M. Barry and A. Wilkinson (eds), *Research Handbook of Comparative Industrial Relations*, Cheltenham, UK and Northampton, MA, USA: Edward Elgar

Basualdo, E. (2006), *Estudios de Historia Económica Argentina*, Buenos Aires: Siglo XXI.

Basualdo, V. (2009), *Los delegados y las comisiones internas en la Argentina. Una mirada de largo plazo, desde sus orígenes hasta la actualidad*, DGB Bildungswerk, Friedrich Ebert Stiftung, Buenos Aires: CTA y FETIA.

Bonnet, A. (2007), *La hegemonía menemista. El neoconservadurismo en Argentina, 1989–2001*, Buenos Aires: Prometeo.

Chitarroni, H. and E. Cimillo (2007), 'Resurge el sujeto histórico? Cambios en el colectivo del trabajo asalariado: 1974–2006', *Lavboratorionline*, **8**(21).

Cohen, S. (2006), *Ramparts of Resistance: Why Workers Lost their Power, and How to get it Back*, London: Pluto Press.

Doyon, L. (2006), *Perón y los trabajadores. Los orígenes del sindicalismo peronista 1943–1955*, Buenos Aires: Siglo XXI.

Etchemendy, S. and R. Collier (2007), 'Down but not out: union resurgence and segmented neocorporatism in Argentina (2003–2007)', *Politics and Society*, **35**(3), 363–401.

Fernández, A. (1997), 'Flexibilisación laboral y crisis del sindicalismo', Buenos Aires: Espacio Editorial.

Fernández, A. (1998), *Crisis y Decadencia del Sindicalismo Argentino*, Buenos Aires: Editores de América Latina.

Ghigliani, P. (2010), *The Politics of Privatisation and Trade Union Mobilisation: The Electricity Industry in UK and Argentina*, Düsseldorf: Peter Lang.

Ghigliani, P. and A. Schneider (2010), 'Dinámica social y protesta laboral en el área metropolitana de Buenos Aires y el Gran La Plata durante la presidencia de Néstor Kirchner (2003–2007)', in *Seminario Internacional: Historias del Trabajo en el Sur Global*, Brazil: Florianópolis.

Harvey, D. (2005), *A Brief History of Neo-liberalism*, Oxford: Oxford University Press.

Hyman, R. (2001), *Understanding European Trade Unionism: Between Market, Class and Society*, London: Sage.

Iñigo Carrera, N. (2007), 'Strikes in Argentina' in van der Velden (ed.), *Strikes Around the World, 1968–2005, Case-studies of 15 Countries*, Amsterdam: Aksant.

James, D. (1990), *Resistencia e integración. El peronismo y la clase trabajadora Argentina 1946–1976*, Buenos Aires: Sudamericana.

Kosacoff, B. (2010), '*Marchas y contramarchas de la industria argentina (1958–2008)*', Collection Projects Documents, Buenos Aires: CEPAL/United Nations.

Levitsky, S. (2003), *Transforming Labor-Based Parties in Latin America: Argentine Peronism in Comparative Perspective*, New York: Cambridge University Press.

Murillo, M. (2001), *Labor Unions, Partisan Coalitions, and Market Reforms in Latin America*, Cambridge: Cambridge University Press.

Palomino, H. (2005), 'Los cambios en el mundo del trabajo y los dilemas sindicales', in J. Suriano (ed.), '*Nueva Historia Argentina. Dictadura y Democracia*', Buenos Aires: Sudamericana.

Peralta-Ramos, M. (2007), *La economía política argentina: poder y clases sociales (1930–2006)*, Buenos Aires: Fondo de Cultura Económica.

Pozzi, P. (1988), *La oposición obrera a la dictadura (1976–1982)*, Buenos Aires: Editorial Contrapunto.

Pozzi, P. and A. Schneider (1994), *Combatiendo el capital*, Buenos Aires: El Bloque.

Schvarzer, J. (1996), *La industria que supimos conseguir. Una historia politico- social de la industria argentina*, Buenos Aires: Planeta.

Thwaites Rey, M. (2003), *La Desilusión Privatista. El Experimento Neo-liberal en la Argentina*, Buenos Aires: Eudeba.

Villanueva, E. (ed) (1994), *Conflicto Obrero. Transición política, conflictividad obrera y comportamiento sindical en la Argentina 1984–1989*, Buenos Aires: Universidad Nacional de Quilmes.

5 Neo-liberal evolution and union responses in Australia

David Peetz and Janis Bailey

INTRODUCTION

It's the first national general strike in Australia. Around the country, on 12 July 1976, union members are pounding the streets, carrying placards proclaiming 'Hands off Medibank!', loudly protesting the new conservative government's plans to dismantle the national health insurance scheme established just two years earlier. The demonstrations have limited attendance, because there is no public transport to take people to them. But this is not the biggest problem with the strike. In fact, between a quarter and a half of union members have gone to work anyway, despite the transport problems (Donn 1979). Lasting, as planned, for only one day (quite typical for Australian strikes), it places no ongoing pressure on the government to give in to the union demands. Indeed the government refuses to negotiate with the unions and makes no changes to its plans for health insurance. The first national general strike is a fizzer. So it is also the last.

Thirty years later, and union members are on the streets again, in bigger numbers than in 1976 – over 100 000 of them. This is no national strike. People have come here on the way to work or taken time off to attend. It would be illegal to strike over this issue. The leading banners of these very orderly demonstrations read 'Your rights at work: worth fighting for'. Over 20 years after neo-liberalism took hold in Australia, this is a fight about laws that threaten the very survival of the union movement. The demonstration itself is hardly decisive – more about keeping up morale among union activists than directly persuading the government to change its laws. The real action is happening on the telephone, in workplaces and community halls, and on television screens around the country. The demonstration is part of a two-year campaign that spectacularly achieves what it set out to do: defeat the conservative government that threatened to cripple unionism.

These two events illustrate several aspects of Australian unionism. They point to unions' need for favourable state policies; to union efforts, sometimes successful, sometimes not, to achieve them; and to the unions' reliance on having Labor, rather than conservative, governments in office. They show

how union tactics have been shaped by the legislative framework, indeed habituated by the arbitration system in place for most of the last century (hence strikes were short and used to alert employers and tribunals to union intent) and have had to change since the end of arbitration. The alterations in the legislative framework themselves point to the changes wrought by neo-liberalism. And the events indicate how even the large scale manifestations of union anger that have challenged key state policies have not fundamentally challenged the economic system or the philosophies guiding it.

At the core of economic policy in Australia since the 1980s has been neo-liberalism. The term typically refers to a set of ideas supporting adherence to free market philosophies and a minimum of state intervention that maintain the interests of capital. In Australia, this set of ideas has also been referred to as 'economic rationalism' (Pusey 1992), 'economic fundamentalism' (Argy 1998), 'economic liberalism' (Stilwell 2002) and 'market liberalism' (Quiggin 2010). Its purpose is to create conditions to boost company profits and increase the returns to owners of capital. As in many other countries, neo-liberal policies found increasing favour with Australian governments from the mid-1980s. Labor came to government in Australia at that time when social democratic parties in many larger countries were in opposition (Pierson and Castles 2002: 697). Hence, in Australia, the midwife for neo-liberalism was ostensibly a social democratic government, with strong ties to the union move-ment (Lavelle 2010) and governing in a political context where state regula-tion rather than direct state provision is the norm (Pierson and Castles 2002: 688). Thus neo-liberalism in the 1980s operated within a quasi-corporatist, highly centralised incomes policy negotiated with the trade union movement. For this reason the approach to industrial relations reform was gradualist – at least until the mid-1990s – and, overall, less drastic than the government's approach to economic reform more generally.

This early period of Australian neo-liberalism we refer to as 'constrained neo-liberalism'. When a conservative coalition government (comprising 'the 'Liberal' and 'National' Parties) took office in 1996 under Prime Minister John Howard, policies favouring capital over labour reached their high point, yet in the arena of industrial relations they were so interventionist that, modi-fying a remark used by one of the business-funded free market lobbyists, we refer to the Howard years as 'Stalinist neo-liberalism'. Thus neo-liberalism in Australia has a distinct flavour because it has never been applied in its pure, full glory, with different governments focusing on different aspects of it – Labor emphasising the benefits that greater reliance on markets would allegedly bring to workers or at least consumers, the conservatives more will-ing to set aside market principles in order to meet the interests of capital.

The ascension of the Labor government in 2007 brought to office Kevin Rudd, who then wrote a major essay explicitly decrying neo-liberalism (Rudd

2009), yet whose policies remained heavily influenced by liberal market economics. As nothing has risen to take the place of neo-liberalism, ideas discredited by the global financial crisis – such as the efficient markets hypothesis, the benefits of privatisation, and the notion of 'trickle down' ideas – still underpin the thinking of many policy makers. The ideas are, as Quiggin (2010) argues, like zombies: 'neither alive nor dead'. So we refer to the Rudd years as a period of 'revisionist neo-liberalism'.

While neo-liberalism emerged as a dominant philosophy among elites in the late twentieth century, it is also important to recognise that it is not a philosophy that ever attained widespread acceptance in the community at large. For example, opinion polls have typically shown the majority of voters support import quotas and oppose privatisation (Murray and Peetz 2010). In the realm of industrial relations, sympathy towards unions has increased over the past two decades (despite major falls in union membership) and voters consistently opposed the WorkChoices reforms of the Howard government (Murray and Peetz 2010). As will be demonstrated, unions were able to mobilise and help shape public opinion in order to oppose and eventually bring down the government that had introduced WorkChoices (Muir 2008).

Elsewhere in this volume, Gall, Hurd and Wilkinson (see Introduction) develop a four-fold categorisation of union responses, which we characterise as follows: 'accommodatory' (globalisation is good or progressive and unions and their members can benefit from it where the companies, sectors or economies can successfully compete – a mutual gains agenda); 'protective' (unions advocate that workers need some strategic protection/state action in order to compete fairly as well as to protect them from the worst effects of globalisation and the 'race to the bottom'); 'reformist oppositional' (unions believe in opposition to corporate globalisation and advocate social democracy as an alternative in order to socialise the capitalist economy); and 'radical oppositional' (unions believe in opposition and resistance to capitalist globalisation and advocate socialism as the alternative). In the context of a sceptical public, the move to neo-liberalism has occurred principally among business and policy elites, and the response of unions has ranged from accommodatory to oppositional. This chapter describes the phases of neo-liberalism in Australia and union responses to them, commencing with analysis of Australian unions before the rise of neo-liberalism.

UNIONS BEFORE NEO-LIBERALISM

The dominant ideology of Australian unions for much of the twentieth century has been described as 'labourism'; that is, a belief in parliamentary politics, protection for local industry and arbitration unionism. Traditionally, labourism

– a term borrowed from the British 'new left' – has been contrasted with 'socialism'. While the short-hand term labourism masks a more complex picture of labour movement ideology, it remains a useful descriptor for characterising union movement ideology in Australia. Labourism's relationship to capitalism is analogous to the terrain covered by the 'protective' and 'reformist oppositional' approaches to neo-liberalism.

Understanding the ALP-union movement relationship is essential to understanding unions pre-neo-liberalism. The histories of the union movement and the Australian Labor Party (ALP) are inextricably interwoven. Unions created the ALP in the various Australian colonies (Buckley and Wheelwright 1988: 198–200). In international terms, the ALP was an early example of an electorally successful working-class party, although it has never chosen to 'challenge the fundamentals of Australian capitalism' (Patmore and Coates 2005: 125). It has been portrayed as 'a vehicle for working-class aspirations, albeit flawed' (Shor 1999: 68) and even a 'capitalist workers' party' (Bramble and Kuhn 2009: 282).

Working class aspirations were cemented with early and extensive state regulation of the employment relationship via conciliation and arbitration legislation in 1904. These laws were seen as an example to working class movements elsewhere and as a way to secure collective representation in the wake of unsuccessful strikes that had decimated the union movement in the 1890s (Rowse 2004: 22). Arbitral tribunals would settle disputes by establishing 'awards' which had the force of law and which set minimum wages and conditions for individual industries and occupations. These often contained conditions, such as sick pay, that in other countries were provided by the state, leading to a distinctive Australian public policy dubbed 'the wage earners' welfare state' (Castles 1994). Unions were officially recognised by and incorporated into the arbitral system, to such an extent that some writers considered unions had become an arm of the state (Howard 1977). Union reliance on arbitration varied over time and between unions (Rimmer 2004: 314), but it meant that many unions focused much of their energies on arguing before tribunals rather than developing workplace union structures (Crosby 2005). Provided the movement had a militant heartland willing to take action and achieve strategic gains, other unions could then rely on tribunals and awards to generalise those gains across their membership as a whole, even in workplaces with little local activism. The strategies of many unions (with some exceptions) were underpinned by a belief that, under pressure, the state (in particular Labor governments and the arbitration system) could deliver real gains for their members and balance the power of employers. Thus the ALP-union relationship was symbiotic, albeit at times with significant tensions. The ALP needed unions for electoral success and unions needed the ALP (in power) to pursue the reforms union leaders favoured.

Nevertheless, labourism was never hegemonic. The syndicalist Industrial Workers of the World (IWW) was active in Australia for a short period during and just after World War I (Burgmann 1995, Shor 1999: 69). The Communist Party of Australia (CPA) then became an important force from the 1920s to the 1950s (Macintyre 1998; O'Lincoln 1985) in manufacturing, mining, transport and even education and clerical occupations (Bramble 2008: 8; Sheridan 1989). After the war, the union movement ruptured politically when conservative 'industrial groups' of members were established to campaign against Communist union officials, leading to a decline in Communist influence and splits in the union movement and in the ALP that kept Labor out of government federally until 1972 (Scalmer 1998). Reflecting divisions in the international communist movement, the CPA itself split in the early 1960s and again in 1971, and it gradually ceased to have any major influence on unions (O'Lincoln 1985).

Militancy was a contested strategy within the union movement. On the one hand, union officials had to deal with some in their rank and file who were more militant than they, and who sometimes engaged in unauthorised action, for example in car plants, the post office and mines (Bramble 2008; Murphy 1983; Tierney 1996). On the other hand, a large proportion of their membership, especially those forced to join by compulsory membership provisions, were not at all interested in action. Through the 1960s and 1970s, nearly 40 per cent of union members voted for conservative political parties (Leigh 2006). Members were thus on average considerably more politically conservative than their leadership: a survey of 84 union officials found none voted for conservative parties at the 1977 election (unpublished data from a survey in Spillane 1981). While left-wing unions were more ready to use strike action (Bramble 2008: 21), both they and moderate union leaders in the end relied on the same core strategies; that is, using short strikes to leverage favourable outcomes through arbitration. And the taking of industrial action was inconsistent with the values of arbitration, which was established to do away with the need for strikes. So despite a relatively healthy level of density, the public legitimacy of Australian unions was among the lowest in western countries (Peetz 2002), adding further to the difficulty facing union leaders in organising sustained, large-scale mass actions.

As factions' powers waxed and waned, one of the most significant ideological changes within the union movement in the 1970s was the increasing demands for gender equity. Women sought from the first to widen unions' industrial agendas, with communist and left-wing unions providing room for women's struggles (Ellem 1999). Critical advances towards reducing the gender pay gap were made through arbitration courts in 1969 and 1972 (Whitehouse 2004: 226–236), although in some cases there was industrial action, including a national strike by clerical workers in 1975 (Fieldes 1994).

Peak councils and individual unions established women's caucuses and some unions overturned bans on female labour (Bevege 1980). The proportion of women workers who were union members rose from 35 to 49 per cent cent between 1969 and 1982 (Rawson 1986: 26) and the number of female union officials grew, although modestly.

While sections of the union movement resisted capital and advocated socialism, most unions favoured strategic state protection delivered by the arbitration system and did not significantly challenge capitalism. Through the twentieth century, unions dominated the formal structures of ALP outside Parliament, and provided many of the aspiring politicians who entered Parliament as well as, until recently, the bulk of the ALP's funds (Bramble and Kuhn 2009: 287), but their influence on decisions of the Parliamentary executive gradually declined. Still, ties linking the ALP and unions at organisational, factional and personal levels have been responsible for 'moderating the politics of the unions and delivering parliamentary power to the ALP' (Ellem and Franks 2008: 57). Thus the relationship between the industrial and political wings of the labour movement resulted in gains for unions but muted their militancy until a period of turmoil in the early 1970s, to the detriment of the newly elected ALP Government. The then Prime Minister, Gough Whitlam (1985: 201), later rued the lack of a close working relationship between unions and his government. Labor's economic credibility was seriously damaged by rising unemployment and inflation in the context of a 'wages explosion' and this was a significant factor in its early defeat in 1975 (ironically, Whitlam had taken Australia's first major step towards free trade and confronted Labor's protectionist trade tradition by cutting tariffs by 25 per cent in July 1973). The conservative Fraser government redistributed income from labour to capital (in part by dismantling the Medibank national health insurance scheme) but failed to prevent a large rise in unemployment in 1982, leading to its defeat in 1983 and the return of Labor under Prime Minister Bob Hawke, former president of the ACTU. In the meantime, both Labor and the unions had fundamentally reconsidered their relationship. The outcome would reshape the Australian economy and labour market.

CONSTRAINED NEO-LIBERALISM UNDER THE ACCORD

Two weeks before the 1983 election, the Labor Party and ACTU finalised a prices and incomes 'Accord'. The Whitlam government's problems with economic management led both wings of the labour movement to conclude that an incomes policy was necessary to address simultaneously high unemployment and inflation. The Accord provided for guaranteed wage rises, mostly linked to the consumer price index, but with moderation in wage claims exchanged for 'social wage' benefits in universal health care and spending on education, welfare and public housing, as well as targeted tax cuts. Leaders of the ACTU and government met regularly and unions had an unprecedented influence on national economic policy (Singleton 1990). This signalled a temporary and stark reversal of the long term decline in union influence on the Parliamentary executive.

At the same time there were major structural changes within the union movement. The ACTU until 1982 had held limited sway over its constituents – a union leader told one of the authors that year the ACTU 'couldn't deliver a letter'. Yet in 1983 it assumed centralised control over virtually the whole of the union movement. The few dissident unions, such as the Food Preservers Union and the Builders Labourers Federation, were disciplined and at times excluded from benefits the arbitration system delivered (Ross 2004). One unaffiliated union, the airline pilots, which sought to break the wages guidelines of the time, was essentially destroyed by the actions of the government, the military (whose pilots flew planes during the strike) and the ACTU (Smith 1990). The ACTU's central control within the movement arose not from the peak body's constitution, but from its authority in negotiating with government and from the regulatory powers of the arbitration tribunal, which had responsibility for implementing (albeit with an independent mind) the wages provisions of the Accord agreements. Within government, the key structural change was in the relationship between party and bureaucracy. The Whitlam government's relationship with top bureaucrats, especially Treasury, had been poisonous, with catastrophic consequences. The Hawke government instead embraced the bureaucrats it inherited from the conservatives, one of whom later left to become a leading neo-liberal activist, and relied heavily on them for advice.

Long before the shift to 'enterprise bargaining', the Labor government was initiating a programme of market-leaning reforms in product and financial markets. Most importantly, in December 1983, all exchange rate controls were lifted and many aspects of financial markets were deregulated. This was probably the single most important step towards neo-liberal policies. It set up what would be seen by some commentators as a conflict between (unregulated) financial markets and (regulated) labour markets, but would perhaps be better portrayed as a conflict between financial markets and civil society. Through the remainder of the 1980s product markets were deregulated, 'competition policy' reforms were introduced, and from 1986 public assets were privatised when a collapse in the terms of trade and volatility in financial markets engendered a sense of economic crisis (such that some feared possible intervention by the International Monetary Fund) (Kelly 1992: 207). Over the next few years, government-owned airlines, banks and numerous other corporations were controversially sold (Quiggin 1998).

How was it that such neo-liberal reforms could be pursued while unions had such influence on the Government? The ACTU was actively involved in negotiating responses to changing economic circumstances. From 1985, the Accord was constantly renegotiated – in the end, this happened seven times during the five terms of the Hawke and Keating Labor governments, as economic circumstances changed, pressures within the union movement altered and policy orthodoxies evolved within the government. The renegotiated Accords focused on minimising the cost flow-through of exchange rate movements and removing regulatory impediments to workplace efficiency, culminating in the complete abandonment of nationally centralised wage fixation in 1991 and its replacement by a system of enterprise-level wage bargaining, with 'safety net' increases available to those unable to bargain. While the increasingly influential Business Council of Australia initiated the debate on 'enterprise bargaining', the ACTU eventually pushed the idea enthusiastically. It saw it as a means of releasing wage pressures, alerting employees to the benefits of union membership, taking authority away from a recalcitrant arbitral tribunal which had not fully implemented the Accord's provisions, and establishing a more worker-friendly version of an enterprise-focused system that it expected would be put in place anyway by resurgent conservative parties at some time in the future. The move to enterprise bargaining signalled an end to the primacy of arbitration that had dominated industrial relations for almost a century.

Unions did not restrict themselves to industrial issues and the Accord provided legitimacy for union ventures into a range of economic and social policy arenas. The ACTU in the latter half of the 1980s put forward an alternative model of economic management that contrasted with the neo-liberal model of market liberalisation and privatisation. The most prominent manifestation of the ACTU's strategy was the report *Australia Reconstructed* that arose from a government-sponsored mission by key ACTU personalities, including leaders of the powerful left-wing metalworkers union, to northern Europe. Described as 'the most comprehensive policy manifesto ever published by the mainstream Left in Australia' (Scott 2006), it recommended that Australia model itself on Scandinavia and develop not only a more refined incomes policy but also industry planning, active manpower policy, education and training, and employee participation in decision making (ACTU/TDC 1987). At the same time, unions expressed opposition to several of the product market reforms being pursued by the government. They successfully influenced the development of adjustment strategies for key industries such as steel and vehicle manufacturing. However, unions were ineffective in opposing the broad thrust of the deregulatory agenda, or in shaping the government's macroeconomic strategy after 1985. It was one thing to be able to negotiate policies regarding specific industries where they had a strong presence and could back their position with the implied threat of economic disruption; it was another altogether to successfully challenge the hegemony of ideas that the Treasury and related departments had, when no one in government believed that unions could organise economic disruption over issues few workers understood and were motivated by. The union approach through this period was thus a combination of 'protective' and 'reformist oppositional', becoming deeply engaged in the decision making process regarding labour market policy, particularly industrial relations policy, and successfully gaining protection for workers in a number of industries adversely affected by economic liberalisation, but not effectively challenging the emerging neo-liberal paradigm among key policy makers.

In short, in the 1980s unions put forward elements of an alternative, progressive social democratic framework, but a combination of circumstances meant that the programme failed to take hold. While there were a range of union responses to the quasi-corporatist arrangements of the Accord, political and industrial dissent was muted. The Accord's emphasis on the 'social wage' highlighted redistributive issues and encouraged unions to travel further down a social democratic path, developing links between the wage system, the labour market and social welfare issues such as child care, superannuation (pensions) and health care. These links were but fleetingly made, however, as the perceived imperatives of the newly liberated financial markets and employer agendas came to dominate the Accord's socially redistributive emphasis. This was a period of significant structural change in the economy, from manufacturing to services, and from the public sector to the private. The ambitious ideals of *Australia Reconstructed* were challenged and ultimately defeated by the Treasury vision of globalisation and accompanying product market reforms. The shift to enterprise bargaining failed to reverse the decline in union density that had commenced in the early 1980s, as employers took advantage of weak union organisation to displace unions altogether from many workplaces (Peetz 1998). Ironically, despite a return to high unemployment, the conservative parties unexpectedly failed to defeat the Labor government in the 1993 election, mainly because of their radical policies on industrial relations, health care and, most visibly, a goods and services tax. It took another three years, and a considerable softening of their political platform, before the conservative parties gained government once more.

STALINIST NEO-LIBERALISM UNDER HOWARD

In March 1996, the Liberal and National Parties won a national election. Lacking control of the upper house (Senate), they were forced to negotiate compromises on their new legislative regime for industrial relations with the centrist Australian Democrats party. Unions lobbied the Democrats but to little effect. In the main, the new Workplace Relations Act contained most of the conservatives' IR policy: the introduction of individual contracts ('Australian Workplace Agreements' or AWAs) that could be inconsistent with (though not, in net terms, lower than) minimum standards set out in awards, non-union 'collective' agreements, prohibitions on compulsory unionism under the banner of 'freedom of association', restrictions on when industrial action was legal, harsher sanctions for unions breaching restrictions on industrial action, and limits on the matters that could be covered by awards or arbitrated by tribunals. The clear intent was to reduce union power. What credibility unions had was shattered by the 'Cavalcade to Canberra', a protest to Parliament House that unexpectedly led to violent scenes in and around the building that were widely reported in the media (Bailey and Iveson 2000).

Within this newly established framework, employers pursued specific sectoral strategies, often actively encouraged by the government. In the highly unionised coal mining industry, employers made use of new laws to open non-union mines and victimise or dismiss union activists in existing mines. The meat industry, telecommunications and some areas of the public service were also targeted. The most dramatic and celebrated strategy, however, was on the waterfront. Just before Easter 1998, one of the two major employers, Patrick Corporation, dismissed its entire unionised workforce and replaced it with a non-union workforce employed under AWAs by a contractor. For the government, this would be Australia's version of the 1984 British miners' strike, a defining moment as the government expected the union would call a national strike and be destroyed by the Workplace Relations Act and trade practices prohibitions on secondary boycotts. But despite considerable internal pressure the union did not act as predicted, eschewing a national strike as 'community' pickets mobilised around the docks. With strategic advice from the ACTU, it challenged the action in the courts, using the Workplace Relations Act's provisions on freedom of association against the government and Patrick, alleging that a conspiracy by them breached the law. Eventually under High Court instructions the unionists were reinstated and their replacements on AWAs were themselves sacked. The union had to accept redundancies to improve productivity as part of the settlement, so the employer achieved some significant gains from the process, but as the waterfront remained unionised the outcome was a major defeat for the government.

Elsewhere union responses to the employer and government agenda were mixed. In every industry union density fell during the Howard years, by the largest amounts in those industries where concerted employer deunionisation strategies (including use of AWAs) were used. Unions also became involved, with limited efficacy, in specific campaigns on matters such as the US-Australia Free Trade Agreement. Having lost all political influence at the national level, unions focused on internal reforms. Particularly after the ascension of Greg Combet (an architect of the waterfront response) to leadership of the ACTU in 1999, the peak body increasingly prioritised the development of union 'organising' strategies, based on renewing union influence at the workplace level and redirecting power to members in the workplace (ACTU 1998). Unions in this period began to move to a more 'organising' focused approach but did so slowly, intermittently and unevenly. The agenda was gradually accepted by most in spirit if not in practice. The precipitous falls in union membership that occurred each year through the 1990s plateaued. Membership through the next decade oscillated around 1.8m. Density, though, continued to decline (ABS 2010).

Notably, the shift to organising did not appear to align with the traditional left-right divide within the union movement. An embrace of organising did not equate to any fundamental challenge to the governance of capitalism or neoliberalism. But it did mean a fundamental challenge to the governance systems of unions, and where successful would lead to a shift in power relations at the workplace.

The conservative government was re-elected three times, most importantly in 2004 when it obtained for the first time an unexpected majority in the Senate in its own right. Almost immediately it began preparing a new legislative regime. It was introduced into the Parliament in November 2005 under the name of WorkChoices, supported by a media campaign that commenced even before the details of the new law were announced and eventually cost over A$130m (approximately US$100m).

WorkChoices introduced further restrictions and heavier penalties on unions undertaking industrial action, imposed major limitations on union officials' right to enter workplaces, took away many remaining powers of the independent tribunals, and sought to make state jurisdictions redundant. Most significantly, it abolished protection against unfair dismissal for all workers in firms with fewer than 101 employees, and in all cases where employers could claim 'operational reasons' as part of the justification for dismissal, and it enabled AWAs to undercut minimum award provisions for penalty rates, overtime pay and other 'protected conditions'.

While on the one hand espousing the rhetoric of enabling employers and employees to determine enterprise-level outcomes for themselves without third party intervention, the government's 1388 pages of legislation, 414 pages of regulations and 890 pages of explanatory memoranda – 2692 pages in total – sought to intervene in micro-level relations in a partisan fashion to a degree unprecedented in Australia or elsewhere in the OECD. If an agreement contained provisions that offended the federal Minister – for example, provisions for unfair dismissal protections or union training – the parties were liable to heavy fines. One corporate lobbyist likened it to the 'old Soviet system of command and control, where every economic decision has to go back to some central authority and get ticked off' (quoted in *The Age* 26 March 2006). Hence we describe it as 'Stalinist neo-liberalism', extending a trend that commenced under the Workplace Relations Act.

The union response was to launch what the beleaguered Minister later called the 'most sophisticated political plan that we have seen in Australia' (Hockey 2007). In sharp contrast to the debacle of the 'Cavalcade to Canberra', this campaign, known as 'Your Rights at Work' (YR@W), involved a highly coordinated combination of media campaigns, grassroots activism and mass actions, with large numbers of union members in marginal electorates (parliamentary seats decisive to the election outcome) telephoned directly by their union. Particular emphasis was placed on framing the campaign to emphasise the impact of WorkChoices on individual (vulnerable) employees and 'working families', rather than on unions as institutions which were the true target of WorkChoices (Muir and Peetz 2010). Once the law came into effect, AWAs routinely reduced employment conditions. Numerous stories emerged in the media (many strategically released by unions) of workers having pay and conditions cut through AWAs, often in combination with the threat, or actuality, of dismissal.

Funded by a levy on unionists and costing a quarter of the government's campaign, the YR@W campaign bore more than a passing resemblance to the election campaign of Barack Obama a year later in the US. It drew heavily on the principles of 'organising' that the ACTU had been encouraging for several years, and indeed was coordinated by the former co-director of the ACTU's organising centre. The YR@W campaign united left and right unions. The Howard Government was defeated in the 2007 election. Prime Minister Howard lost his Parliamentary seat. WorkChoices was recognised as the single issue that contributed most to this outcome by the ALP, Liberal and National Party campaign directors and victorious and defeated candidates (Muir and Peetz 2010). Polls consistently showed clear majority opposition to WorkChoices and that industrial relations was the key vote-switching issue (*Sydney Morning Herald* 2 November 2007; Essential Research 2007). Among people who had voted for the Liberal Party in 2004, some 36 per cent disapproved of WorkChoices and, of those, half switched to Labor or the Greens at the 2007 election. No other issue was as important in causing voters to switch parties (AES 2007). The swing against the government was 1.3 to 2 per cent higher in electorates that had featured local YR@W campaigns (Spies-Butcher and Wilson 2008).

Union strategy in this period combined 'protective' and 'reformist opposition' approaches to neo-liberalism. In this period, particularly towards its close, unions' industrial and very specific political agendas – notably, their survival and the defeat of the Howard government – necessarily dominated over any kind of broad vision of, let alone action for, economic and social reform. In contrast to the Accord when unions developed an alternative vision of the economy, in this period of Stalinist neo-liberalism they focused narrowly on their continuing existence. At a time of great challenge to its members' wages and conditions and their collective workplace rights, unions saw a political solution – rather than one based on industrial action and militancy – as appropriate. But they were probably correct in assessing that, with only 18 per cent density, they no longer had the industrial capacity to bring the country to its knees through direct action alone, and any attempt to do so would have instead reinforced the government's rhetoric about irresponsible and thuggish unions. Ironically, a movement which had been dismissed as irrelevant due to its low density showed it still had the capacity to bring down a government.

YR@W brought to an end a law that would have certainly seen a further major decline in unionism. However the campaign did not, in itself, lead to any increase in union membership. Though applying organising principles to political action, if anything, it diverted union energies away from workplace member organising. Still, it mobilised Australian popular sentiment against one of the core elements of neo-liberalism – the philosophy of 'individualism' (Stilwell 2002) – and closed the widening gap that had emerged between elite practice and popular opinion on this issue. Policy makers who attempted to go this far down the neo-liberal path in future would do so at great peril. In that sense, it was a successful challenge to a key element of neo-liberalism. But the campaign did not construct a broad alternative vision to the edifice of neo-liberalism.

REVISIONIST NEO-LIBERALISM UNDER RUDD

The defeat of the Howard government brought to office Labor Prime Minister Kevin Rudd, a man with probably fewer links to unions than any previous Labor leader. Shortly before the government's first term ended, he was replaced as leader by his deputy, Julia Gillard – who had also been until then the Minister for Workplace Relations, among other portfolios. The subsequent election saw the government lose its comfortable majority and hang onto office only with assistance from several independent and minor party parliamentarians, an unusual outcome in Australian political history.

Rudd positioned his government as part of 'the reforming centre' (Rudd 2008a) with a political philosophy 'beyond Left and Right' (Rudd 2008b) that emphasised 'balance' (Rudd 2006). In an essay written after his party won government, he spelt out his position on the global financial crisis, proclaiming that 'the great neo-liberal experiment of the last 20 years has failed ... the emperor has no clothes', and urging a need 'to reach beyond Keynes' (Rudd

2009). He argued that the neo-liberal values of 'liberty, security and prosperity' should be combined with those of 'equity, community and sustainability' (Rudd 2006: 6). Rudd emphasised the role of faith in politics, placing himself in the tradition of progressive, Christian social democracy (Rudd 2006: 7). Yet Rudd's bold rhetoric was not matched by bold action. Indeed his slide from electoral dominance (for most of his leadership, polls indicated he would more than double his majority at the next election) to doom can be dated to his failure to follow through on his claim to confront the greatest crisis wrought by neo-liberalism – the threat posed by climate change. A second critical moment was a failure to effectively manage an attempt to increase taxation on the hugely profitable mining sector. These failures reflected not just personality but also structural problems with Labor in Government: 'he had little courage and was part of a cabinet that almost universally lacked courage' (Gittins 2010: 2). His successor, Gillard, though different in many respects – an avowed atheist, Australia's first female Prime Minister, possessing an inclusive style, an industrial lawyer experienced in acting for unions – showed no greater boldness. The revisionist neo-liberalism of the Rudd-Gillard years reflected not so much a belief in the benefits of markets, or a determination to serve the interests of capital, as a lack of determination to challenge the interests of capital. Both leaders – and the Labor Party generally – could be characterised as embodying the 'Third Way' (see Scanlon 2001), although neither leader used this phrase.

The 'Fair Work' policy that Labor took to the 2007 election bore the signatures of both Rudd and Gillard, in form and content. Stewart characterised the Fair Work Act as 'an exercise in political pragmatism' with 'little that is conceptually novel' (2009: 23–24). The Act continued the push towards a fully national industrial relations system begun under Howard. Importantly for unions, the new Act abolished AWAs, largely reinstated unfair dismissal laws, emphasised collective bargaining with a new requirement to 'bargain in good faith', established new statutory employment standards – including on redundancy pay, long service leave, and the right of parents of young children and those with disabilities to request (but not necessarily receive) flexible working arrangements – and expanded individual protections against victimisation and discrimination (Stewart 2009). The Act contains a new 'low paid bargaining stream' that may assist some low-paid, award-reliant workers – mainly women – to gain better wages and conditions via arbitrated decisions by Fair Work Australia, somewhat unusual in that arbitration has largely been abolished for most workers (Cooper and Ellem 2009: 10). The first case, for aged care workers (who are predominantly women) had commenced at the time of writing. The new law retained a number of WorkChoices provisions unpopular with unions, particularly in relation to union rights of access to workplaces and penalties for illegal industrial action. In addition, restrictions on the content of collective agreements were only partially removed (a breach of Labor's pre-election promises) and unions did not regain the principal status they had under the old award system.

Union responses to the Fair Work Act have been mixed. ACTU President Sharan Burrow's address to the 2009 ACTU Congress 'strove to strike a balance between celebrating the change of government and noting that the job of reform must continue' (Davis 2009: 170), which is a neat summation of the unions' generally muted criticism of the Fair Work Act. A formal resolution at the Congress took issue with the Act in a number of ways relating to agreement-making and industrial action (Davis 2009: 172). But the loudest opposition was reserved for the Rudd government's refusal to abolish coercive regulatory arrangements, established under the Howard government, in the building and construction industry (see Allan *et al.* 2010). Julia Gillard, one of the invited speakers, was greeted by Congress delegates, all in yellow T-shirts provided by the Construction, Forestry, Mining and Energy Workers Union bearing the message 'One Law For All' and demanding abolition of the coercive agency (Davis 2009: 173–175). It seems clear unions will continue to work, formally and informally, towards small changes in the Fair Work Act, though the removal of the special provisions governing the construction industry are a priority. Unions are also likely to continue to pursue variants of the organising approach. Some of the provisions of the Fair Work Act provide opportunities for reformist action by unions, particularly with respect to equal pay and the low paid, and the Act does not inhibit (but nor does it facilitate) the organising agenda within unions.

The Rudd and Gillard governments present a considerable paradox. We term their dominant philosophy 'revisionist neo-liberalism'. On the one hand, the ALP in office decried the extremes of neo-liberalism, while on the other hand maintaining a heavy reliance on market mechanisms and introducing only moderate changes to labour regulation. For the labour movement, this was a more benign environment than the Howard years, with a somewhat less constraining environment for organising and bargaining. On unions' part, however, a modified form of labourism remains the dominant ideological frame. In a nutshell, revisionist neo-liberalism stimulated revisionist labourism – revisionist in the sense that unions had a range of internal revitalisation strategies, but maintained their faith in the parliamentary process, focusing their energies on media commentary and lobbying ministers on the new governments' changes to labour law, but eschewing industrial campaigns. Some opportunities opened up for unions under revised legislation, but there were no signs of major union challenges to the dominant revisionist neo-liberalist paradigm.

While there were some isolated challenges within the union movement to revisionist neo-liberalism, unions lacked a coherent alternative framework, and focused on adapting to the new environment rather than challenging it. They advocated the need for strategic state action, and welcomed the ALP government's reforms while strongly criticising them for not going far enough. Overall, they did not significantly threaten the ALP's 'revisionist neo-liberal' agenda. Nor do they have the same capacity to influence it as in the past. In 1993, under the Accord, ACTU negotiators regularly met with government officials to draft the major legislative reform of the time, the Industrial Relations Reform Act. In 2008, with density less than half that at the peak of the Accord, the unions played no such role in drafting the Fair Work Act; though they met with government, they had no more status than business lobbyists in designing the act. They lacked the organisational power to force the Government to enact further reforms in industrial relations, and lacked the ability to mobilise ideas in the community sufficiently to force a government rethink on broader economic or social issues. Yet while union influence on Labor cabinet policy is probably lower than at almost any time during the preceding century, the formal and informal links are still there, such that in the Rudd period three former ACTU presidents, as well as former secretary Greg Combet, represented the ALP in the national Parliament. These structural relationships, which attract recurring media interest, have been insufficient to offset the structural power of capital and the ideology that serves it, neo-liberalism.

CONCLUSION

Union strategy has varied over the past century or so between advocating a need for 'protective' state action on the one hand to 'reformist oppositional' stances on the other. The latter took the form of muted opposition to corporate globalisation in the form of industry policies in the Accord years, and advocacy of social democracy as an alternative in order to 'civilise' the capitalist economy. This largely reflects two factors: unions' role (now largely disappeared) within the arbitration system, and their long established links to the ALP and hence parliamentary politics. Arbitration unionism was intermixed with militant action at various periods, though since the 1970s militancy, measured by strike action and in other ways, has diminished. Australian unions were in some ways 'trapped' by a state that was more activist than most in the industrial relations arena. Accepting the benefits of relatively comprehensive industrial relations laws which moderately compress wage relativities and thus assist the low paid (who are often not members of trade unions), Australian unions reaped certain benefits for members and non-members alike, but then had to accept the restraints that come with an interventionist state role. This pattern reached its zenith with the Accord (Lavelle 2010: 59).

The Accord broadened the terrain on which unions could legitimately traverse and provided, albeit briefly, a moment where they put forward something resembling an alternative social democratic vision for the economy to the emerging, constrained neo-liberalism. But it could not decisively counter the power of those neo-liberal ideas within the state bureaucracy and at the same time exacerbated the already critical weakness of unionism at the workplace. Unlike the Scandinavian unions on which Australian unions wished to model themselves, they could not simultaneously be active and effective in both the national and workplace spheres.

So it was that a Labor government from 1983 to 1996 oversaw the introduction of neo-liberalism into Australia. Keating, in assessing the Hawke and his own Labor governments, was later to write that they both 'had a greater belief in markets than our conservative counterparts' (Keating 1999, cited in Lavalle 2010: 60). Some political analysts have suggested that government action – specifically, the constant renegotiation of the Accord – was 'a response to the press of events rather than arising from a carefully prepared programme' and 'was not driven by a will to reposition the ALP ideologically' (Pierson and Castles 2002: 686, 698), but there is little doubt that, when it came to office, the Hawke/Keating government was more amenable both to market-based policies and to corporatist negotiation than its predecessors, and it is perhaps this contradiction that best explains events over its period. Under Howard, neo-liberal social policy measures, particularly those relating to welfare reform, were extensively developed (Bessant *et al.* 2006), not an issue previous Labor governments had particularly addressed. These changes occurred alongside ongoing economic reform and, from 1996 but particularly from 2006, very significant industrial relations change. Yet the latter had many interventionist elements that shifted it from a market model. For the Howard government, the key element of neo-liberalism was about supporting capital against organised labour, and if that meant moving away from markets to a form of Stalinist neo-liberalism, so be it.

As the desperate need for workplace union development was revealed and responded to, the breadth of union vision outside the workplace narrowed. The need for survival under Stalinist neo-liberalism rather focused the collective mind. However, a union movement with a focused mind was successful in achieving its principal goal. There are few union movements in the world which can claim to have peacefully overthrown a government. For a movement that was, according to some, doomed, it was a remarkable achievement.

While Australian unions, with some exceptions, neglected the creation of workplace activism until recent years, they now advocate organising approaches. Such approaches increasingly emphasise union education of activists, which has the capacity to broaden workers' understanding of workplace and class issues. Organising based union renewal strategies also emphasise the promotion of union values among employees, of developing linkages with other groups in the community and of corporate campaigning. Yet unions have not developed a modernised class politics to underpin the new emphasis on workplace activism. The forms of exploitation highlighted by YR@W epitomised class relations, but the substance of the campaign highlighted a more moderate philosophical agenda based on 'working families' and 'vulnerable people (seemingly non-unionists) ... helplessly caught up in the system' (Wanna 2010: 19). Unions have been electorally successful but, arguably, less so industrially. While the ALP-union relationship has changed over the past century, it still continues to dampen overt class politics. There is no sign at this point of a radical oppositional response to the Labor government's revisionist neo-liberalism. Australia's relative prosperity compared to other countries, and the lack of a coherent new philosophical position on the part of trade unions, suggests radical opposition is unlikely to dominate any time soon.

REFERENCES

Allan, C., A. Dungan and D. Peetz (2010), '"Anomalies", damned "anomalies" and statistics: construction industry productivity in Australia', *Journal of Industrial Relations*, **52**(1), 61–79.

Argy, F. (1998), *Australia at the Cross Roads: Radical Free Market or a Progressive Liberalism*, Sydney, NSW: Allen and Unwin.

Australian Bureau of Statistics (ABS) (2010), *Employee Earnings, Benefits and Trade Union Membership*, cat no 6310.0, Canberra: ABS.

Australian Election Study (2007), *Australian election study 2007*, Canberra: Australian National University.

Australian Council of Trade Unions/Trade Development Council (ACTU/TDC) (1987), *Australia Reconstructed*, Canberra: Australian Government Publishing Service.

Australian Council of Trade Unions (1998), *Unions@Work*, Melbourne, UK: ACTU.

Bailey, J. and K. Iveson (2000), '"The Parliaments call them thugs": public space, identity and union protest', *Journal of Industrial Relations*, **42**(4), 517–34.

Bessant , J., T. Dalton, P. Smyth and R. Watts (2006), *Talking Policy: Making Social Policy in Australia*, Sydney, NSW: Allen and Unwin.

Bevege, M. (1980), 'Women's struggle to become train drivers in Melbourne 1956–1975', in E. Windschuttle (ed.), *Women, Class and History: Feminist Perspectives on Australia 1788–1978*, Melbourne, UK: Fontana/Collins, pp. 437–52.

Bramble, T. (2008), *Trade Unionism in Australia: A History from Flood Tide to Ebb Tide*, Melbourne, UK: Cambridge University Press.

Bramble, T. and R. Kuhn (2009), 'Continuity or discontinuity in the recent history of the Australian Labor Party?', *Australian Journal of Political Science*, **44**(2) 281–94.

Buckley, K. and T. Wheelwright (1988), *No Paradise for Workers: Capitalism and the Common People in Australia 1788–1914*, Melbourne, VIC: Oxford University Press,.

Burgmann, V. (1995), *Revolutionary Industrial Unionism: The Industrial Workers of the World in Australia*, Cambridge: Cambridge University Press.

Castles, F. (1994), 'The wage earners, welfare state revisited: refurbishing the established model of Australian social protection, 1983–1993', *Australian Journal of Social Issues*, **299**(2), 120–45.

Cooper, R. and B. Ellem (2009), 'Fair Work and the re-regulation of collective bargaining', *Australian Journal of Labour Law*, **22**(3), 284–305.

Crosby, M. (2005), *Power at Work: Rebuilding the Australian Union Movement*, Sydney, NSW: Federation Press.

Davis, E. (2009), 'The ACTU Congress of 2009', *Labour History*, **97**, 169–83.

Donn, C. B. (1979), 'The ACTU, trade union congresses, and nationwide general strikes', *Labour History*, **37**, 78–85.

Ellem, B. (1999), 'Women's rights and industrial relations under the postwar compact in Australia', *International Labor and Working-Class History*, **56**, 45–64.

Ellem, B. and P. Franks (2008), 'Trade union structure and politics in Australia and New Zealand', *Labour History*, **95**, 43–67.

Essential Research (2007), *National Opinion Poll: Summary Report*, Melbourne, VIC: Essential Research.

Fieldes, D. (1994), 'The fight for equal pay in the Australian insurance industry, 1972–75', in R. Callus and M. Schumacher (eds), *Current Research in Industrial Relations*, Sydney, NSW: Proceedings of the 8th AIRAANZ Conference, pp. 481–507.

Gall, G., R. Hurd and A. Wilkinson (2011), 'Labour unionism and neo-liberalism', in G. Gall, R. Hurd and A. Wilkinson (eds), *International Handbook on Labour Union Responses to Neo-Liberalism*, Cheltenham, UK and Northampton, MA, USA: Edward Elgar.

Gittins, R. (2010), 'Outlook for Australian politics and government in 2011', presentation to the Australian Business Economists Annual Forecasting Conference, Sydney, NSW, accessed at http://rossgittins.blogspot.com/2010/12/outlook-for-australian-politics-and.html.

Hockey, J. (2007), interview on *AM*, Australian Broadcasting Corporation, 13 June, accessed 6 June 2011 at www.abc.net.au/am/content/2007/s1949620.htm.

Howard, W. (1977), 'Australian trade unions in the context of union theory', *Journal of Industrial Relations*, **19**(3), 255–73.

Kelly, P. (1992), *The End of Certainty: The Story of the 1980s*, Sydney, NSW: Allen and Unwin.

Lavelle, A. (2010), 'The ties that unwind? Social democratic parties and unions in Australia and Britain', *Labour History*, **98**, 55–75.

Leigh, A. (2006), 'How do unionists vote? Estimating the causal impact of union membership on voting behaviour from 1966 to 2004', *Australian Journal of Political Science*, **41**(4), 537–55.

Macintyre, S. (1998), *The Reds: The Communist Party of Australia from origins to illegality*, Sydney, NSW: Allen and Unwin.

Muir, K. (2008), *Worth Fighting For: inside the Your Rights at Work Campaign*, Sydney, NSW: University of NSW Press.

Muir, K. and D. Peetz (2010), 'Back from the dead – the Australian union movement and the defeat of a government', *Social Movement Studies*, **9**(2), 215–28.

Murphy, D. (ed) (1983), *The Big Strikes: Queensland 1889–1965*, St Lucia, QLD: University of Queensland Press.

Murray, G. and D. Peetz (2010), 'Ideology down under and the shifting sands of individualism' in C. Azais (ed.), *Labour and Employment in a Globalising world: Autonomy, Collectives and Political Dilemmas*, Brussels: PEI Peter Lang, pp. 229–46.

O'Lincoln, T. (1985), *Into the Mainstream: The Decline of Australian Communism*, Sydney, NSW: Stained Wattle Press.

Patmore, G. and D. Coates (2005), 'Labour parties and the state in Australia and the UK', *Labour History*, **88**, 121–41.

Peetz, D. (1998), *Unions in a Contrary World*, Melbourne, VIC: Cambridge University Press.

Peetz, D. (2002), 'Sympathy for the devil? Attitudes to Australian unions', *Australian Journal of Political Science*, **37**(1), 57–80.

Pierson, C. and F. Castles (2002), 'Australian antecedents of the Third Way', *Political Studies*, **50**(4), 683–702.

Pusey, M. (1992), *Economic Rationalism in Canberra: A Nation-building State Changes its Mind*, Melbourne, VIC: Cambridge University Press.

Quiggin, J. (1998), 'Social democracy and market reform in Australia and New Zealand', *Oxford Review of Economic Policy* **14**(1), 76–95.

Quiggin, J. (2010), *Zombie Economics*, Princeton, NJ: Princeton University Press.

Rawson, D. (1986), *Unions and Unionists in Australia*, Sydney, NSW: Allen and Unwin.

Rimmer, M. (2004), 'Unions and arbitration' in J. Isaac and S. Macintyre (eds), *The New Province for Law and Order*, Melbourne, VIC: Cambridge University Press, pp. 275–315.

Ross, L. (2004), *Dare to Struggle, Dare to Win! Builders Labourers Fight Deregistration, 1981–94*, Melbourne, VIC: Vulgar Press.

Rowse, T. (2004), 'Elusive middle ground: a political history', in J. Isaac and S. Macintyre (eds), *The New Province for Law and Order*, Malbourne, VIC: Cambridge University Press, pp. 17–54.

Rudd, K. (2006), 'Faith in Politics', *The Monthly*, October.

Rudd, K. (2008a), 'Australia 2020: setting our nation's sights for the future', presentation to Sydney Institute Annual Dinner, accessed 8 April 2010 at www.pm.gov.au/node/5836.

Rudd, K. (2008b), address to the business forum with the AI Group, accessed 8 April 2010 at www.pm.gov.au/node/5513.

Rudd, K. (2009), 'The global financial crisis', *The Monthly*, February.

Scalmer, S. (1998), 'Labour's golden age and the changing forms of workers representation in Australia', *Journal of the Royal Australian History Society*, **84**(2), 186–93.

Scanlon, C. (2001), 'A step to the left? Or just a jump to the right? Making sense of the third way in government and governance', *Australian Journal of Political Science*, **36**(3), 481–98.

Sheridan, T. (1989), *Division of Labour: Industrial Relations in the Chifley Years 1945–49*, Oxford: Oxford University Press.

Shor, F. (1999), '"Virile syndicalism" in comparative perspective: a gender analysis of the IWW in the United States and Australia', *International Labor and Working-Class History*, **56**, 65–77.

Singleton, G. (1990), *The Accord and the Australian Labour Movement*, Melbourne, VIC: Melbourne University Press.

Smith, G. (1990), 'From consensus to coercion: the Australian air pilots dispute', *Journal of Industrial Relations*, **32**(2), 238–53.

Spies-Butcher, B., and S. Wilson (2008), 'Election 2007: did the union campaign succeed?', **32**(2), *Australian Review of Public Affairs*, accessed 6 June 2010 at www.australianreview. net/digest/2007/05/spies-butcher_wilson.

Spillane, R. (1981), 'Attitudes to Australian industrial relations: the influence of political affiliation' *Human Resources Management Australia*, **18**, 17–21.

Stewart, A. (2009), 'A question of balance: Labor's new vision for workplace regulation', *Australian Journal of Labour Law*, **22**(1), 3–50.

Stilwell, F. (2002), *Political Economy: The Contest of Economic Ideas*, Melbourne, VIC: Oxford University Press.

Tierney, R. (1996), 'Migrants and class in postwar Australia', in R. Kuhn and T. O'Lincoln (eds), *Class and Class Conflict in Australia*, Melbourne, VIC: Longman, pp. 95–113.

Wanna, J. (2010), 'Business and unions', *Australian Cultural History*, **28**(1), 15–22.

Whitehouse, G. (2004), 'Justice and equity: women and indigenous workers', in J. Isaac and S. Macintyre (eds), *The New Province for Law and Order*, Melbourne, VIC: Cambridge University Press, pp. 226–36.

Whitlam, G. (1985), *The Whitlam Government 1972–1975*, Melbourne, VIC: Viking.

6 Britain: how neo-liberalism cut unions down to size

John McIlroy

INTRODUCTION

Neo-liberalism in Britain evolved through four broad stages. It developed after 1945 as an ideological critique of the Keynesian social-democratic consensus. Distilled in the work of Hayek, it penetrated the political class, reaching state agendas with the proto-monetarism of Callaghan's Labour administration after 1976. Stoked by the crisis of oil and profitability this second period of practical influence developed after 1979: the Thatcher governments broke gradually, tentatively, cumulatively, decisively, with the post-war settlement (Harvey 2005). By 1990, neo-liberalism structured the policies of state and capital. The neo-liberalisation of the Labour Party facilitated by Conservative success produced a third stage: the ascendancy of neo-liberalism, reflected in a new consensus. In government from 1997, New Labour purveyed a more sophisticated, populist neo-liberalism. It maintained the core of Thatcherism, marginalised social democracy and exposed 'Third Way' nomenclature as cosmetic (McIlroy 2009a, 2009b). A fourth period of crisis, financial turmoil and recession commenced in 2008. It saw defeat for New Labour and a Conservative-Liberal Democrat coalition after the 2010 election. There was no return to Keynesianism: the platforms of all major parties remained neo-liberal, cuts in state expenditure to rescue the system remained common ground. Alternatives remained weak: candidates of the Trade Union and Socialist Coalition (TUSC) received on average 371 votes. Recomposition rather than unravelling of a damaged British neo-liberalism appears most likely (Harvey 2010).

My conceptualisation of neo-liberalism is elaborated in my earlier writing. Neo-liberalism expedites tendencies to global economic integration pushing markets towards deregulation, privatisation and subordination to discipline exercised through the major powers' dominance of international institutions. At the heart of universalising and restructuring commodification, rehabilitating markets and restoring profitability, lies an offensive against socialist ideas and trade unions characterised as impediments to markets and efficient exploitation of labour. Neo-liberalism attempts to claw back Keynesian concessions and redistribute resources from labour to capital. Prioritising low inflation and inequality, it privileges monetarism, often disdaining active fiscal policy. A stronger financial sector permeates market activity (McIlroy 2009a: 27–31). Imperfectly realised, neo-liberalism does not, as its crisis affirms, duplicate liberalism or discard the state. It is no more uniform, coherent or successful than Keynesianism. Compared with America, Britain still possesses an extensive welfare state and strong unions. There are varieties of neo-liberalism. It is applied in distinctive contexts with different configurations of class forces. It changes to face challenges: 'If we eschew monolithic frameworks and remain sensitive to historical difference and historical shifts within the paradigm, neo-liberalism serves as a useful way of understanding and conceptualising developments within capitalism since the 1970s' (ibid 30).

The distinctiveness of British experience is denoted in my characterisation of 1979–1997 as 'pioneering', 'experimental', 'destructive' neo-liberalism. Governments broke progressively from social democracy, learning which aspects of ideology were realisable rather than simply applying pre-existing programmes. They demolished key features of Keynesianism. In contrast, New Labour applied 'constructive', 'creative' neo-liberalism. It employed the state to support markets; it reconciled and integrated casualties of the Conservatives, notably trade unions. British neo-liberalism encountered success – subordinating labour and the left, restoring profitability – and failure – the crisis since 2008 (McIlroy 2009b: 63–97). This chapter expands these points. It details how trade unionism has been debilitated and domesticated. Membership has fallen, workplace organisation has been undermined, national leadership is defined by subordination to New Labour and inability to educate members about neo-liberalism as a prerequisite to combating it. British unions have been confirmed as reactive economic actors. They have failed to compensate through pro-active political power building. The following section outlines the development of neo-liberalism in the birthplace of capitalism and the policies of successive governments. The third section examines the reaction of trade unionists to 'destructive' neo-liberalism. This is followed by exploration of New Labour's policies in government and union responses. The chapter concludes with categorisation of union reactions over three decades.

BRITISH NEO-LIBERALISM

Accompanying Labour's overture, neo-liberalism burgeoned among Conservatives disturbed by growing state intervention, progressive taxation, falling profits, strong unions, socialist ideas and cultural change corrosive of capitalist discipline. In government, 'a step by step' approach mingled ideology, opportunity and state craft. Removal of obstacles opened new avenues. Success sharpened radical appetites. The speed with which neo-liberalism surged to supremacy remains surprising. In comparison with America, Britain was a stronghold of social democracy, collectivism and continuity in industrial relations. Destruction was the price of progress. Neo-liberalism needed states to make states behave differently: to strengthen the market, extend competition, diminish the public sector and unions (Clarke 2001: 104). The institutions of social-democratic corporatism, like the National Economic Development Council, were dismantled. Privatisation and commercialisation of the public sector proceeded from gas and telecommunications through electricity and steel to buses, railways and mines. Monetarism; high interest rates; removal of controls over capital movements; deregulation of industry; regressive, corporate-friendly taxation; and withdrawal of the Keynesian commitment to full employment, laid the ground for devastation of trade unionism (Coates 1989; McIlroy 1995).

In accordance with neo-liberalism's discourse of individualism and entrepreneurialism, state support for collective bargaining and organised labour was incrementally reduced through abolition of the statutory recognition procedure, the Fair Wages Resolutions, and Wages Councils. The process climaxed with removal of the responsibility of the Advisory, Conciliation and Arbitration Service to encourage collective bargaining. The closed shop was outlawed, limits on strikes restrictively reset and complex systems of balloting before industrial action and in union elections imposed. More unusual in the neo-liberal problematic was creation of state commissions to protect members against legal abuse and safeguards for strikebreakers in lawful disputes. Withdrawal of legitimacy entailed decreased access to government and curtailed representation on shrinking quasi-governmental organisations for union leaders, depicted *in extremis* as 'the enemy within'. Industrial relations was decollectivised, the century-old, union-friendly 'voluntary system' laid to rest (Davies and Freedland 1993, 2007).

Britain's declining economic and political fortunes justified restoration of the natural order. Antipathy to trade unionism, presented in the 1979 manifesto in terms of excessive power and militancy, became embedded in conceptions fundamentally antagonistic to collectivism. Industrial relations policy was increasingly influenced by the eternal narratives of Hayek and the gestation of neo-liberalism during the Keynesian era (McIlroy 1995: 194–9). It was rarely explained as a conjunctural response to the expansion and integration of global production, trade and finance or technological innovation which liberated capital. The initiation of deregulation at home and abroad through the international economic institutions was justified in terms of general efficiency and the interests of the City of London, rather than invocation of 'globalisation' (Coakley and Harris 1992: 39–42). Nonetheless, blossoming of the 'strong state and free market' (Gamble 1988) was attended by acceleration of trends towards internationalisation of the economy. There were moves from manufacturing to services, industry to finance, an increasingly diverse, fragmented and unequal workforce, and enhanced flexibility and insecurity at work. Innovation was facilitated by decentralisation of labour regulation to the enterprise and what was increasingly a smaller workplace. Such tendencies militated against trade unionism and rendered construction of solidarity more precarious (Hyman 1999). Impelled by a changed context, the recession of 1980–1982, sharper competition in product markets, sustained unemployment, fragile unions, primed with new ideological and legislative weapons by the state, employers cut costs. Disillusioned with the strategies of the 1970s, they bypassed shop stewards, neglected workplace collective bargaining, dismantled national bargaining and demanded further relief from regulation and 'burdens on business'. Restructured industrial relations were based on restoration of management prerogative and the rhetoric, and in fewer cases, reality, of HRM (Charlwood 2007; Gospel 2005).

A major achievement was the marginalisation, then neo-liberalisation of the Labour Party and creation of a new consensus. By the mid-1990s, Labour's adaptation to neo-liberalism culminated in its embrace. Acceptance of the new settlement and securing employer support was deemed indispensable by leaders of the re-branded New Labour for reasons of electability, governance and personal preference. Winning a majority required shredding social democratic commitments and reinvention as an unambiguous and more effective representative of capital than the Conservatives. It necessitated a more socially inclusive, effectively legitimated neo-liberalism, resourced by a more active state. New Labour politics assumed states depended increasingly on profit-maximising capital, which depended for competitive edge on skilled, adaptable labour (Hay 1999). Support for innovation was influenced by electoral impotence and the perceived benefits of Conservative change, including weakened unions, as well as the divisive detriments of higher unemployment, greater inequality, inadequate productivity, and social conflict. By 1997, flight from social democracy was justified by invocation of the limits globalisation placed on political choice and state interference in markets, the centrality it accorded national competitiveness and the gains to be garnered if the economy cut with the grain of globalisation rather than resisting it (Hay 2006).

Several points require emphasis in relation to this contested concept. First, tendencies to globalisation are real and important although uneven and incomplete (Held and McGrew 2002; Ravenhill 2008). The process contains positive possibilities for capital; its development is frequently exaggerated (Hirst and Thompson 1999; Kleinknecht and ter Wengel 1998) and its benefits brittle – as the present crisis emphasises. Second, the kind of globalisation that has taken shape represents part of the programme of neo-liberalism aimed at expanding markets and weakening unions (Albo 2007). It is an integral aspect of that project of capitalist accumulation, centred on removing barriers to it. It is not an exogenous economic process (Piven 1995). It is the product of 'explicit or implicit political decisions, not of some implacable economic determinism' (Moschonas 2002: 261). Third, the limits of globalisation, the fact that the world market is neither fully integrated nor classically competitive and the state neither obsolescent nor impotent suggests that politicians still possess choices, and that workers are not powerless in the face of capital (Dunn 2008). Fourth, New Labour's iron law – globalisation determined policy – rationalised and obscured its leaders' active choice of neo-liberalism (McIlroy 2009a).

New Labour's replacement of Clause IV of the party constitution, 'to secure for the producers by hand and brain the full fruits of their industry', with a declaration commending 'the enterprise of the market and the rigours of competition' encapsulated the party's transformation. With New Labour in power from 1997, the Conservative emphasis on controlling inflation and credibility in financial markets remained. Depoliticisation of economics was extended with powers devolved to the Bank of England to govern monetary policy. The stress on deregulation, privatisation, competitive labour costs and a business-friendly environment was sustained. There were attempts to curb redistribution of income at the bottom, combat poverty and stimulate the supply side through tax credits, workfare, a national minimum wage and expansion of training to promote skills, flexible labour, social mobility and competitiveness (Cerny and Evans 2004; Shaw 2007). Expenditure rose – targeted at education and health. The economic growth and consumer spending which took off from the early 1990s depended on a 'permanent debt economy', a 'privatised Keynesianism', based on rising housing markets and easy credit (Crouch 2009).

Industrial relations policy was decisively managerialist. Legitimising restoration of unilateral decision-making, New Labour was anxious about productivity, how to placate its social-democratic constituency and control and propitiate the unions, given their still significant role in party policy and finance, as well as past commitments. The solution was to sanction managerial trade unionism. New Labour acknowledged employers' concerns that bolstering collectivism risked recreating its ability to obstruct the market and impede the state. Assuaging anxieties motivated attempts to recompose unions as servants of capital. Their role was to lubricate labour markets, improve human resources and deliver services to workers through contracts with the state. The strategic importance New Labour placed on this approach, as distinct from employing it to conciliate union leaders, remains unclear (McIlroy 2009b). Conservative legislation was substantially maintained. A spavined recognition procedure and feebly-enforced minimum wage distinguished New Labour within neo-liberalism. Reversing the Conservatives' opt-out from the European Union's Social Chapter, New Labour adulterated EU initiatives as its predecessors had done. Individual rights dictated by considerations of flexibility and human resource management, from dismissal to parental leave, were extended. There was enhanced access to government and renewed union presence on quangos. Influence operated at the margins; employer voice remained dominant. The remaking of trade unionism was offered minimal legal but generous financial sustenance, via the Partnership at Work Fund, the Union Learning Fund and the Union Modernisation Fund. The objective was to persuade labour to collaborate with capital and galvanise productivity (McIlroy 2009b).

New Labour proved successful in consolidating and civilising the Conservative legacy and normalising neo-liberalism. It presided over growth, higher profits, a relatively protected education and health service and rising living standards, paid for by flexibility, insecurity and intensification of work. Blair and Brown reinforced the ascendancy of finance and services and contraction of manufacturing. Developing dissatisfaction can be seen in the declining vote in 2001 and 2005 and unpopularity over Iraq. The shallow foundations of success were exposed when the bubble burst in 2008 (Bootle 2010; Callinicos 2010). There was no reversion to social democracy which could strengthen workers. A trillion pounds was pumped into banks with minimal accountability. Government research confirmed New Labour had maintained the unequal society forged by Thatcher. The Chancellor promised cuts 'tougher and deeper than Thatcher' and New Labour entered the 2010 election locked in 'a neo-liberal dead end' (*Guardian* 12 March 2010). It too produced convergence: Conservative leader David Cameron became 'the heir to Blair' (Snowdon 2010). In that context, we turn to examine union responses to three decades of British neo-liberalism.

UNION RESPONSES: RESISTANCE, ACCOMMODATION AND CONSEQUENCES, 1979–1997

In 1979 13.2m workers, 57 per cent of the labour force, were union members and there were 300 000 workplace representatives (Charlwood and Metcalf 2005; Clegg 1979: 51–52). Entrenched in the corridors of political power, trade unionism was:

> Moving in the direction of a stronger, more inclusive collectivism better able to provide, albeit still inadequate, protection to workers ... If restricted, variable and contingent, its reach, its legitimacy, its social presence, measured by membership,

density, legislation and access to government, its potential to mobilise its members and its ability to bargain with the state were greater than at any other time in its history. (McIlroy 2007: xxiv)

Positive judgements require qualification. Strategies of concertation with the state had faltered, because of economic problems and political failures but also because of sectionalism. From the mid-1960s, industrial struggle was characterised by a degree of grassroots initiation and independence. This diminished after 1974. Unions were identified with inflation and, as the 1978–9 'Winter of Discontent' confirmed, social disruption. Membership growth was handed to unions. It stemmed from favourable legislation, an inflationary context and incomes policies which attracted 'paper members'. Organising was the province of stewards and, outside the salariat, peripheral to union concerns. There was detachment between political and representational processes which embraced a minority and membership mobilisation. There was little compelling exposition of the case for collectivism. There was inadequate articulation between union activists and the Labour Party left, attempts at an alternative economic strategy made little impact on governments, while from 1974 the Communists and the Trotskyist groups were in decline (Hyman 1984: 217–35; Hyman 2007). It is unhelpful to compare contemporary realities with ideal versions of trade unionism. These difficulties were nothing new; relative to the past, strengths outweighed weaknesses. What was novel – at least since the 1920s – was the impending relentless state assault. The extent and duration of unemployment during the 1980–82 recession, as well as state abstention from intervention, were crucial. Membership was in decline before the legislation took effect. Reaction was restricted but united. The TUC 'Day of Action' in May 1980 stressed demonstrations not strikes and the response was patchy. However, the Wembley Principles, adopted to combat the 1982 Employment Act, provided the basis for a response which on paper exceeded the successful approach to the Conservative legislation of 1971. The TUC general council was empowered to call and coordinate industrial action in support of unions facing legal action under the new statutes (TUC 1982: 20).

TUC staff were cautious. So were right-wing unions of skilled workers, who resented erosion of relativities under Labour's incomes policies, notably the Amalgamated Engineering Union (AEU) and the Electricians Union (EETPU). The Wembley Principles were pushed through by the left, the Transport and General Workers' Union (TGWU) and the National Union of Mineworkers (NUM), in alliance with the centre, led by the temporarily radicalised leadership of the General, Municipal and Boilermakers' Union (GMB). Dominated by socialists after 1981 with the election of Arthur Scargill as president, the NUM emerged as the spearhead for a projected struggle: transcending the miners' strikes of the 1970s, it would mobilise the labour movement, provoke governmental crisis and produce a left Labour adminis-tration. Headed by Tony Benn, this would implement policies based on plan-ning, nationalisation, workers' participation and control of foreign trade. Thatcher's retreat over pit closures in 1981 invigorated this perspective (Routledge 1993: 80–137). Unity on paper did not prosper in practice. The general council's refusal to support the printworkers' union, the National Graphical Association, in its 1983 dispute with *Messenger* newspapers, proved a landmark. The TUC decision that affiliates should boycott state funds for state-imposed ballots was undermined because the AEU and EETPU refused to observe it. Together with smaller bodies, they stood for co-operation with government and, after Thatcher's second electoral victory, TUC staff moved to orchestrate accommodation. The 1983 *TUC Strategy* announced 'the new realism'; it recalled past collaboration with Conservative administrations and aspired to a modified corporatism. Its lack of grasp of still developing neo-liberalism was underlined by the response: the banning of trade unionism at the government's GCHQ communication centre (McIlroy 1992, 1995: 245–61).

The year-long miners' strike of 1984–85 sparked by pit closures repre-sented the apex of resistance. It embodied a challenge to pioneering neo-liberalism and attracted widespread support. The TUC made no attempt to organise solidarity action as distinct from endeavouring to broker a deal. It questioned whether it could provide financial assistance in the face of the new legislation. The climate was also engendering caution among activists and members. Attempts by unions, particularly the TGWU, to encourage solidarity action collapsed. The miners' defeat sealed the demise of aspirations to chal-lenge the state on the industrial front and constituted a watershed in the evolu-tion of British neo-liberalism (Beckett and Hencke 2009). The TUC now concurred that acceptance of state funds was a matter for union discretion. In the early years of Thatcherism it had sponsored extra-parliamentary campaigns, although initiatives such as the People's Marches for Jobs of 1981 and 1983 had been pushed through by affiliates against TUC opposition. The 'battle of ideas' was fought in union workshops and one-day schools. Mainstream TUC education, financed by the state, accepted the correlative 'non-political' edict and submitted to government intervention in programmes (McIlroy 1993).

In contrast with the 1960s and 1970s, there was little action from below, orchestrated by unofficial bodies such as the Liaison Committee for the Defence of Trade Unions and organised by stewards (McIlroy and Campbell 1999). Continuing anti-union legislation strengthened centralised control as workplace organisation waned (Undy *et al.* 1996). Resistance persisted. The TGWU, the Society of Graphical and Allied Trades and the National Union of Seafarers defied the law and had their assets sequestrated. Sectional militancy was typically unsuccessful and the accommodation lobby placed further pressure on unity. In 1988 the EETPU's pursuit of business unionism, which included poaching members and acting as an employment agency for Rupert Murdoch in the 1986 Wapping dispute, prompted its expulsion from the TUC. Despite resilient combativity, reflected in the fight against the poll tax and privatisation of the mines in the early 1990s, more sophisticated strategies of adaptation to neo-liberalism were crystallising (McIlroy 1991, 1992).

John Monks, influential even before appointment as TUC general secretary in 1993, constructed a majority coalition based on reworking earlier tendencies and foregrounding developments in the EU: its social dimension provided a vision and a spine. 'Modernisation' privileged a politics predicated on extension to Britain of an idealised model of the social market, social partnership, social dialogue and protections for labour perceived as successful in Europe. It postulated a practice in which unions would become 'partners' with employers and purveyors of HRM in reconstructed, high-cost, high-value enterprises. The TUC would become more of a pressure group. Affiliates would devote greater attention to recruitment through provision of services, particularly financial services, and embed organising in everyday practice (Taylor 1994). Piloted by the AEEU (a merger of the AEU and EETPU), the GMB and the Shop, Distributive and Allied Workers (USDAW), unions such as the TGWU and the public sector Unison, espoused partnership and stomached doubts about the EU. Monks prepared for partnership with the Conservatives; they would not reciprocate. Progress depended on governmental change. To that end, the unions endorsed political convergence as the Labour Party assimilated to the new landscape, accepting most of the anti-union legislation (Hay 1999). Opposition was the prerogative of a left coalition of small unions led by the NUM.

By 1996, resistance within accommodation transmuted into adaptation to neo-liberalism and aspiration for modification centred on social partnership and productivity coalitions with employers. A debilitating illusion was conviction that Labour Party leaders conceived the future as union leaders did. It was neo-liberalism not 'stakeholding' (Hutton 1995) which entered the party's soul. But despite doubts about New Labour, most union leaders went along with it as the only alternative to continuing attrition; indeed they were complicit in its making. There were divisions: the vote on removal of Clause IV was split, with the AEEU championing change and Unison opposing it. Opposition was muted: the only organised response was the establishment of the tiny Socialist Labour Party (SLP) by Scargill which recruited a sprinkling of officials and activists from the miners', rail and bakers' unions. Most unions mobilised behind New Labour in the 1997 election, while the SLP recorded a negligible vote (McIlroy 1998, 2000).

The consequences of neo-liberalism were devastating. In the steepest sustained decline in history, membership diminished, from 13.2m to fewer than 8m and density from 57 per cent to 34 per cent. TUC membership dropped from 12.1m to 6.8m. TGWU membership halved. NUM membership fell from 250 000 miners in 1979 to fewer than 7000 by 1996. A consolation was that public sector membership held up: the major unions, the National and Local Government Officers (NALGO) and the National Union of Public Employees (NUPE) who merged in 1993 to form Unison, suffered minimal loss (McIlroy 1995: 385–421). The scope of collective bargaining and its dominance in employment regulation declined. Little over 40 per cent of workers in establishments of more than 25 employees had their pay determined by collective bargaining at the end of the Conservative era, compared with 75 per cent at its inception (Brown *et al.* 2000). Union representatives were present in 40 per cent of such establishments compared with 54 per cent in the early 1980s. At 218 000, the estimated number of representatives suggested resilience. But their negotiating role was considerably more restricted than in the 1970s: in half of establishments with union representatives, no negotiations of any kind occurred (Cully *et al.* 1999: 14–16).

Blyton and Turnbull (2004: 336–340) distinguished three phases in the decline of the strike. 'Coercive pacification' characterised the period 1980–1985, with an average of 1300 strikes and 9.8m days lost (including the miners' strike), compared with an average of 2300 strikes and 11.6m days lost 1975–1977. This was followed by a period of 'calculative bargaining', as unions adapted to change with an average of 800 strikes and 3.5m days lost 1986–90; and a phase of 'economic pacification and legal self-restraint' with only 250 strikes and 650 000 days lost, 1991–1996. By the mid-1990s, strikes were usually of one or more days, sometimes repeated, rather than all-out stoppages; the legislation was scrupulously observed. If leadership failings were evident, there was no groundswell of opposition from below. Workers were less willing to support militancy. Coercion was one instrument of change but acquiescence had a material basis. Incomes became more dispersed, work intensified and with union decline the protections they offered were less effective across a segmented working class. However, average take-home pay grew by 2.4 per cent between 1979 and 1999, faster than between 1974 and 1979 (McIlroy 2009a: 39–40).

UNION RESPONSES: ACCOMMODATION, RESISTANCE AND CONSEQUENCES, 1997–2010

The arrival of New Labour in government ensured unions faced an improved environment compared with the Conservative years. They were weaker actors. They possessed reduced power and diminished capacity to influence the workplace or Whitehall. Economic growth; low inflation; expansion of jobs, despite hidden unemployment; rising average earnings, an increase which could not generally be ascribed to weaker unions; and reduced bargaining coverage, all ensured that the context was less favourable to union revival than some conceded, certainly compared with 1964–1979 (but see Willman and Kelly 2004: 2–4). State support for trade unionism able to define and pursue an autonomous mission remained absent. The deficiencies of a fragile recognition procedure and a minimum wage which after 12 years reached £5.80 an hour, were gradually exposed (Gall 2007). Piecemeal repair of rights ravaged by the Conservatives, and the extension of human resource legislation intended to stimulate flexibility and competitiveness, on work–life balance and parental leave, was minimal and difficult to enforce. Legislation on strikes remained inferior to that in comparable jurisdictions and violated international conventions; the revised balloting provisions continued to prove potent in impeding mobilisation (Dickens and Hall 2006). Far from bolstering the EU social model, New Labour sought to neo-liberalise it. Social partnership initiatives such as the Low Pay Commission were sparse and spasmodic rather than systemic (Taylor 2009).

Relief after the unrelenting roll-back of the Conservative years, renewed access to government and enhanced, although still marginal, influence, as well as state funds and involvement in training policy, ensured New Labour enjoyed support from union leaders in its first term. They believed the government would retreat from infatuation with employers; a second term promised resumption of social-democratic policies and further concessions (McIlroy 2009b: 176–80). From 2002, discontent accompanied realisation that the parsimonious legislative programme was substantially a last instalment, a remnant of the past not a portent of the future. Privatisation, the Public Finance Initiative and Foundation Hospitals were flashpoints as unions began to grasp that New Labour was not to be reasoned out of its neo-liberal trajectory. Dissatisfaction from below percolated upwards stimulating election of critical, outspoken leaders, 'the awkward squad', in Amicus, the Communication Workers' Union (CWU), the Fire Brigades Union (FBU), the Public and Commercial Services Union (PCS), the TGWU and the rail unions (Murray 2003). The FBU dispute 2002–3 constituted a significant confrontation between a frustrated union and New Labour. The government demonstrated its neo-liberal credentials in a performance four-square with that of its Conservative predecessors (Seifert and Sibley 2005).

Industrial action continued at a historically low level. Strikes were short and concentrated in the public sector. While the majority followed legislative requirements, some unofficial stoppages slipped through the net. Most remained defensive. But strikes in Royal Mail, the fire service and rail were characterised by anger and aggression (Gall 2006). The two faces of trade unionism, protest and acquiescence, deference by union representatives inside the party to policies their members opposed, were evident over Iraq. Major unions affiliated to the Stop the War Coalition. But at the 2002 Labour Party conference the four biggest unions connived to suppress debate on the issue (McIlroy 2009c: 180–81). Respect, a 'united front' of expelled Labour MP George Galloway, Asian community politicians and the Trotskyist Socialist Workers Party, was a product of this period. Like the SLP it achieved little and soon split. Pressure from activists influenced ephemeral cuts in finance to New Labour from affiliated unions. The disaffiliation of the FBU and the Rail, Maritime and Transport Workers' Union (RMT) in 2004 was important; but their combined membership was around 120 000. It became clear that fixtures of 'the awkward squad', Derek Simpson (Amicus), Tony Woodley (TGWU) and Billy Hayes (CWU), had no intention of following them or mounting more than verbal pressure on Blair. They were to the left of their predecessors but, given the constraints they confronted, not really very left.

Heery (2005) observed the cyclical nature of cooperation and conflict: conflict subsided as elections approached. Before the 2005 contest, cracks were papered over in the Warwick Agreement. The government promised to implement a list of demands. Yet the volatility of intersecting processes of accommodation and antagonism was underlined by the Gate Gourmet dispute in 2005. It demonstrated that resistance and solidarity strikes were still possible as BA baggage handlers walked out in support of catering staff. It also affirmed such action was unlawful: unless repudiated it opened a union to injunctions and damages. The TGWU complied with the law and the incident represented a costly reverse. But it provoked a resurgence of agitation for reform around the Trade Union Freedom Bill, ultimately unsuccessful as New Labour stood firm (Hendy and Gall 2006).

The outcome of Warwick confirmed the impasse. It hardly touched the anti-union laws, the necessity for a robust recognition procedure, improved individual rights, or privatisation. Government acceptance that bank holidays would not constitute part of annual leave and extension of protection of strikers against dismissal were useful but limited (McIlroy 2009c: 185–6). By 2005, the emphasis on partnership was fading while Simpson and Woodley were raging against government negativity towards the EU social dimension which ensured that 'British workers had the worst conditions in Europe' (*Guardian*, 30 June 2004). Protest remained divorced from action. At Labour Party conferences, unions coordinated support for motions critical of government policy but organised no ensuing campaigns for change in policy which would have stimulated conflict within the party. They were apprehensive about internal struggle. When, in 2008, the party leadership demanded removal of voting on contemporary issues from the conference agenda, union leaders bent the knee, depriving themselves of an important weapon, albeit one they were not prepared to deploy to maximum impact (McIlroy 2009c: 189–92).

Disputes over pensions, privatisation and pay persisted in the public sector involving the PCS, Unison and the UCW, while the railways continued to be a cockpit of industrial action. Nonetheless, Unison joined Unite in rendering Brown's election as Blair's successor a formality by refusing to support MPs who promised pro-union change. One union even broke its conference mandate to support Brown (*Labour Research*, June 2008). As recession unfolded with wage freezes and redundancies, there were strikes, by public sector workers, occupations and disputes over recruitment. They were aggressive in approach but defensive in demands. Some ended in acceptable compromise, some in success. They did not herald 'a qualitative shift in the situation' (Kimber 2009: 11). There was no transformation at the top. The leaders of the big unions blamed the bankers and placed their trust in the government, which bailed out the banks. The culture remained one of complaint and illusion combined with compliance, lubricated by access to government and state funds. TUC deputy leader Frances O'Grady 'argued that Labour could secure a new term in office if it pledged a "new kind of economy" where equality and fairness took the place of free-market greed' (*Morning Star*, 12 March 2010). But New Labour had spent 13 years promoting a new kind of economy which privileged the free market and neglected fairness and equality. The leopard appeared unlikely to change its spots. Underpinning faith in New Labour was the belief – it had some justification, although it ruled out any possibility of creating an alternative to supporting a neo-liberal party – that there was no other choice. As the general secretaries of Unite put it:

> Our political agenda is of course dominated by ... the unequivocal need to defeat the Tories and secure a fourth term for Labour ... the choice for trade union members ... will be straightforward – continue the progress made by Labour with, we would hope, additional commitments to protect people from the effects of the bankers' crisis, or go back to the policies of the 1980s ... Those in our movement hoping for a 'third option' to a Labour government or the Tories are deluding themselves. (*Morning Star*, 23 November 2010)

The leaders of Unison, the GMB, USDAW agreed. For Unite, 'Reclaiming Labour' entailed extending influence with MPs – despite lack of success since 1992. Union leaders made scant attempt to analyse neo-liberalism or engage it in a 'battle of ideas' which asserted the relevance of solidarity, equality and internationalism (Hyman 1999). There was greater resort to 'globalisation' to explain things. TUC statements did not diverge from New Labour analysis, although they nodded towards greater equality. The basic argument was: 'the UK gained from the globalisation of trade and industry but the gains were not spread evenly ... whilst we cannot resist globalisation we can shape it towards progressive ends' (TUC 2006: 57; 2007: 55).

Evidence of unions shaping globalisation towards progressive ends is scarce. When it threatens jobs and engenders resistance, examples of support-ive action are negligible (Stirling 2010). In the 2010 BA dispute, the TUC pursued a deal based on wage reductions, not global solidarity. There was talk of strikes in Europe and boycotts by American unions. But no action, unsur-prising given the dearth of solidarity action in Britain; members of the TUC-affiliated pilots' union declared themselves 'neutral' but flew planes worked by strike-breakers. TUC thinking was eclectic. New Labour's skills strategy, which financed union involvement, was acceptable although it disregarded TUC policy. Policy on employment legislation, welfare and taxation, also justified by globalisation, was perceived as aberrant (McIlroy and Croucher 2009).

As the artificially homogenised 'awkward squad' disintegrated, and members subsided into amenability, a minority forcefully rejected neo-liberal politics. The PCS provided a contrast to the 'complain outside election peri-ods, comply when the chips are down' approach of Unison. The latter's lead-ership talked tough about funding yet pumped millions of pounds of members' money into New Labour, simultaneously disciplining activists who thought like the PCS leaders. With 300 000 members the PCS is a sizeable organisa-tion facing the firing line on pensions, cuts and wages with a socialist programme calling for increased expenditure, extensive nationalisation, repeal of the anti-union laws, redistributive taxation and withdrawal from Afghanistan and Iraq. It has sought to strengthen workplace organisation and politicise members. Its leaders believe in mobilisation to combat neo-liberalism (Serwotka 2007; Upchurch *et al.* 2008).

PCS leaders have organised sectoral and national strikes. They are constrained by an unfavourable balance of forces and lack of support from fellow public sector unions. In 2008, coordination of action over public sector pay – TUC policy – collapsed when Unison and Unite took their claims to arbitration, isolating the PCS. It proved unable to redeem pledges of a return to national bargaining. It was forced to compromise over reduced pensions for new recruits. It called off national industrial action over pay in 2008 after a narrow pro-strike vote. There are conflicting views on the impact strikes with-out strike pay have on low-paid members in comparison with selective action with pay. Leaders campaign for an alternative to New Labour. But the PCS is not affiliated to Labour because of socialist considerations; but because a 'non-political' membership considered supporting Labour too radical. The union rules out affiliation with any party, new or old.

With 79 000 members concentrated in one, privatised and decentralised, industry and traditions of successful militancy, the RMT, which takes rena-tionalisation of the railways seriously, mounted more adventurous political initiatives. A minority of its executive around general secretary Bob Crow favour a new party while the leadership backs the National Shop Stewards'

Network intended to revive militant workplace organisation (Darlington 2009). The RMT sponsored a slate, No2EU in the 2009 European elections. This embodied a traditional strand of labour movement Europhobia and achieved slight success. The pull of Labourism on a union which left New Labour over support for the Scottish Socialist Party (SSP) was demonstrated in the failure of the RMT to sponsor TUSC in the more important British general election in 2010 – although Crow offered personal support. The FBU, with 44 000 members and a tradition of militancy, has likewise baulked at working towards an organised political alternative in the wake of quitting Labour. It endorses leftwing campaigns and leftwing Labour MPs. Even its radical general secretary, Matt Wrack, acknowledges improved relations with New Labour and the derisory votes garnered by candidates to Labour's left (*New Statesman*, 14 September 2009).

These unions affiliate to a Trade Union Co-ordinating Group along with five small, left-led unions – the Bakers' Union (the only Labour affiliate), the National Union of Journalists, the Prison Officers' Association, the Probation Officers and the United Road Transport Union – with Labour MP, John McDonnell, as convenor. The CWU is noticeably absent given its left reputation. There are divisions between its mail and telecommunications sections; the left is stronger in the former where the threat of restructuring has been greatest. The UCW has a tradition of local militancy and rank-and-file networks. Since 2005 it has confronted privatisation, wage cuts and work intensification which have enhanced the importance of national leadership. Guerrilla warfare on the ground has been tempered by moderate attitudes at the top. Two well-supported national disputes in 2007 and 2009 terminated in compromise while the leadership around former 'awkward squad' icon, Billy Hayes, discouraged disaffiliation from New Labour (*New Statesman*, 14 September 2009).

Opposition to New Labour failed to muster meaningful alternatives to neo-liberalism and remained of limited weight. It mobilised sections of the leadership and activists, not wider layers of members. It reflected economic dissatisfactions more than a turn to the left. The socialist organisations which sustain left caucuses are divided and on the margins of the political mainstream. To observe the minority nature of developments in a few unions but assert that 'it nevertheless represents a qualitative shift in union strategy and political orientation' (Upchurch *et al.* 2009: 172) is to magnify matters and lend exaggerated political cohesion and direction to a circumscribed process. There is nothing in Britain approaching *Die Linke* in Germany or even the Anti-Capitalist Party in France. The SLP, the SSP, which also split, Respect and TUSC have been tried and found wanting.

On the ground, unions, left and right, responded to New Labour neo-liberalism with overlapping strategies to reverse decline.

Sleeping with the Enemy: Partnership involves unions formally committing themselves to working with management to secure the success of the enterprise in return for recognition; and exchanging support for HRM and job flexibility for employment security. Partnership agreements are rare because of employer antipathy, government refusal to provide legislative support, the pressures institutionalised co-operation places on union independence and the delicate balance between conflict and collaboration in the employment relationship (Kelly 1996, 2004). There is little evidence that this strategy, in which most unions have engaged at one time or another, has significantly increased membership or that initiatives like the European Works Council have extended partnership (Upchurch 2009).

Organising the Unorganised: Influenced by American and Australian experience, this approach identifies employers as the problem and mobilisation to secure recognition and membership and embed organising in workplace activity as the answer. There are tensions between conflict-based organising and simultaneous invocation of partnership, top-down management by the TUC – which established a flourishing Organising Academy – and union leaders, and the call for rank-and-file ownership, at a time of rank-and-file quiescence. The socialist inspiration which characterised organising in the past is largely absent. Experience has been mixed (Gall 2009). But organising has failed to transform practice or reverse decline although it may have contributed to stemming it and increased membership in specific situations (Daniels 2009).

Selling Services: In the 1990s, there was stress on treating workers as consumers and attracting them to unions by expanding and improving services, particularly financial services (Heery 1996). The 'service model' enjoyed renewed prominence with the assertion that provision of educational and training opportunities by union learning representatives could stimulate recruitment. Research points the other way: workers join for protection at work, not for help with home insurance or course fees (Waddington and Whitston 1997). Again there is inadequate evidence that this aspect of partnership with employers has improved union fortunes (McIlroy 2008).

Bigger Means Better: Unions have pursued mergers to achieve economies and efficiencies of scale. There were 170 unions in 2008, 233 in 1997. The major public sector merger of the 1990s, which created Unison, was complemented by the private sector amalgamation of Amicus, itself the product of merger activity, and the TGWU to form Unite in 2007. Whether 'huddling together' does improve finances, performance and participation, given transaction costs and enhanced bureaucracy, remains questionable (Willman 2004).

Going Global: Unions continued to engage in the ETUC, Global Federations and the International Trade Union Confederation. Unison allied with unions in Germany and Italy, Unite with the largest private sector organisation in America. The TUC and affiliates produced pamphlets and courses on globalisation (Croucher and Cotton 2009). They contained no distinctive analysis or strategy. Progress in implanting global challenges in trade unionism and its responses to neo-liberalism remains slender. Unions are less active than their European counterparts in initiating international action (Erne 2008). Confronted with job loss through takeovers or relocation, they have looked to the British state, not global solidarity (Stirling 2010).

The agency of workers during these years failed to stop – although it slowed – decline prompted by changes in the role of the state, capitalist organisation and employment, and ultimately and centrally the impact of change on attitudes which influence workers to join unions. Overall membership decreased to 6.8m by 2008 with density at 27.4 per cent. It was beginning to decline in the public sector, dropping from 59 to 57 per cent. With density at 15.5 per cent the private sector constituted non-union territory. TUC membership fell from 6.7m in 1997 to 6.2m in 2008 (Barratt 2009). Collective bargaining contracted at the same rate as during the 1980s. It covered a minority of workers and its agenda remained restricted (Brown and Nash 2008). By 2004, there were 128 000 workplace representatives in establishments with 25 or more employees compared with 330 000 in the early 1980s and less than 50 per cent of that total worked in the private sector (Charlwood and Forth 2009).

The 'union premium', the wage advantage membership grants trade unionists as against comparable non-members, diminished (Blanchflower and Bryson 2003) and the dispersion of wages persisted (Addison *et al.* 2007). Strikes stayed in the doldrums and there was no major demonstration of rank-and-file unrest. This perhaps reflects the consolidation of individualised consumerism in the context of rising earnings – for some. They were paid for in an unequal society (Butler and Watt 2007) by longer hours, more intensive work, increased stress and unhappiness (Layard 2006). By 2010 a squeeze on real wages was underway (*Labour Research* March 2010).

CONCLUSION

It is difficult to classify the responses to neo-liberalism over 30 years of a variety of organisations representing millions of workers, short of more elaborate analysis. In terms of the reactions suggested in the introduction to this book – acceptance of neo-liberalism, seeking protections within it, advocacy of social democratic or socialist alternatives – the dominant tendency has been to accept neo-liberalism in practice, simultaneously pursuing adjustments and demanding restoration of modified social democracy. Urging the latter's continued relevance, most unions pursued protections for members and mutual gains through partnership with employers, with restricted success. A minority advocated socialist solutions. Such blunt categorisation underestimates the differences within and between organisations. It elides distinctions within and between leaders, staff, activists, workplace representatives and members. It neglects context and change. Eclectic and opportunist, constrained by the state, capital and the multifarious attitudes of union members, embodying posture and action, union politics can resist conventional labels. Should we, for example, term the politics of leaders who finance, and campaign for New Labour, despite disagreements, 'neo-liberal'? Given acceptance of neo-liberalism in practice, should we talk of 'neo-liberal trade unionism' superseding 'social-democratic trade unionism'? At the risk of underplaying complexity, we can offer a more precise if still general and tentative taxonomy of response.

The first Thatcher government provoked a posture of organised defiance. This involved a codified response from the TUC, and general animosity to emergent neo-liberalism. It was predicated on the speedy return of Labour, although, throughout the decade, a third of trade unionists voted Conservative. Conceptions of Labour's mission varied from social-democratic – revival of corporatism – to socialist – the alternative economic strategy. Influenced by electoral failure, the second phase, 1983–6, produced fragmented responses and defeat for both confrontation and cooperation. The miners' strike embodied antagonistic mobilisation. Although unsuccessful, it arrested compromise and compliance by the TUC and unions such as the AEU and EETPU, processes fundamentally curtailed by government implacability. The third period, 1986–92, was one of regroupment around the TUC which isolated the EETPU. A phase of adaptation to neo-liberalism and relative acquiescence based on failure of electoral politics and industrial confrontation unfolded. Despite fissures the unions accepted the need for change in Labour Party policies. The onslaught could not be stemmed industrially. Electoral failure necessitated political revisionism. These years saw attention to renewal and the first stabs at organising and partnership. Finally, between 1992 and 1997, more sophisticated adaptation to neo-liberalism was combined with development of a compelling alternative. TUC visions of social partnership were shared by most affiliates. The unions *en bloc* opposed neo-liberalism. Their alternative politics had moved from neocorporatism and Bennism in the early 1980s towards the social market and 'stakeholding' by the mid-1990s. They embraced 'Rhine capitalism' as against 'Anglo-American neo-liberalism', Jacques Delors' conception of the EU as against globalisation.

Approval, and the ascendancy of partnership, as ideology not practice, characterised New Labour's first term, centred on concessions to settle accounts with its past. Union leaders confused this with restoration of social democracy. It was a requiem for 'Old Labour'. The advent of 'the awkward squad', the firefighters' dispute and Iraq marked the second stage, 2002–5, a time of disillusion and discontent. Partnership ran out of steam. There was yearning for social-democratic politics at one end of the spectrum and socialism at the other. Union leaders realised they had misread the signs: government did not share their enthusiasm for social partnership and regulation which would protect workers from globalisation or revision of the Conservative laws. Dissatisfaction was circumscribed by conviction that New Labour remained preferable to the Conservatives and dissension would damage its electoral prospects. The period 2006–10 saw recomposition of earlier tendencies. The leadership of Unite, Unison, the GMB, emerged as benevolent critics. Asserting social-democratic policies, they accepted the substance of second-stage neo-liberalism, with its apparently eternal growth, gains from globalisation, and increased living standards. They criticised its attitude to privatisation and legal protection for workers. But they continued to fund New Labour. This remained unchanged by crisis. If New Labour politics represent a variety of neo-liberalism, the politics of the union mainstream represent a social-democratic variant of neo-liberalism. At the other end of the spectrum, leaders of the PCS, RMT and smaller unions appraised neo-liberalism as antipathetic to strong trade unionism. They perceived it as pivoting on the myth that the market and the private is always preferable to the planned and the public, to the detriment of their members' interests. This group advocated socialist solutions to the economic crisis and mobilisation to stave off its effects.

Sustained decline and enhanced employer power mean that conditions for effective opposition and resurgence have progressively deteriorated – although the case of the RMT demonstrates what can be achieved in adverse circumstances. On the whole, the ambitions of union leaders have diminished. They inflate small achievements. Allowing for an unfavourable balance of forces, they are averse to risk – in launching strikes, defying the law, challenging government policy or looking for alternatives. Limited traditions of solidarity and rank-and-file initiative have been eroded, debilitating democracy and mobilisation. There is little unity in action and inadequate attempts to construct it. In the 'battle of ideas', unions have been ineffectual. They publish no weekly, let alone daily, paper. They proved incapable of exploiting radio, television and the internet. Education has concentrated on training in technique not issues and strategy. Unions have failed to influence public agendas with programmes for market regulation, enhanced equality and stronger protection for the vulnerable. Political resources have diminished. The Labour left has dissolved, groups to its left exercise slender influence, socialist ideas have less purchase than 30 years ago. Workers possess reduced awareness of what they have in common with other workers and diminished consciousness that they constitute part of a class with interests which conflict with the interests of capital. The structural nature of that conflict suggests, although it is far from fated, that at some point we shall see resurgence of resistance. The forces to fuel it are presently absent and it is difficult to discern evidence of their gestation. There are no full stops in history but a revival of trade unionism appears unlikely in the foreseeable future. If neo-liberalism is about remodelling labour, eroding working-class power and restoring ruling-class domination, it has met with significant success in Britain.

REFERENCES

Addison, J., R. Bailey and S. Siebert (2007), 'The impact of deunionisation on earnings dispersion revisited', *Research in Labour Economics*, **26**, 337–64.
Albo, G. (2007), 'Neo-liberalism and the discontented', in L. Panitch and C. Leys (eds), *Socialist Register 2008*, London: Merlin Press, pp. 374–83.
Barratt, C. (2009), *Trade Union Membership 2008*, London: Department for Business Enterprise and Regulatory Reform.
Beckett, F. and D. Hencke (2009), *Marching to the Fault Line: The 1984 Miners' Strike and the Death of Industrial Britain*, London: Constable
Blanchflower, D. and A. Bryson (2003), 'Changes over time in union relative wage effects in the UK and US revisited', in J. Addison and C. Schnabel (eds), *International Handbook of Trade Unions*, Cheltenham, UK and Northampton, MA, USA: Edward Elgar, pp. 197–245.
Blyton, P. and P. Turnbull (2004), *The Dynamics of Employee Relations*, Basingstoke: Palgrave Macmillan.
Bootle, R. (2010), *The Trouble with Markets*, London: Nicholas Brealey.
Brown, W., S. Deakin, D. Nash and S. Oxenbridge (2000), 'The employment contract: from collective procedures to individual rights', *British Journal of Industrial Relations*, **38**(4), 611–29.
Brown, W. and D. Nash (2008), 'What has been happening to collective bargaining under New Labour? Interpreting WERS 2004', *Industrial Relations Journal*, **39**(2), 91–103.
Butler, T. and P. Watt (2007), *Understanding Social Inequality*, London: Sage.
Callinicos, A. (2010), *Bonfire of Illusions: The Twin Crises of the Liberal World*, Cambridge: Polity Press.
Cerny, P. and M. Evans (2004), 'Globalisation and public policy under New Labour', *Policy Studies*, **25**(1), 51–65.
Charlwood, A. (2007), 'The de-collectivisation of pay determination in British establishments, 1990–1998', *Industrial Relations Journal*, **38**(1), 33–50.
Charlwood, A. and D. Metcalf (2005), 'Appendix: trade union numbers, membership and density', in D. Metcalf and S. Fernie (eds), *Trade Unions: Resurgence or Demise?*, London: Routledge, pp. 231–9.
Charlwood, A. and J. Forth (2009), 'Employee representation', in W. Brown, A. Bryson, J. Forth and K. Whitfield (eds), *The Evolution of the Modern Workplace*, Cambridge: Cambridge University Press, pp. 74–96.
Clarke, S. (2001), 'The state, globalisation and phases of capitalist development', in R. Albritton, M. Itoh, R. Westra and A. Suege (eds), *Phases of Capitalist Development: Booms, Crises and Globalisations*, Basingstoke: Palgrave Macmillan.
Clegg, H.A. (1979), *The Changing System of Industrial Relations in Great Britain*, Oxford: Blackwell.
Coakley, J. and L. Harris (1992), 'Financial globalisation and deregulation', in J. Michie (ed.), *The Economic Legacy 1979–1992*, London: Academic Press, pp. 37–57.
Coates, D. (1989), *The Crisis of Labour: Industrial Relations and the State in Contemporary Britain*, London: Philip Allen.
Crouch, C. (2009), 'Privatised Keynesianism: an unacknowledged policy regime', *British Journal of Politics and International Relations*, **11**(3), 382–99.

Croucher, R. and E. Cotton (2009), *Global Unions, Global Business*, London: Middlesex University Press.

Cully, M., S. Woodlands, G. O'Reilly and G. Dix (1999), *Britain at Work*, London: Routledge.

Daniels, G. (2009), 'In the field: a decade of organising', in G. Daniels and J. McIlroy (eds), *Trade Unions in a Neo-liberal World: British Trade Unions under New Labour*, London: Routledge, pp. 254–82.

Darlington, R. (2009), 'Leadership and union militancy: the case of the RMT', *Capital and Class*, **99**, 3–33.

Davies, P. and M. Freedland (1993), *Labour Legislation and Public Policy: A Contemporary History*, Oxford: Clarendon Press.

Davies, P. and M. Freedland, (2007), *Towards a Flexible Labour Market: Labour Legislation and Regulation since the 1990s*, Oxford: Oxford University Press.

Dickens, L. and M. Hall (2006), 'Fairness – up to a point: assessing the impact of New Labour's employment legislation', *Human Resource Management Journal*, **16**(4), 338–56.

Dunn, B. (2008), *Global Political Economy: A Marxist Critique*, London: Pluto Press,.

Erne, R. (2008), *European Unions: Labour's Quest for a Transnational Democracy*, Ithaca, NY: ILR Press.

Gall, G. (2006), 'Research note: injunctions as a legal weapon in industrial disputes in Britain, 1995–2005', *British Journal of Industrial Relations*, **44**(2), 327–49.

Gall, G. (2007), 'Trade union recognition in Britain: an emerging crisis for trade unions?', *Economic and Industrial Democracy*, **28**(1), 78–109.

Gall, G. (2009) (ed), *The Future of Union Organising: Building for Tomorrow*, Basingstoke: Palgrave Macmillan.

Gamble, A. (1988), *The Free Economy and the Strong State: The Politics of Thatcherism*, Basingstoke: Macmillan.

Gospel, H. (2005), 'Markets, firms and unions: a historical-institutionalist perspective on the future of unions in Britain', in S. Fernie and M. Metcalf (eds), *Trade Unions: Resurgence or Demise?*, London: Routledge, pp. 19–44.

Harvey, D. (2005), *A Brief History of Neo-liberalism*, Oxford: Oxford University Press.

Harvey, D. (2010), *The Enigma of Capital: And the Crises of Capitalism*, London: Profile Books.

Hay, C. (1999), *The Political Economy of New Labour: Labouring Under False Pretences*, Manchester: Manchester University Press.

Hay, C. (2006), 'What's globalisation got to do with it? Economic interdependence and the future of European welfare states', *Government and Opposition*, **41**(1), 1–22.

Heery, E. (1996), 'The new new unionism' in I. Beardwell (ed), *Contemporary Industrial Relations: A Critical Analysis*, Oxford: Oxford University Press, pp. 175–202.

Heery, E. (2005), *Trade Unionism under New Labour: The Shirley Lerner Memorial Lecture*, Manchester: Manchester Industrial Relations Society.

Held, D. and A. McGrew (2002), *Globalisation/Anti-Globalisation*, Cambridge: Polity Press.

Hendy, J. and G. Gall (2006), 'British trade union rights today and the Trade Union Freedom Bill', in K. Ewing (ed.), *The Right to Strike: From the Trade Disputes Act 1906 to a Trade Union Freedom Bill 2006*, Liverpool: Institute of Employment Rights, pp. 247–77.

Hirst, P. and G. Thompson (1999), *Globalisation in Question:The International Economy and the Possibilities of Governance*, Cambridge; Polity Press,.

Hutton, W. (1995), *The State We're In*, London: Cape.

Hyman, R. (1984), *Strikes*, London: Fontana.

Hyman, R. (1999), 'Imagined solidarities: can the unions resist globalisation?' in P. Leisink (ed.), *Globalisation and Labour Relations*, Cheltenham, UK and Northampton, MA, USA: Edward Elgar, pp. 94–115.

Hyman, R. (2007), 'Afterword: what went wrong?', in J. McIlroy, N. Fishman and A. Campbell (eds), *The High Tide of British Trade Unionism: Trade Unions and Industrial Politics, 1964–79*, Monmouth: Merlin Press, pp. 353–64.

Kelly, J. (1996), 'Union militancy and social partnership', in P. Ackers, C. Smith and P. Smith, (eds), *The New Workplace and Trade Unionism*, London: Routledge, pp. 77–109.

Kelly, J. (2004), 'Social partnership agreements in Britain: labour cooperation and compliance', *Industrial Relations*, **43**(1), 267–92.

Kimber, C. (2009), 'A new period of class struggle', *Socialist Review*, September.
Kleinknecht, A. and J. ter Wengel (1998), 'The myth of economic globalisation', *Cambridge Journal of Economics*, **22**, 637–47.
Layard, R. (2006), 'Happiness and public policy: a challenge to the profession', *Economic Journal*, **116**, C24–C33.
McIlroy, J. (1991), *The Permanent Revolution? Conservative Law and the Trade Unions*, Nottingham: Spokesman.
McIlroy, J. (1992), 'Ten years for the locust: the TUC in the 1980s', in D. Cox (ed.), *Facing the Future*, Nottingham: University of Nottingham, pp. 147–94.
McIlroy, J. (1993), 'Tales from smoke-filled rooms', *Studies in the Education of Adults*, **25**(1), 42–63.
McIlroy, J. (1995), *Trade Unions in Britain Today*, Manchester: Manchester University Press.
McIlroy, J. (1998), 'The enduring alliance? Trade unions and the making of New Labour, 1994–97', *British Journal of Industrial Relations*, **36**(4), 537–64.
McIlroy, J. (2000), 'New Labour, new unions, new Left', *Capital and Class*, **71**, 11–46.
McIlroy, J. (2007), 'Reflections on British trade unions and industrial politics', J. McIlroy, N. Fishman and A. Campbell (eds), *The High Tide of British Trade Unionism: Trade Unions and Industrial Politics, 1964–79*, Monmouth: Merlin Press, pp. xv–xl.
McIlroy, J. (2008), 'Ten years of New Labour: workplace learning, social partnership and union revitalisation in Britain', *British Journal of Industrial Relations*, **46**(2), 283–313.
McIlroy, J. (2009a), 'A brief history of British trade unions and neo-liberalism: from the earliest days to the birth of New Labour', in G. Daniels and J. McIlroy (eds), *Trade Unions in a Neo-liberal World: British Trade Unions under New Labour*, London: Routledge, pp. 21–62.
McIlroy, J. (2009b), 'A brief history of British trade unions and neo-liberalism in the age of New Labour', in G. Daniels and J. McIlroy (eds), *Trade Unions in a Neo-liberal World: British Trade Unions under New Labour*, London: Routledge, pp. 63–97.
McIlroy, J. (2009c), 'Under stress but still enduring: the contentious alliance in the age of Tony Blair and Gordon Brown', in G. Daniels and J. McIlroy (eds), *Trade Unions in a Neo-liberal World: British Trade Unions under New Labour*, London: Routledge, pp. 165–201.
McIlroy, J. and A. Campbell (1999), 'Organising the militants: the Liaison Committee for the Defence of Trade Unions, 1966–1979', *British Journal of Industrial Relations*, **37**(1), 1–31.
McIlroy, J. and R. Croucher (2009), 'Skills and training: a strategic role for trade unions or the limits of neo-liberalism?', in G. Daniels and J. McIlroy (eds), *Trade Unions in a Neo-liberal World: British Trade Unions under New Labour*, London: Routledge, pp. 283–315.
Moschonas, G. (2002), *In the Name of Social Democracy, The Great Transformation, 1945 to the Present*, London: Verso.
Murray, A. (2003), *A New Labour Nightmare: The Return of the Awkward Squad*, London: Verso.
Piven, F. (1995), 'Is it global economics or neo laissez-faire?', *New Left Review*, **213**, 107–14.
Ravenhill, J. (2008), *Global Political Economy*, Oxford: Oxford University Press.
Routledge, P. (1993), *Scargill: The Unauthorised Biography*, London: HarperCollins.
Seifert, R. and T. Sibley (2005), *United They Stood: The Story of the Firefighters' Dispute, 2002–2004*, London: Lawrence and Wishart.
Serwotka, M. (2007), *The Future of Public Services under Labour*, Hertfordshire University Business School working paper no. 3.
Shaw, E. (2007), *Losing Labour's Soul? New Labour and the Blair Governments, 1997–2007*, London: Routledge.
Snowdon, P. (2010), *Back from the Brink: The Inside Story of the Tory Resurrection*, London: Harper Collins.
Stirling, J. (2010), 'Global unions: chasing the dream or building the reality?', *Capital and Class*, **34**(1), 107–14.
Taylor, G. (2009), 'Europe: the double-edged sword of justice? New Labour, trade unions and the politics of Social Europe', in G. Daniels and J. McIlroy (eds), *Trade Unions in a Neo-liberal World: British Trade Unions under New Labour*, London: Routledge, pp. 342–67.
Taylor, R. (1994), *The Future of Trade Unions*, London: Andre Deutsch.
Trade Union Congress (TUC) (1982), *Industrial Relations Legislation*, London: TUC.
TUC (2006), *Congress 2006: General Council Report*, London: TUC.

TUC (2007), *Congress 2007: General Council Report*, London: TUC.

Undy, R., P. Fosh, H. Morris, P. Smith and R. Martin (1996), *Managing the Unions: The Impact of Legislation on Trade Union Behaviour*, Oxford: Clarendon Press.

Upchurch, M. (2009), 'Partnership: New Labour's Third Way?', in G. Daniels and J. McIlroy (eds), *Trade Unions in a Neo-liberal World: British Trade Unions under New Labour*, London: Routledge, pp. 230–53.

Upchurch, M., M. Flynn and R. Croucher (2008), 'The activist as subject: political congruence and the PCS activist', Bristol: British Universities Industrial Relations Association Conference.

Upchurch, M., G. Taylor and A. Mathers (2009), *The Crisis of Social Democratic Trade Unionism in Western Europe: The Search for Alternatives*, Farnham: Ashgate

Waddington, J. and C. Whitston (1997), 'Why do people join unions in a period of membership decline?', *British Journal of Industrial Relations*, **35**(4), 515–46.

Willman, P. (2004), 'Structuring unions: the administrative rationality of collective action', in J. Kelly and P. Willman (eds), *Union Organisation and Activity*, London: Routledge, pp. 73–85.

Willman, P. and J. Kelly (2004), 'Introduction', in J. Kelly and P. Willman (eds), *Union Organisation and Activity*, London: Routledge, pp. 1–6.

7 Unions in China in a period of marketisation

Fang Lee Cooke

INTRODUCTION

Existing studies on Chinese unions have mostly been critical of the All-China Federation of Unions (ACFTU) – the only union that is recognised by the Chinese government. The ACFTU is one of the eight 'mass organisations' (non-government organisations) in China that operate under the leadership of the Chinese Communist Party (CCP). It has been heavily criticised for its institutionally incapacitated position and operational inefficacy (Clarke 2005; O'Leary 1998; Taylor *et al.* 2003; and others). What has been the response of the ACFTU in the process of China's marketisation informed by neo-liberalism? This chapter addresses this question by first providing a brief historical overview of the transformation of the Chinese economic policy and structure since 1978 that has witnessed the radical state sector reform and the emergence of the market economy. We then review the impact of marketisation on two major groups of Chinese workers: the state-owned enterprise (SOE) workers and the rural migrant workers. In the third main section, we critically evaluate the attitude and role of the ACFTU in response to the changing nature of employment relations in the state sector and the poor working conditions of workers in the private and foreign-funded firms. We do so in view of the political and resource constraints of the ACFTU. We also investigate new initiatives and modes of organising from the ACFTU in response to the new dynamics of employment relations and the rising level of labour disputes, notably in the export-oriented manufacturing sector. Tensions inherent in the ACFTU's multiple functions are highlighted, particularly its subordination to the CCP on the one hand and its role in defending workers' rights on the other. Finally, we discuss the roles of other organising bodies, including international bodies, and workers' self-organising in light of the inefficacy of the ACFTU. The chapter concludes that the prospect of any substitute of the ACFTU in the labour movement in China is remote and that while the ACFTU's response to workers' representational needs has been inadequate, it has nevertheless played a positive, albeit moderate, role in pushing for a tightened legislative framework and in monitoring labour standards.

MARKET ECONOMY WITH SOCIALIST CHARACTERISTICS

The ideology of neo-liberalism, marked by minimalised state intervention and the maximalised role for the market/private sector as observed in major western economies and other less developed economies such as Chile and to some extent India, has never been fully embraced in China. The state has also increased its role as a regulator in order to provide an orderly market. Despite the rapid growth of the private sector as a key feature of China's economic development in the last three decades following its open door policy enacted in 1978, neither has the role of the state been minimised nor has the freedom granted to the private sector been a smooth process. Instead, the growth of the private sector has been heavily influenced by the ebbs and flows of political support in the 1980s and 1990s (Parris 1999; Saich 2001). During the state planned economy era (1949–1978), private economy – symbolic of capitalism – was marginalised due to its ideological clash with socialism. This state suppression was gradually replaced by state support during the reforming period since the 1980s when the private sector was called upon to absorb displaced workers from the state sector and the new labour force.

In the Seventh National Party Congress in the 1988, it was announced that private enterprises with more than eight employees were to be given legal status. This was the first time since the early 1950s (Parris 1999). This progress, however, received a temporary setback after the Tiananmen Square Event in 1989. Deng's relaunch of economic reform in 1992 breathed new life into the private sector. The growth rate was at its highest between 1993 and 1995, fuelled by Deng's influential speech during his famous tour of Southern China and the consequent relaxation of government policies in supporting the development of individual and private economies. The spirit of Deng's speech, or more precisely economic reform policy as projected in his speech, was to glorify private entrepreneurship and allow a minority of people to get rich first. This reflects the neo-liberalism ideology in which the uneven distribution of the spoils of growth was justified in order to stimulate economic growth. In 1997, the then Premier Zhu Rongji announced that poor-performing SOEs were given three years to reform themselves through downsizing, closure and privatisation of smaller ones (see below for impact on workers). By 1998, the sector was given full political legitimacy. Full legal rights were granted to the private sector in 2000 (Child and Tse 2001; Parris 1999).

In the meantime, the Chinese government has been actively attracting foreign direct investment (FDI) through a range of favourable policies and became one of the top FDI recipient countries in the world. A significant proportion of the FDI entered the Chinese market as foreign-invested enterprises (FIEs) or joint ventures (JVs) with Chinese firms. Similar to the growth of the domestic private sector, the growth of FIEs has been under some regulatory constraints. In the 1980s, foreign firms must form joint ventures with local firms to operate in China. It was not until the mid-1990s when foreign firms were granted rights to operate as wholly foreign-owned businesses. In the 1980s and 1990s, the majority of the FDI came from overseas Chinese from Hong Kong, Macao and Taiwan. They operate primarily in the export-oriented manufacturing sector, importing some of the poor labour management practices. It was not until the mid-1990s when FDI from western economies started to enter the Chinese market in full force.

A distinctive feature in the marketisation process of the Chinese economy has been the continuing presence of state intervention, through legislation and policy regulations at the central level and a hands-on approach at the local level. As Khanna (2007) argued, the Chinese government is often the entrepreneur itself in its current vigorous economic growth. Governments at all levels continue to be heavily involved in businesses, and the largest and best performing firms tend to be state-owned or invested. It should be noted also that a countervailing view holds that the ever-present state intervention has been precisely the obstacle to the development of a strong private sector in China (Nolan 2001; Huang 2008 and others). Indeed, not all government interventions are legitimate. It has been widely reported that some local government officials abuse their power to gain personal advantage from private employers in the name of the government. So much so that private firms do not want to grow larger or operate at night time to conceal the size of their business and production from greedy officials.

Therefore, instead of embracing a neo-liberalism model led by business elites and the private sector, the Chinese government has adopted a state centric approach in which the state actors are the political entrepreneurs who craft neo-liberalism (Prasad 2006). In the Chinese context, the government has played the role of the developmental state, which has been crucial in the rapid economic development of East and Southeast Asian countries in recent decades (Öniş 1991; Zhu 2004 and others). This is characterised by a strong commitment to growth, productivity, competitiveness and privatisation of property and market in the absence of a commitment to social equality and welfare. It is also marked by a relatively high level of state intervention in the process of marketisation via various state agencies, often managed by elite bureaucrats (Öniş 1991). The economic transformation of China since the 1980s shared many of these characteristics (Cooke 2012).

What complicates matters, however, is the local developmental state (decentralisation) model that the Chinese state has adopted (Zhu 2004). Each province and municipality is responsible for its own economic development. Key performance indicators are set by the higher authority and used to benchmark local bureaucrats' performance during their terms of office. As a result, local state agencies have a high level of flexibility and autonomy in pursuing their own interests, often in an opportunistic manner (Zhu 2004). This flexibility and autonomy may not be officially endorsed by their central state master. Rather, it is often the outcome of active resistance and local strategy to overcome institutional constraints (Oliver 1997). In doing so, local institutional actors actively identify and recreate policy gaps and spaces within which to operate. They act as the gate keepers as well as the players, albeit increasingly in a disguised manner, to pursue their own agenda which are not necessarily in line with that of the central government (Cooke 2012).

The change of government leadership to Premier Wen Jiabao and President Hu Jintao in 2003 marked the beginning of the pursuit of an economic development policy that emphasises social justice, social harmony and environmental protection. This is an important departure from an efficiency-driven economic development policy pursued by their predecessors typically influenced by the economic thinking of Deng Xiaoping – the architect of modern Chinese economic development. It is a response to the increasing level of pressure that the government has been subject to, both at home and abroad, to grow China's economy in a more humanistic and responsible way. The primary objective of the state intervention in employment relations is two-fold: to provide a greater level of protection to the workers, and to facilitate enterprises to establish harmonious employment relations as part of its agenda to build a harmonious society (Warner and Zhu 2010). Much of what has happened in employment relations and the changing roles of the unions in China's marketising economy needs to be understood in this context.

MARKETISATION AND IMPACTS ON WORKERS

Marketisation has had significant impacts on two major groups of workers: workers in the SOEs and workers in the private firms and FIEs. The majority of the latter are (rural) migrant workers. While downsizing of SOEs started in the early 1990s, it was Premier Zhu's three-year reform programme for SOEs in the late 1990s that witnessed the displacement of state sector workers *en mass*. Employment relations in the state sector were once portrayed as harmonious, with workers participating in the democratic management of the workplace and production activities through their union organisations and workers' representatives. The ongoing reforms in SOEs in the last two decades have led to profound changes in the employment relationships between the workers and their state employers. For the SOE workers, the end of job-for-life, the reduction of extensive workplace welfares, including social security provisions, and the introduction of production and performance-based reward systems have been the most dramatic consequences. In 1978, some 78 per cent of the urban workers were employed in the state sector; this was dropped to less than 24 per cent by 2009 (*China Statistical Yearbook 2010*). These changes have undermined, and in some cases practically ended, the paternalistic bond between the state employer and its workers. A significant proportion of the labour discontent and disputes come from those who are negatively affected by these changes (Cooke 2011a).

Meanwhile, the opening up of the economy has attracted millions of rural migrant workers to seek employment in the urban area. Indeed, they have played a pivotal role in China's contemporary economic development. The inflow of rural migrant workers to urban areas started in the late 1980s and by 2006, they made up 58 per cent of the workers in the industry sector and 52 per cent in the service sector (The State Council 2006). Initially working in manufacturing plants, construction sites and as domestic helpers, they are now working in a wide spread of industries and occupations, but primarily in private firms, foreign-invested sweatshop plants and the informal sector where labour standards are low and employment regulations often violated. The vast majority of them have no written employment contract, little training, few rest days, no social security and little health and safety protection. They work extensively long hours, live in poor conditions and are largely un-organised and un-represented (Chan 2001; Lee 2007; Pun and Smith 2007 and others). Delay of wage payment is common, especially in the construction industry (Cooke 2008a). The adversarial employment condition endured by rural migrant workers is a legacy of the highly non-egalitarian socialist development strategy adopted by the government in which the urban development has been ironically achieved at the expense of the rural population (Meng 2000; Solinger 1999).

It has been observed (Gallagher 2005) that the opening up of the Chinese economy to foreign investments prior to the reform of the state sector has served to legitimise the labour reforms of the latter. The government was able to project the country's economic development as a collective national goal which affects the whole population and requires all to participate. Within this paternalistic and nationalistic framing, competitive pressures on the Chinese workers are legitimised, so is the endurance of the negative impacts on the minority for the greater good of the nation as a whole. It is important to note that the SOE workers never had the ability to negotiate their rights and benefits. It was given to them by their state employer. The withdrawal of the state protection has rendered the SOE workers exposed to market competitions. It requires them to redraw their social contract and re-establish their social identity and power base. While they are resisting and adapting to this new reality, the national economic development continues to propel, thanks to the availability of the rural migrant workers who are willing to take any jobs and work anywhere and anytime. In some ways, the existence of the latter in the urban economy undermines the ability of the SOE workers to advance their rights and benefits. The externalisation and semi-marketisation of the social security provisions (pension, work-related injury compensation, maternity entitlement, sick pay and unemployment benefit) further opens up opportunities for employers to find innovative ways, often with the tacit support of the local government, to avoid or reduce their legal responsibility. This gives further incentives to employers to hire migrant workers instead of local urban residents.

UNION RESPONSES

Marketisation and the ensuring radical changes in the labour market and employment relations called for the unions to respond with new strategies and organising techniques. In this section, we assess the role of the ACFTU and its grassroots organisations in the reform process. It is important to note that the unions' power and ability to respond to the Chinese variant of neo-liberalism needs to be evaluated in the context of the legal rights of the workers, the ACFTU's relationships with the state and the employer, and how these two institutional actors impose constraints as well as create opportunities and sites for unionism.

Legal Rights of the Chinese Workers

To understand the role of the ACFTU it is important, first of all, to establish the scope of legal rights of the workers and their representing body. It has been argued that, with 'the major exception of freedom of association', the labour standards established by the series of labour laws and regulations of China 'are not markedly inferior to those of comparable countries and indeed many developed nations' (Cooney 2007: 674). Since the 1990s, a number of legislative and administrative regulations have been issued by the government that provide a basic framework under which the labour market is regulated in principle. Major laws include: Labour Law of China (enacted in 1995) and the three laws enacted in 2008, that is, the Labour Contract Law, the Employment Promotion Law and the Labour Disputes Mediation and Arbitration Law. In addition, the then Ministry of Labour and Social Security issued a special regulation on minimum wage in 2004. The rising level of labour disputes accompanying the privatisation and marketisation of the economy has made it imperative for the state to improve legal protection and labour standards; and the continuing growth of the economy has made it possible to do so (Chan 2009), since neither the state nor the employer can use expense as the excuse for not raising labour standards.

However, labour rights stipulated in these laws focus on individual rights, such as contracts, wages, working conditions and social security, whereas collective rights, particularly 'the rights to organise, to strike, and to bargain collectively in a meaningful sense' are largely absent (Chen 2007: 60). In this sense, labour rights in China are defective because the lack of collective rights is a contributing factor that 'render workers' individual rights vulnerable, hollow, unenforceable, or often disregarded' (Chen 2007: 77).

It should be noted that collective rights are not totally absent from China's labour legislation. 'Both the Labour Law and the Union Law, for example, contain clauses on the rights to organise although defined vaguely and abstractly' (Chen 2007: 65). Collective bargaining is perhaps the most significant collective right of the Chinese workers, although its implementation, like other regulations, remains problematic. In 1994, the unions have been given the official role to represent workers for consultation with employers. This position of the unions has been reinforced and expanded in subsequent labour laws. However, without the right to organise independently and the right to strike, the right to collective bargaining is meaningless as it does not give workers any real power to bargain with employers (Chen 2007). The ACFTU's drive to promote the collective consultation system since the early 1990s and the signing of collective contracts in more recent years has been no more than a 'single-minded pursuit of numerical growth' with little substantive gains for the workers beyond what has been stipulated in the labour laws (*China Labour Bulletin* 2009: 39). Workers were rarely consulted, in some cases were not even aware of the terms and conditions agreed, as was reported in the Wal-Mart case (*China Labor News Translations* 2008).

Structural Constraints of the ACFTU – Party-state Dependence

The ACFTU operates under the leadership of the Chinese Communist Party. The union-CCP tie dates back to the 1920s (the union was founded on 1 May 1925) when grassroots union organisations served as the CCP member recruitment bases and provided vital support to the CCP by mobilising workers to participate in the revolutionary movement. Under the socialist state planned economy system, labour and management were perceived to share the same interests, unions' activities were focused on the promotion of productivity, the provision of welfare and entertainment for the employees under the leadership of the CCP, although union officials would be consulted for disciplinary and dismissal matters. The governance structure of the ACFTU branches are in the form of a vertical and horizontal reporting line. ACFTU organisations are under the dual control (or 'leadership' as it is described) of the local government at their level and their organisational branch of a higher level. Union officials at the branch level are normally appointed by the local governments.

Government officials and ACFTU officials at the local government level are managed in similar ways to civil servants as prescribed in the Civil Servants Law (Cooke 2011b).

Since the mid-1990s, the initiative of direct elections for the grassroots union officials (particularly enterprise union chairmen) has been adopted in a number of coastal provinces, albeit often in a piecemeal manner (Howell 2008). It was hoped that direct election of union officials at the enterprise level 'will help stabilise labour relations and reduce spontaneous unrest' (Howell 2008: 853). It is believed that elected union chairmen and representatives will be more accountable to their member workers. This bottom-up approach can help ACFTU to enlarge its base in the private sector and strengthen the links between the higher and lower levels of union organisations. It is also seen as a step forward towards democratisation of the mass organisation (Howell 2008). However, a diverse range of tactics and practices were found at the local level in terms of how the union chairman was to be elected and who should qualify as candidates. While direct election of union chairmen at the enterprise level is 'encouraged' by the ACFTU, elected candidates may not be approved by the higher union authority or the local government for various reasons (*China Labour Bulletin* 2009; Howell 2008). Even when accepted, elected union officials may find their effort to defend workers' rights undermined by all quarters. Grassroots union officials and representatives also face job loss threats or victimisation if they side with the workers, despite the Union Law's stipulation against victimisation.

In theory, 'Unions shall represent and protect the legal rights and interests of workers independently and autonomously and develop their activities according to the law' (the Labour Law 1995, Chapter 1, Article 7). In practice, this proposition is rarely fulfilled and union officials have been heavily criticised for their lack of professional competence and political will to carry out their prescribed functions. More broadly, the divergence of labour-capital interests and the resultant conflicts that arise pose tremendous challenges to the ACFTU organisations to demonstrate their continuing value to employers, state and workers simultaneously. This requires them to reconstitute their traditional functions (Clarke and Pringle 2009) to gain identifications from new bases of workers constituency and to reduce resistance from employers in the private sector at the same time.

While some critics of the ACFTU (including Lee 2007; Taylor and Li 2007) argue that party dependence is its fundamental problem in representing the workers, others (including Clarke 2005; Clarke and Pringle 2009) argue that 'the limitations of post-socialist unionism are structural, rather than an expression of ideological and political legacies and constraints' (Clarke 2005: 13). Clarke (2005: 14) noted that some of the once Communist party-led unions in post-socialist Central and Eastern European countries had not been able to sustain themselves after they became independent and have had to turn to political patronage to secure 'their institutional reproduction'. However, we should not assume that the ACFTU has played merely a subservient role to the CCP and simply acted as dependent agents of the government. Instead, the relationship between the CCP and the ACFTU has not always been smooth. There have been several attempts of the ACFTU to gain more autonomy in light of the marketising economy, the growing discontent of the workers with the ACFTU and the emerging attempts of autonomous union organising. For example, 'the 11th ACFTU Congress in October 1988 called for 'drastic changes', including greater independence for the unions to enable them to head off the threat of independent worker organisations' (Clarke and Pringle 2009: 86). The ACFTU has pressed strongly for the collective regulation in labour legislation. Senior ACFTU leadership used their positions in the top level of government bodies to lobby for labour legislation (Clarke and Pringle 2009). The ACFTU also provided strong support to the students and autonomous workers' unions during the Tiananmen Square event in 1989. However, efforts of the ACFTU to gain independence have been suppressed by the CCP-state (Sheehan 1999; Clarke and Pringle 2009). Each round of failed power struggles was followed by the tightened grip of the CCP-state over the ACFTU and labour movements especially when the state or government was the target of the movement. The ACFTU's request for more autonomy and greater influence in policy and legislation processes was granted only in exchange of accepting the CCP leadership (Howell 2008). Similarly, attempts to form autonomous workers' unions were crushed, as was the case during the Tiananmen Square event (Cooke 2011a). Under the tight control of the CCP, grassroots union organisations are relatively homogeneous and carry out similar functions.

Resource Dependence and Constraints

Financial constraint is a key issue for the development of the ACFTU grass-roots organisations. The declining level of union membership and funding from the government to the ACFTU during the late 1990s and the mid-2000s has led the 'resource crisis' of the ACFTU (Liu *et al.* 2011). For example, the total number of full-time union officials nation-wide had dropped to 0.46m in 2004 compared with 0.56m in 1990 (*China Labour Statistical Yearbook 2008*). Between 2001 and 2004, union organisations underwent a period of restructuring and downsizing as part of the state sector reform. This retrenchment took place in the context of the expansion of the union functions and the rising number of grassroots union organisations and members. Under the threat of job losses and financial penalty (such as deduction of bonus) for failing to achieve performance targets, union officials now work beyond their normal hours and duties (Cooke 2008b).

Financial constraints impair the opportunity for capacity building and solidarity for ACFTU grassroots organisations. Research (including Cooke 2011b) suggests that there was limited interaction between workplace union representatives and union officials at the district branch level to consolidate union strengths and to develop activities to maximise their resource and impact due to resource constraints. Financial constraints also affect the development of union officials and representatives, with those at the grassroots level being the most affected. To compensate for the deficiency of union representatives at the workplace level, the ACFTU attempts to 'professionalise' grassroots union leaders by parachuting in union officials from the higher level to participate in negotiation with the management at the enterprise level (Chen 2007).

The Expanding Functions of the ACFTU Organisations

The institutional function of the ACFTU has been both 'representative' and 'administrative' (Warner 2008). Under the state planned economy mode, the core function of the unions was three-fold: production (problem solving teams, skill contests to enhance productivity), life (social welfare and wellbeing), and education (skill training, behavioural and moral development). The latter two were organised in order to maximise productivity. It was not until 1988 (during the 11th ACFTU National Congress) when the fourth dimension, to defend workers' interest, was listed as one of the new functions of the unions (Feng 2006). From then on, the four basic functions of the ACFTU were listed as: to defend workers' interests, to represent workers in participating in the management of the company, to develop mass production activities, and to raise the quality of the workforce (Feng 2006).

In reality, the most important function of the ACFTU at the grassroots level is to maintain stability of the society, as admitted by union officials (Cooke 2011b). This means that they may have to perform a policing role during labour unrests and demonstrations. The second most important role is then to protect workers' rights. We need to be reminded that the union's role in labour disputes resolution is not through organising industrial actions, but through monitoring the labour standards and enforcing the labour regulations. When the labour disputes are a result of direct conflicts between the state (employer) and the workers, union officials typically play a mediator role and at times side with the management (Clarke 2005; O'Leary 1998). Nevertheless, 'the ACFTU is credited with its effort to promote the pro-labour legislation' (Chen 2007: 65), particularly in drafting the Labour Contract Law and Labour Disputes Mediation and Arbitration Law. It must be noted that the promulgation of the Labour Contract Law has caused strong opposition from the employers and FIEs through their international lobbying bodies. The final version of the Labour Contract Law reflects the compromise of the state in response to the demands of the employers and their representing bodies (see Cooke 2009 for more detailed discussion).

Unions' Recruitment Drive and the Changing Constituency

The ACFTU is the largest national union body in the world, measured by its official membership on paper (Warner and Zhu 2010). Union membership level has been consistently high at over 90 per cent since 1990 at workplaces where union organisations were established (see *China Statistical Yearbook 2010*). According to the ACFTU, union membership reached 212m members at the end of 2008. There were more than 1.7m grassroots union organisations across the country and over 77 per cent of the workforce were unionised (*China Labour Bulletin* 2009). Generally speaking, in organisations where a union unit is established, union membership level is high for both men and women, with women's membership level less than 3 per cent lower than that of men's. It must be noted here that the high level of membership in recognised workplaces is not necessarily an indication of union strength. Once a union unit is established in a company, it is virtually mandatory for its employees to become a member.

The expansion of union membership since the mid-2000s is necessarily a result of the ACFTU's national recruitment drive in an attempt to organise the rural migrant workers. The union's response to the growing presence of rural migrant workers as a potential group to be organised and represented had largely been passive until the mid-2000s. This is despite the fact that the ACFTU at all levels were instructed by the government in late 1994 to launch a campaign 'to set up unions in all the non-unionised foreign-invested enterprises, with the ultimate declared purpose of implementing collective bargaining' (Chan 1998: 1223). Under the Chinese socialist administrative system, farmers did not fall within the constituency base of the ACFTU because they were not classified as 'the working class' which was a privilege reserved for urban workers. Since rural migrant workers working in the urban areas still carry their administrative status of rural residents, they have failed to gain the union's attention as targets for organisation (Cooke 2007).

Rampant exploitation and the rising level of health and safety problems in sweatshops and construction sites that accompanied the rapid expansion of the urban economy has meant that organising and representing rural migrant workers became an urgent priority. In August 2003 the ACFTU officially classified rural migrant workers in urban areas as 'members of the working class' and required union organisations to organise rural migrant workers (*Yangcheng Evening News* 8 August 2003). The ACFTU's strategy was to recruit as many rural migrant workers as possible into the union, disregarding where they were from, what types of job they did, how long they worked or whether they were in employment (*Workers' Daily* 25 February 2005). As such, the ACFTU was criticised for being 'more concerned with meeting quotas than establishing genuinely representative workers' organisations' for effective representation (*China Labour Bulletin* 2009: 32). Despite the ACFTU's recruitment drive and their clear representational needs, few of the rural migrant workers have heard of the phrase 'union', even fewer were being represented, as unions face formidable barriers to recognition by employers (Cooke 2008b).

This diversification of union constituency consequential of the marketising economy presents different opportunities as well as challenges to the unions. It also calls for them to adoption of different roles, organising strategies and activities at the grassroots level to address multiple issues if the unions were to maximise their utility. This poses significant challenges to the grassroots union organisations as well as those at the policy making level because the needs and grievances of these groups are framed distinctively within the boundary of class, educational level, occupational and social identity that cannot be readily transcended (Perry and Selden 2000).

Organising Initiatives

As China's economic transformation deepens in the last two decades, the ACFTU grassroots organisations become an active labour market broker, providing training and employment services to displaced SOE workers as well as migrant workers. Meanwhile, the ACFTU is fully aware of its responsibility to the Party-state in maintaining 'social harmony' by containing labour unrest. To this end, a number of initiatives have been adopted by the ACFTU to organise those outside the state sector, targeting especially at the rural migrant workers and foreign-invested firms. These initiatives represent both hard and soft approaches. As mentioned earlier, the ACFTU launched a national recruitment drive in 2003 that had led to the recruitment of over 70m rural migrant workers into the union by the end of 2008. In mid-2008, backed by the Party-state, the ACFTU launched an intensive three-month campaign to 'unionise the Fortune 500' whose unionisation rate in China was significantly lower (less than 50 per cent) than the average unionisation rate (73 per cent) in overseas-invested companies as a whole. This had led to a rapid increase of unionisation rate to over 80 per cent by September 2008 (*China Labour Bulletin* 2009: 32). In addition, the ACFTU maintains that 'it would not allow companies to bypass the unionisation process by setting up proxy-organisations such as 'employee welfare clubs' and 'employee entertainment clubs' funded by the two% of payroll that by law should go to the union' (*China Labour Bulletin* 2009: 32).

In conjunction with these high profile campaigns, two major strategies have been adopted by the unions to organise the migrant workers (the word 'organising' is used in broad terms here, although we are aware of the debates of 'organising' and 'servicing' models in the western unionism literature). One is 'workplace organisation': to gain recognition at the workplace and then unionise the workers with the support of the company. However, gaining employer recognition remains a difficult task given the persistent resistance of domestic private firms and FIEs (Cooke 2007). The other way of organising is 'distant organisation': to recruit migrant workers (those already in employment or are seeking jobs) outside the workplace with services packages as inducement. This is usually carried out by operating in the labour market and in ways similar to what Kelly and Heery (1989: 198–199) classify as a 'distant expansion' recruitment strategy.

However, these organising techniques are essentially logistic innovations, whereas the key issue here is for the union to gain power and be able to prevent rampant exploitation and mistreatments at the workplaces. Without recognition by the employer, union effectiveness is questionable as it is more difficult for the union to represent workers collectively outside the workplace. In addition, workers' dependence on the union and union impact are likely to be weakened where union organising attempts are duplicated and diluted by other functional bodies offering similar services in the labour market (see below). While this service-oriented mode of organising has some tangible effects in increasing union memberships, the rural migrant workers may be unionised but not necessarily organised in the strict sense. Union density is not a reliable indicator of union strength, especially where the main function of the union is to provide services rather than organising to press for improved working conditions (Cooke 2007).

ALTERNATIVE FORMS OF REPRESENTATION AND SELF-ORGANISING

As noted above, the ACFTU is not the sole organising body in the labour market servicing the workers. There are a number of organisations, both public and private, which are gearing up to organise the (rural migrant) workers and provide somewhat similar services to them. These include: the local governments (mainly the labour authority), job centres, employment agencies, training centres and legal centres. These organisations emerge as a result of certain governmental initiatives or business opportunities. They may be the branch outs or sub-contractors of local government departments. Their primary goal may not necessarily be serving the workers, even less so in organising them. Nonetheless, they constitute major alternative sources of service provision and official representational function for workers (see Cooke 2007; 2009 for further discussion).

At the international level, foreign client firms operating at the upper end of the product market and international NGOs are increasingly playing a role in monitoring the labour standards and legislative compliance in China, particularly in the export-oriented manufacturing sector. While foreign client firms use corporate social responsibility (CSR) as their leverage to raise the labour standard of Chinese supplier firms, this pressure has had both positive and negative effects to the Chinese workers (Cooke 2009; Harvey 2009). Others (such as Howell 2008) critique that the discourse of CSR may be merely a hypocritical device to protect the western market. For the international NGOs and domestic ones under international patronage, they provide financial, medical, legal, educational and emotional support to the workers in sweatshop plants through some forms of organising primarily outside the workplaces (Pun and Yang 2004; Lee and Shen 2008 and others). These services are provided within an institutional environment that is largely absent of a civil society tradition and at times hostile to the embeddedment of non-CCP-led NGOs. Nevertheless, the promulgation of the Labour Contract Law and related regulations has undoubtedly provided NGOs with more legal instruments to carry out their work.

The emerging monitoring role of the foreign client firms and the growing presence of NGOs may undermine the operational legitimacy of unions and their ability to fulfil the range of functions prescribed to them by the state. That said, the institutional position of NGOs is far from secure, as they rely on external resource support on the one hand and the tolerance of the CCP-state on the other, and can easily be isolated through political discourse. Similarly, foreign client firms may look to other countries for their suppliers when the price of Chinese suppliers becomes comparatively uncompetitive. The somewhat transient and precarious nature of foreign client firms and NGOs in their labour standards monitoring role may regenerate sites which formal monitoring channels have not been able to reach (Cooke 2009).

Nonetheless, the emergence of the above new forms of organisation that provide services and support to aggrieved workers, despite the smallness in scope of services and limitations in effects, has forced the ACFTU to develop similar lines of services. For example, the ACFTU are now sponsoring and operating a significant proportion of the job centres, training centres, and legal advice centres nation-wide. Some local ACFTU organisations have reportedly approached NGOs and black lawyers for collaboration (Clarke and Pringle 2009).

The inability of the ACFTU grassroots branches and other formal channels to organise workers to protect their employment terms and conditions have also led to attempts of self-organising by aggrieved Chinese workers. These activities are often spontaneous and event specific, targeting at the workplace level or the local governments. They take the form of wild cat strikes, walk-outs and street protests (Chan 2001; Chen 2003; Lee 2007 and others). These labour protests are not confined to rural migrant workers in sweatshop plants and workers in the SOEs who have either been displaced or are suffering from low wages due to financial deficit of the firm. Other occupational groups such as taxi drivers in major cities and school teachers in remote and poor areas have also taken to the street as the last resort to protest against their low income as a result of harsh taxation by the taxi companies or wage arrears by the local government employer (*China Labour Bulletin* 2009). It is interesting to note that workers' applications for setting up unions (including aggrieved taxi drivers) have been rejected by the ACFTU branches with the reason that 'unions should be organised by the enterprise' (*China Labour Bulletin* 2009: 35).

The year 2010 marked the turning point of labour-capital power imbalance through a string of high profile strike actions organised by workers themselves in a number of foreign-invested manufacturing/brewery plants in various major cities. These include, for example, Honda in Foshan and Zhongshan, Hyundai in Beijing, Toyota in Tianjin, Brother in Xi'an, Panasonic in Shanghai, and Carlsberg in Chongqing. Demands for higher wages and better working conditions were the main reason for the strikes. These strikes have yielded positive results – all employers have agreed to a substantial pay rise of between 20 and 40 per cent after rounds of negotiation (*Guardian* 11 June 2010).

Successive industrial actions of various forms that have taken place across a number of industries and the country suggest that Chinese workers are becoming more aware of their rights and less tolerant when their rights have been grossly breached. Emboldened by the promulgation of the Labour Contract Law and Labour Disputes Mediation and Arbitration Law, they 'have demonstrated the ability to organise large-scale and effective protests' (*China Labour Bulletin* 2009: 31). Despite being illegal, strikes remain a highly effective way of resolving labour disputes due to the government's eagerness to contain social discontent. However, this is often not without cost to those who organise the collective actions (Chen 2003; 2006 and others).

It is significant to note that in past strikes, the government has mobilised forces to curtail protests and suppressed media coverage. In the string of strikes in foreign-owned plants in 2010 as noted above, the Chinese authority has verged on the supportive, claiming that the workers' demands were 'reasonable' (Milne 2010). Another reason for the authority's tacit support of the strike actions is the pressure the government has been facing to increase wages in order to address the growing inequality in income and to stimulate internal demand for consumption to offset drops in exports as a result of the 2008 global financial crisis. Supporting workers' actions against foreign capital also enables the government to direct any labour discontent away from its direction by developing nationalist sentiment. Thus, it is easier for workers' self-organising in FIEs in China. Once they are organised, they have the prospect of influencing domestic private firms, where labour practices are similar to those of FIEs. Similarly, there is a stronger chance for international labour unions and organisations to work with the Chinese state and the ACFTU to target FIEs than domestic Chinese firms to push for union recognition and improvement of labour standards.

CONCLUSIONS

This chapter has reviewed the political background of China's marketisation process which started in the late 1970s. It outlined how this economic reform has brought fundamental changes to the SOE workers on the one hand, and created new opportunities forms of farmers who became migrant workers in the urban industrial sector on the other. The ACFTU organisations' response to this process of marketisation is evaluated against the backdrop of their structural and resource constraints. The lack of independence of the union, the absence of right to strikes, and the economic determinism that informed much of the economic transformation period until recent years has meant that neither the unions nor the workers had much scope to voice their concerns and stem the tides of capitalism introduced in a socialist mode, or for some, under the socialist disguise. It is true that marketisation has brought significant improvement to the living standards of the majority of the population, including the families of the rural migrant workers, but the cost and risks associated with this has largely been borne by the individuals and collectively by the society in the case of environmental degradation.

However, it is important to note that the Chinese government has never accepted, and certainly not admitted in public, a full swing of neo-liberalism as that found in the US and the UK. On the contrary, the role of the state remains vital at various levels. Indeed, the role of the state as an employer has been significantly reduced, in terms of both the size of its workforce and the level of employment conditions. But its role as an economic manager and a market regulator has remained constant, as evidenced in its regular interventions to the market through legislation and policy regulations. The marketisation process is described by the government as 'marketising the economy with socialist characteristics' and that a 'crossing the river by feeling the stones' (gradual) approach has been adopted in contrast to the former Soviet Union's radical (shock therapy) model.

Within this broader politico-economic context, the responses of the ACFTU to the Chinese variant of neo-liberalism can be seen as straddling, somewhat loosely, between the first two categories outlined by Gall in this volume. That is, the ACFTU believes that marketisation and globalisation (by introducing FDI into China) are good for the Chinese economy and its people as a whole and should be supported, albeit this may be a coerced agreement and conditional support given the lack of political independence of the ACFTU. On the basis of this broader consensus to and support of marketisation, the ACFTU has been pushing for a more extensive and up-to-date provision of labour legislation and leading unionisation campaigns. As a number of authors have noted (including Taylor and Li 2007; Chan 2009), the role the ACFTU plays in influencing pro-labour legislation has not been given sufficient credit. Similarly, the positive attitude and efforts of at least a proportion of the union officials need to be acknowledged instead of simply branding them as an incompetent and even corrupted group indifferent to workers' needs and sufferings.

It must be emphasised that unions' response to the marketisation has largely been passive, reactive and episodic, and any strategy espoused by the ACFTU has mainly been achieved in numbers rather than in substantial and substantive improvements to the workers. Nevertheless, the ACFTU is responding to, albeit belatedly and slowly, the changing nature of employment relations by adopting new initiatives and strategies to organising the workers, with particular reference to the rural migrant workers. These include, for example, collective negotiation, collective contract system, tripartite consultation system, direct election, and welfare and other services. However, political, institutional and organisational constraints largely determine how far these changes can go (Liu *et al.* 2011). As Warner (2008) observed, the ACFTU plays multiple and at times conflicting roles, including being labour market actors, vehicles of anti-capitalist mobilisation, and agents of social integration.

Finally, in view of the ineffectiveness of the ACFTU, the roles of international organising bodies remain crucial in protecting Chinese workers' rights. These include: the role of International Labour Organisation in promoting labour standards and decent work, the role of international media in reporting human rights issues, the role of foreign client firms in pressing for corporate social responsibility and the role of NGOs in providing support to workers. But one should not have any illusion that any independent organising bodies would emerge to become a mainstream organiser of the labour movement in China without the backing of the CCP-state. Given the political role of the ACFTU and fundamental ideological differences, the prospect of strengthening relationships between the ACFTU and labour organisations of other countries remains unclear. In the meantime, 'with any fundamental union reform still in the distant future, we can expect workers increasingly to find their own ways to organise and resist workplace exploitation' (Howell 2008: 863).

ACKNOWLEDGEMENT

Part of this chapter draws on Cooke (2012).

REFERENCES

Chan, A. (1998), 'Labour relations in foreign-funded ventures', in Greg O'Leary (ed.), *Adjusting to Capitalism: Chinese Workers and their State*, Armonk, NY: M.E. Sharpe, pp. 122–49.

Chan, A. (2001), *China's Workers under Assault: The Exploitation of Labour in a Globalising Economy*, Armonk, NY: M. E. Sharpe.

Chan, C. (2009), 'Strike and changing workplace relations in a Chinese global factory', *Industrial Relations Journal*, **40**(1), 60–77.

Chen, F. (2003), 'Industrial restructuring and workers' resistance in China', *Modern China*, **29**(2), 237–62.

Chen, F. (2006), 'Privatisation and its discontents in Chinese factories', *The China Quarterly*, **185**, 42–60.

Chen, F. (2007), 'Individual rights and collective rights: Labour's predicament in China', *Communist and Post-Communist Studies*, **40**(1), 59–79.

Child, J. and D. Tse (2001), 'China's transition and its implications for international business', *Journal of International Business Studies*, **32**(1), 5–21

China Labour Bulletin (2009), '"Going it alone": the workers' movement in China (2007–8)', *China Labour Bulletin Research Reports*, accessed at www.clb.org.hk.

China Labor News Translations (2008), 'Promising Wal-Mart trade union chair resigns over collective contract negotiations', accessed at http://news.ifeng.com/opeinion/200807/0729.

China Labour Statistical Yearbook 2008 (2008), Beijing: China Statistics Press.

China Statistical Yearbook 2010 (2010), Beijing: China Statistics Press.

Clarke, S. (2005), 'Post-socialist trade unions: China and Russia', *Industrial Relations Journal*, **36**(1), 2–18.

Clarke, S. and T. Pringle (2009), 'Can party-led trade unions represent their members?', *Post-Communist Economics*, **21**(1), 85–101.

Cooke, F. (2007), 'Migrant labour and trade union's response and strategy in China', *The Indian Journal of Industrial Relations*, **42**(4), 558–84.

Cooke, F. (2008a), 'The dynamics of employment relations in China: an evaluation of the rising level of labour disputes', *Journal of Industrial Relations*, **50**(1), 111–138.

Cooke, F. (2008b), 'China: labour organisations representing women', in K. Broadbent and M. Ford (eds), *Woman Organising: Women and Union Activism in Asia*, London: Routledge, pp. 34–49.

Cooke, F. (2009), 'The enactment of three new labour Laws in China: unintended consequences and emergence of "new" actors in employment relations', presentation to the Regulating for Decent Work: Innovative Regulation as a Response to Globalization Conference of the *Regulating for Decent Work* network, Geneva: International Labour Office.

Cooke, F. (2011a) 'Employment relations in China', in G. Bamber and R. Lansbury (eds), *International and Comparative Employment Relations*, 5th edn, London: Sage and New South Wales, Australia: Allen and Unwin Pty Ltd, pp. 307–29.

Cooke, F. (2011b), 'Gender organizing in China: a study of female workers' representation needs and their perceptions of union efficacy', *International Journal of Human Resource Management*, **22**(12), 2558–74

Cooke, F. (2012), *Human Resource Management in China: New Trends and Practices*, London: Routledge.

Cooney S. (2007), 'China's labour law, compliance and flaws in implementing institutions', *Journal of Industrial Relations*, **49**(5), 673–86.

Feng, G. (2006), 'The "institutional weaknesses" of enterprise trade unions and their formative context', *Society*, **26**(3), 81–98.

Gallagher, M. (2005), *Contagious Capitalism: Globalisation and the Politics of Labour in China*, Princeton, NJ: University Press.

Harvey, A. (2009), *The China Price: The True Cost of Chinese Competitive Advantage*, London: Penguin Books.

Howell, J. (2008), 'All-China Federation of Trade Unions beyond reform? The slow march of direct elections', *The China Quarterly*, **196**, 845–63.

Huang, Y. (2008), *Capitalism with Chinese Characteristics: Entrepreneurship and the State*, New York: Cambridge University Press.

Kelly, J. and E. Heery (1989), 'Full-time officers and trade union recruitment', *British Journal of Industrial Relations*, **27**(2), 196–213.

Khanna, T. (2007), *Billions of Entrepreneurs: How China and India are Reshaping Their Futures and Yours*, Boston, MA: Harvard Business School Press.

Lee, C. (2007), *Against the Law: Labor Protests in China's Rustbelt and Sunbelt*, Berkeley, CA: University of California, Berkeley.

Lee, C. and Y. Shen (2008), 'The anti-solidarity machine: labor NGOs in China', in *International Conference 'Breaking down Chinese Walls: The Changing Faces of Labor and Employment in China'*, Ithaca, NJ: Cornell University.

Liu, M., C. Li and S. Kim (2011), 'The changing Chinese trade unions: a three level analysis', in P. Sheldon, S. Kim, Y. Li and M. Warner (eds), *China's Changing Workplace*, London: Routledge.

Meng, X. (2000), *Labour Market Reform in China*, Cambridge: Cambridge University Press.

Miles, R. and C. Snow (1978), *Organizational Strategy, Structure and Process*, New York: McGraw-Hill.

Nichols, T. and W. Zhao (2010), 'Disaffection with trade unions in China: some evidence from SOEs in the auto industry', *Industrial Relations Journal*, **41**(1), 19–33.

Nolan, P. (2001), *China and the Global Economy*, London: Palgrave.

O'Leary, G. (1998), 'The making of the Chinese working class', in G. O'Leary (ed), *Adjusting to Capitalism: Chinese Workers and the State*, Armonk, NY: M. E. Sharpe, pp. 48–74.

Oliver, C. (1997). 'Sustainable competitive advantage, combining institutional and resource-based views', *Strategic Management Journal*, **18**, 697–713.

Parris, K. (1999), 'The rise of private business interests', in M. Goldman and R. MacFarquhar (eds), *The Paradox of China's Post-Mao Reforms*, Cambridge, MA: Harvard University Press, pp. 262–82.

Perry, E. and M. Selden (2000), 'Introduction: reform and resistance in contemporary China', in E. Perry and M. Selden (eds), *Chinese Society: Change, Conflict and Resistance*, London: Routledge, pp. 1–19.

Prasad, M. (2006), *The Politics of Free Markets: The Rise of Neoliberal Economic Policies in Britain, France, Germany and the United States*, Chicago, IL: University of Chicago Press.

Pun, N. and C. Smith (2007), 'Putting transnational labour process in its place: the dormitory labour regime in post-socialist China', *Work, Employment and Society*, **21**(1), 27–45.

Pun, N. and L. Yang (2004), 'The Chinese working women's network', *Against the Current*, accessed at www.solidarity-us.org/atc/113luce.html.

Saich, T. (2001), *Governance and Politics of China*, Basingstoke: Palgrave.

Solinger, D. (1999), *Contesting Citizenship in Urban China: Peasant Migrants, the State, and the Logic of the Market*, Berkeley, CA: University of California Press, Berkeley.

The State Council (2006), *Report on Rural Migrant Workers in China*, Beijing: The State Council of China.

Taylor, B., K. Chang and Q. Li (2003), *Industrial Relations in China*, Cheltenham, UK and Northampton, MA, USA: Edward Elgar.

Taylor, B. and Q. Li (2007), 'Is the ACFTU a union and does it matter?', *Journal of Industrial Relations*, **49**(5), 701–15.

Warner, M. (2008), 'Trade unions in China: in search of a new role in the "Harmonious Society"', in J. Benson and Y. Zhu (eds), *Trade Unions in Asia: An Economic and Sociological Analysis*, London: Routledge, pp. 140–56.

Warner, M. and Y. Zhu (2010), 'Labour-management relations in the People's Republic of China: whither the "harmonious society"?', *Asia Pacific Business Review*, **16**(3), 267–81.
Zhu, J. M. (2004), 'Local developmental state and order in China's urban development during transition', *International Journal of Urban and Regional Research*, **28**(2), 424–47.

8 France: union responses to neo-liberalism
Sylvie Contrepois

INTRODUCTION

Despite the large victory of the left wing parties during the presidential national elections in 1981, the neo-liberal vogue spread very rapidly in France. Neo-liberalism is defined by Dumenil and Lévy (2001: 1) as the 'ideological expression to the return to hegemony of the financial fraction of the ruling class'. It expressed itself through financialisation of the French economy, privatisations of large companies and deregulation of labour legislation. Significantly, as early as 1984, the freezing of public sector wages became an entrenched and firm policy (*politique de rigueur*), prompting the Communist Party's ministers to leave the government, under pressure from its electorate. The shift towards neo-liberalism also affected the unions, which were increasingly becoming destabilised as a result of the weakening of the security of the labour force. Their place in the industrial relation system was directly challenged by a range of measures. The crises that they experienced during the 1980s and the 1990s placed them among the weakest of any union movements in Europe and created an abundant literature that explored the likelihood of their survival in a society more and more governed by neo-liberal concepts. A minority of analysts and commentators thought that they were simply destined to disappear under the tide of the neo-liberal onslaught. According to these analyses, the crisis revealed the ineffectiveness of the unions as 'mediating bodies' that had for a certain period usurped the sovereign power of citizens. Alternatively, others argued that the union decline was the result of the capitalist system's considerable adaptive capacity, which had become able to neutralise collective conflicts via the development of participative human resource management techniques (Durand 1996).

The force of these arguments became more difficult to repel from the beginning of the second millennium. However, some other arguments, developed during the same period from the 1980s onwards, have equally lost their value. These analysed the union crisis as a process whose eventual end point will be the transformation of unions into institutions fully integrated into the capitalist system. Some raised the emergence of an era of service unionism (Rosanvallon 1988; Labbé and Croisat 1992). Nonetheless, relative membership stability and the reappearance of collective conflicts, still largely led by union organisations, have in recent years made commentators more cautious in their forecasts. Most of them now identify three main challenges unions face in order to retain their position as major actors in civil society, namely taking into account the growing diversity of the workforce, launching a new independent and alternative project to counter neo-liberalism, and developing interventions articulated at national, European and global levels (Andolfatto and Labbé 2007a; Mouriaux 2009). Several studies (Béroud and Bouffartigue 2009; Contrepois 2003) show how these challenges are, at least partially, being taken up. In order to understand the changes taking place, the concept of the 'subversive institution' (Contrepois 2005a) is deployed. This concept allows us to understand the full complexity of the union movement, taking into account both its role as a 'representative institution' – defined as a stable group of actions or practices that help regulate the way society works (Contrepois 2005b) – and as a 'social resistance movement' whose strength, while fluctuating, is, nonetheless, being continuously renewed (see also Cohen 2006). The chapter begins by examining the restructuring of French capital and the role of state action. Several state reforms have effectively increased the competition between unions and other forms of independent representation, and the chapter sketches out these outcomes. Finally, the chapter focuses upon analysing the renewal of union capacity and union objectives in the light of the way unions have responded to neo-liberalism through their strategies and actions.

LEFT AND RIGHT NEO-LIBERALISM

French Capital Restructuring

The 1973 oil price hike and slowing down of the world economy is often associated with the beginning of the crisis in France and the acceleration of the restructuring of French capital. The first noticeable trend has been the reduction in size of workplaces by workers employed in a context where companies are becoming much bigger than they were 30 years ago as a concentration of capital develops. In 2006, one third of workers were working in companies employing more than 1000 workers, compared to 27 per cent in 1985 (Cottet 2010). By contrast, 38 per cent of workers were in workplaces of fewer than 20 people in 2006, as against 34 per cent in 1985 (Cottet 2010). While this is the general trend, the situation varies to the particular sectors. The industrial sector became weaker, shedding on average 1.7 per cent of its workforce per year from 1979 to 2006, such that 4.5m citizens worked in this sector in 1979, compared to 3m by 2006 (Cottet 2010). This decrease occurred mainly in large plants of more than 1000 workers, which employed 23 per cent of the industrial workforce in 1979 but only 13 per cent in 1994 (Cottet 2010). During the same period, small plants with fewer than 50 workers increased their share of employment of the industrial workforce from 22 per cent in 1979 to 33 per cent in 1994 (Cottet 2010). This trend is mainly linked to the increased use of subcontracting. After 1994, the size of workplaces by workers employed remained stable but those with more than 1,000 workers increased their relative weight, employing 40 per cent of the industrial workforce in 1994 and 45 per cent in 2006. By contrast, services grew rapidly, employing twice as many workers in 2006 than in 1979. In this sector, small workplaces and enterprises dominate as has traditionally been the case. From 1990, these companies began to develop formal alliances and their size grew rapidly. The retail sector has also grown, but in a different way. The size of shops has become bigger as has the size of the companies. In 2006, 29 per cent of these workers in food retailing worked in small shops (compared to 48 per cent in 1979) and 71 per cent worked in super- and hyper-markets.

A second trend is linked to globalisation. Jefferys (2003: 161) noted that 'Compared to one-third non-French ownership of all French publicly quoted firms, the flagship French groups are on average even more exposed to non-French shareholders, and this exposure is increasing'. The share of the top 40 quoted firms on the French Bourse held by non-French residents was 41 per cent or 45 per cent if France Télécom and Orange are excluded (*Le Monde* 15 June 2001). The same study found still higher levels of foreign ownership among large French finance capital. Thus, AGF (54 per cent owned by the German giant, Allianz) was 73 per cent foreign-owned, Axa was 52 per cent foreign-owned, BNP-Paribas 40 per cent and Crédit Lyonnais 35 per cent. The growth in the number of French firms significantly exposed to global stock market influence is directly linked to the deliberate retreat of the state. A third trend is the privatisation of large companies from 1986, under the cohabitation President Chirac's government. Some of these companies such as Paribas or Saint-Gobain had been nationalised in 1981. The vogue of privatisation included several industrial companies and banks, but also parts of the strategic public services like EDF (electricity), GDF (gas), SNCF (railway), Air France (airway) and hospitals. This trend has continued until the present day, whatever the political leanings of the various governments in office. Between 1986 and 2002, 3000 public companies employing 1m workers were privatised.

The banking sector provides a significant example of the restructuring which occurred as a result of these processes from the beginning of the 1980s. The 1984 Banking Law specifically encouraged inter-bank and inter-sector competition. Beginning in 1986, and continuing up to the state's disposal of its last 10 per cent of Crédit Lyonnais in 2002, a major part of French banking was placed back into private hands. From July 1994 the European insurance market has been totally open to full competition (Bellando *et al.* 1994: 125–136). There have been major waves of both national and international bank take-overs and mergers forming huge international groups, while the traditional divisions between retail and mutual banking, on the one hand, and banking and insurance on the other, have become increasingly blurred. The scale of such mergers is staggering. The dividing lines between financial products are collapsing and the degree of concentration across the sector is growing. Whereas intra-bank competition was once 'gentlemanly,' it is now frantic and desperate. Globalisation has thus led to changes in the scope of the banking market (which is now increasingly international), and in the content of the banking product (now much more focused on selling services than ever before) (Regini *et al.* 1999).

According to Jefferys (2003: 128), despite these transformations the French state remains at the heart of the organisation of relations between capital and labour. Three factors help explain this huge influence: the massive budget it wields – the French government accounts for 44 per cent of the country's gross domestic product in taxes and social security deductions; its role in appointing the chief executives of all the nationalised companies in which it holds all or a majority of shares; and the six million people it effectively employs along with the up to two million more whose wages it pays at one step removed. Depending on how the counting is done, this means the state employs between one in five and one in four of the whole French active working population, and nearly one third of all those in salaried employment.

Finally, a fourth phenomenon must be noted. In a context of high level of company profitability, the share of wages as a percentage of added value decreased from the middle of the 1980s. After 1990, it stabilised under the level it was in the 1960s. At the same time, the rate of company investment was decreasing from the 1950s (Bournay and Pionnier 2007). Linked to strategic management decisions prioritising the financial market, this double-sided phenomenon had several effects. One of these was the slowing down of purchasing. Its growth has been on average 2 per cent per year since 1975 instead of the 5.6 per cent between 1960 and 1975. Another direct effect is the stabilisation of high levels of unemployment. This reached 9 per cent at the beginning of the 1980s, then comprising between 10 per cent and 12 per cent during the 1990s, and between 8 per cent and 10 per cent since 2000. Also, because of labour law deregulation, labour contracts themselves became more casual and more often reduced to part-time jobs. As a result, the number of people living under the French poverty line has been growing, with 0.5m added to their number per year between 2002 and 2008. The number of poor thus comprised between 4.3m and 7.8m in 2008, depending on the definition used.

The Evolution of the French Institutional Framework

It is in such a context that the French state attempted to modify the institutional place of the unions. First of all, the *'ordre public social'* has been challenged over recent decades as the role of the unions in company-level bargaining has altered. At the same time, the rules governing union representation have been changed and more protection against being victimised for union activity was introduced. The *'ordre public social'* is a fundamental principle of labour law and a specific feature of French employment relations (Morin 1994). It assures priority in law to collective agreements, and provides a legal hierarchy between different levels of agreement. Collective agreements are only permitted to improve existing terms and conditions for workers and they do so within a juris-dictional framework that stipulates that national level inter-sector agreements hold sway over sector-level agreements, and that the latter hold sway over company-level agreements. From 1982, when authorisation was first given to the conclusion of agreements that were less favourable than the law in terms of the organisation of working time, this structure has been progressively under-mined. Just over a decade later, with the national-level agreement of 31 October 1995 and the law of 12 November 1996, derogations started to be permitted in the rules governing the conduct of negotiations as far as SMEs were concerned. The 1980s and 1990s witnessed a series of legislative measures encouraging the decentralisation of collective bargaining and encouraging workplace-level nego-tiations. In this situation, the two Aubry laws (of 1998 and 2000) contributed to the joint development of both company- and sector-level negotiations.

Still more recently the Lifelong Learning and Social Dialogue law of 4 May 2004 generalised the possibility of making agreements involving derogations from higher level agreements in lower level negotiations (at sector or at company level), and thus modified the traditional hierarchy of agreements. From this point on, company-level agreements were no longer obliged to comply with the sector agreements, unless these expressly indicated there was a compulsory sector minimum in one of four areas: a minimum wage, job clas-sifications, additional social welfare protection, and professional training. And at the same time, sector agreements no longer had to respect the minima deter-mined by national-level agreements unless, again, the latter expressly required it. A second significant development concerns the evolution in the rules governing union representation. A 1966 law decreed that five employee union confederations should have the permanent status of representative unions. The five are the Confédération Générale du Travail (CGT), the Confédération Française et Démocratique du Travail (CFDT), the Confédération Générale du Travail-Force Ouvrière (FO), the Confédération Française des travailleurs Chrétiens (CFTC) and, only in relation to white collar and managerial work-ers, the Confédération Générale des Cadres (CGC).

In 1982, the same full legal recognition was given to the five confederations at company level, even if they did not have a presence in the firm. Thus, until 2008, however many members they had, and however many workers voted for them, the five main legally-recognised confederations effectively held a monopoly over the right to put up candidates in the first round of works council elections in all companies, without having to prove that they were representative of a firm's workers. In addition, they were officially endowed with a whole range of responsibilities, principally the elaboration and implementation of work regulations, as well as the management of social welfare organisations. As a result of their participation in these missions, the state, the jointly–run welfare organisations and many companies ensured that they received the necessary legally-backed means to carry them out: facility time paid by public sector firms and large companies was put at the disposal of both confederations and sector union federations, as well as grants.

Also, on the basis of these representation rules, representatives of unions in France have been given the right to negotiate agreements on the terms and conditions of work in the profession or the company. But, since 6 November 1996 decision of the Constitutional Court Council alternative methods of collective bargaining are now permitted in companies that do not have union delegates, although a union role is still maintained. The Council (*Official Journal* 13 November 1996: 16531) decided, in effect, that 'workers who had been elected or who held mandates guaranteeing their representation can also participate in the collective determination of working conditions as long as their interventions has neither the object nor the effect of placing obstacles to the interventions of the representative union organisations'.

Furthermore, the law passed on 20 August 2008 abolished the legally-binding representative status for the five main unions and introduced new criteria for representation. There are now seven of these, and each has to be met. They concern respect for republican values, union independence, financial transparency, the length of time the union has existed, its influence, its number of members and the numbers who vote for it. This final criterion is the central one for the whole reform, and it will be measured at every election forcing all the unions to regularly prove their representativeness. Thus, in the workplace elections the only recognised unions will be those that have exceeded the minimum level of 10 per cent of all votes. The 20 August 2008 law also includes a section about the validity of collective agreements. From 1 January 2009, company-level agreements will only be valid if the unions signing them secured at least 30 per cent of the votes in the first round of the relevant workplace elections. This measure will become law in 2012 for sector-level and national-level agreements.

One final aspect of the recent reforms concerns the tightening of the rules over union victimisation. In France, union freedom has carried constitutional weight ever since the preamble to the 1946 Fourth Republic Constitution, and referred to in the Fifth Republic Constitution of 1958, guaranteed both the individual right to belong to a union and the right to act as a unionist: 'Every person can defend their rights and interests through union activity and through joining a union of their choice'. Every person, whatever their gender, age or nationality, has the option of joining a union of their choice, where there are several. The law thus outlaws any difference in treatment between unionists and non-unionists, both at recruitment and throughout a person's career. To support these rights and, following the two equality 2000 European directives a law passed on 16 November 2001, the burden of proof of discrimination changed in the Labour Code. From this moment on, it was only necessary for an employee to show to the judge 'evidence pointing to direct or indirect discrimination', and in the light of this evidence it became the responsibility of the employer 'to prove that their decision was based on facts that had nothing to do with any form of discrimination'. The judge would then determine the case after having ordered all the investigations he considered necessary.

FRENCH UNION STRENGTH AND POWER TODAY

The impact of these economic and legal transformations on French unionism was real but not unequivocal. Over the last three decades, unions have lost both members and a wider audience but simultaneously increased their presence within the workplace.

Membership and Influence Decline

Several studies have tried to assess the scale of union membership decline. The experts conclude that membership declined by more than half, falling from a little over four million in the aftermath of World War II to around two million by the end of the 1990s, a level that has now been stabilised. A changing economic structure is one of the major explanations for this decline. The shift away from huge traditional industrial firms towards both many more SMEs and towards very large national and international groups of privately-owned limited liability companies have contributed to make union presence more difficult. At the same time, the national workforce doubled in size. The result of these two tendencies is that in 60 years, French union density has been fallen to a quarter of what it was, from 25 to 6.5 per cent (Amossé and Pignoni 2006). Andolfatto and Labbé (2007b: 11), for their part, calculated that 'around the start of the twenty-first century there were 1.9m union members, of whom 1.7m were not-retired, equivalent to a union density of 7.2%, the lowest level of all major developed countries. This situation is new ... While the machinery remains very solid, unionism has lost the members and activists that in the past ensured its social roots and legitimacy.' Their estimate is based on figures from the population census provided by the National Statistics Institute (INSEE) and on corrections they carried out to the information provided by the union confederations. The unions' own figures at the start of the 2000s indicated 3.2m working and retired members. The three biggest confederations, the CGT, the CFDT and FO, declared 675 000 to 800 000 members (Andolfatto and Labbé 2007b: 79). According to the figures provided by the confederations, French union density would be somewhere between 12 and 14 per cent, taking into account the proportion of retired workers included in the calculation. This long-term decline must, however, be seen in perspective. Thus, as Mouriaux shows (1998: 49–113, 2009), French union members were very thin on the ground from the very beginning. The period of the '30 glorious years' thus constitutes an exception, linked to the very particular post-war context. It is also the case that there has been a relative stability in union numbers during the 1990s.

The trend is very similar in terms of participating in elections. The numbers actually voting in Employment Tribunal elections (*prud'homales*) fell from 7.8m in 1979 to 4.8m in 2008, while the numbers entitled to vote rose from 12.7m to 18.7m. This produced a spectacular fall in the proportion voting: down from 61 per cent in 1979 to 25.5 per cent in 2008. The fall in participation is much less in the other employment-linked elections that take place within private companies and public sector organisations. In the elections for works council delegates, for example, participation has only fallen by 8 percentage points over 40 years, declining from 72 per cent in the 1966/1967 two-yearly election cycle to 63 per cent in 2005/2006. The trend has also been less clear over time, with increases taking place at certain moments. However, the share of the total vote going to the five main union confederations has fallen significantly, benefiting non-union candidates. From the 1990s, they have taken the largest single share of the vote: 29 per cent in the 1990/1991 election cycle compared to 15 per cent in 1966/1967. This phenomenon is primarily linked to the extension of works council elections into the SME sector as, over the same period, the total number of works councils rose from 8600 to 25 000. The unions found it very difficult to get candidates to stand in SMEs. It is important, however, not to overstate the importance of this trend, since the proportion of non-union affiliated works council delegates has declined somewhat in the 2000s. Thus, non-union candidates only received 23.5 per cent of the votes cast in the 2004/2005 electoral cycle. The other side of this coin is, thus, an increasing proportion of workplaces where elected union representatives are present.

A Stronger Organisational Presence but Less Power

According to Amossé and Pignoni (2006: 405), 'The organisational presence of unions has become stronger: in 2004 more than half of all wage earners reported that a union was present within their company or public sector organisation, and that most of the welfare state funds they contribute to are managed jointly by the employers and the unions'. This 'union renewal' experience was examined by Dufour (2005) in research on works councils funded by the Ministry of Labour (DARES). Analysing the results of the election cycles from 1998/1999 and 2000/2001, he found that the advance of the 'union voice' was clearly linked to a retrenchment of the 'non-union voice' in the context of a significant decline in electoral participation. At the same time, within the SMEs, the extension of the 'union voice' appeared to be a sign of a trend towards the 'normalisation' of practices in relation to employee representation and union presence. On the basis of a complementary case study examination of 19 workplaces, Dufour (2005: 116) concluded that most of the situations studied were quite fragile, whatever the characteristics of the workplace and the longevity of a employer-union relationship: 'With only two exceptions, the teams of representatives we met did not have continuous structured relations with their unions, although there were some individual contacts. The unionisation of employee representatives, and particularly of works councils, is becoming increasingly an individual matter'. In concluding, Dufour examined the employer's position in relation to the employee representative institutions. He concluded that management is now more respectful of the institutions and unions. But union weakness on the ground, the lack of articulation between the different representative institutions, the individualisation of representative mandates and the difficulties in finding new representatives, have all confirmed that these institutions are highly fragile, and often only have a formal existence.

Employee representative institutions now cover practically all French workplaces with more than 20 workers. Reading it, if we take the two possible polar positions, there is at least one representative institution present in almost every workplace with more than 500 workers, and in two-thirds of workplaces with between 20 and 49 workers (Jacod 2007). This stronger institutional presence does not mean that unions extended their power accordingly. In 2002, Béroud *et al.* (2003) produced a report called 'Working time reductions and industrial relations: the consequences of negotiations for the 35-hour week on company-level industrial relations'. On the basis of research in 12 firms that had moved on to the 35-hour week, they concluded that the decentralisation of negotiations had helped shift the balance of forces away from the unions. In particular, Béroud *et al.* (2003: 159) noted that:

faced with the problems of training the negotiators, of keeping close links with grass-roots, and of keeping the workers as fully informed as possible about the course of the negotiations, on what were often very technical issues, the unions were simply overwhelmed by the scale of the task, that was also spread over several months. Isolated, they were required to respond to complex draft proposals that needed technical knowledge while also having to satisfy the workers' expectations and to relieve their concerns. (Beroud *et al.* 2003: 1159)

A second study by Kerbourch *et al.* (2008) specifically examined the 4 May 2004 law on derogations in company-level agreements. They concluded that derogations were rarely used by the employers and that many sectoral agreements continued to specifically rule out the possibility. According to them, the employers did not really require them. Their research suggested that small firms used to prefer to negotiate with elected personnel representatives rather than with union delegates, while big firms were often satisfied with the quite flexible body of rules that already made up their sectoral collective agreements. Kerbourch *et al.* (2008: 52) argued 'From this angle some employer representatives clearly expressed their wish that sector and company-level negotiations didn't start competing with each other, as the result would be to weaken the sector. The idea should remain that company-level negotiation should limit itself to the issues that had not been negotiated at sector level (the logic of complementarity)'. In the end, Kerbourch *et al.* (2008: 2) found that 'the law had had paradoxical effects on the articulation of levels of negotiation, and in particular had led to strengthen the power of the sectoral agreements over the terms and conditions of workers in the different sectors.'

Finally, the measures improving the chances of legal redress in cases of union victimisation appear to have had a small effect. One of the indicators on this issue is the number of dismissals of protected workers (such as union delegates, works councillors, personnel delegates, and health and safety representatives). These have been relatively stable for quite a long time, varying each year between 10 000 and 13 000 employer requests to the Labour Inspectorate, of which slightly more than 80 per cent are accepted. Something like three-quarters of these dismissals are of non-unionists, and in their case there are not only a higher proportion of employer requests, but also they are more likely to have their dismissals accepted. Where union representatives are dismissed, half of all cases involve members of the CGT. Another indicator of the partial effectiveness of steps taken against union victimisation is the numbers of claims on this issue put before the Employment Tribunals (*les tribunaux de prud'hommes*). Since the application of the 2001 law, all the unions have taken up this question and have developed a systematic way of establishing claims linked to wage discrimination, to discrimination in career prospects, to redundancies or to favouritism shown towards one union to the detriment of others. Cases taken up in this way have often been fought successfully.

Among the cases that have recently been taken to courts in France are ones against Snecma, Compagnie des wagons lits, IBM, Arcelor-Mittal, Caisse d'épargne, primaire d'assurance maladie, Sagem, the Agence France Presse and Renault Trucks.

So, the reforms have had different consequences for the unions. The 'ordre public social' remains essentially unchanged. In theory, the unions still retain a relatively significant weight in the way the whole system is regulated. But, in a context where the balance of forces is less favourable, national and sector level agreements now only lay down the absolute minimum regulations, and finally leave much wider room to manoeuvre to the employers. Consequently, the decentralisation of negotiations places greater responsibility on the work-place level activists who are not always equipped to deal with challenge of the complex issues they face. The situation has been worse where the employee representatives are non-union because they have fewer resources to call upon than the union representatives, who at least can benefit from the technical, human and logistical support of their organisation. These non-union represen-tatives are even more vulnerable to redundancies than are their union equiva-lents.

ARE FRENCH UNIONS STILL SUBVERSIVE?

French unions are bedevilled and gripped in contradictions. On the one hand, they are well embedded institutions, and on the other, they little manifest power. This paradox makes them dependent upon the strategic renewal of the social movements of which they are a part. If subversion is to be 'actions that trouble, that turnover the existing state of things, laws or established princi-ples' (French Language Larousse Dictionary 1972 edition), we can suggest the hypothesis that as voluntary organisations the unions include many with such views of turning over the existing order.

Strategic Choices and Demands Driving Contestation

The French union movement reacted in different ways to the changes it under-went. From the 1980s, the two biggest confederations, the CGT and the CFDT, shifted their political orientation. The CGT partially renounced its commitment to 'class struggle' in order to join the European Union Confederation. It still believed in opposition and resistance to capitalist globa-lisation but no longer advocated socialism as the alternative. The CFDT aban-doned its support for workers' control (*autogestion*) and adopted a more pragmatic attitude, accepting most of the proposals made by the employers and right-wing governments. It argued that workers need some strategic protection/state action in order to compete fairly and successfully as well as to protect them from the worst effects of neo-liberal globalisation and 'the race to the bottom'. As a result of these changes of direction, divisions occurred and gave rise to new radical union federations like SUD. The activists from this kind of federation reject socialism as an alternative but believe in opposition and resistance to capitalist and neo-liberal globalisation. SUD as member of G10 (group of ten independent trade unions) contributed to create the French branch of the alter-world organisation, ATTAC. Moreover, a number of major labour conflicts took place, sometimes beyond the control of union organisations. Some of these started in the national railway company, SNCF, and spread to the rest of the economy (in 1988, 1995 and 2003). Other strikes – often responses to job cuts – remained limited to single companies but became famous for their radicalism and their length.

For the last 30 years, the right to work has been a headline demand of the union movement. The CGT, for example, has thus developed two new demands that it is putting at the centre of most of its struggles: one being for 'a new status of waged work', and the other being for 'occupational social security'. In both cases, the demands aim to attach cumulative and transferable social rights to the individual, so they can be moved from one firm to another in order to enable occupational mobility to take place while guaranteeing there are sufficient resources to support it. The other main demands – for wages, union rights, training and so on – are not less important, and it is quite common to see leaflets from all different unions presenting lists of all the changes they deem necessary. Nonetheless, a certain coherence between these different demands is being developed in union discourse around two strong arguments: the recognition of the vital role of workers in society, who cannot be treated as simple inputs like factors of production, and the pushing forward in opposition to financial logic of the concept of 'social efficiency'.

Contrepois (2003) noted that the unions are not allowing themselves to be trapped by analyses based on property rights, as laid down in substantive law. Instead, claiming recognition of the legitimacy of the workgroup, they often use the prerogatives provided to them by the company-level representative institutions to intervene on economic issues. The company strategy, its management methods, its industrial policies are, thus, all objects of systematic analysis and of union positions. The defence of a productive capacity and of public services then appear as an objective that is closely linked to the improvement in collective guarantees for the workers. These general positions, however, do not always lead to specific proposals being made by the unions. Thus, for example, in response to a management attempt to tighten the criteria for assessing productive efficiency, the unions will not necessarily propose other ways of carrying out an assessment. Yet this absence of concrete counter-proposals does not itself signify the absence of alternative approaches.

Rather, the union approach is to raise their demands at the level of social efficiency in society rather than attempt to respond at the level of the individual company. In this context, it appears difficult to categorise workers' demands in terms of 'defensive' (such as, for example, the retention of acquired employment and welfare rights) or 'offensive' (which could be for giving back productivity gains to the workers or for alternative modes of management). From a more general perspective, the preservation and improvement of collective guarantees can be understood as part of the process of asserting the importance of the work collective. The fact there is a relative consensus around this dynamic, however, does not mean there are not many and divisive debates among the unions about which are the actual demands to be raised. This review of the demands being raised suggests that the unions are trying in practice to raise broad projects and strategic visions about power. A major effort is being deployed to put in place procedures that will permit some control to be exercised over major management decisions.

Renewal of Union Strength

However much they have become institutionalised, French union organisations remain essentially voluntary organisations which workers are free to recognise as representing their interests or not. Examining the means by which they have been able to renew some of their strength shed some light on the way they are responding to neo-liberalism. Union membership has become more diverse, and now includes, most significantly, technicians and other workers from 'intermediate professions', as well as managers and women. One significant trend is the increase in public sector union representation. According to Andolfatto and Labbé's (1997b: 133–7) estimates, it appears that, in the mid-1990s, unions were most strongly represented in the teaching profession, in civil service and local public government and welfare administration, as well as in the medical and social work professions. The iron and steel industry ranked only fourth. It was closely followed by the transport and public utilities industries, by the postal and telecommunication services, and by the energy sector. This shift towards public sector union membership, which was slowed somewhat by the waves of privatisation since the early 1980s, is part of a wider phenomenon, namely a reorientation to the service economy. Indeed, the first three sectors in which unions are well represented are principally composed of clerical and technical workers and managers, which suggest that the archetypal French union member is now a white-collar worker.

The presence of women within the unions has also increased, although equal gender representation is still far from common at every level of the union hierarchy. Women now account for roughly 30 per cent of membership, and roughly 15 per cent to 20 per cent of union executive bodies. This is, of course, an average rate, as their representation varies widely from one organisation to another, and from one type of leadership responsibility to another (Contrepois 2006). We know little, by contrast, about the presence of ethnic minority workers and the more vulnerable categories of workers within the unions. From various testimonies and academic work, we assume it is quite low. According to union officials, it remains exceedingly difficult to reach out to the more vulnerable categories of workers in today's economy or to make headway in the less highly-concentrated industries. Despite numerous voluntarist initiatives reported, there has been little progress either in unionising workers in subcontractor firms or, more generally, in small firms. Nor has there been much success in organising part-time workers, workers on fixed-term contracts, or the unemployed.

Béroud *et al.* (2007: 25) examined the problems for union recruitment, summarising the situation:

> The relation between precarious workers and collective action seems to unfold within a dilemma: on the one hand, the voluntarism of the current representation structures is absolutely necessary to try and reach out to workers who find themselves structurally outside the constituencies of these structures; on the other hand, the creation of a specific identity for precarious workers also appears to fail to enable them to assert themselves within the representative arrangements of the totality of workers and to stimulate change from within. (Béroud *et al.* 2007: 25)

We can note that the union presence changes in relation to the transformation of the working class, albeit with a certain time lag. The main factors explaining the lag include the problems of mobilising groups whose legitimacy is denied, the presence of identity issues and the material organisation of production relations.

Motives for Union Activism

Studies of an industrial area in the Paris region towards the end of the 1990s (Contrepois 2003) and in the bank sector in the early 2000s (Contrepois and Jefferys 2004) showed that the dynamics of pro-union propensity and of union activism remained essentially based on the desire to collectively defend workers' occupational interests. In both, interviewee respondents explained their decisions to join a union and this suggested only very weak generational differences. Volition to join usually took place as a result of the unions' search for candidates to stand in workplace elections or of specific appeals to do so from an existing union. Among the white collar and management workers, those who unionised did so more clearly with a view to defending their own rights. But overall, the mechanisms at the origin of union propensity remained similar, closely correlated with the work situation that individuals found themselves in. Those activists studied still tended to refer to distinctive and independent cultures of struggle, often including anti-capitalist elements. Although the content of their activism has been significantly modified by the evolutions that have taken place in the role of representatives and in union strength, the findings suggested that activists' guiding motivations have changed surprisingly little, still being largely focused around the demand for social justice. Finally, the propensity of workers to organise to defend their interests appears to be more or less related to the objective conditions in which they find themselves. Work organisation and the traditions left by history are the principal factors in this. When they do organise themselves, workers still tend to choose a union organisation. And most often, this is a union affiliated to one of the five representative union confederations. Two basic reasons explain this. First, the unions are theoretically independent and lasting structures with the capacity to organise collective action. Next, the representative union confederations have more room to manoeuvre than do the others. It is also the case that the representative union confederations are also attempting, with more or less success, to implement strategies aiming to maintain as wide a membership base as possible, in response to the evolving labour market. Despite their weakness, they still largely cover the whole country and remain accessible to a very large number of workers.

Continuing Conflict

The union movement still plays a key role in the organisation of most disputes, even if it is sometimes overwhelmed or overtaken by self-organising groups of workers. But where this does happen, workers' 'coordinations' often effectively comprise a consensual way of democratically managing inter-union rivalries, at the same time as giving access to workers who refuse to choose between the different unions. Until recent years, the official measurement of labour conflict was mainly performed through an indicator established by the government departments that dealt with labour issues: individual days not worked due to strike action (*journées individuelles non travaillées pour fait de grève* or 'JINT'). This indicator has declined nearly continuously since the 1970s. The Ministry of Labour counted 3m JINT in the private sector at the end of the 1970s, but only 250 000 to 500 000 JINT in the middle of the 1990s. Only the period between 1995 and 2003 and probably the years 2009 and 2010 represented departures from this declining trend in open labour conflicts. The number of national strike days and inter-sector strike actions which exceptionally increased during those years concerned essentially the public sector and major nationalised companies. According to Béroud *et al.* (2008: 12–21), the scope of investigation covered by the official statistical monitoring system has major bias and ignores many collective labour disputes. A recent survey conducted by the French Ministry of Labour shows that after having taken into account other forms of action over and beyond the two days of strike action, the propensity for collective disputes has actually intensified during the last decade. In 30 per cent of establishments, the management acknowledged that at least one form of dispute had occurred between 2002 and 2004. This proportion was only 21 per cent between 1996 and 1998 (Béroud *et al.* 2008: 29). This increase, equally noted from answers provided by staff representatives, concerns all sectors. It contrasts with the decline in the number of JINTs recorded in the statistics, from 999 400 JINTs for the years from 1996 to 1998, down to 665 300 JINTs for 2002–2004. All forms of dispute, therefore, do not evolve in the same way. The increase in the proportion of establishments with disputes without work stoppages (up by 6.9 per cent) is much more pronounced than that of establishments having experienced collective disputes with work stoppages (up by 2.4 per cent). In addition, the frequency of short work stoppages has increased, whereas the number of strikes of more than two days is the only type of action to have slightly declined between the two periods studied.

Other research provides further information about union methods. One study (Contrepois 2003) in the industrial area of Corbeil-Essonnes observed three main strategies. One was based on a systematic investment in the industrial relations' representative institutions, with the main aim of making them take up union concerns. This often led the representatives to go beyond the legal limits that strictly circumscribe their rights to social matters to go into the areas of economics and management. The consequence was that not only were the employers required to explain their strategies and questioned publicly on the 'societal' relevance of their choices, but that their ability to act is also more strictly regulated. Increasingly vigilant about the application of rules, unions often demanded that clauses specifying control mechanisms are included in agreements, and hesitated less and less in taking up legal proceedings to enforce them. A second strategy was based on the mobilisation of public opinion. The strike, in particular, is becoming a media event. It provides, as such, an opportunity to look for alliances in the associative and political worlds, and to appeal to the local population, asking them to take up a position. The third strategy was based on the focusing upon directly talking to workers when the cooperation of individuals is needed, but also on creating ways of directly and more effectively consulting the workers. This happens indirectly, through union members going to their fellow workers, and directly, in particular through a greater and more systematic use of information technology. The direct democracy which is being developed here is an echo of the strong aspirations for it that were expressed by the coordination movement of the 1980s.

CONCLUSION

In the early twenty first century, French unions remain institutions whose strength is based on a very broad legal and regulatory arsenal that the neo-liberal orientations of several governments have so far been unable to desta-bilise. They may be characterised by their insertion into a system of national and international rules that define the forms of worker collective representa-tion. This insertion involves a dialectical relationship: it is as much the subject, as active player as it is the object that is acted upon. If the unions must, them-selves, conform to the procedures and accept the processes and the formal rules prescribing what actions they may take, they can at the same time act to try and modify these rules and procedures (Reynaud 1993). At the same time, they retain the fragility and vulnerability of voluntary organisations which draw their *raison d'être* from challenging the dominant power relations. The idea of 'subversive' unionism that we have used here referred to two main hypotheses. The first proposes a relative continuity over time in the value systems that underlie activist involvement and political demands. The rejec-tion of human exploitation, the promotion of ideas of dignity, of individual and collective self-fulfilment, and of solidarity today make up, as they did yesterday, the key levers used to challenge the basis of the current system's work and social organisation. And even if pragmatism is currently in vogue, this group of counter-values continues to strongly structure work relations, and more widely, the expressions of French citizenship. The second hypothesis concerns the strategies chosen by the unions. Anxious to preserve their inde-pendence, they currently prioritise a collective and transversal approach that goes beyond the frontiers of the workplace; they remain committed to consult-ing their base, and they seek to create or improve the balance of forces in their favour through externalising conflicts. The concept of 'subversive institution' allows an understanding of both these of these as well as their continuities in all their complexity. It throws light upon a paradox often emphasised by foreign observers surprised by the big gap between the ideological importance of the French union movement and its numerical weakness.

REFERENCES

Amossé, T. and M. Pignoni (2006), 'La transformation du paysage syndical depuis 1945', in INSEE (ed.), *Données Sociales – La Société Française*, Paris: INSEE, pp. 405–12.

Andolfatto, D. and D. Labbé (2007a), *Histoire des syndicats (1906–2006)*, Paris: Seuil.

Andolfatto, D. and D. Labbé (2007b), *Les syndiqués en France, Qui? Combien? Où?*, Paris: Editions Liaisons.

Bellando, J., H. Bouchaert and A. Scher (1994), *L'assurance dans le marché unique*, Paris: La Documentation française.

Béroud, S. and P. Bouffartigue (2009), *Quand le travail se précarise, quelles résistances collectives?*, Paris: La Dispute.

Béroud, S., J. Denis, G. Desage, B. Giraud and J. Pélisse (2008), *La lutte continue? Les conflits du travail dans la France contemporaine*, Paris: Editions du Croquant.

Béroud, S., J. Denis, C. Duffour, A. Hege and J. Pernot (2007), *Flexibilité et action collective. Salariés précaires et représentation syndicale*, Paris: DARES.

Béroud S., L. Chelly and J. Capdevieille (2003), *Working time reductions and industrial relations: the consequences of negotiations for the 35-hour week on company-level industrial relations*, Paris: DARES.

Bournay J. and P. Pionnier (2007), *L'économie française : ruptures et continuités de 1959 à 2006*, *Insee Première*, no 1136, Paris: INSEE.

Cohen, S. (2006), *Ramparts of Resistance: why workers lost their power, and how to get it back*, London: Pluto Press.

Contrepois S. (2003), *Syndicats, la nouvelle donne. Enquête au cœur d'un bassin industriel de la région parisienne*, Paris: Syllepse.

Contrepois, S. (2005a), 'Unionism: roads to renewal', *Labor History*, **46**(3), 362–8.

Contrepois S. (2005b), 'De la pertinence du concept "d'institution subversive" pour penser le syndicalisme de salariés contemporain', Communication aux dixième journées de sociologie du travail, Rouen.

Contrepois S. (2006), 'France: un accès encore inégal et partiel aux différentes sphères de la représentation syndicale', *Recherches féministes*, **19**(1), 25–45.

Contrepois, S. and S. Jefferys (2004), *Globalisation, Relocation and the Challenge to Bank Trade Unions in France and Britain*, Lisbon: European Congress of International Industrial Relations Association.

Cottet V. (2010), 'Depuis trente ans, les grandes entreprises concentrent de plus en plus d'emplois' *Insee Première*, no 1289, Paris: INSEE.

Dufour C. (2005), Etude sur la re-syndicalisation des comités d'entreprise (CE), in recherches et études financées par la DARES.

Dumenil, G. and D. Lévy (2000), *Crise et sortie de crise: Ordres et désordres néolibéraux*, Paris: Presses Universitaires de France.

Durand, J. (1996) (ed), *Le syndicalisme au futur*, Paris: Syros.

Jacod, O. (2007), 'Les institutions représentatives du personnel: davantage présentes, toujours actives mais peu sollicitée par les salariés' DARES, *Premières synthèses, premières informations*, no 05-1.

Jefferys, S. (2003), *Liberté, Égalité and Fraternité at Work: Changing French Employment Relations and Management*, Basingstoke: Palgrave.

Kerbourch J., O. Mériaux and C. Seiler (2008), *Evaluation de la loi du 4 mai 2004 sur la négociation d'accords dérogatoires dans les entreprises*, Documents d'étude de la DARES, no140, Paris: DARES.

Labbé, D. and M. Croisat (1992), *La fin des syndicats?*, Paris: Logiques sociales l'Harmattan.

Morin, M. (1994), *Le droit des salariés à la négociation collective, principe Général du droit*, Paris: LGDJ.

Mouriaus, R. (1998), *Crises du syndicalisme français*, Montchrestien: Coll Clefs politique.

Mouriaux, R. (2009), *Le syndicalisme en France*, Coll Que-Sais-je: PUF.

Regini, M., K. Kitay and M. Baethge (1999), *From Tellers to Sellers: Changing Employment Relations in Banks*, Cambridge, MA: MIT Press.

Reynaud, J. (1993), *Les règles du jeu*, Paris: Armand Colin.

Rosanvallon, P. (1988), *La question syndicale*, Paris: Calmann Lévy.

9 German unions facing neo-liberalism: between resistance and accommodation

Heiner Dribbusch and Thorsten Schulten

INTRODUCTION

In the autumn of 2010, only two years after the bankruptcy of Lehman Brothers ushered in the financial crisis, it seems the German economy was in the process of recovery: exports were taking off again and officially registered unemployment was about to reach its lowest level since the early 1990s. But the balance sheet for the unions has not been so healthy. They realise that, while government and employers in late 2008 were receptive to involving them in corporatist crisis management, their more far-reaching goals were dismissed. From the viewpoint of the German unions, the crisis has confirmed the failure of neo-liberal policies. As the president of the Confederation of German Unions (DGB) pointed out at its 2010 congress, 'Neo-liberalism, deregulation and privatisation were enormous errors. They have led the economy and society down a blind alley'. Consequently, he called for a 'new order' to create a society that was characterised by 'understanding, fairness, solidarity and with good jobs for everyone' (Sommer 2010, our translation). The character and contours of such a 'new order', however, are far from clear. During the past three decades, unions in Germany have mainly focused on defending the principles of 'Rhenish capitalism' (Albert 1993), a model which has its roots in the post-war development in western Germany.

The German union movement, which emerged in the post-war years, is largely dominated by one large confederation, the DGB, and its comparatively few affiliated unions. Their point of reference has been a post-war class compromise which was based on the unions' acceptance of a free market economy and the overarching aim of competitiveness in exchange for solid protection of workers, strong union rights and a comprehensive welfare state. It included a highly institutionalised system of industrial relations which helped to integrate unions into the 'social market economy'. Neo-liberalism in Germany is opposed by the DGB because it calls for an end to this arrangement. This opposition can be labelled 'social democratic' in so far as it strives to maintain the regulation of capitalism, rather than its abolition. At industry and company level, we find a slightly different picture. Here we find a practice of social partnership whereby the acceptance of the paradigm of competitiveness by unions and works councils favours a position of 'qualified and conditional support' towards neo-liberal restructuring. The latter is perhaps most often not welcomed but tolerated as long as it promises at least to protect the works councils' constituencies from the worst-case scenario of high unemployment.

In this chapter, we describe and discuss the responses of unions to neo-liberalism in Germany against the background of the institutional framework of industrial relations and the shift in the balance of power in favour of employers that has been apparent since the mid-1990s. The chapter is organised in four parts. The first examines the post-war class compromise, including sketching the balance of power, drawing on concepts of labour power developed by Wright (2000) and Silver (2003) and introducing the main union organisations and the institutions of industrial relations. The second describes the various phases, main projects and socio-economic impact of neo-liberal restructuring in Germany. The third then analyses the different union responses, ranging from new corporatist arrangements to open resistance and unions' claims for renewed social and economic regulation. Finally, the fourth summarises the arguments and gives an overview of how unions have reacted to the current global financial crisis.

POST-WAR CAPITALISM AND UNION INTEGRATION

Following the defeat of National Socialism and against the background of the division of Germany and the Cold War the (western) 'German Model' emerged on the basis of a national class compromise which included the corporatist integration of unions. The economic development of German post-war capitalism was mainly based on three pillars (Berghahn and Vitols 2006): First, there was a highly competitive manufacturing sector specialising in high quality production in branches such as automobiles, electronics, chemicals, engineering and machine building. These sectors were the main promoters of an export-oriented development model which formed the backbone of Germany's post-war 'economic miracle'. Second, there was a dense network of cross shareholdings and interlocking directorates between major German companies and the large universal banks which created a specific form of corporate governance allowing for a high degree of stability and a more long-term strategic company development. Third, German post-war capitalism also contained a relatively comprehensive public sector, including some important national monopolies in the network industries such as the postal service, telecommunication and railways and a strong municipal sector comprising public transport, energy, waste disposal and social services. The economic

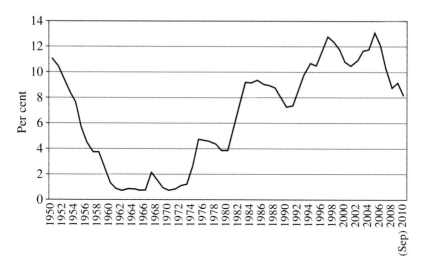

Figure 9.1   Unemployment rate 1950–2010 (annual averages (except September 2010) in per cent)

Source: Federal Employment Agency's own calculation.

Note: Unemployment as percentage of all wage earners, excluding self-employed.

success of German post-war capitalism allowed a continuous improvement of living standards for large sections of the working class and created the material basis for the corporatist integration of German unions. Until the mid-1970s the overall balance of power was comparatively favourable for workers and unions. *Structural power* of labour grew as unemployment declined in the second half of the 1950s, reaching such a low level in the early 1960s that employers looked for workers outside Germany and the European Economic Community (see Figure 9.1).

Up to the 1980s the associational power of workers was expressed in a growing number of union members, although overall net density oscillated between 30 per cent and 35 per cent (Ebbinghaus and Visser 2000: 324–325). Metal manufacturing in general, and the car industry in particular, emerged as strongholds of unionism with workers having particular disruptive power because of the key role these industries played in the export-driven 'economic miracle' of the 1950s and 1960s. A further pillar of unionism was the public service sector, including the national postal and rail services. The development of the institutional power of German unions was based on these primary sources of labour power (Brinkmann and Nachtwey 2010). This institutional power found its main expression in the legal security of unions, their influence via works councils and board-level co-determination and in a comprehensive collective bargaining system based on an extended net of sectoral collective agreements.

The Institutional Framework

The conservative Christian Democrats won the first national elections in western Germany in 1949 and set the cornerstones of the institutional framework of industrial relations. Its most characteristic feature is the 'dual system of interest representation' based on unions and employers who are solely responsible for collective bargaining, and works councils as the main workplace employee representation bodies (*cf.* Müller-Jentsch and Weitbrecht 2003). Industrial action is only lawful in the context of collective bargaining and the sole privilege of unions and employers (*cf.* Dribbusch 2007). Political and general strikes are outlawed. At workplace level, employee representation in the private sector is governed by the Works Constitution Act (*Betriebsverfassungsgesetz*, BetrVG) which was first introduced in 1952 and substantially amended in 1972 and 2001. The works council is not a union structure as all employees have the right to vote and to stand as candidates. The works council has a number of information, consultation and co-determination rights but is not involved in collective bargaining and has no right to call industrial action. Most works councillors are members of one of the DGB-affiliates. They are often members of unions' bargaining commissions and elected as local, regional and national delegates to union conferences. An important feature of German industrial relations is the co-determination at board level. It was first established in its most far-reaching form in 1951 in the coal, iron and steel industry where calls for nationalisation had been most powerful. The 1976 Co-Determination Act (*Mitbestimmungsgesetz*) introduced so-called parity co-determination for public limited companies with more than 2000 employees, whereby both employees and union representatives have the same number of seats in the supervisory boards as the shareholders. Works council and board level representation are intertwined as leading works councillors are usually also elected to sit on the supervisory board. A further pillar of the post-war framework was the development of a comprehensive welfare state which insured workers against major risks through compulsory health, unemployment and pension insurance schemes. These schemes were funded equally by employers and employees while the individual contributions depended on the individual wage levels.

The union landscape is dominated by the Confederation of German Unions (*Deutscher Gewerkschaftsbund*, DGB), the largest union confederation in Germany which represents almost 80 per cent of all union members in Germany (Table 9.1). There are two union confederations outside the DGB: the German Civil Service Association (DBB) and a small Christian Union

Table 9.1   Unions in Germany (2009)

	Members
Confederation of German Unions (DGB)	**6 265 000**
DGB affiliates:	
German Metalworkers' Union (IG Metall)	2 263 000
United Services Union (ver.di)	2 138 000
Mining, Chemicals and Energy Union (IG BCE)	687 000
Building, Forestry, Agriculture and the Environment Workers' Union (IG BAU)	325 000
German Education Union (GEW)	258 000
Transport, Service and Networks Union (TRANSNET)	219 000
Food, Beverages, Tobacco, Hotel, Restaurants and Allied Workers' Union (NGG)	205 000
Police Union (GdP)	169 000
German Civil Service Association (DBB)	1 283 000
Christian Union Confederation (CGB)	283 000
Non-affiliated unions*	270 000
In total	**8 100 000**

*   Estimation by WSI.

Source: DGB, DBB and CGB.

Confederation (CGB) notorious for undercutting terms and conditions negotiated by DGB affiliates (Dribbusch 2009). Finally, there are a number of non-affiliated, mostly professional unions. The DGB and its affiliated unions consider themselves to be a unitary and non-partisan movement, though affiliates have traditionally had close ties and a privileged partnership with the Social Democratic Party of Germany (*Sozialdemokratische Partei Deutschlands*, SPD). An established role is also held by a small Christian wing with special relations to the Christian Democratic Party (CDU). More recently a significant number of unionists have become affiliated to the new Left Party (*Die Linke*).

Social Partnership and Militancy

The post-war class compromise was ideologically legitimised by the idea of a 'social market economy'. First promoted by the conservative Christian Democrats, it was later adopted by the Social Democrats and finally became – by and large – a point of reference for German unions (*cf.* Hyman 2001:

116–23). Its expression in industrial relations was the concept of 'social part-nership' (*Sozialpartnerschaft*) as opposed to socialist class struggle. At its core was the assumption that 'social partners' might have diverging bargaining interests but share the overarching interest of reconstructing the German econ-omy and restoring and expanding its competitiveness. The class compromise was materially founded on an essentially export-led growth strategy which was able to provide both high profits, substantial concessions to unions and signif-icant improvements in the welfare system. Steadily increasing wages, shorter working time and paid leave were not only regarded by union officials as genuine achievements but also helped to integrate much of the working class into the post-war western German order. The extended presence of unionists in the works councils and the holding of seats in the supervisory boards favoured the accommodation. Until the 1970s social partnership had become dominant in union practice in particular at workplace level although some unions such as the Metalworkers' Union, IG Metall or the Printworkers remained reluctant to fully embrace the accompanying rhetoric (*cf.* Markovits 1986). Manufacturing the relationship between management and works councils could be described as 'productivity coalition' (Windolf 1989: 3). In public services the transition from union representation to management was often rather fluid and allowed for the heads of administration to be part of the union and vice versa.

Conflict has never been fully absent from German industrial relations. Major gains in pay and conditions could only be reached following industrial action including massive lock-outs (Dribbusch 2007). Unofficial action helped to enforce workers' interests at the shop floor level (Birke 2007; Dribbusch 2010: 151–3). However, compared to other OECD countries such as Canada, Italy, France or the UK, overall strike levels in Germany have always been low (*cf.* Dribbusch 2010; Shalev 1978: 15; Velden *et al.* 2007). This is widely regarded as a competitive advantage. Unions often point with pride to their contribution to industrial stability although differences between employers and unions have remained. Whereas employers have reclaimed absolute discretion in management affairs, unions have insisted on the expansion of co-determination rights. In order to characterise the ambivalent relation between institutional cooperation and the fundamental conflict of interest, German labour relations have often been described as a system of 'conflict partnership' (Müller-Jentsch 1999).

NEO-LIBERAL RESTRUCTURING OF GERMAN CAPITALISM

Neo-liberalism in Germany does not substantially differ from that found in other countries in its striving for deregulation, privatisation and the retrenchment of public ownership and social security. It differs in form as it builds on the existing industrial relation framework which the German neo-liberal mainstream wants to modify but not fully abolish. It is specific to the time frame and the political constellations by which it was implemented.

Three Phases of Neo-liberal State Intervention

As the post-war boom came to an end in the mid-1970s, Germany was faced with much lower growth rates and increasing unemployment, and following the resultant crisis of the post-war regime, German capitalism entered a long-lasting period of neo-liberal state intervention which can be divided into three phases: For many observers the first phase had already started in the mid-1970s when the German Central Bank took a fundamental shift towards a more restrictive monetarist policy (Streeck 1994). As price stability became the exclusive focus of monetary policy the former period of Keynesian macro-economic policies with its commitment to full employment came to an end. At the political level, the beginning of German neo-liberalism is usually associated with the change in government in 1982, when the small liberal Free Democratic Party (FDP) broke its former coalition with the SPD and created a new coalition government with the CDU. The new conservative-liberal government originally presented a wide ranging neo-liberal agenda claiming a necessity to improve the climate for investors in Germany namely by reducing direct and indirect labour costs. In practice, however, the CDU with a then still influential labour wing remained reluctant to fully break with the post-war class compromise, so that neo-liberal reforms were only gradual and did not question the basic institutions of German capitalism (*cf.* Jacobi *et al.* 1992: 240–41).

A second phase of neo-liberal reforms started in the early 1990s with German unification. In East Germany, integration into the western market economy led to a deep transformation crisis with an extensive process of de-industrialisation and a sharp increase in unemployment. As a consequence of this, massive transfer payments from west to east Germany became necessary, which created a major structural burden and long lasting imbalances between the two parts of Germany. In 2010 GDP per capita in east Germany was still only 70 per cent of the western level, while unemployment rates continued to be more than twice as high. A third phase of more radical neo-liberal state intervention in Germany started at the end of the 1990s. Ironically, it was promoted by a centre-left coalition of the SPD and the Green Party (*Bündnis90/Die Grünen*), which came into power in 1998 after 16 years of a conservative-liberal government. Following 'new' Labour in Britain, leading parts of the SPD were at that time very much influenced by ideas of a new 'Third Way' which claimed to offer a modernisation strategy beyond neo-liberalism on the one hand and the 'old' Keynesian-style policy of the 1970s on the other hand. However, in practice the red-green government launched a couple of more fundamental reforms in the fields of economic, social and labour market policy which led to a much more radical neo-liberal restructuring of German capitalism.

Major Policy Fields of Neo-liberal Restructuring

There were at least three major policy fields which were at the core of neo-liberal restructuring in Germany. The first was the liberalisation and privatisation of public services, which marked 'a fundamental break with the modus operandi of the post-war interventionist welfare state' (Streeck 2009: 71). It took place in three successive waves (Brandt and Schulten 2008). The first wave of privatisations started in the second half of the 1980s and focused on the few western German industrial companies which were still state-owned. It was continued at a much larger scale after 1990 in eastern Germany. During the 1990s a second wave of privatisations focused on the deregulation of former public monopolies in areas such as telecommunication, railways, public transport and energy. The most important initiatives were the privatisation of the Federal Postal Services, and the Federal Rail Service, which was finally realised in 1994 after Christian Democrats and Liberals won the support of the SPD. The latter was necessary because the privatisation required a two-thirds majority in parliament in order to change the German Constitution. Finally, a third wave of privatisations gained momentum after the turn of the millennium at local level with a focus on sectors such as municipal housing, waste disposal, street cleaning, hospitals and other health and social services. It was supported by a fiscal and tax policy of the then *red-green* government which increased the budget problems of many municipalities.

The second major field of neo-liberal restructuring in Germany was the liberalisation of financial markets and the respective changes in corporate governance. While some financial market reforms were already executed by the conservative-liberal government, it was the red-green coalition which passed the decisive legislation to disentangle interlocking capital and raising the attractiveness of Germany as a financial market place (Cioffi and Höpner 2006). Among other points, the red-green government had abolished the previously high levels of taxation on capital gains which made the purchase and sale of company shares much more attractive. At the same time major German banks had shifted their strategies towards investment banking and became less interested in supporting the traditional German company networks. Consequently, Germany saw some far-reaching changes in the ownership structure of large companies which for many observers marked an end of the traditional close company and banking relations of the 'Germany Inc' (Streeck 2009). This development also led to major changes in corporate governance, where the position of the traditional stakeholders (including unions) were significantly weakened in favour of the shareholders with a pronounced shift from orientation on long-term company developments towards more short-term profit expectations. Finally, the third core field of neo-liberal restructuring in Germany was social and labour market policy. In the 1990s, there was a dominant discourse according to which major reforms of the welfare state were deemed necessary in order to limit its increasing costs, which were seen to be the result of Germany's unfavourable demographic development. As social security in Germany is mainly financed by joint contributions of workers and employers, the overall aim of neo-liberal reforms was to limit or even reduce non-wage labour costs, in order to strengthen the competitiveness of German capital. Regarding pension and health insurances one major strategy was to limit employers' contributions by reducing the benefits from the standard system and promoting additional private insurance to be paid exclusively by the workers. Moreover, the retirement age was extended from 65 to 67.

Regarding labour market policy, some neo-liberal reforms such as the relaxation of fixed-term employment dated back to the mid-1980s. During the 1990s, the conservative-liberal government had continued with some reduction of dismissal protection and a partial repeal of sick pay. However, the more radical changes in labour market policy were introduced after 2002, during the second term of the red-green government. It first repealed almost all restrictions on temporary agency work which led to a fast growth of temporary agency workers. Furthermore, in 2003 the government introduced a comprehensive neo-liberal action programme called *Agenda 2010* which aimed at increasing the pressure on recipients of state benefits to re-enter the labour market. The government adopted the so-called 'Hartz-Reforms', which were named after the then labour director of Volkswagen and member of IG Metall, who was leading a commission to work out proposals that inspired the subsequent legislation. Among other points the 'Hartz-Reforms' applied statutory protection against dismissal only to companies with more than ten employees, rather than the previous five, and introduced cuts in the length of unemployment benefits. Most importantly recipients of unemployment benefits were obliged to accept every legal job offered to them, even at levels below collectively agreed rates.

Economic Restructuring of German Capitalism

After the end of Germany's long period of post-war prosperity a profound process of economic modernisation and restructuring gained momentum. The large-scale introduction of information technology was coupled with new management techniques and aggressive cost-cutting strategies. These changes could best be observed in the car industry which was one of the pioneers in changes that finally affected both manufacturing and the public sector alike. Since the mid-1980s, restructuring in the car industry had been dominated by the adaptation of largely Japanese production concepts which gained prominence under the headings of 'lean production' and 'just in time' manufacturing. In the 1990s new markets and opportunities appeared and international competition became further intensified and several waves of restructuring followed (Jürgens and Krzywdzinski 2008). Strategic decision making was centralised and management had to fulfil increasing expectations of shareholders with regard to returns on capital. Every operation came under scrutiny in order to find ways of cost cutting. Suppliers were put under increasing pressure by manufacturers to lower prices. Domestic outsourcing of operations, an extended flexibilisation of production and a reorganisation of the production chain were further elements of this process. Companies were divided into business units which had to compete as so-called profit centres, not only with external suppliers but with other units within the organisation. International benchmarking became the norm. As a consequence, workers saw themselves confronted with successive waves of demands by management to accept cuts in labour costs in order to maintain competitiveness as a prerequisite to keeping their jobs.

One major result of the neo-liberal restructuring of German capitalism was that many companies in Germany could significantly improve their competitiveness. As a result, the export-oriented growth strategy, which had always been a characteristic feature of German capitalism, became further intensified. The value of German exports measured in per cent of the Gross Domestic Product increased from around 25 per cent in the mid-1970s to 32 per cent in 1990 and – after a short period of decline as a temporary result of German unification – accelerated to more than 47 per cent in 2008, which is by far the largest value among larger capitalist economies (Figure 9.2).

German export industries were promoted by very moderate wage increases and a significant reduction of real unit labour costs. At the same time the domestic demand in Germany remained systematically underdeveloped. As a result of this, the overall economic performance was relatively weak in comparison to most other OECD countries (Joebges *et al.* 2009).

UNIONS IN THE FACE OF NEO-LIBERALISM

The neo-liberal restructuring of German capitalism manifested that the high days of the post-war class compromise were over. This development went along with a significant shift in the power relations between unions and employers.

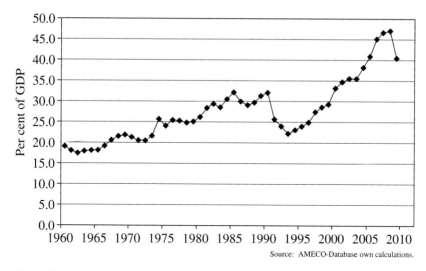

Source: AMECO-Database own calculations.

Figure 9.2   Exports as percentage of GDP in Germany

Shifts in the Balance of Power

The single most important factor in undermining the structural power of labour was the steady increase of unemployment which had already begun in western Germany in the late 1970s but gained momentum in unified Germany when the short-lived unification boom came to an end in the mid-1990s (*cf.* Figure 1). Unemployment peaked in 2005 when about 5m people were officially registered as unemployed. This was accompanied by an increasing casualisation of the workforce which found its main expressions in a substantial growth of fixed-term contracts, marginal part-time jobs, temporary agency work and low-paid jobs in general. Finally, the public sector underwent fundamental changes due to privatisation and liberalisation. As a result, in the period after the early 1990s more than 2m jobs were either cut or moved outside the public service. This went along with a substantial decline in associational power of labour which was expressed by a severe decline in union membership. In 1991, following German unification the DGB membership peaked at an unprecedented 12m following the integration of members of the former eastern German unions only to dramatically decline in the following years (Figure 9.3). By 2009 membership in DGB-unions had almost halved down to 6.3m members although a few affiliates have managed to slow down or even stop the decline since about 2005.

Overall net union density covering all German unions was estimated by the Institute of Economic and Social Research (WSI) to stand in 2009 just below

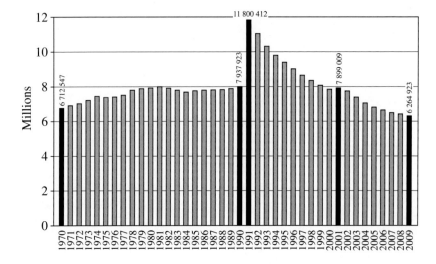

Figure 9.3   DGB Membership 1970–2009

Source: DGB.

the 20 per cent mark. Furthermore, the Blairite shift in the German social democracy in the late 1990s meant that unions lost their privileged partnership with the party and their established channels of communication with the government became less influential than in previous decades. Union power was further damaged when bargaining coverage started to decline in the late 1990s. The institution of the sectoral agreements began to crumble when employers left employers' associations or chose to opt out of collective agreements. Faced with this decline in power, which did not come overnight but developed over a longer period, unions mainly focused on the defence of the existing institutional framework of industrial relations – mainly by creating new forms of competitive corporatism and to a lesser extent by organising open protests and resistance to neo-liberal reforms.

The Emergence of Competitive Corporatism

The term 'competitive corporatism' was originally introduced by Rhodes (1998) to analyse the new nationally-negotiated social pacts, which emerged in Europe during the 1990s, and to distinguish them from traditional forms of social corporatism developed in the post-war period in the framework of Keynesian macroeconomic policies. In contrast to neo-liberalism with its focus on free market policies, the concept of competitive corporatism is founded on the idea that institutionalised co-operation between capital, labour and the state is a better and more efficient way to improve competitiveness. With regard to neo-liberal globalisation, competitive corporatism offers a strategic concept for the unions to redefine their role under a changed political and economic environment. While accepting the paradigm of national competitiveness, the unions have advocated for a 'high-road strategy' according to which competitive advantage could best be won through investments in education and training, an excellent infrastructure and a highly motivated and productive workforce. The latter, in particular, requires an important role for unions and works councils, as they are able to mediate potential conflicts at industry and company level.

In order to tackle successive economic crises, German unions have developed a long tradition of corporatist crisis management which had its origins in the handling of the downsizing of the coal industry and was further developed during the restructuring of the steel and ship building industries in the 1970s and 1980s (*cf.* Esser 1982). The latter restructurings met the Metal Workers' Union in a position of strength and employers had to weigh the costs of unilateral crisis solutions against the advantages of a more consensual approach. The result was a process of so-called 'socially acceptable job cuts'. Its main instruments were extensive early retirement schemes, re-training programmes, the placement of workers in so-called job creation companies and financial incentives for 'voluntary' redundancy. The government subsidised these instruments by adjusting the social security system in a way which made early retirement attractive to both employers and employees. This form of corporatist crisis management was largely perceived by unions to be a success and remained a point of reference way beyond the 1980s.

Faced with new challenges in the 1990s, the unions felt trapped in a dilemma. They still shared in principle the employers' economic objective of maintaining and improving international competitiveness but had greater difficulties dealing with the consequences. The environment for competitive corporatism had changed. Nevertheless, seeing no feasible alternatives, unions opted for a renewal of the class compromise rather than to call it off. The leadership of IG Metall surprised the public in 1995 with a proposal for a so-called 'Alliance for Jobs' (*Bündnis für Arbeit*) whereby wage restraints were offered in exchange for job guarantees. The proposal was mainly responded to at company level. Since the mid-1990s, works councils and management in a growing number of companies have concluded so-called 'pacts for employment and competitiveness' (Seifert and Massa-Wirth 2005). The main difference to former crisis pacts was that works councils now had to deal not only with companies in crisis but with returning demands for cost cuts and concessions in highly profitable industries as well. The 'productivity coalitions' turned into new 'coalitions for competitiveness' (Rehder 2002) whereby the employees' side accepts the management's objective of cost cutting in exchange for limited job guarantees. In 1998, the red-green government estab-lished a national tripartite 'Alliance for Jobs, Training and Competitiveness' which finally failed in 2003. Opposition within the unions had grown as employers insisted on wage moderation but persistently refused any sound job guarantees. Forms of 'competitive corporatism', however, survived at sectoral and company level and retained a strong influence on unions' bargaining policy.

Decentralisation of Collective Bargaining and Union Response to Low Wages

The collective bargaining system has become partially eroded. From the mid-1990s to 2009 the proportion of workers covered by a collective agreement declined from 80 to around 60 per cent (Bispinck and Schulten 2010). Bargaining coverage is particularly low in east Germany and in private services. Moreover, even in sectors still having high bargaining coverage there has been a strong trend towards decentralisation. A major expression for this has been the increasing use of so-called opening clauses, which allowed for deviations from the sectoral standards at company level (Bispinck and Schulten 2010). In the beginning so-called 'hardship clauses' were restricted to organisations in serious economic difficulties. Later on the use of opening clauses was also allowed with the aim of improving competitiveness and the terms of investment. In metalworking, for example, IG Metall settled on a landmark agreement in 2004, which institutionalised and accelerated the decentralisation process. Parts of the unions have seen this strategy of 'organ-ised decentralisation' via opening clauses as a way to prevent a further erosion of sectoral bargaining. Others hope to regain a certain regulative control over diverging developments at company level. The decline of unions' bargaining power since the mid-1990s has been mirrored in a partial extension of weekly working times and a strong decline in the wage share. In particular, since the turn of the millennium wage developments in Germany have been extremely restrictive and far below wage increases in most other OECD countries. Second, there has been a strong increase of the overall wage dispersion mainly through a rapid extension of the low wage sector. As bargaining coverage declined and low pay expanded, the idea of a national statutory minimum wage gained ground among German unions. In the beginning this campaign was only supported by the service sector unions, while the Metal and Chemicals workers' unions in manufacturing criticised the idea – saying it was counter to the principle of autonomous collective bargaining. Eventually, at the national congress of the DGB in 2006, the demand for the introduction of a statutory minimum wage won the support of a broad majority. The campaign which followed was the most successful German unions had started for decades. Although a national minimum wage had not been achieved by 2010, successive surveys have demonstrated overwhelming public support and have continued to put pressure on parliament and the political parties.

Protest and Resistance

There have also been various projects of neo-liberal state intervention where the unions organised open protests and resistance. In the late 1980s the unions campaigned against the privatisation of the post and rail services but in line with their strictly legalistic tradition abstained from calling political strike action. Civic protests against privatisation only gained momentum in the late 1990s when local authorities privatised utilities and public hospitals. These movements found support from unions which were sometimes the driving forces behind occasionally successful local plebiscites (Mittendorf 2008).

When in 1996 the conservative-liberal government passed legislation to partly repeal the existing regulations on sick pay, attempts to implement these changes were answered by a wave of unofficial strikes notably in the car industry. The protests finally led to collective agreements in almost all industries guaranteeing the old sick-pay regulations. The legal status quo was then restored in 1999 by the red-green coalition. Similar action, however, was largely absent when the red-green coalition turned to more radical neo-liberal policies. The 'Hartz-Reforms' led to massive protests on the streets in 2004 – in particular in eastern Germany. In April 2004 the unions organised a 'political action day' with about half a million participants. When the 'grand coalition' of Conservatives and Social Democrats extended the legal retirement age in 2007 the IG Metall district of Baden Württemberg organised rallies and walk-outs involving almost 70 000 employees. The general scepticism and reluctance within the unions towards such political action left these protests largely isolated and without lasting effects.

Global reorganisation of production chains, greater exit-options for employers and the expansion of structural unemployment have put workers since the mid-1990s on the defensive. No conflict on concessions resulted in a longer official dispute. Some negotiations saw unofficial stoppages frequently complacently tolerated by the works councils. Most of these protests remained comparatively marginal, given the concessions at risk. With recurring demands for concessions, however, a feeling grew in some plants that 'enough is enough'. The most spectacular acts of resistance took place in 2004 in the car industry. In July protest meetings and short stoppages in several plants of Daimler-Benz showed that workers were angry about a new massive cost-cutting package. A day of action called by IG Metall saw some 60 000 workers walk out in what turned out to be the largest protests at Daimler in post-war history. The final compromise was followed by a debate in which union activists criticised the majority in the company works council that the struggle had not been intensified and extended to other companies. In October 2004, the workers at the GM-Opel car plant in Bochum stopped production for six days in unofficial action to protest against plans to cut several thousands of jobs across Europe (Gester and Hajek 2005). This wild-cat strike which initially was neither organised nor controlled by the works council, won huge media coverage and was widely perceived by many employees as an act of legitimate self-defence. To the disappointment of activists, however, it did not spread to other GM sites. Emblematic of a number of similar disputes since 2003 was in 2006 the official six-week strike of 1700 workers at the AEG Nuremberg site of the multinational company Electrolux (Artus 2006). In the end the management's decision to close the site was not turned over but the action did help employees to win increased sever-ance payments. The damaging consequence of privatisation for the bargaining power of employees in the public sector was exposed in a series of long-last-ing strike disputes in western Germany in 2006. These strikes were entirely defensive and triggered by public employers' demands for a general extension of working time. The service sector union ver.di managed to mobilise new groups of employees in public child care and the health service but this could only partly compensate for the lack of strike effectiveness caused by the privatisation and out-sourcing of key sectors such as public transport and util-ities (Dribbusch and Schulten 2007).

Revitalising the Union Movement

Against the background of diminishing organisational power, German unions have started to discuss and develop new political strategies which aim at a revitalisation of the union movement. Two strategic approaches in particular are discussed within the union movement (Urban 2005). The first has a kind of 'back-to-the-roots' attitude and wants to concentrate the union activities on the 'core businesses': collective bargaining and workers interest representa-tion at company level. Its basic assumption is that unions will only overcome their crisis if they regain strength at company level. In contrast to that, the second approach wants to strengthen the union voice in the overall political arena by promoting social movement unionism and seeking new alliances with other social movements. Both approaches do not necessarily compete with each other but could form complementary parts of a comprehensive strategy.

Since 2005, first ver.di, then IG Metall and the building workers union IG BAU, have also picked up elements of Anglo-Saxon campaigning and organ-ising models (Bremme *et al.* 2007; Wetzel 2009). IG Metall launched a number of campaigns with a strong emphasis on strengthening the union at the workplace by involving and mobilising members. These new approaches are not undisputed in the union. One campaign labelled 'Better not cheaper' (*Besser statt billiger*) focuses on innovation and demands prior to expert coun-selling on alternatives if companies want to implement cost-cutting programmes and make use of opening clauses to deviate from agreements. Critics see a potential danger that this furthers the erosion of sectoral collec-tive agreements whereas the defenders of the campaign argue that deviations take place anyway and that it is better to do this at the table and combined with a mobilising strategy, rather than under the table and in back-room negotia-tions. An important element of the new IG Metall strategy is that any agree-ment to concessions at company level must be bound to prior approval of members. The union reports rising union density in organisations not only where concessions could be defeated but also if they were approved following intense membership involvement.

Mobilising members and workers with the aim of strengthening the union's organisational power has also been a major element in a partly revised bargaining strategy of ver.di in the public and private service sector since 2006. This has included an extended involvement of members in industrial action, a fight-back strategy towards employers who want to avoid collective bargaining existing agreements and a closer consultation of members and activists on collective bargaining results. However, the fact that the annual number of disputes in which ver.di was engaged quadrupled – from 36 in 2004 to 163 in 2009 – reflected not only a greater militancy of the union but was also an indicator for an increasing aggressiveness of employers.

UNION RESPONSES: BETWEEN RESISTANCE AND ARRANGEMENT

Following the categorisation laid out in the editorial introduction to this book, the leading position within the German union movement regarding neo-liberal globalisation can be qualified as a 'social democratic opposition' insofar as it does not seek to abolish capitalism but defend and modernise its regulation. In order to avoid a downward spiral of competition of social and labour stan-dards, the unions argue in favour of a 'social market economy' with strong workers protection and union rights, a comprehensive welfare state and a Keynesian macroeconomic policy which – against the background of an increasingly internationalised economy – should be coordinated at European or even at a global level. At company and industry level, however, union policy has often been rather contradictory. In the area of collective bargaining, for example, the unions traditionally rejected claims for wage restraint as counter productive to growth and employment but finally often agreed to rather moderate increases or even made concessions which undermined existing standards. Of course, unions did not want to follow a policy of concession bargaining but felt pressed by a changing competitive environment. Persistently high levels of unemployment made the safeguarding of jobs a priority and paved the way to concession bargaining – in particular as no feasible alternative to western capitalism was at hand and socialist ideas substantially discredited by the reality of the German Democratic Republic. To this is added the fact that German unions in manufacturing had their strongholds precisely in the export driven industries which were the backbone of the German economy. This linked the existence of unions in these sectors, and even more so the works councils, to the economic success of the companies involved. Unions are convinced that the best way to serve their members' interests is to assist in improving competitiveness by way of a high-road strategy (Dribbusch and Schulten 2009). This arrangement of unions and works councils with the paradigm of competitiveness favours a position of 'qualified and conditional support' towards neo-liberal restructuring. As there is often no clear cut between a high-road and a low-road strategy, companies usually aim to get both higher productivity and lower costs. Consequently, 'competitiveness' became the core concept in Germany to justify wage restraint and social concessions.

Recent Union Strategies: Responses to the Global Economic Crisis

With the wide-ranging economic crisis in the years 2008 and 2009, the discourse on more fundamental changes to the current social-economic system gained new prominence within German unions. In May 2009, the DGB had even organised a large 'congress on capitalism' which brought together unionists, progressive politicians, critical academics and representatives from various other social movements (see: www.kapitalismuskongress.dgb.de). Within the unions this has been widely interpreted as a fundamental crisis of a 'finance-dominated free-market capitalism' which documented the principle failure of more than two decades of neo-liberalism. Consequently, many unionists have called for a fundamental 'change of course' (Huber 2010) or the creation of a 'new order' (Sommer 2010) which has to be based on an alternative socio-economic model. While only a small minority within the unions discuss socialist alternatives to capitalism, the contours of an alternative model as seen by the majority of the unions largely represent a modernised version of Rhenish capitalism. The unions have basically demanded an extensive re-regulation of financial markets, more active state intervention and a re-strengthening of social and labour market institutions. Furthermore, the unions have argued for a redistribution of income and wealth in order to fight the growing inequality in Germany. The latter has also been seen as a major precondition to strengthening domestic demand in order to overcome the one-sided fixation on export surpluses.

As Germany's export-oriented strategy has made a major contribution to the development of huge global economic imbalances, there is a growing awareness among the unions that Germany could not simply continue with this strategy. Therefore, most unions have called for a rebalancing of the German economy through a strengthening of its domestic market. Under the conditions of the global economic crisis, however, the various sectoral unions follow different political priorities reflecting the immediate interests of their constituencies (Uellenberg van Dawen 2009). The service sector union ver.di has advocated diminishing the dependency on exports by fostering the expansion of the service sector, especially in public services such as education, health, care and other social services. In contrast to that, the industrial unions IG BCE and IG Metall have put their emphasis on pushing the state to secure the core manufacturing companies which have been hit hardest by the current crisis. As a short-term measure, for example, IG Metall has successfully pushed for the introduction of a so-called car scrap bonus, which was a temporary financial incentive offered by the government for buyers of a new car who traded in their old car for scrap. Moreover, the unions have called for a new industrial policy which is intended to help certain industries to keep their competitiveness and to promote an ecological restructuring towards more sustainable production.

Considering the current union debates on the consequences of the global economic crisis, there is at least one point which has the potential to go beyond a modernised form of Rhenish capitalism – that is the issue of economic democracy (Hirschel and Schulten 2010). During the past decades the unions registered that the existing forms of co-determination were neither sufficient to counter the increasing structural power of capital, nor to defy the growing dominance of shareholder value orientation. Moreover, the unions have self-critically admitted that through the institutions of co-determination they were often incorporated in problematic management decisions, including the determination of extraordinarily high payments for managers (Huber 2010). As a consequence of this, the unions demand a far-reaching democratisation including a significant enlargement and extension of co-determination rights which should give workers' representatives a real say in economic decisions (Allespach *et al.* 2010, Huber 2010, Urban 2010). For example, IG Metall would like to extend the co-determination rights on the supervisory board, according to which decisions on plant closures, relocations or mass redundancies would need a two-thirds majority of the board. Such a regulation, which already exists in accordance with a special law at the German car producer Volkswagen, would *de facto* give veto power to the workers on plant closures.

Originally, there was much hope among the unions that with the global economic crisis the era of neo-liberalism would come to an end (Bsirske 2009). In the meantime, however, the enforcement of an alternative socio-economic model has become uncertain. So far, none of the unions' wider-ranging political propositions have been picked up by either the 'grand coalition' government of Christian and Social Democrats or by the conservative-liberal coalition which came to power in autumn 2009. A sustainable political mobilisation for a more far-reaching reform agenda did not take place and two calls in 2009 for national rallies – of which only one was officially supported by the DGB unions – did not receive the broad response the organisers had hoped for. Instead there was a revival of 'corporatist crisis management' (Urban 2010) whereby the unions became an important ally for capital in getting support from the state in order to tackle the economic difficulties and to safeguard jobs. The corporatist crises management took place at company as well as at political level. At company level, for example, managers, works councillors and unionists often jointly negotiated with the state in order to get money from the 'recovery funds'. At political level employers' associations and unions have together successfully lobbied the government to extend the possibilities of short-time work which allow companies to reduce labour costs without making workers redundant while the workers receive a state benefit for the time not worked. The widespread use of short-time work has been one major reason for 'Germany's job miracle', that is a very low increase in unemployment compared to all other OECD countries.

As for the unions, the corporatist crisis management was a relative successful strategy towards securing jobs, they continued on this path even in their collective bargaining policy. Unprecedented in its bargaining history IG Metall decided to enter into the 2010 bargaining round without having tabled a specific pay demand. In the final settlement, reached in February 2010, the union agreed to rather moderate pay increases in combination with provisions aimed at safeguarding employment by way of reductions in working time, with only partial pay compensation and an extension of short-time work. A similar deal for moderate wage increase in exchange for job security was made in April 2010 in the chemical industry. In the so-called 'Crisis Pact for the Chemicals Industry' both the unions and the employers' association agreed that 'their common understanding of a social market economy and of responsible social partnership is crisis-proof and without alternative.' Furthermore, they continued to say that the overall aim of the 'Crisis Pact' was to '*sustainably secure the competitiveness of the chemical industry* in Germany by way of a long-term personnel policy thereby increasing employees' chances to be employed' (our emphasis and translation).

The recent pay agreements in Germany have been criticised by some economists as being too low to boost domestic demand and for following the old pattern of improving competitiveness through wage restraint which has been analysed as a 'beggar-thy-neighbour' policy (Flassbeck 2010). In contrast to the industrial unions, ver.di had started its 2010 bargaining round in the public sector with a comparatively high wage claim. It justified its demands with the need for substantial wage increases as an important tool towards strengthening private demand which for ver.di is crucial to overcoming the economic crisis. However, the final agreement settled in February 2010 has also provided for only moderate wage increases. While the public budgets of many municipalities were increasingly negatively affected by the economic crisis, large parts of ver.di were rather sceptical whether the union would have had the mobilising capacity to fight successfully for a better result.

What Future for the Unions?

For the unions the global economic crisis has created a rather contradictory situation. Although the crisis has made the failure of neo-liberalism rather obvious, it makes it even more difficult to fight for more fundamental changes as the organisational power of the unions remains weak, while the structural power has become even further diminished. There is, however, at least a temporary increase of institutional power as both the employers and the state have an interest to integrate the unions into a strategy of corporatist crisis management. For the state it is still the union's ability to control possible militancy and spontaneous social eruptions which might become even more important when the costs of the crisis are placed upon the mass of working people (Urban 2010). This view is shared by influential factions within the employers' camp, notably those representing large corporations in manufacturing who are neither interested in smashing the unions nor abandoning sectoral collective bargaining but seek to redefine 'social partnership' to their benefit. The new esteem of unions is volatile and it is quickly withdrawn when unions seem to break with crisis cooperation and push for more fundamental changes. If unions cannot regain structural and organisational power their institutional power will always be founded on a precarious basis (Brinkmann and Nachtwey 2010: 21).

This is not ignored in the German union movement. The vice chair of IG Metall, Detlef Wetzel (2009: 352), who is responsible for organising and campaigning, stresses that 'the old days of the Rhenish Capitalism with a social compromise on which we could build for a long period of time are over – and they will not return' (our translation). Officials and activists in many industries experience that the terms of trade have changed for unions. Collective agreements no longer define the minimum – but rather the maximum levels of pay and conditions. With successive concessions the on-top payments have largely disappeared and the low pay sector is expanding. While extended short-time work prevented deteriorating development of the labour market it is also evident that the growing number of temporary workers was largely left unprotected. The fact that in recent years the annual number of disputes has increased reflects not only a greater militancy of the union but is also an indicator for an increasing aggressiveness on the side of employers. But if the environment changes then unions need to change as well. It is against this background that more confrontational organising and campaigning tactics are gaining ground. Regaining bargaining and mobilising power is a prerequisite for unions not only to approach employers from a position of strength but also to challenge the still dominating neo-liberal policies in Germany.

REFERENCES

Albert, M. (1993), *Capitalism Against Capitalism*, London: Whurr.

Allespach, M., A. Demirovic and L. Wentzel (2010), 'Demokratie wagen! Gewerkschaftliche Perspektiven in der Wirtschaftskrise', *Blätter für deutsche und internationale Politik*, **55**(2), 95–105.

Artus, I. (2006), 'Strike action to save the life of a plant is followed by its "honourable death": the conflict at AEG in Nuremberg', *Transfer*, **12**(4), 563–75.

Berghan, V. and S. Vitols (eds) (2006), *Gibt es einen deutschen Kapitalismus?*, Frankfurt: Campus.

Birke, P. (2007), *Wilde Streiks, im Wirtschaftswunder. Arbeitskämpfe, Gewerkschaften und soziale Bewegungen in der Bundesrepublik und Dänemark*, Frankfurt am Main and New York: Campus.

Bispinck, R. and T. Schulten (2010), 'Sector-level bargaining and possibilities for deviations at company level: the case of Germany', Eurofound project on the functioning of sector level wage bargaining systems and wage setting mechanisms in adverse labour market conditions.

Brandt, T. and T. Schulten (2008), 'Privatisation and liberalisation of public services in Germany: the postal and hospital sectors', in M. Keune, J. Leschke and A. Watt, A. (eds), *Privatisation and liberalisation of public services in Europe*, Brussels: ETUI, pp. 37–66.

Bremme, P., U. Fürniß and U. Meinecke (eds) (2007), N*ever work alone. Organising – ein Zukunftsmodell für Gewerkschaften*, Hamburg: VSA.

Brinkmann, U. and O. Nachtwey (2010). 'Krise und strategische Neuorientierung der Gewerkschaften' *Aus Politik und Zeitgeschichte* (13–14), 21–9.

Bsirske, F. (2009), 'Gewerkschaftliche Alternativen in der Krise des Finanzmarkt-Kapitalismus' in R. Brenner (ed.), *Kapitalismus am Ende?* Hamburg: VSA, pp. 22–5.

Cioffi, J. and M. Höpner (2006), 'The political paradox of finance capitalism: interests, preferences, and center-left party politics in corporate governance reform', *Politics & Society*, **34**(4), 463–502.

Dribbusch, H. (2007), 'Industrial action in a low-strike country: strikes in Germany, 1968–2005', in S. van der Velden, H. Dribbusch, D. Lyddon and K. Vandaele (eds), *Strikes Around the World, 1968–2005: Case Studies of 15 Countries*, Amsterdam, Netherlands: Aksant, pp. 267–97.

Dribbusch, H. (2009), 'Konkurrierende Tarifpolitik: Herausforderungen für die DGB-Gewerkschaften', *WSI-Mitteilungen*, **62**(4), 193–200.

Dribbusch, H. (2010), '60 Jahre Arbeitskampf in der Bundesrepublik. Ein Überblick', in R. Bispinck and T. Schulten (eds), *Zukunft der Tarifautonomie. 60 Jahre Tarifvertragsgesetz: Bilanz und Ausblick*, Hamburg: VSA, pp. 145–68.

Dribbusch, H. and T. Schulten (2007), 'The end of an era: structural changes in German public sector collective bargaining', in P. Leisink, B. Steijn and U. Veersma (eds), *Industrial*

Relations in the New Europe. Enlargement, Integration and Reform, Cheltenham, UK and Northampton, MA, USA: Edward Elgar, pp. 155–76.

Dribbusch, H. and T. Schulten (2009), 'German trade unions between neoliberal restructuring, social partnership and internationalism', in A. Bieler, I. Lindberg and D. Pillay (eds), *Labour and the Challenges of Globalization: What Prospects for Transnational Solidarity?*, London: Pluto Press, pp. 178–98.

Ebbinghaus, B. and J. Visser (2000), *Trade Unions in Western Europe since 1945*, London: Macmillan.

Esser, J. (1982), *Gewerkschaften in der Krise: die Anpassung der deutschen Gewerkschaften an neue Weltmarktbedingungen*, Frankfurt: Suhrkamp.

Flassbeck, H. (2010), 'Putting employment security first will diminish demand – a warning from Germany', *Global Labour Column*, (13), accessed at www.global-labour-university.org/fileadmin/GLU_Column/papers/no_13_flassbeck.pdf.

Gester, J. and W. Hajek (eds) (2005), *Sechs Tage der Selbstermächtigung. Der Streik bei Opel in Bochum Oktober 2004*, Berlin: Die Buchmacherei.

Hirschel, D. and T. Schulten (2010), 'Wirtschaftsdemokratie contra Krisenkapitalismus. Über den notwendigen Kurswechsel der Gewerkschaften', *Blätter für deutsche und internationale Politik*, **11**, 75–81.

Huber, B. (2010), 'Kurswechsel für Deutschland. Die Lehren aus der Krise' in B. Huber (ed.), *Kurswechsel für Deutschland*, Frankfurt: Campus, pp. 13–89.

Hyman, R. (2001), *Understanding European Trade Unionism. Between Market, Class and Society*, London: Sage.

Jacobi, O., B. Keller and W. Müller-Jentsch (1992), 'Germany: codetermining the future?', in A. Ferner and R. Hyman, R. (eds), *Industrial Relations in the New Europe*, Oxford: Blackwell, pp. 218–69.

Joebges, H., A. Schmalzbauer and R. Zwiener (2009), 'Der Preis für den Exportweltmeister Deutschland: Reallohnrückgang und geringes Wirtschaftswachstum', Düsseldorf: IMK Studies 4.

Jürgens, U. and M. Krzywdzinski (2008), 'Relocation and East-West competition: the case of the European automotive industry', *International Journal of Automotive Technology and Management*, **8**(2), 145–69.

Markovits, A. (1986), *The Politics of the West German Trade Unions. Strategies of Class and Interest in Growth and Crisis*, Cambridge: Cambridge University Press.

Mittendorf, V. (2008), 'Bürgerbegehren und Volksentscheide gegen Privatisierung und die Rolle der Gewerkschaften', in T. Brandt, T. Schulten, G., Sterkel and J. Wiedemuth (eds), *Europa im Ausverkauf*, Hamburg: VSA, pp. 310–29.

Müller-Jentsch, W. (ed) (1999), *Konfliktpartnerschaft*, Munchen: Rainer Hampp.

Müller-Jentsch, W. and H. Weitbrecht (eds) (2003), *The Changing Contours of German Industrial Relations*, Munchen: Rainer Hampp.

Rehder, B. (2002), 'Wettbewerbskoalitionen oder Beschäftigungsinitiativen? Vereinbarungen zur Standort- und Beschäftigungssicherung in deutschen Großunternehmen', in H. Seifert (ed), *Betriebliche Bündnisse für Arbeit*, Berlin: Edition Sigma, pp. 87–102.

Rhodes, M. (1998), 'Globalisation, labour markets and welfare states: a future of 'competitive corporatism?' in M. Rhodes and Y. Mény (eds), *The Future of European Welfare. A New Social Contract?*, London: Macmillan, pp. 178–203.

Seifert, H. and H. Massa-Wirth (2005), 'Pacts for employment and competitiveness in Germany', *Industrial Relations Journal*, **36**(3), 217–40.

Shalev, M. (1978), 'Lies, damned lies and strike statistics: the measurement of trends in industrial conflict', in C. Crouch and A. Pizzorno (eds), *The Resurgence of Class Conflict in Western Europe since 1968. Vol. 1 National Studies,* Basingstoke: Macmillan, pp. 1–19.

Silver, B. (2003), *Forces of Labour*, Cambridge: Cambridge University Press.

Sommer, M. (2010), 'Gerechtigkeit in der Krise – Solidarisch in die Zukunft. Für eine neue Ordnung – Ordnung in den Köpfen und Ordnung im System', presentation to 19th DGB Congress, Berlin.

Streeck, W. (1994), 'Pay restraint without incomes policy: constitutionalized monetarism and industrial unionism in Germany', in R. Boyer, R. Dore and Z. Mars (eds), *The Return to Incomes Policy*, London: Francis Pinter, pp. 118–40.

Streeck, W. (2009), *Re-Forming Capitalism: Institutional Change in the German Political Economy*, Oxford: Oxford University Press.
Uellenberg van Dawen, W. (2009), 'Arbeitskampf in Krisenzeiten', *Blätter für deutsche und internationale Politik*, **54**(10), 57–64.
Urban, H. (2005), 'Wege aus der Defensive. Schlüsselprobleme und –strategien gewerkschaftlicher Revitalisierung', in H. Detje, K. Pickshaus and H. Urban (eds), *Arbeitspolitik kontrovers*, Hamburg: VSA, pp. 187–212.
Urban, H. (2010), 'Niedergang oder Comeback der Gewerkschaften', *Aus Politik und Zeitgeschichte* (13–14), 3–7.
van der Velden, S., H. Dribbusch, D. Lyddon and K. Vandaele (2007), (eds), *Strikes Around the World, 1968–2005: Case Studies of 15 Countries*, Amsterdam. Netherlands: Aksant.
Wetzel, D. (2009), 'Gewerkschaftliche Erneuerung ist möglich', in M. Crosby (ed.), *Power at work. Die Rückgewinnung gewerkschaftlicher Macht am Beispiel Australiens*, Hamburg: VSA, pp. 349–62.
Windolf, P. (1989), 'Productivity coalitions and the future of European corporatism'. *Industrial Relations*, **28**(1), 1–20.
Wright, E. (2000), 'Working class power, capitalist interests, and class compromise', *American Journal of Sociology*, **105**(4), 957–1002.

10 India, neo-liberalism and union responses – unfinished business and protracted struggles
Ernesto Noronha and David Beale

INTRODUCTION

India is a very large, expanding economy with a population of over 1000 million, a labour force of approximately 43 per cent and with 30 per cent living in urban locations (Labour File 2008; National Sample Survey 2007; World Bank 2010a). India covers an area roughly similar to the size of Europe, with 28 states and seven union territories, and it is a very diverse country economically, politically and culturally, alongside extremes of poverty and wealth. Government is based on parliamentary democracy, though experiences considerable regional tensions and conflicts between its state-level governments and central government (Sinha 2005). Information technology, telecommunications and business process outsourcing are rapidly growing employment sectors and of increasing significance globally (World Bank 2010a).

While the impact on India of neo-liberalism gathered pace in the 1990s, the country's industrial relations trajectory has been influenced considerably by British colonialism, the independence struggle and the country's post-independence political economy (Bhattacherjee and Ackers 2010: 107–112). Prior to 1947, the independence movement was dominated politically by the Indian National Congress (commonly referred to simply as Congress), while unions organised to fight for independence and workers' rights primarily through the communist-led All India Trade Union Congress (AITUC) (Candland 2007: 22–23). Following independence, Congress quickly set up its own national union federation – the Indian National Trade Union Congress (INTUC) – as a labour adjunct of the party (Bhattacherjee and Ackers 2010: 107). In the following years, a proliferation of opposition parties gradually emerged of the left, right and regional interests, and mirrored by the emergence of many national union federations with strong party political affiliations. These included the Bharatiya Mazdoor Sangh (BMS), which has close links to the Hindu fundamentalist Bharatiya Janata Party (BJP), and the Centre of Indian Trade Unions (CITU), affiliated to the Communist Party of India – Marxist (CPM). Although much more recently

167

non-party affiliated union national centres have been established, the political factionalism of unionism is still largely institutionalised within Indian
industrial relations.

For essentially 40 years after 1947 under successive Congress administrations, India had close ties with the Soviet Union, embraced a strong state
sector, established tight controls on foreign investment and maintained a
relatively interventionist legal framework for industrial relations, influencing dispute resolution and workers' employment rights. However, the benefits to workers of the latter and of unionism have been restricted to the
formal sector of the economy, representing less than ten per cent of the
workforce today (World Bank 2010b); and there are ongoing pressures in
India to substitute informal for formal employment. In spite of this and the
considerable political fragmentation of unionised labour, the impact of
unionism on the Indian economy and society more generally is not an
obscure or marginal question, and the unions may have more power and
influence than a first glance could suggest (Teitelbaum 2006). At the same
time, workers and the poor are engaged in a desperate struggle to make their
voices heard in Indian society, with economic and social inequalities on a
vast scale. As the World Bank itself admits, there are two Indias – one that
is doing well out of the country's impressive economic growth rates and
another centred on 300 million people below the poverty line (World Bank
2010a). Others pose the issues more starkly, citing 400 million people without access to electricity, 150m unemployed, 78 million homeless, 80 per
cent of health services controlled by the private sector and only affordable
to the privileged few, and an estimated 200 000 suicides by peasants due to
their debts and a crisis of agriculture among the rural poor (New Socialist
Alternative 2009; Patnaik 2009: 29). In this context, India has undergone
major changes in the last two decades. There has been a clear departure from
the state-led political economy of the Nehru era and India has emerged as the
fourth biggest economy in the world (Government of India 2009), with an
average growth rate for 2004–2008 of 9 per cent (World Bank 2009).
However, in some respects, this shift towards a neo-liberal agenda has been
gradual, hesitant and contradictory.

We now turn to outline the government's and employers' agenda, including the broad trends and developments, labour law reform, the formal/infor-
mal labour divide and comments on key employment sectors. Then, we look
at union response in formal employment, union response in the informal
sector, and the government and employer backlash. Finally, the conclusion
highlights the key elements of union response to date and comments on the
potential for strengthening the union challenge to neo-liberalism in the
future.

GOVERNMENT POLICIES AND EMPLOYERS' INITIATIVES

The year 1991 is frequently identified as a turning point in terms of Indian central government policy and neo-liberalism. Then, India faced a fundamental fiscal crisis, brought about by economic, political, domestic and international factors (Candland 2007: 99–100). As a result, the government secured assistance from the IMF, linked to a structural adjustment package. In addition to two immediate currency devaluations, the package included policy initiatives with the ultimate objective of privatisation, the removal of licensing regulations for private investment, reduced restrictions on foreign direct investment (FDI), tariff reductions and deregulation of capital markets (Balasubramanyam and Mahambare 2001; Candland 2007: 100; Hensman 2010: 112–13; Uba 2008: 863). Also, the impact of the WTO from its foundation in 1995 – with India as a founding member – further weakened trade restrictions, liberalised FDI and reduced restraints on public sector activities (Hensman 2010: 113). Furthermore, these developments all took place in the wake of the collapse of India's traditional ally, the Soviet Union.

However, the notion of 1991 as a watershed needs to be qualified. First, an increasing political and economic instability followed Indira Gandhi's 1975–1977 state of emergency, which essentially ended the Congress Party dominance that had endured since independence. Some have argued that the 1975–1977 regime was the initial trigger for economic liberalisation, with Indira Gandhi's *de facto* overtures to business at the time (Candland 2007: 95). Certainly, the general economic trajectory between 1977 and 1991 was a gradual and partial drift towards deregulated economic policies. Second, following 1991, neo-liberalist reforms on a nation-wide basis have occurred but have been relatively gradual and within limits, especially regarding privatisation (Ahluwalia 2002; Candland 2007: 91; Sinha 2005: 18–20; Uba 2008: 863). While central government has restructured some public sector organisations as state-owned enterprises on a commercial basis (known as public sector units or PSUs in India) with partial equity sales, this process – at least as initiated by central government – has often stopped short of full-scale privatisation. Between 1990 and 2003, government privatisation revenues came mainly from minority share sales in banking, oil and gas, plus full privatisation of a few manufacturing enterprises and the restructuring of the telecommunications organisation as a PSU (Kikeri and Kolo 2005). According to Uba (2008: 863–4), by 2004 central government had fully privatised ten and partially privatised 47 out of 244 public sector enterprises, while Candland (2007: 100) suggests a slightly more conservative picture. Central government caution – a feature of both Congress and BJP-led administrations – has seemingly focused on fear of public unpopularity, union opposition and electoral defeat. Many of the state governments within India have, however, been less cautious in implementing privatisation (Sinha 2005: 19; Uba 2008: 865–6). The politics and dynamics of these developments are complex, somewhat paradoxical and have an important 'federalised' dimension.

To cite a particular example, the Left Front state government of West Bengal led by the CPM was less cautious in advocating restructuring and privatisation than the Congress-led central government. While this case conforms to the turn by most communist parties in favour of the market in the context of the post-Soviet era, of China's 'socialist market' policies and of globalisation, it may also have roots in the traditional grievances felt by West Bengal regarding central government and the resulting adversarial relationship historically (Sinha 2005: 99–105), in conjunction with the CPM's hegemony in West Bengal through its period of continuous government there since the late 1970s, inhibiting union opposition and electoral challenges from the left in that state. Additional explanatory factors common to other Indian states include the competition between state governments to attract investment and promote development, arguably linked to the influence of political patronage and the selective application of such policies affected by politicians' vested interests (Uba 2008: 864). At the same time, evidently, Congress-led *central* governments have gained from encouraging such a devolved process of privatisation while being relatively cautious themselves, thus often avoiding electoral and union opposition nationally. Regarding industrial relations, the unwillingness of successive central governments to implement reforms may also have encouraged inter-state competition to attract investment on the basis of driving down labour standards (Bhattacherjee 1999: 11). Typically linked to such inter-state competition is the 2005 Special Economic Zones (SEZ) Act. By 2007, 404 SEZs had been formally approved, covering 54 280 hectares (Sampat 2008). The gusto with which the central government approved SEZs is indicative of its increasing role as promoter of corporate-led economic growth, linked to aggressive land acquisition and its transfer to 'developers' (ibid). Those people displaced were potentially pushed into a private arena with their compensation negotiated by the market, with government effectively abdicating responsibility for rehabilitation (ibid).

LABOUR LAW REFORM?

A fundamental employer and government neo-liberal objective in India has been to deregulate the formal sector of the economy. Formal sector workers have the best legal protection, are largely public sector and are most likely to be union members. India is generally recognised as having some of the strongest legal protection for formal sector workers anywhere in the world (Teitelbaum 2006) and, alongside Indian employers and government, the World Bank has demanded root and branch labour law reform (Jenkins 2004). Thus, the formal sector's legal framework is constantly under employer and government attack, which is seen as a significant piece of unfinished business from the 1990s economic reform programme. The employers have also campaigned vigorously for an unrestricted right to hire and fire workers, known as the 'exit policy' (Hensman 2001). Planned labour law reform sought to make irrelevant prior government permission required to close down workplaces and retrench labour where more than 100 workers were employed – an important feature of India's labour law framework (Singh 1995). Employers argued that labour flexibility and market restructuring would ultimately expand employment opportunities (for a critical assessment, see D'Souza 2010). A systematic campaign was carried out by employers' associations to revise (a) the Contract Labour Act, especially Section 10, with the aim of removing all restrictions on contract labour usage, and (b) the Industrial Disputes Act, 1947. Provision V B of the latter, introduced in 1976, specified that all business units employing 300 or more workers must obtain state government permission before implementing dismissals or closures – amended to all units employing 100 workers or more in 1982 (Hensman 2001).

Arguably, central to this has been a conscious policy of employers and successive governments to shift labour from the formal to informal sectors – with the latter defined in terms of small unregistered workplaces, casual and sub-contracted labour, and any other workers who are excluded from employment protection legislation and union rights (Hensman 2010).[1] However, government and employer-led attacks on labour rights may pre-date 1991, essentially driven by a domestic agenda and dynamic, which implies that the 1991 crisis and WTO developments have provided Indian government and employer interests with opportunities for developing this agenda (ibid).

With Indian labour law reform a politically risky proposition for central government, the latter decided on a 'federalist' strategy, on the basis of encouraging the non-enforcement of labour protection by state governments, linked to inter-state competition to attract investment. As a result, confrontation with unions is more likely to be isolated within states and sequential, rather than united and simultaneous on an all-India basis; and employers and governments can also develop their tactics state by state (Jenkins 2004; see also Bhattacherjee 1999). The Andhra Pradesh state government was the first to overhaul its contract labour regulations fundamentally, resulting in other states' employers' associations demanding similar legal amendments (Jenkins 2004).

SUBVERTING THE FORMAL–INFORMAL LABOUR DIVIDE

Thus, central government worked covertly to undermine the legal framework (Datt 2008), increasingly enabling employers to bypass the law (Hensman 2001) and weakening the formal sector by allowing employers to decentralise production and sub-contract various operations to smaller businesses. Legal violations regarding workplace closures were often ignored; and employers imposed more flexibility over wage payments, provident funds, leave encashment and gratuity (Noronha and Sharma 1999). Dismissals and closures continued unabated throughout the 1990s. In Mumbai alone, plants belonging to Ciba Geigy, Abbott Laboratories, Roche Pharmaceuticals, Hoechst, Boots, Boehringer-Mannheim and Parke-Davis were closed, demolishing some of the best jobs available anywhere in India, especially for women. This was achieved mostly by Voluntary Retirement Schemes, which in practice often intimidated, coerced and misinformed workers, creating 'a fear psychosis' (personal interviews with plant-level unionists, 1993–9). This led to a reduction in the formal *nature* of jobs and a simultaneous increase in their informal *nature*. According to the Economic Survey (2009–10), the employment growth in the formal (organised) sector grew at 1.20 per cent per annum during 1983–94 but decelerated to –0.03 per cent pa between 1994 and 2007

Table 10.1   Relationship between sector and type of employment (UPSS)

Formal / Informal sector	Total Employment (Millions)		
	Informal/ Unorganised Workers	Formal/ Organised Workers	Total
1999–2000			
Informal/Unorganised sector	341.3 (99.6)	1.4 (0.4)	342.7 (100.0)
Formal/Organised sector	20.5 (37.8)	33.7 (62.2)	54.2 (100.0)
Total	361.8 (91.2)	35.1 (8.8)	396.9 (100.0)
2004 – 2005			
Informal/Unorganised sector	393.5 (99.6)	1.4 (0.4)	394.9 (100.0)
Formal/Organised sector	29.1 (46.6)	33.4 (53.4)	62.5 (100.0)
Total	422.6 (92.4)	34.8 (7.6)	457.4 (100.0)

Note: Figures in brackets are percentages.

Source: NSSO 55th and 61st Round Survey on Employment-Unemployment, Computed in *Report on Conditions of Work and Promotion of Livelihoods in the Unorganised Sector*, NCEUS, 2007, p. 4.

(Government of India 2010). This decline was mainly due to a decrease in employment in public-sector establishments from 1.53 per cent growth 1983–94 to –0.57 per cent cent decline in 1994–2007. With regard to the informal sector, the National Commission for Enterprises in the Unorganised Sector (NCEUS) estimated that the total employment in the country during 1999–2000 was 396.9m with 361.8m being of an informal nature, while in 2004–5 the total estimated employment was 457.4m with 422.6m being informal in nature (Table 10.1). In fact, the employment of a large number of informal workers is now the norm, which enables companies to combine a strict dual labour market with flexibility-linked wages to minimise costs (Suresh 2010).

BUSINESS PROCESS OUTSOURCING AND TELECOMMUNICATIONS SECTORS

Business process outsourcing (BPO) (including call centres) and telecommunications in India are internationally significant and rapidly developing sectors (World Bank 2010a). Regarding the former, globalisation has been the catalyst, with 0.77m workers directly employed (NASSCOM 2010). Although the annual growth rates for its workforce – which expanded by more than 26 per cent between 2001 and 2007 (NASSCOM 2003, 2006 and 2007; Noronha and D'Cruz 2009a: 34–43; Taylor *et al.* 2007) – slowed down due to recession, revenue grew by 6 per cent totalling US $12.4bn in 2010 (NASSCOM 2010). India is the main beneficiary of global BPO developments, with considerable labour cost advantages and a large, well-qualified, English-speaking labour pool, encouraging the location of higher value processes in India alongside lower end call centre and back office services (NASSCOM 2006; Noronha and D'Cruz 2009a: 35,41). Central and state governments have particularly encouraged foreign and domestic investment in this sector through incentives, deregulation and the use of SEZs. The primary BPO centres are New Delhi and the National Capital Region, Mumbai, Bangalore, Chennai and Hyderabad, although BPO investment is emerging in smaller cities as well (NASSCOM 2006: 94, 216–31; Noronha and D'Cruz 2009a: 37, 40). Thus, India's BPO sector has provided a significant expansion of jobs for the middle classes. In contrast, Indian telecommunications has a long history of state ownership (BSNL 2009). However, central government re-organised it into two separate departments in the mid-1980s (ibid) and the great global changes to information and communication technologies in this period created a momentum, in terms of on-going re-organisation and increasing orientation to the rapidly shifting and redefined product markets in the sector. In this regard, India's experience with telecommunications had some similarities to other countries, and in 2000 as part of its neo-liberal agenda, the government restructured it on a commercial basis as a PSU – Bharat Sanchar Nigam Ltd (BSNL) (ibid) – although to date full privatisation has not occurred.

UNION RESPONSE IN THE FORMAL SECTOR

Between 1991 and 1994 and in response to the neo-liberal turn in government policy, four all-India general strikes substantially disrupted the economy, even though the two largest union federations (BMS and INTUC) refused to partic-ipate in the first strike and gave little subsequent support (Candland 2007: 109–11; Uba 2008: 875). These strikes triggered negotiations and industry-specific discussions but failed to achieve a jointly managed restructuring process. However, it appears that anti-privatisation protests significantly increased subsequently, at least until 2003 (Uba 2008: 872–3). Uba's data exclude protests organised by political parties and include both those organ-ised by unions and by social movements and other groups. This suggests that popular opposition to privatisation – including that of the unions – was resilient in this period. At the same time, the 1998–2004 BJP-led central government pushed the neo-liberal agenda forward, with banking unions defeated over new legislation to allow increased private investment, with restructuring of electricity in Uttar Pradesh undeterred by labour protests and agitation, and with a defeat for unions over privatisation in the aluminium sector (Uba 2008: 876–7). Unions in conjunction with various social move-ments fought back with major anti-privatisation protests in the electricity and oil sectors in 2001 and 2003 (ibid). Uba's invaluable empirical data indicates three further points: a much greater propensity in the 1991–2003 period for anti-privatisation agitation by CITU and AITUC than by BMS and INTUC; an increasingly diverse range of protest methods in addition to strikes; and a decline in such union agitation in 2004 with the election of the Congress-led United Progressive Alliance government, which was dependent on left parties to stay in power and initially more hesitant vis-à-vis privatisation (Uba 2008: 874–6).

This picture of union response in the formal sector is substantially compli-cated by a combination of party political allegiances, central-state government relationships and distinctive regional factors, creating apparent paradoxes and inconsistencies in union responses. An exclusively ideological assessment of Indian unions *per se* is quite often an inadequate predictor of their response and, in particular state and political contexts, some unions have vigorously supported or opposed specific restructuring initiatives and private investment projects in apparent contradiction to their own ideological position. This has in fact been in response – and frequently subservient – to political party interests that are often defined in terms of a combination of party ideology, pragmatism and vested interest. Generally, unions have had a relatively more consistent response and posed stronger opposition to neo-liberalist initiatives when the dispute has been one with central government. In addition, the *de facto* promotion by successive central governments of their economic reform programme at a state level, mediated through state-level politics and via the dynamics of central-state government relations and inter-state-competition, has played a big part in creating the complexities and contradictions of union response to the neo-liberal agenda. It has also increased significantly the challenges to unions in terms of fragmentation and division, and thus made effective union opposition to the neo-liberal agenda considerably more difficult. Thus, arguably, union opposition to neo-liberalism at a state level has often been weakened by party political allegiances and with the respective parties often driven as much and sometimes more by a combination of opportunism and a determination to promote economic development at any price than by ideology.

However, Teitelbaum (2006) challenges the notion that Indian labour is essentially fragmented, weak, and dominated by political division. He argues that labour activism has resulted historically in a thick web of pro-worker labour legislation that has withstood the pressures of economic liberalisation. Unions have actively opposed privatisation and thus Indian labour has not been quiescent (Uba 2008). Similarly, Candland (2007) argues that unions have substantially inhibited economic reforms compared with Pakistan. Also, most of the big union federations make extensive use of their party affiliations in terms of political lobbying and this also needs to be seen as part of the union movement's critical response to the neo-liberal agenda, especially on an all-India basis, and unions have prevented some privatisations through such methods (Candland 2007: 111–14).

Another argument about union response concerns the link between workers' rights and international trade (Hensman 2010). This suggests that the International Labour Organization (ILO) core labour standards should be incorporated as a 'social clause' in international trade agreements. Although some Indian workers' organisations have supported this proposal, all the main national unions have rejected it as a protectionist measure favouring developed economies, a challenge to India's national autonomy and advancing a combined agenda of imperialism and neo-liberalism. In short, they consider labour standards to be a domestic issue (Hensman 2010). However, Hensman (2010) argues that these unions are actually supporting the neo-liberal agenda by advocating enforceable protection for capital but not for labour. She distinguishes between neo-liberalism and globalisation (Hensman 2010: 112–16), arguing that the former goes much further than the latter through World Bank and IMF demands on countries to devalue currencies, increase interest rates, cut government expenditure, deregulate the economy and privatise. On this basis, she highlights the different reasons for opposition to globalisation by the right (principally the BJP and its union federation, BMS) and the communist left (principally the CPM and implicitly its union federation, CITU), while emphasising the enthusiasm of the BJP for a neo-liberalist and anti-worker domestic agenda.

Regarding union response in the BPO/call centre and telecommunications sectors, there are interesting contrasts between them. BPO/call centre employees are largely non-unionised. This is in spite of many of them believing that unions are necessary to protect their interests and the existence of several call centre workers' organisations, such as the Union for ITES Employees (UNITES Professional), the West Bengal Information Technology Services Association (WBITSA) and the Young Professionals Collective (YPC) (D'Cruz and Noronha 2010). Human resource policies may have encouraged the slow pace of unionisation, including a focus on individualism, travel arrangements peculiar to the Indian context, the particular organisation of work, the acquired professional identity, fear of employer backlash, avoidance of conflict and employee turnover. This situation may lead to a combination of traditional union and professional association functions in the emerging collective organisations. The UNITES call centre union has also advocated partnership with employers as the only viable option, aimed to re-establish some union legitimacy and credibility (Noronha and D'Cruz 2009b).

In sharp contrast, the leading union nationally organising manual telecommunication workers in BSNL Ltd was the communist BSNL Employees Union (BSNL EU), a CITU affiliate. It had majority union membership in BSNL and had secured sole collective bargaining rights on an all-India basis through successive official union membership verifications since 2004 (Beale 2009). Although collected in Gujarat alone, there is some empirical evidence to suggest that the union aggressively opposed full-scale BSNL privatisation nationally (Beale 2009). Following its restructuring in 2000, both BJP and Congress-led central governments hesitated to take the next step and fully privatise BSNL, and the power, influence and anti-privatisation position of BSNL-EU seems to have been a significant factor in this situation (Beale 2009). The union's anti-privatisation policy and strategy was evident in the union's internal communications, campaigns, education, training and organisation of members, and its willingness to organise industrial action and protest if necessary. This case lends some support to the argument that Indian unions can be a force to be reckoned with when able and willing to challenge employers on an all-India basis and confront central government directly in relation to privatisation threats and the neo-liberal agenda – contrasting with more difficult battles that unions have waged in particular states as a result of the devolved strategy of employers and government.

In the BSNL-EU case, the union's CPM links did not seem to limit substantially its anti-privatisation stance, unlike CITU unions in CPM-led West Bengal. More generally, CITU/CPM ties appear to have been a bit less problematic for CITU union opposition to neo-liberalism on an all-India basis than has been the case in West Bengal, in spite of the inhibiting effects of CPM's participation as a junior partner in the Congress-led United Progressive Alliance central government. Thus, regardless of the factors that frequently qualify and compromise the influence of ideology on Indian union response, empirical data about BSNL-EU indicates that its communist-informed ideology was an important driver of its militancy and methods (Beale 2009).

THE RESPONSE OF UNIONS AND LABOUR-FOCUSED NGOS IN THE INFORMAL SECTOR

However, in general terms the patron-client relationship between political parties and unions may have weakened somewhat over the years (Bhattacherjee 2001; Candland 2007: 157; Mani 1995; Venkata Ratnam 2003: 247), thus providing space for new forms of unionism distinct from both party-affiliated and enterprise unionism (Hammer 2010 and others). An important example is the National Centre for Labour (NCL), a membership-based organisation that transcends political party affiliations, placing little emphasis on ideology but much emphasis on solidarity (Venkata Ratnam 1999). NCL provides a national co-ordinating and representative function for various workers' organisations, including unions, cooperatives and non-governmental organisations (NGOs), for a wide range of informal workers (Sinha 2004). Its demands include a national minimum wage, full employment, sickness and disability protection, provident fund rights, maternity benefits and crèche facilities, as well as adequate housing, equal educational opportunities, better health care, access to adequate essential goods through the public distribution system[2] and rights regarding natural resources (Venkata Ratnam 1999). Founded more recently in 2006, the New Trade Union Initiative (NTUI) is a progressive/left social and political organisation but unassociated with any political party. NTUI claims 200 affiliated unions and 500 000 members across India (Gillan 2008; Tewari 2010), using a small but established base in the formal sector to recruit non-union labour and is committed to internal democracy, international solidarity and gender equality (Gillan 2008). Organisationally, it focuses both on workplaces and on workers' communities (Tewari 2010), promoting coalition building with various social movements and civil society to represent workers' rights and interests more effectively (Gillan 2008).

These initiatives have affected the traditional unions strategically. The competition has pushed most leading national union centres to start expanding their activities with informal labour (Gillan 2008), prioritising women and casual/contract workers in union discourses, public campaigns and new union organising initiatives. In 2007, official government statistics for verified union membership within central union organisations revealed a dramatic increase in recent years (Table 10.2) and this could be attributable partly to these efforts of traditional union centres.

Table 10.2   Membership of Selected Central Trade Unions, 1989 and 2002 (millions)

Union	1989	2002
INTUC	3.51	3.95
BMS	1.88	6.22
UTUCLS	1.23	0.84
HMS	1.84	3.34
TUCC	0.27	0.73
AITUC	1.06	3.44
CITU	1.03	2.68
All trade unions	12.39	24.88

Source: Verification of Membership of Central Trade Unions, Government of India, Ministry of Labour cited in Das (2008: 971).

Over the last decade major left unions have experimented tentatively with participation in campaigns and selective coalition building with non-party organisations and social movements that are often supported by NGOs. However, this has been problematic, with concerns about 'co-option' and 'politicisation' of social movements, and such alliances potentially tempered by mutual suspicion. Many union federations – not least CITU – have strongly criticised NGOs as aiding the employers' agenda and acting to displace unions (Centre of Indian Trade Unions 2007). Unions argue that they are organisations of workers and accountable to them, while NGOs are not membership-based workers' organisations and are actually accountable only to their donors. Arguably, the advocacy process of NGOs remains confined to reconciliation with capitalism and the left union federations believe this weakens the mass, class-based democratic movement (Centre of Indian Trade Unions 2007). Most unions regard NGOs as management's accomplices, with corporate codes of conduct serving to avoid unionisation and companies enthusiastically adopting such codes also often oppose unionisation. For instance, in

Bangalore a number of units that supply Nike, Gap and Wal-Mart abhor unions but subject themselves to regular checks by these companies' local agents regarding labour standards' implementation (Roychowdhury 2005). Suspicion also prevails over the code monitoring mechanisms and unions argue that they are inevitably a more credible body to do this than NGOs. When NGOs audit compliance, they may be able to assess visible safety and child labour standards but cannot spot wage, overtime or freedom of association violations (Nathan and Posthuma 2010). Thus, while there may be a role for NGOs in monitoring standards, involving unions would seem essential. In their defence, NGOs' intervention through labour codes arguably implies a 'third way', supplementing government legal regulation and collective bargaining (Shyam Sundar 2003).

Thus, some say unions also need to maintain a distinct identity regarding the wider social movement (Sengupta 2009). With relatively superior material resources and familiarity with the state's legal-institutional framework, unions may provide the more inchoate popular movements with valuable advice, focus, strategy and leadership. However, labour's involvement with various societal groups and social and political struggles, could dissipate individual unions' energies and resources, and existing members may begin to feel that membership does not carry any special advantage in comparison with other workers' movements and organisations.

THE PUNITIVE BACKLASH OF EMPLOYERS AND GOVERNMENT

Overall, in spite of many complex challenges, problems and compromises, Indian unions continue to be a significant obstacle to the neo-liberal agenda of successive central and state governments and employers. Unions and workers have paid a price for this and strikes are often blunted by contract labour replacing strikers, with company thugs sometimes hired to intimidate union leaders (Adve 2005). Lockouts are also a common employers' weapon used to pressurise workers to accept humiliating conditions of work and to retrench them (Datt 2008). Indeed, the proportion of strikes has fallen quite dramatically, while the proportion of lockouts has risen substantially (Table 10.3).[3] Further initiatives in this war of attrition between capital and labour have been the continuous attempts by employers to circumvent unions altogether, by pressurising workers to sign new contracts individually and make pledges of good behaviour, even though 'good conduct' undertakings are illegal – thus deterring some workers from participating in collective action (Adve 2005; Roychowdhury 2005).

Another common management practice is to organise workers into plant-

Table 10.3   Disputes by Strikes and Lockouts in India

	Strikes			Lockouts		
Year	Number	Workers Involved ('000)	Man-days* Lost ('000)	Number	Workers Involved ('000)	Man-days* Lost ('000)
1994	808	626	6651	393	220	14332
1995	732	683	5720	334	307	10570
1996	763	609	7818	403	331	12467
1997	793	637	6295	512	344	10738
1998	665	801	9349	432	488	12713
2000	426	1044	11959	345	374	16804
2001	372	489	5563	302	199	18204
2002	295	900	9665	284	199	16921
2003	255	1011	3206	297	805	27050
2004	236	1903	4829	241	169	19037
2005	227	2723	10801	229	191	18864
2006	243	1712	5318	187	98	15006

*   Man-days rather than working days is the official term used by the Indian Government.

Source: Ministry of Labour and Employment, Govt of India & Ministry of Finance, Govt of India (11307)

level teams and various internal workers' committees that focus on relatively non-political issues, such as the quality of canteen or transport services; and these management-driven associations compete with the more established, party-affiliated unions for workers' attention and allegiance (Adve 2005; Sengupta 2009). For instance, at Hyundai's South India plant, the management refused to recognise the union but instead signed a wage settlement with the workers' committee, arguing against recognition of party-affiliated unions (Thaindian News 2009). Workers joining party-affiliated unions in such workplaces usually face suspension and dismissal, with management ignoring external union leaders, insisting on individualised dealings with workers and refusing to participate in tripartite discussions (Roychowdhury 2005).

Similarly, although Indian labour laws do not prevent the formation and registration of unions inside SEZs, in practice investors and zone authorities discourage unionisation and SEZ companies have been granted public utility status by the respective state governments under the 1947 Industrial Disputes Act, which prohibits recourse to strikes without conciliation. Also, responsibility for industrial dispute resolution within SEZs rests with a development commissioner (an executive appointed by central government's Ministry of Commerce) and this tends to disfavour workers' interests (Murayama and Yokota 2009).

In addition, the inter-state competition that encourages close state government-employer relations through various financial incentives has been accompanied sometimes by brutal police methods aimed to crush workers' and unions' demands. One glaring example has been the ruthless violence by state police against striking Honda Motor and Scooters India employees (Adve 2005). While some workers were charged with murder, no case was filed against management for imposing an illegal undertaking on workers that restrained them from joining unions. Similarly, the Left Front Government of West Bengal also used the police and CPM cadres to repress people in Singur, in encouraging Tata Motors to establish its small car factory there (Datt 2008). Another example concerned the Uttar Pradesh (UP) State Government, which used the Essential Services Maintenance Act (ESMA) and the National Security Act to attack its own workers in the UP Electricity Board's strike in January 2000. Similarly, the Tamil Nadu (TM) State Government used the Tamil Nadu ESMA in September 2002 to suppress the TM State Government employees' strike. Furthermore, the Supreme Court declared in 2003 that both central and state government employees have no fundamental, legal, moral or equitable right to go on strike (T.K. Rangarajan v. Government of Tamil Nadu and Others 2003 SOL Case No. 429); and the judiciary reversed its own judgment on contract labour absorption in the case of Steel Authority of India (Datt 2008).

CONCLUSION

To summarise, the Indian government and employers' neo-liberal agenda came to the fore in the 1990s, key determinants being India's 1991 fiscal crisis, IMF and World Bank demands arising from this and India's participation in the WTO from 1995. However, a gradual departure from the dominant, post-independence Nehruvian model was evident from the mid-1970s. Also, from the mid-1990s onwards direct and explicit central government endorsement of neo-liberal policy remained relatively gradual and cautious in practice, with a desire to avoid unnecessary national confrontations over the issues with unionised labour and the wider populace. Instead, a devolved government-employer strategy emerged to promote neo-liberalism on a state by state basis, thus exploiting competition between state governments to attract investment. Central to the neo-liberal agenda in India has been (a) a programme of restructuring and where possible ultimately privatisation of public sector organisations; (b) extensive debate about labour law reform, which threatened to weaken workers' rights; (c) attempts to deregulate the formal/organised employment sector and expand the informal labour force; and (d) the very rapid establishment and growth of SEZs. Combined with wider popular opposition to the neo-liberal agenda, Indian unions overall have played a role in deterring a more rapid pace of change, and in limiting the confidence of central government and employers to confront the Indian union movement on the national stage, in a set-piece battle with the aim of inflicting a decisive defeat on the unions. Nationwide strikes, labour campaigns and protests against the neo-liberal agenda continue to occur and to pose a challenge to central government and employers.

However, we conclude that this has not been on the basis of a consistent and comprehensive opposition to capitalism by any of the main union federations or in clear pursuit of an explicit socialist agenda. At one extreme, in spite of BMS' occasional participation in demonstrations and strikes with other unions, and its critical nationalist rhetoric regarding some aspects of globalisation (linked as it is to the BJP), the BMS leadership has actually embraced neo-liberalism and argued for a 'mutual gains' agenda. In practice, INTUC's response to neo-liberalism would seem to vary between a similar mutual gains position and support for a regulated labour market; at most, its rhetoric may occasionally call on social democratic concepts in its Nehruvian tradition. INTUC is also frequently compromised by its close, top-down affiliation to Congress, a party that has done so much to promote neo-liberalism in recent decades. As for the big communist union federations, AITUC and CITU do pose a more significant opposition and can rally substantial support in national strikes and demonstrations targeted at central government. They are, however, hampered by the willingness of their respective political parties to endorse some elements of the neo-liberal agenda. CPM (to which CITU is linked) is criticised from the left, especially for its participation as a junior partner in the Congress-led 2004–9 central government and in light of CPM-led state government policies in West Bengal (New Socialist Alternative 2009 for instance). The new union centres, NCL and NTUI, may have advantages in combating neo-liberalism by rejecting both party links and any kind of mutual gains perspective, but NCL has also been criticised by CITU for its engagement with 'undemocratic' NGOs. Clearly overall, Indian unions face considerable, complex challenges in terms of neo-liberalism and they desperately need to unionise informal sector workers; to be more effective in enforcing basic legal rights in the workplace; to ensure union political affiliations are decreasingly an obstacle to workers' solidarity and to find a way through the issue of union-party links.

In short, central government and employers, and clearly the World Bank, consider there to be much unfinished business in India in terms of the neo-liberal agenda, while in spite of their weaknesses the Indian unions have engaged in a myriad of protracted struggles – but neither side has been able or willing to inflict a decisive defeat on the other. However, the immense pressures from below in terms of the enormity of workers' grievances and the utter desperation of India's poor are undoubtedly an important factor in this situation – as demonstrated, for example, by the impressive September 2010 all-India general strike (Centre of Indian Trade Unions 2010; New Socialist Alternative 2010) – and this indicates very considerable potential to push the balance of power in favour of the unions. Even the Hindu fundamentalist BMS faces fundamental, relentless pressures to reconcile its party's traditional, nationalist, elitist and communalist agenda with the day-to-day demands of its poverty-stricken rank and file members. As for CPM (and CITU), in spite of its ideological association historically with class struggle and the most exploited sections of society, it is experiencing a growing challenge from more radical sections of the labour force and the rural poor as a result of its concessions to neo-liberalism, especially but not only in West Bengal. CITU and AITUC in particular may well face growing pressure from their membership to adopt a more militant and anti-capitalist position or face new divisions and splits. The immense upward pressures from the poor and the millions of downtrodden workers also indicate considerable possibilities for new union organisations. Overall, this does suggest great potential for the Indian union movement to develop and mount a more effective challenge to neo-liberalism than it has to date, although if realised this may be in spite of rather than because of the leadership of the main, existing party-aligned union federations.

An additional key factor concerns the ability and willingness of unions to mobilise on an all-India basis in pursuit of workers' own needs and demands, rather than being driven primarily by the campaigns of the main existing parties and by regional and local interests. In India, this is clearly a difficult task and much more so in some employment sectors than others. But if this were to happen alongside a more representative and growing union movement, that began to organise the vast number of informal workers and cut across the many divisions within the Indian labour force, this would threaten to defeat the central government neo-liberal agenda and greatly inhibit employers and state governments in its pursuit.

NOTES

1.   The terms 'unorganised' and 'informal' sector are used interchangeably in the Indian context, as are the terms 'organised' and 'formal' sector. The National Commission for Enterprises in the Unorganised Sector (NCEUS) adopted the following definition of the unorganised sector: 'The unorganised sector consists of all unincorporated private enterprises owned by individu-

als or households engaged in the sale and production of goods and services operated on a proprietary or partnership basis and with less than 10 total workers' (Kannan and Papola 2007).
2.   The Department of Public Distribution is charged with the prime responsibility of the management of the food economy of the country. The twin objectives of the department are to ensure remuneration rates for Indian farmers and the supply of food grain at reasonable prices to consumers through the public distribution system.
3.   However, perhaps this picture needs to be treated with some caution, since official statistics do not report political strikes (Uba 2008: 873–4). Uba (ibid) also shows that protest against privatisation more generally rose substantially in the 1991–2003 period, although Table 10.3 does refer to the different time frame of 1994–2006.

REFERENCES

Adve, N. (2005), 'Living to fight another day: the attack on Honda's workers', *Economic and Political Weekly*, **40**(37), 4015–19.
Ahluwalia, M. (2002), 'Economic reforms in India since 1991: has gradualism worked?', *Journal of Economic Perspectives*, **16**(3), 67–88.
Balasubramanyam, V.N. and V. Mahambare (2001), 'India's economic reforms and the manufacturing sector', Lancaster University Management School working paper 2001/010.
Beale, D. (2009), 'Indian public sector trade unionism in Modi's Gujarat: compromise, incorporation or defiance?', presentation to British Universities Industrial Relations Association annual conference, University of Cardiff.
Bhattacherjee, D. (1999), 'Organized labour and economic liberalization in India: past, present, and future', International Institute for Labour Studies discussion paper, DP/105/1999, ILO, Geneva.
Bhattacherjee, D. (2001), 'The evolution of Indian industrial relations: a comparative perspective', *Industrial Relations Journal*, **32**(3), 244–63.
Bhattacherjee, D. and P. Ackers (2010), 'Introduction: employment relations in India – old narratives and new perspectives', *Industrial Relations Journal*, **41**(2), 104–21.
BSNL (2009), '150 years of Indian telecommunication', accessed at www.bsnl.co.in/150/index.html.
Candland, C. (2007), *Labor, Democratization and Development in India and Pakistan*, London: Routledge.
Centre of Indian Trade Unions (CITU) (2007), 'Report of the General Secretary', presented at the 12th Conference of the CITU, Chennai.
Centre of Indian Trade Unions (2010), 'Historic general strike on 7th September 2010 rocks the country', accessed at http://citucentre.org/press_release/details.php?id=399& phpMyAdmin=3a7a0d985d532b349002380a96a45723.
Das, S.K. (2008), 'Trade unions in India: union membership and union density', *Indian Journal of Labour Economics*, **51**(4), 369–982.
Datt, R. (2008), 'Emerging trends in trade union movement', *Mainstream*, **41**(20), accessed at www.mainstreamweekly.net/article678.html.
D'Cruz, P. and E. Noronha (2010), 'Employee dilemmas in the Indian ITES-BPO sector', in J. Messenger and N. Ghosheh (eds), *Offshoring and Working Conditions in Remote Work*, Basingstoke and Geneva: Palgrave Macmillan and ILO.
D'Souza, E. (2010), 'The employment effects of labour legislation in India: a critical essay', *Industrial Relations Journal*, **41**(2), 122–35.
Gillan, M. (2008), 'Parting of the ways: trade unions, NGOs and social movements in India', presentation to the Biennial Conference of the Asian Studies Association of Australia, Melbourne, VIC.
Government of India (2009), 'Indian economy: economic indicators from 1991', accessed 14 May at http://business.gov.in/indian_economy/eco_indicators.php.
Government of India (2010), 'Economic survey 2009–2010', accessed at http://indiabudget.nic.in/es2009–10/esmain.htm.

Hammer, A. (2010), 'Trade unions in a constrained environment: workers' voices from a new industrial zone in India', *Industrial Relations Journal*, **41**(2), 168–84.

Hensman, R. (2001), 'The impact of globalisation on employment in India and responses from the formal and informal sectors', CLARA working paper no.15, Amsterdam, Netherlands.

Hensman, R. (2010), 'Labour and globalization: union responses in India' *Global Labour Journal*, 1(1), 112–31.

Jenkins, R. (2004), 'Labor policy and the second generation of economic reform in India', *India Review*, **3**(4), 333–63.

Kikeri, S. and A. Kolo (2005), 'Privatization: trends and developments', World Bank policy research working paper no. 3765.

Labour file (2008), 'Increase in labour force', Labourfile News Service, 14 March.

Mani, M. (1995), 'New attempt at workers' resistance: National Centre for Labour', *Economic and Political Weekly*, **30**(40), 2485–6.

Murayama, M. and N. Yokota (2009), 'Revisiting labour and gender issues in export processing zones:cases in South Korea, Bangladesh and India', *Economic and Political Weekly*, **44**(22), 73–83.

NASSCOM (2003), *Strategic Review 2003*, New Delhi: NASSCOM.

NASSCOM (2006), *Strategic Review 2006*, New Delhi: NASSCOM.

NASSCOM (2007), *India ITES-BPO Strategy Summit 2007: Background and Reference Source*, New Delhi: NASSCOM.

NASSCOM (2010), *Strategic Review 2010*, New Delhi: NASSCOM.

Nathan, D. and A. Posthuma (2010), 'Conclusion', in A. Posthuma and D. Nathan (eds), *Labour in Global Production Networks in India*, New Delhi: Oxford University Press, pp. 348–71.

National Sample Survey (2007), *Employment and Unemployment Situation in India 2004–05, NSS 61st Round, July 2004–June 2005*, New Delhi: Ministry of Statistics and Programme Implementation, Government of India.

New Socialist Alternative (2009), 'Countrywide elections have begun', accessed at www.socialistworld.net/doc/3544.

New Socialist Alternative (2010), '7th September general strike will herald a new wave of radicalisation!', accessed at http://socialism.in/?p=37.

Noronha, E. and R.N. Sharma (1999), 'Displaced workers and withering of welfare state', *Economic and Political Weekly*, **34**(23), 1454–60.

Noronha, E. and P. D'Cruz (2009a), *Employee Identity in Indian Call Centres: The Notion of Professionalism*, New Delhi: Response Books.

Noronha, E. and P. D'Cruz (2009b), 'Engaging the professional: organising call centre agents in India' *Industrial Relations Journal*, **40**(3), 215–34.

Patnaik, P. (2009), 'The crisis of the left', *Economic and Political Weekly*, **44**(44), 27–32.

Roychowdhury, S. (2005), 'Labour activism and women in the unorganised sector: garment export industry in Bangalore', *Economic and Political Weekly*, **40**(22), 2250–5.

Sampat, P. (2008), 'Special economic zones in India', *Economic and Political Weekly*, **43**(28), 25–9.

Sengupta, M. (2009), 'Economic liberalization, democratic expansion and organized labour in India: towards a new politics of revival?', *Just Labour: A Canadian Journal of Work and Society*, **14**, 13–32.

Shyam Sundar, K.R. (2003), 'Organizing the unorganized', accessed at www.india-seminar.com/2003/531/531%20k.r.%20shyam%20sundar.htm.

Singh, G. (1995), 'Who needs an exit policy anyway?', *Economic and Political Weekly*, **30**(23), 1359–60.

Sinha, P. (2004), 'Representing labour in India', *Development in Practice*, **14**(1–2), 127–35.

Sinha, A. (2005), *The Regional Roots of Developmental Politics in India: A Divided Leviathan*, Bloomington, IN: Indiana University Press.

Suresh, T. (2010), 'Cost cutting pressures and labour relations in Tamil Nadu's automobile components supply chain', in A. Posthuma and D. Nathan (eds), *Labour in Global production networks in India*, New Delhi: Oxford University Press, pp. 251–71.

Taylor, P., D. Scholarios, E. Noronha and P. D'Cruz (2007), *Employee Voice and Collective Formation in the Indian ITES-BPO Industry*, Bangalore, India: UNITES.

Teitelbaum, E. (2006), 'Was the Indian labour movement ever co-opted? Evaluating standard accounts', *Critical Asian Studies*, **38**(4), 389–417.

Tewari, M. (2010), 'Footloose capital intermediation, and the high road in low wage industries', in A. Posthuma and D. Nathan (eds), *Labour in Global production networks in India*, New Delhi: Oxford University Press, pp. 146–65.

Thaindian News (2009), 'Labour trouble brews again in Hyundai Motor', accessed at www.thaindian.com/newsportal/business/labour-trouble-brews-again-in-hyundai-motor_100281375.html.

Uba, K. (2008), 'Labor union resistance to economic liberalization in India: what can national and state level patterns of protest tell', *Asian Survey*, **48**(5), 860–84.

Venkata Ratnam, C. S. (1999), 'Indian trade unions in the informal sector: finding their bearings. Nine country papers', *Labour Education*, **3**(116).

Venkata Ratnam, C. (2003), *Negotiated Change: Collective Bargaining, Liberalisation and Restructuring in India,* New Delhi: Sage Publications.

World Bank (2009), 'India at a glance', accessed at http://devdata.worldbank.org/AAG/ind_aag.pdf.

World Bank (2010a), 'India country overview April 2010', accessed at www.worldbank.org.in/WBSITE/EXTERNAL/COUNTRIES/SOUTHASIAEXT/INDIAEXTN/0,,contentMDK:20195738~pagePK:141137~piPK:141127~theSitePK:295584,00.html.

World Bank (2010b), 'India country strategy 2009–12', accessed at http://www.worldbank.org.in/WBSITE/EXTERNAL/COUNTRIES/SOUTHASIAEXT/INDIAEXTN/0,,contentMDK:22006280~pagePK:141137~piPK:141127~theSitePK:295584,00.html.

11 Russian unions after communism: a study in subordination

Sarah Ashwin

INTRODUCTION

Russia's neo-liberal reform programme combined the 'textbook economics' of 'market fundamentalists' (Stiglitz 2002: 138) with a long governmental tradition of 'callous economic radicalism' (Rosefielde 2001: 1159) – an unholy alliance often referred to as 'market Bolshevism'. Utopian experiments are facilitated by the absence of effective constraint on government action and Russian society in the 1990s was unable to offer such restraint. Along with the rest of Russian civil society, Russian unions were weak and ill-prepared for the whirlwind of transformation. On the eve of reform, Russia's unions were divided into two camps: the anti-communist independent unions, and the former communist unions which had organised 99 per cent of Soviet employees (including managers). The former broadly supported economic reform, while the latter, though they were far more critical, had little credibility. At the time, it seemed that the independent workers' movement might represent the future of Russian unionism, with the former communist unions decaying along with the system of which they were an integral part. But the strike wave of 1991, which looked like a promising beginning, instead turned out to be the high point in the influence of the independent workers' movement. Independent unions proved unable to expand beyond their small base in mining and transport, and remain tiny in comparison with the former communist unions. Although independent trade unions also exist in health, education and municipal transport, their main significance is to act as a spur to the former communist unions to improve their representation of members. In analysing Russian unions' response to neo-liberal structural adjustment, this chapter therefore focuses on the latter, those to which the overwhelming majority of Russian union members belong.

When the Soviet system collapsed in 1991 the former communist unions had only just asserted their independence from the Communist Party, were remote from their members and subordinate to enterprise management. Thus, as economic reform began, Russia's recently renamed Federation of Independent Trade Unions was confronted not only with the strategic task of developing a response to neo-liberalism, it also faced the more fundamental challenge of defining a new *raison d'être*. In the period 1991–3, the FNPR tried to oppose neo-liberal reform, but this policy merely served to expose the union's dependence on the government, and weak relationship with its members. The union's attempted resistance ended in failure and, after a change in leadership, the FNPR adopted the conciliatory policy of 'social partnership'. This facilitated the institutional survival of the unions, but did little to defend their members. While the unions pursued partnership, 'shock therapy' continued largely unopposed. In this article, I argue that Russian unions' response to neo-liberalism can only be understood in relation to the wider challenge they faced in defining a new role. All union movements define their strategies 'under circumstances directly encountered, given and transmitted from the past', but in the Russian case these circumstances were particularly unpropitious. The chapter begins with an overview of neo-liberal reform in Russia. It then traces and explains the FNPR's path from resistance to conciliation, concluding with an assessment of the unions' role in the Putin era.

MARKET BOLSHEVISM

Although Russia's route to the market was not as short as expected, it was certainly nasty and brutish. This was in large part because the attempted 'shortcut to capitalism' neglected to establish the basic institutional prerequisites of a functioning market economy (Stiglitz 2002: 139). 'Shock therapy' began in the absence of an appropriate social safety net; banking laws; bankruptcy laws; anti-monopoly regulation, to name some of the most glaring omissions. Most importantly, although Russia was supposedly a democracy, little emphasis was placed on the establishment of the rule of law, with the implementation of economic reform encouraging rather than inhibiting lawlessness. The most dramatic examples of this tendency were Yeltsin's military assault on the Russian parliament in 1993 because of its resistance to reform, and the routine use of non-payment of wages and pensions as a form of economic management. Both practices were accepted by the international financial institutions as necessary evils of the reform era. The development of lawlessness brought devastating social consequences, and arguably established the preconditions for the rolling back of the democratic gains of the 1990s in the new century, as Russians opted for authoritarian government in preference to the Hobbesian 'war of all against all' which began to take hold in the Yeltsin era.

Russia followed a standard structural adjustment package of liberalisation, stabilisation and privatisation which conforms to the definition of neo-liberalism laid out in the introduction. The specific features of neo-liberalism *à la Russe* stem from the speed with which the programme was introduced, the lack of appropriate institutions, and the lack of constraint over the ruling elite which encouraged reckless and corrupt implementation. Most prices were freed overnight in January 1992, plunging Russia into hyperinflation, and wiping out savings. This inflation was then controlled by high interest rates and strict control of the money supply – so-called 'stabilisation'. It is widely agreed that this caused a liquidity crisis which denied enterprises the funds they required for restructuring, and set in train a reversion to barter as the economy was 'de-monetised'. Routine non-payment of wages was a result of this policy, including on the part of the government which were regularly delayed paying the wages of 'budget' (public) sector employees. The first two steps in the reform programme set the stage for a very corrupt privatisation process. The elimination of savings meant that private individuals had no money with which to invest. This was formally compensated for by the voucher privatisation scheme of 1992–4 which allowed employees to receive a share in the ownership of their enterprises either through a give-away (in the first variant allowed in the law) or through the use of the vouchers which were distributed to the population (the second variant). In the first variant the majority of shares remained in the hands of the State Property Committee for subsequent sale, as opposed to 49 per cent in the second variant. Even under the second variant, managers remained firmly in control of the enterprises (Clarke 1996). Meanwhile, the lack of liquidity implied by stabilisation left enterprises on the verge of bankruptcy, and unpaid workers desperate for money – which meant that shares could be acquired for knock-down prices. The consolidation of ownership was completed by the 1995 loans-for-shares scandal, in which the government acquired loans from private banks, many of them owned by friends of the government. Shares in state enterprises were put up as collateral, creating instant billionaires when the government defaulted on the loans. Enterprises ended up in the hands either of their owners, or of political insiders with close relationships with the government. Meanwhile, since there was no money available for restructuring, the easiest way for the new owners to make money was through asset stripping – which was endemic.

The outcomes of this programme were 'what the critics of shock therapy predicted – only worse' (Stiglitz 2002: 187). The decline in Russia's GDP in the 1990s was steeper and deeper than that experienced during the Great Depression in the US (Connor 2000: 199; Rosefielde 2001: 116); indeed, Russia is said to have endured the 'deepest and most sustained recession in world history' during the reform era (Clarke 1999: 1). This led to a devastating decline in living standards for the majority of the population. In mid-1998 statistical real wages were a little over half their 1985 level. Moreover, this decline was accompanied by a huge growth in inequality, implying the position of poorest had declined even further (Clarke 1999: 120). Unemployment was not as high as was expected, reaching 9.7 per cent in 1996, and rising to a peak of 13.2 per cent in 1998 (Goskomstat 2003: 130). Comparatively low unemployment was little cause for celebration, however, since it merely reflected the fact that labour was so cheap and flexible that enterprises had little reason to shed staff. Enterprises routinely resorted to late payment of wages, short time and enforced leave during the 1990s, and encountered little protest from workers who continued to work without pay for months at a time (Ashwin 1999).

State support also declined substantially and failed to meet new needs. For example, by 2000 child benefit amounted to only six per cent of the state-defined child subsistence minimum (Clarke, 2002: 4). During the 1990s only a small proportion of those unemployed according to the Labour Force Survey were registered with the Employment Service and eligible for benefits. This reached a maximum of 37 per cent in 1996, but in most years of the decade ranged from 14 to 25 per cent (author's calculations using Goskomstat 2000: 84). It is thus not surprising that by 2001 more than a quarter of Russians were living below the subsistence minimum (Goskomstat 2003: 189), itself a very strict poverty line, equal to approximately a third of the Soviet poverty line.

The social impact of this was most visible in mortality rates – particularly among working-age men. One estimate places the number of premature deaths caused by the shock therapy of 1990–98 as high as 3.4m (Rosefielde 2001). Male life expectancy plummeted in the reform era, declining from 64.2 in 1989 (Goskomstat 2002: 105), to a low of 57.5 in 1994. It then recovered to 61.3 in 1998, only to fall back to 58.4 in 2002 (Goskomstat 2003: 117). Meanwhile, female life expectancy remained more constant, declining from 74.4 in 1989 (Goskomstat 2002: 105) to a nadir of 71.1 in 1994, followed by a stabilisation at over 72 between 1996 and 2002 (Goskomstat 2003: 117). Researchers searching for the causes of this catastrophe have cited the 'state of confusion, uncertainty and calamity' experienced by Russians in the face of 'dramatic changes in the labour market' – in short, severe social stress (Shkolnikov *et al.* 1998: 2008–9).

Stuckler *et al.* (2009) arguing rapid mass privatisation programmes in the former Eastern bloc were associated with a short-term increase in mortality rates of working-age men, also showed that social capital (as measured by the proportion of the population who belonged to at least one social organisation) significantly reduced this association. In Russia, neither economic policy nor its impact was ameliorated by 'social capital'. The lack of collective agency is well captured by the words of one cabinet minister of the early Yeltsin era, who remarked that Russians reacted to reform by 'going into their homes and dying' (Standing 1996: 250). There was some protest in response to the reform programme – there were sporadic, spontaneous strikes, particularly in response to wage delays of more than six months. But these strikes were rarely led by FNPR affiliates, and had little impact on their policy. Overall the Russian case is one of union failure to challenge or ameliorate neo-liberalism. Its effects were devastating, and the unions offered no significant protection to their members even in the face of flagrant violation of basic elements of labour law, notably the requirement to pay wages on time. As will be seen in the next section, however, it was difficult to pursue a more assertive policy given the unions' past.

POST-SOVIET UNIONS ON THE EVE OF REFORM

In developing their responses to neo-liberalism, all union movements are constrained by their histories: their accumulated resources (or lack thereof); political alliances; ideological traditions; repertoires of collective action, and so on. But in the Russian case the constraints on strategic choice were particularly compelling. These resulted from the unions' history as agents of the state and management, rather than as workers' representatives. The unions entered the transition era with no experience of representation let alone mobilisation, and a weak relationship with their members. This left them dependent for survival on the state at central level and enterprise management at the base – a condition which was hardly conducive to the development of a strategic response to economic reform.

Soviet unions were never intended to represent workers' interests, because supposedly there could be no conflict of interest between workers, and their vanguard, the ruling Communist Party. Instead, they performed a variety of state and managerial functions. At enterprise level, unions were charged with enforcing labour discipline, raising productivity through means such as 'socialist competition', and administering the social and welfare infrastructure of enterprises, a duty they acquired in the Stalin era. Over time this became the most important role of unions. Acting as both an agent of state social policy and an adjunct of management they administered not only social insurance but the vast social infrastructure of the Soviet enterprise: the housing waiting list; kindergartens; holiday vouchers and complexes; health facilities; allotments, as well as the social programme of enterprises. They also provided financial assistance to their members, helping with expenses such as funeral costs. Some of these services were funded by the state social security fund which the unions used to administer, some by enterprises, and the remainder by union dues (Ashwin and Clarke 2003: 17–22).

This presented obvious problems during the transition era. While they often complained that unions did not represent them, workers expected unions to provide social services. Most visits to union offices concerned these services rather than representational issues, and union presidents were judged by indicators such as the quality of the New Year's presents (see Ashwin 1999: 93, 2004: 32). To antagonise management was to risk losing control of this social empire, which constituted the basis of unions' historic relationship with their members. On the other hand, building a different relationship with members would require unions to develop their representational capacity – which would imply siding with workers in opposition to management.

Unions' relationship with the state was equally problematic. In addition to administering the state social security fund, the unions also ran the health and safety inspectorate. Meanwhile, they had been granted vast property by the state in their capacity as managers of the social sphere – tourist organisations, clubs and cultural centres, libraries, pioneer camps and sporting facilities. They also had organisational privileges such as the automatic check off of union dues. Again, this meant they entered the reform era with a lot to lose.

In some respects, the unions were quick to respond to the challenges of the reform era. The All-Union Central Council of Unions (VTsSPS) asserted its independence from the Party as early as 1987, and was later replaced by a new General Confederation of Unions (VKP) in October 1990, in which the organisations of what were still the republics of the Soviet Union, and the branch unions, had a greater degree of autonomy. Meanwhile, from the spring of 1990, the official branch organisations began to establish republican organisations. At this time the Russian confederation, the FNPR, was established, again asserting its independence of the Party and state, but also fighting for greater independence from the VKP. The branch unions – organised on an industry basis, with all the workers (and managers) in a particular industry belonging to the same union – initiated similar name changes and declarations of reform (Ashwin 1999: 84–85).

The inclusion of the word 'independent' in the FNPR's name was an acknowledgement of the fact that with the demise of communism the justification for state-dependent unions had disappeared. To survive, unions had to assert their claim to fulfil the usual function of unions: defence of workers' interests. And indeed, many reformers within the movement had a genuine desire to perform this function. The problem was that independence could only be based on a relationship with union members – something union leaders candidly admitted they did not have. Indeed, in 1992 the then vice-president of the FNPR, Vladimir Kuzmenok, acknowledged during an interview that the unions had been a 'state within a state' and had very weak links with their members. He had no illusions: if the government imprisoned the whole of the FNPR leadership not one worker would lift a finger to defend them (ICFTU 1992). But developing a new relationship with members based on defence of their interests was an uncertain endeavour, especially given workers' distrust of the unions. In short, achieving genuine independence was a great deal more arduous than deciding on a name change.

The FNPR's rebranding had little impact on its structural organisation which has retained its Soviet form. As in the past, primary organisations are affiliated to a regional branch committee (*obkom*), and the obkoms are affiliated to regional federations (uniting different branches) and to the central committees of their branch unions. Meanwhile, some unions also have district and town committees (see Ashwin and Clarke 2003: chapter four for more details on their structure and membership). The preservation of Soviet-era structures underlines the institutional resilience of the FNPR: in a period of transformation the union has retained its integrity and much of its infrastructure. Even more significantly, the union has retained a significant proportion of its membership: the FNPR still organises approximately 45 per cent of employees (Kozina 2009: 25).

The main difference from the Soviet era lies in the FNPR's abandonment of democratic centralism as the principle of union governance. This has given autonomy to member organisations, and has destroyed the ability of the centre to enforce policy down what is referred to as the union 'vertical'. A key result of the policy has been the ability of the enterprise organisations to retain a greater proportion of dues, up from an average of 67 per cent in the mid-1980s to around 80 to 85 per cent in the mid-1990s (Ashwin and Clarke 2003: 88). Thus, the centre has been weakened in both financial and political terms, and all higher organisations of the union are now in the position of having to prove their efficacy to primary organisations they purport to service.

ATTEMPTED RESISTANCE TO NEO-LIBERALISM

Attempting to find its feet in the post-communist environment, the FNPR faced conflicting pressures. The union was anxious not to antagonise the Yeltsin government which had the power to remove its considerable institutional privileges. But at the same time, the FNPR faced pressure to respond to the government's 'shock therapy' programme which was plunging its supposed constituency into poverty. Despite internal tensions, the union leadership eventually adopted a policy of opposition to economic reform. As will be seen below, this attempted resistance above all revealed the structural constraints on FNPR policy making. The union proved unable to chart an independent course, and was eventually forced back into the familiar position of building collaborative relations with the government.

From the outset, the FNPR was aware of its vulnerability. When Yeltsin had banned political organisations from the workplace in July 1991, there had been an immediate fear that the FNPR unions would also fall under this decree. Gorbachev set a further dangerous precedent when he nationalised the property of the Communist Party in August 1991. Yeltsin's suspension of the Communist Party, which was followed by its banning in November 1991, renewed fears that an attack on the unions would follow. The independent unions, which had played a major role in supporting Yeltsin's rise to power and had good connections in his entourage, were clamouring for the abolition of the FNPR and the nationalisation of its property. In September 1991 it was made known that a draft decree to this effect sat on Yeltsin's desk, awaiting only his signature. The threat of dissolution receded as the autumn progressed however, not least because the government realised that it was impractical to dissolve the unions given the wide range of social and welfare functions they fulfilled.

The immediate response of FNPR to Yeltsin's reform programme was to try to establish its credentials as the representative of its members' interests. The FNPR leader, Igor Klochkov, called 'unity of action' days for Oct 21–6 1991, despite Yeltsin's appeal to the unions to enter into negotiations with the government over its reform plans. However, FNPR's attempted display of strength back-fired when its demonstrations attracted a derisory turn-out. A warning strike called for November was cancelled, supposedly on the grounds that Yeltsin had accepted FNPR's main demands. After this set-back, the FNPR adopted a more cautious stance announcing a four month moratorium on strikes just as prices were freed in January 1992. The outbreak of spontaneous strikes particularly in coal mining, health and education in response to hyperinflation soon breached this policy. In March 1992 the FNPR issued a Declaration on Socio-Economic Policy which aimed at averting the collapse of production and living standards and included a proposed substantial increase in the minimum wage. Following a visit by Klochkov to Japan, FNPR launched its 'Spring Campaign' through 'Days of Unity of Action of Russian Unions', with the slogan 'Market Prices – Market Wages'. Klochkov threatened to demand the resignation of the government, but the action was not a success because it lacked mass support.

In the absence of the support of its members, FNPR sought to build political alliances with other forces hostile to the reform programme. First, it developed relations with the 'industrial *nomenklatura*', becoming actively involved in the formation of a centre-left 'loyal opposition' around Arkadii Vol'skii's Union of Industrialists and Entrepreneurs, joining with Vol'skii to create the 'Assembly of Social Partnership' in July 1992 and jointly publishing a newspaper, *Rabochaya tribuna*. The initiative came from FNPR, which could not join Vol'skii's centrist party 'Civic Union' because it was constitutionally barred from engaging in political activity. Although Vol'skii's organisation was nominally an employers' body, the leaders of FNPR and VKP played a dominant role FNPR and VKP officials filled one-fifth of the seats at the November 1993 plenum of Vol'skii's Union. The replacement of Gaidar by Chernomyrdin as Prime Minister in December 1992 was at first acclaimed as a victory for the coalition between FNPR and the industrial lobby and boded well for relations between the government and FNPR. However, Chernomyrdin did not live up to expectations and there was no significant change in the course of the government.

Second, the FNPR actively lobbied its interests in the Supreme Soviet of Russia, which was moving into increasingly sharp opposition to Yeltsin. In addition to a union fraction which, according to FNPR, could count on the support of 89 deputies, FNPR had been cultivating connections with non-party political allies, to avoid being accused of engaging in politics, among opposition fractions in the Supreme Soviet and the apparatus of Khasbulatov. In the confrontation between Yeltsin and the Congress of People's Deputies in March 1993 FNPR stood on the side, calling for simultaneous elections of parliament and president in the near future.

Over the summer of 1993, tension increased between Yeltsin and the Supreme Soviet, and in the country as a whole. There were new waves of protest in the regions as the budget squeeze led to public sector wage delays. In the summer the coal miners and workers in defence plants were particularly active, while in September the teachers and scientists took action. FNPR repeatedly warned of growing unrest and unavoidable consequences if the government did not change course. On 26 August the FNPR issued an appeal in which it declared its readiness 'to struggle for the interests of labouring people with all the methods available to unions' (Gritsenko *et al.* 1999: 363). When Yeltsin suspended the parliament on 21 September, the FNPR executive committee openly sided with the latter, declaring that 'the unconstitutional limitation of the activity of one of the branches of power ... can be called nothing other than a *coup d'état*' (Gritsenko *et al.* 1999: 364). It called on workers to use all available means to protest against the unconstitutional actions, and again demanded simultaneous presidential and parliamentary elections.

This policy was a disaster for FNPR. The government responded to the union's 'disloyalty' by freezing the FNPR bank accounts, cutting off their telephones, banning the check-off of union dues, and depriving them of their control of the state social insurance fund, and for the health and safety inspection. After Yeltsin's victory over the parliament, FNPR hastily retreated. Klochkov was forced to resign at an extraordinary congress in October 1993, and the president of the Moscow Federation of Unions, Mikhail Shmakov, was elected in his place. This was not only related to Klochkov's failed policy of confrontation, but also to the centralising tendencies of his leadership (see Ashwin and Clarke 2003: 43–44). Shmakov, who had been open critical of the confrontational stance of Klochkov and had developed a policy of 'social partnership' with the Moscow city administration, was ideally placed to develop more conciliatory relations with the government.

This failed attempt to define an oppositional stance clearly revealed the constraints on union strategy. It highlighted the FNPR's inability to mobilise its members – its calls for action met with little response, and only served to reveal its weakness. Strikes and protests did occur in reaction to government policy, but these were generally neither led nor effectively coordinated by FNPR-affiliated unions. The events of the period also exposed the FNPR's acute dependence on the government – at any moment the union could be threatened with the nationalisation of its property, or the removal of its privileges. The government's reaction to its support for the parliament during the autumn confrontation showed that this was a real threat. Thus, given its weak relationship with its members, the FNPR's only hope of sustaining a critical stance lay in developing political alliances. However, in an environment in which power relations were relatively unconstrained by institutions, clear rules or ingrained habits this was a risky strategy – particularly if the union ended up on the losing side. In future, the unions were much more circumspect about openly challenging the government.

MODERATION IN THE FACE OF REFORM

After 1993, the unions quickly reoriented. Klochkov's oppositional policy had never commanded unanimous support within the union movement. While the budget-sector unions, such as health and education, and the military-industrial complex were certain losers from the reform programme, other branch unions, particularly the metallurgists, were strongly in favour of the transition to a market economy, which they anticipated would markedly improve the position of their branch and their members. Shmakov's realignment of the unions thus had two dimensions – a move away from confrontation towards conciliation, and a much greater sensitivity to the divergence of interests among the branch unions that made up FNPR. This approach was enacted in broadly three ways: 'social partnership' pursued through dialogue at multiple levels, periodic 'days of action' to emphasise the union line, and political lobbying. Of these, the second was the least important, being little more than ritual display, and achieving very little. Having been scarred by the events of 1993, the unions were very wary of any protest that could be seen as unconstitutional, and for this reason were very cautious regarding demonstrations. The other two components are examined below.

SOCIAL PARTNERSHIP

The strategy of social partnership was highly successful in ensuring the survival and institutional stability of the FNPR unions, but largely ineffective as a response to neo-liberalism. It allowed the union structures at every level to maintain themselves, giving them a much-needed direction in the new environment. But this came at a cost, as the strategy did nothing to develop union independence, and indeed relied on the maintenance of collaborative relations with the relevant power-holders.

The strategy of social partnership was facilitated by government policy which provided a framework in which an elaborate network of social partnership agreements could be developed. In November 1991 Presidential Decree No. 212 'On Social Partnership and the Resolution of Labour Disputes (Conflicts)' provided for the establishment of the Russian Tripartite Commission for the Regulation of Social-Labour Relations (RTK), and similar commissions at branch and regional levels. The RTK was established in 1992 and stands at the apex of a system of branch, regional and sub-regional tripartite (or sometimes bipartite) agreements, with enterprise collective agreements at the base. Thus, union organisations at every level have an institutional framework within which to pursue partnership. FNPR leaders claim that they adhere to the ILO model of social dialogue in which social partners enjoy parity of status and represent distinct interests (Ashwin and Clarke 2003: 132–135). In practice, however, Russian unions do not have the bargaining power to ensure genuine political exchange.

Partnership proved a brilliant vehicle for ensuring the FNPR-unions' integration into the new power structures. This applied at every level. At enterprise level, the ideology of partnership allowed unions to maintain their good (but dependent) relations with management. Since it implied an inability to mobilise the union base, the dependence of the enterprise unions was reproduced throughout the union hierarchy. Nevertheless, 'social partnership' allowed higher union structures to prove their utility both to their internal constituents and the relevant state and managerial bodies.

At the base, 'social partnership' meant that unions avoided the risk of siding with distrustful members against management. They did this in three main ways. First, just as at central level the unions allied with employers in defence of production, so at the base unions tended to act 'as an instrument of the struggle of labour collectives ... against the destructive policies of the post-Communist government' (Ilyin 1996: 68–9). This 'one enterprise' form of unionism provided a framework within which unions could represent a key interest of workers – in the survival of their workplaces. At the same time, it allowed them to serve management through their lobbying activities, which had the additional merit of channelling conflict outside the enterprise (for an example of this see Ashwin 1999: chapter four).

Second, enterprise unions sought to square the demands of members and management by acting as mediators between the two sides, rather than as representatives of their members. Thus, when conflict occurred, enterprise union organisations usually attempted to resolve it through informal negotiations with management. When such an approach failed and members pushed for further action, unions tended to use the elaborate procedures for pursuing collective labour disputes laid down by the law (see Ashwin and Clarke 2003: 127–31 on the complex legal framework) – which generally resulted in months of 'conciliation' but rarely any concessions from management. In using these procedures, unions were able to pose as 'honest brokers' between management and workers – preserving their relationship with the former, while giving the appearance of action to the latter (Ashwin 2004). Only very rarely did unions attempt to mobilise their members against management during collective labour disputes. This tended to occur when there was conflict within the management team, and the union supported the opposition faction (Ashwin and Clarke 2003: 256).

Finally, as far as possible unions continued to provide social services to their members. This was familiar and comfortable territory for union officers, and had the merit of binding members to the union, while not involving conflict with management. But this strategy had serious disadvantages. A substantial part of the unions' own social assets, much of the enterprise social and welfare apparatus and the bulk of the housing stock of enterprises was privatised or transferred to the municipalities during the course of the 1990s, while the removal of social insurance funds from unions' control in 1993 drastically reduced the resources at their disposal. Enterprise unions generally spent over 80 per cent of their income on social services,[1] but they were never able to meet the escalating demand for material assistance in a period of economic crisis. This enormous investment probably helped retain members, but it did nothing to develop a more representational form of unionism. It maintained unions' status as social and welfare providers, while diverting money from activities such as the development of strike funds, which had the potential to foster union strength.

Given that enterprise unions were usually allied with management and keen to avoid conflict, it is not surprising that higher union bodies could not depend on them to support their bargaining positions – at least in anything other than words. Thus, the higher union bodies had to depend on cultivating good relations with their relevant managerial and state interlocutors – both for their survival and to achieve any concessions. This meant that they had to prove themselves 'useful'. There were two main means of doing this. First, they could help the relevant regional or branch interest lobby the central government. Second, they could act as guarantors of social peace, acting to dampen social tension, rather than to using it to push the union agenda. These strategies helped the relevant union bodies to survive, but not to defend workers. Indeed, evidence indicates that union higher bodies were very wary of acting as representatives of their member organisations in disputes when this would bring them into direct conflict with their managerial or governmental counterparts (Ashwin 2004).

The dependency inherent in the form of Russian social partnership was visible in the character of the agreements at all levels. These did little to extend regulation or workers' rights. At enterprise level, even the better collective agreements did little more than re-state the provisions of operative labour law and the branch tariff agreements. At worst, they were confused and included provisions which were, illegally, inferior to those provided by the law and higher agreements (Ashwin and Clarke 2003: 228–9). Likewise, regional tripartite agreements were characterised by general, unenforceable provisions, a tendency to defer rather than initiate action, and repetition of existing law (Ashwin and Clarke 2003: 153–70). Branch tariff agreements were somewhat better in that they included more concrete specifications of the terms and conditions of employment specific to the branch. Although these also tended to keep close to the conditions specified in the law, they did make moderate improvements. For example, in 1999 all but one tariff agreement established a minimum wage higher than that specified by law, although still a long way below the subsistence minimum (Ashwin and Clarke 2003: 150). In all cases there were problems with enforcement, with no sanctions available in the event of non-fulfilment and no prospect of coordinated protest to uphold the agreement. Finally, the general agreements signed at national level during the 1990s replicated these flaws, containing few enforceable provisions. They were also concluded after the budget had been adopted, and thus had no impact on spending commitments.

Overall, the elaborate network of negotiated agreements did little to regulate employment relations during transition. From the base upwards, the system depended on union bodies maintaining good relations with their interlocutors, leading them to avoid confrontation at all costs. This was a huge handicap in a period of economic crisis when violations of labour law were endemic, and workers were impoverished and desperate. Rather than conflict being channelled through the elaborate mechanisms of partnership in a way that could have modified government policy or employer behaviour, it occurred outside the system. It also occurred 'outside' the unions – the waves of anger and energy leaving them largely untouched as they clung to their role as peacemakers and mediators.

Thus, during the 1990s workers were often forced into spontaneous forms of protest to press their demands such as hunger strikes, road and rail blockades, and, in extreme cases, to hostage taking and protest suicide. Such actions were nearly always in protest against late payment of wages, though they tended to be mounted only after four to six months without pay. A classic example of this was the May 1998 'rail wars' during which Russia was split in two by Kuzbass miners blocking the Trans-Siberian railway, while their comrades in Rostov blocked the North Caucasus line, after a wage delay of nearly six months. In areas where there was no site for a sufficiently disruptive blockade, workers could be pushed to even more extreme measures. In the Kuzbass town of Prokop'evsk, for example, which spent the whole of the winter of 1996 to 1997 without wages and heating, the teachers resorted to taking the chief of the education department hostage – something which, while not commonplace, occurred in several different locations during the 1990s. A more tragic act of desperation was protest suicides. In May 1998, for example, there was a wave of public suicides in Rostov, where one miner hanged himself and another threw himself down a mine shaft in drastic pleas for wage debts to be paid to their families (ICFTU 1998). Meanwhile, in 1999 the most notable form of spontaneous action was the establishment of workers' militias to defend enterprises against the imposition of hostile management teams with no commitment to the 'preservation of the labour collective'. The key sites of such protest were the Vyborg Cellulose Paper Combine in Leningrad region; the Kuznetsk Metallurgical Combine and Chernigovski open-cast mine in Kuzbass; the Krasnoyarsk aluminium factory; the Yasnogorsk engineering factory and the Kimovskii radio-technical factory in Tula.

The proliferation of these spontaneous forms of action clearly reveals the extent to which the mechanism of social partnership failed to channel workers' demands. Most of these conflicts concerned late payment of wages, which was not only illegal but also ran contrary to all the various agreements in force which generally repeated the provision from the law regarding the timely payment of wages. The system of social partnership did little to check this mass, systematic violation of labour law. Effective channelling of workers' demands could have put the government's policy of stabilisation – which was responsible for the non-payment crisis – under pressure. This is indeed what happened in Poland where a political backlash resulted in a relaxation of budgetary constraint early in the transition (King 2002). In Russia, however, it was workers who faced pressure – to survive without wages, to be patient, to endure. Meanwhile, with unions effectively promising to maintain social peace, the government could afford to divide and rule, paying out emergency sums of money whenever social tension in a particular area became too threatening, but retaining non-payment as the 'normal' form of budgetary management.

POLITICAL LOBBYING

The FNPR was fully cognisant of its weakness as a bargaining force. For this reason, it also sought to achieve its ends through lobbying and political alliances. Its aims were a moderation of the reform programme in the interests of workers and domestic producers, and the establishment of social guarantees. In terms of the schema of this book, the FNPR strategy can be seen as 'social democratic'. Some qualification is required here, however. In the 1990s the left of Russian politics was dominated by the Communist Party (KPRF), which still had substantial support. In the first round of the 1996 Presidential election, for example, Yeltsin gained 35 per cent of the vote, as compared with 32 per cent for the leader of the KPRF, Gennady Zyuganov. The private sympathies of many in the FNPR fold were also with the KPRF, but a national alliance with the Communists would have been very risky for the unions. The KPRF's strong showing in the 1993 Duma election led the presidential apparatus to emphasise the FNPR's dependence and warn them off allying with the KPRF – in February 1994 the president's allies let it be known that a decree appropriating the union's assets had been drawn up, and only awaited Yeltsin's signature (Ashwin and Clarke 2003: 44). Having experienced the dangers of confrontation, the FNPR took care to choose 'legitimate' centre-left allies, thus avoiding the charge of extremism and the consequences which might result from this. But, while it did not provoke the government, the FNPR's strategy had only modest results.

The FNPR devoted a lot of attention to lobbying in the Duma, and did achieve some successes. For example, in the period 1993–5 it was able to secure rises in the derisory minimum wage, and also claim that it had helped secure repeal of the 'excess wages tax' which penalised enterprises that paid relatively high wages (Ashwin and Clarke 2003: 46). Meanwhile, in the second Duma it also secured some concessions, such as the rejection of the government's draft of a law on the social insurance fund in favour of its own. FNPR's proposals were also taken into account in a new basic law on health and safety signed July 1999 and in the 1999 Law on Employment which included an increase in the rate of unemployment benefit (Ashwin and Clarke 2003: 53). However, in 1996 an attempt to use a change in the Civil Code to ensure that wage payments were given priority over tax payments failed. While it initially slowed the growth of private sector wage arrears, tax receipts slumped and the IMF, concerned about the government's poor tax collection record, suspended its loan. The Finance Ministry, Tax Service and Central Bank then issued a joint instruction to banks, ordering them to ignore the relevant article of the Civil Code and give tax payments priority over wage payments. This revealed the limits of legislative challenge to the government's stabilisation package – its policy would not be diverted through such bureaucratic means (for more details see Ashwin and Clarke 2003: 54–5).

In terms of alliances, in the 1995 Duma election the FNPR joined with Arkadii Vol'skii's Union of Industrialists and Entrepreneurs, to establish the social-political organisation Unions and Industrialists of Russia – Union of

Labour. The organisation made little headway, gaining only 1.59 per cent of the party list vote, well below the threshold to gain Duma representation (Ashwin and Clarke 2003: 49). For the 1999 Duma election the Union of Labour was reconstituted, this time without the industrialists. FNPR threw its support behind the mayor of Moscow, Yuri Luzhkov, and the Union of Labour participated as a founder member in the formation of Luzhkov's organisation *Otchestvo* (Fatherland). The latter then merged with an association of powerful regional governors, Vsya Rossiya (All Russia), to form Otchestvo-Vsya Rossiya (OVR). The FNPR leadership had high hopes for this centrist coalition which favoured greater state regulation of the market, but again its hopes were dashed. In the end, only four unionists were elected on the OVR list, and OVR itself was overtaken in the last stages of the campaign by Yedinstvo (Unity), the 'party of power' supported by Yeltsin and Putin (see Clarke 2001 for more details on the unions' role). The FNPR then had to engage in some frantic repositioning once it became clear that Putin was going to win the 2000 presidential election.

This electoral failure is at first sight surprising, given the union's nationwide infrastructure and membership, which should have been a major boost to the blocs it supported. However, the FNPR's endorsement did not translate into support for these organisations in the regions. The FNPR lacked the unity and discipline to mobilise its member organisations in support of its political ambitions, and was unable to exert significant influence over the voting intentions of its members. This can be traced back to the politics of social partnership. As mentioned above, in order to secure their bargaining relationships the branch and regional unions were obliged to cultivate relations with their interlocutors. This meant that they refused to follow the FNPR line in the elections where this threatened to disrupt their local alliances. For example, in the 1999 elections the regional union organisations only tended to support OVR where the local 'party of power' was allied with this organisation (Clarke 2001). Thus, the FNPR's dream of a centre-left force achieving power remained unrealised, and with it hopes of moderating the reform programme without confrontation.

UNIONS IN THE PUTIN ERA

With the increasing authoritarianism of the Russian government in the 2000s, the instinctive caution of the unions was only strengthened. They were also mollified as the economy finally began to recover from the disaster of the 1990s, wage delays became less common, unemployment fell, and incomes began to rise. This period did not see a major change in union policy, though the opportunities for cultivating oppositional political alliances were reduced.

Nevertheless, the union continued its lobbying in the Duma, and this, as in the past, did secure concessions, most importantly with regard to the new Labour Code. The achievement of a government majority after the 1999 elections meant that it could finally press ahead with long-delayed plans to revise the Labour Code. The government draft of the code proposed a radical deregulation of the labour market, while the unions supported the 'deputies' variant' of the code proposed by a working group of eight deputies from various parties. In the week before the Duma hearing of Labour Code was scheduled on 21 December 2000, the union organised a mass lobbying effort of meetings, demonstrations and a letter-writing campaign to Duma deputies (for more details about the scale of this action see Ashwin and Clarke 2003: 66). The success of this effort was evident when, at the last minute, the government postponed the hearing, to allow a conciliation committee a chance to draw up a compromise variant. This variant, which was eventually signed into law on 30 December 2001, was a significant improvement on the government draft, retaining many of the protective and regulatory features of its Soviet predecessor, and actually advancing the position of workers in some respects (for example prescribing the payment of interest on unpaid wages, and allowing workers to stop work, without pay, after a wage delay of over 15 days). Crucially, from the perspective of the FNPR, its regulation of strikes and collective bargaining weakened the alternative unions, by stipulating conditions only likely to be fulfilled by FNPR-affiliates (for more details see Bronstein 2005).

Chen and Sil (2006: 72) use the evidence of the labour code campaign to suggest 'a much greater convergence between workers' grievances and union agendas' than in the 1990s and a shift away from the unions' past status as 'transmission belts'. This optimistic reading is not supported by other evidence, however. Recent analyses of union behaviour suggest that they have proved unable to extricate themselves from their dependence on management and the state. As Kozina (2009: 27) argues, summarising the findings of recent research, the process of FNPR-unions taking on the role of workers' representatives is happening 'extremely slowly'. At enterprise level, the 'social development of the collective' in the form of sporting and cultural events remains one of their key functions (Plotnikova 2009: 58–9). It is therefore not surprising that analysts expected unions to side with management rather than their own members in conflicts arising from the 2008 financial crisis (Chetvernina 2009: 431). Meanwhile, unions are still wary of confrontation with the state, as can be seen in the FNPR's stance over the issue of the monetisation of benefits. The policy replaced in-kind benefits for pensioners, war veterans and the disabled such as free transport, medicine and local telephone calls with cash payments. Prior to the passing of the law on 22 August 2004, the FNPR had organised protests and proposed 200 amendments to the law to the Duma, many of which were adopted. Nonetheless, the compensation for the loss of benefits was seen to be inadequate, and when the law came into force on 1 January 2005 it provoked outrage, particularly among pensioners. Mass spontaneous protests erupted across the country with pensioners blocking roads, taking control of buses, and assaulting bus conductors. The FNPR, however, did not support the protesters, and indeed was critical of the demonstrations, echoing the state line that various political groups had exploited popular dissatisfaction for their own ends (Ilyin and Filatova 2005). This once again reveals the union's aversion to leading oppositional forces at moments of social confrontation.

Developments in 2006–8 likewise suggest a continuation of FNPR-unions' cautious stance. There was a notable wave of industrial action over this period, mainly in the most prosperous sectors such as fuel and energy and companies with foreign owners (Chetvernina 2009: 426; Germanov 2009: 112–13). But FNPR affiliates were usually marginal in these disputes, which sometimes led to the establishment of alternative unions (Chetvernina 2009: 427). That is, workers pursuing their own interests did not generally feel able to do so through the agency of the FNPR unions. Nevertheless, the strikes did represent a new dynamic in Russian industrial relations. Compared to the strikes of the 1990s which were largely in response to wage delays, these strikes were 'pro-cyclical', the result of rising expectations in a growing economy, thus bringing Russia more in line with trends in established market economies (Green and Robertson 2010). International comparisons and links to international union groups were also important in stimulating worker activism (Germanov 2009: 97).This suggests a potential for union growth and renewal, but the FNPR's ability to harness this is very much open to question.

CONCLUSION

'Shock therapy' was introduced at a time when the unions were very weak. The alternative unions were barely established, while the former communist unions were yet to emerge from their dependence on management and the state. It is thus not surprising that the unions proved so ineffective in defending workers during reform. They failed to channel and lead protest in a way that could have resulted in modification of the reform programme, particularly the devastating 'stabilisation' programme. They were unable to mitigate the impact on workers, and allowed late payment of wages to become a normal form of budget management. The union policy can be categorised as failed social democratic opposition. The unions felt too weak to take risks, but moderation achieved very modest results. The lack of effective social control over the government was a key reason why the economic reform programme in Russia was so brutal and corrupt.

Arguably, however, the unions' caution underlay their key achievement of the era: the maintenance of their institutional integrity. Whether or not this was a worthwhile accomplishment will depend on how the unions acquit themselves in the future. Past form suggests that they will continue to suppress conflict and eschew representation; the risks of doing otherwise are very great. But if worker activism continues to grow during the crisis and recovery the danger of being outflanked by alternative unions may begin to rival the threat of antagonising the powers that be.

NOTES

1. The 2001 ISITO survey of 1454 union presidents from nine regions found that almost half of the income of primary organisations was spent on material assistance to members, and over a third on 'mass cultural work', such as providing vacations and organising celebrations, sporting and cultural events (Ashwin and Clarke 2003: 217–18).

REFERENCES

Ashwin, S. (1999), *Russian Workers: The Anatomy of Patience*, Manchester: Manchester University Press, Manchester.

Ashwin, S. (2004), 'Social partnership or 'a complete sellout'? Russian unions' responses to conflict', *British Journal of Industrial Relations*, **42**(1), 23–46.

Ashwin, S. and S. Clarke (2003), *Russian Unions and Industrial Relations in Transition*, Basingstoke: Palgrave.

Bronstein, A. (2005), 'The new labour law of the Russian Federation', *International Labour Review*, **144**(3), 291–318.

Chen, C. and R. Sil (2006), 'Communist legacies, postcommunist transformations and the fate of organized labor in Russia and China', *Studies in Comparative International Development*, **41**(2), 62–87.

Chetvernina, T. (2009), 'Unions in transitional Russia – peculiarities, current status and new challenges', *South East Europe Review for Labour and Social Affairs*, **12**(3), 407–32.

Clarke, S. (1996), 'The enterprise in the era of transition', in S. Clarke (ed.), *The Russian Enterprise in Transition: Case Studies*, Cheltenham, UK and Northampton, MA, USA: Edward Elgar, pp. 1–61.

Clarke, S. (1999), *New Forms of Employment and Household Survival Strategies in Russia*, Coventry and Moscow: ISITO/CCLS.

Clarke, S. (2001), 'Russian unions in the 1999 Duma election', *Journal of Communist Studies and Transition Politics*, **17**(2), 43–69.

Clarke, S. (2002), *Making Ends Meet in Contemporary Russia: Secondary Employment, Subsidiary Agriculture and Social Networks*, Cheltenham, UK and Northampton, MA, USA: Edward Elgar.

Connor, W. (2000), 'The world of work, employment, unemployment and adaptation', in M. Field and J. Twigg (eds), *Russia's Torn Safety Nets: Health and Social Welfare during the Transition*, Basingstoke: Macmillan, pp. 191–212.

Germanov, I. (2009), 'Samoorganizatsii rabotnikov i protestnaya aktivnost', in I. Kozina (ed.), *Profsoyuzy na predpriyaiyakh sovremennoi rossii, vozmozhnosti rebrendinga*, Moscow: ISITO.

Goskomstat (2000), *Rossiya v tsifrakh 2000*, Moscow: Goskomstat Rossii.

Goskomstat (2002), *Demograficheskii ezhegodnik Rossii 2002*, Moscow: Goskomstat Rossii.
Goskomstat (2003), *Rossiiskii statisticheskii ezhegodnik 2003*, Moscow: Goskomstat Rossii.
Greene, S. and G. Robertson (2010), 'Politics, justice and the new Russian strike', *Communist and Post-Communist Studies*, **43**, 73–95.
Gritsenko, N., V. Kadeikina and E. Makukhina (1999), *Istoriya profsoyuzov Rossii*, Moscow: Akademiya truda i sotsial'nykh otnoshenii.
ICFTU (1992), *Report on the CIS, October 1992*, Brussels: ICFTU.
ICFTU (1998), *Report on the Russian Miners' Strike*, Brussels: ICFTU.
Ilyin, V. (1996), 'Russian unions and the management apparatus in the transition period', in S. Clarke (ed.), *Conflict and Change in the Russian Industrial Enterprise*, Aldershot: Edward Elgar, pp. 65–106.
Ilyin, V. and O. Filatova (2005), 'The political activity of Russian unions', INTAS report accessed at http//go.warwick.ac.uk/russia/intas.
King, L. (2002), 'Postcommunist divergence: a comparative analysis of the transition to capitalism in Poland and Russia', *Studies in Comparative International Development*, **37**(3), 3–34.
Kozina, I. (2009), 'Sotsial'no-ekonomicheskaya transformatsiya i novye vyzovy profsoyuznomu dvizheniyu', in I. Kozina (ed.), *Profsoyuzy na predpriyaiyakh sovremennoi rossii, vozmozhnosti rebrendinga*, Moscow: ISITO.
Plotnikova, E.B. (2009), 'Sotsial'noe partnerstvo v sfere truda i zanyatosti, zachem vlasti profsoyuzy?', in I. Kozina (ed.), *Profsoyuzy na predpriyaiyakh sovremennoi rossii, vozmozhnosti rebrendinga*, Moscow: ISITO.
Rosefielde, S. (2001), 'Premature deaths: Russia's radical economic transition in Soviet perspective', *Europe-Asia Studies*, **35**(8), 1159–76.
Shkolnikov, V., G. Cornia, D. Leon and F. Meslé, F. (1998), 'Causes of the Russian mortality: evidence and interpretations', *World Development*, **26**(11), 1995–2011.
Standing, G. (1996), 'Social protection in Central and Eastern Europe: a tale of slipping anchors and torn safety nets', in G. Esping-Andersen (ed.), *Welfare States in Transition, National Adaptations in Global Economies*, London: Sage, pp. 225–55.
Stiglitz, J. (2002), *Globalization and its Discontents*, London: Allen Lane.
Stuckler, D., L. King and M. McKee (2009), 'Mass privatisation and the post-communist mortality crisis: a cross-national analysis', *The Lancet*, **373**, 399–407.

12 Neo-liberalism, union responses and the transformation of the South Korean labour movement

Dae-oup Chang

INTRODUCTION

This article aims to analyse the nature, forms and effectiveness of the unions' response to neo-liberalism in South Korea. It does so by looking mainly at various responses from the Korean Confederation of Trade Unions (KCTU) and its affiliates and tracing the trajectory of union responses in relation to capital, the state and unorganised workers. This chapter first describes the ways in which the democratic labour movement re-emerged in the 1980s and became an important social force against the repeated attempt of the state and capital to introduce a full-scale neo-liberal reform before the Asian economic crisis of 1997–8. The second analyses the impact of the post-crisis neo-liberal restructuring that involved market liberalisation, privatisation of the public sector and 'irregularisation' of labour. The third examines the response of unions and of the KCTU in particular to neo-liberal reforms. Although the KCTU and democratic unions continue to be leading figures in challenging neo-liberal reforms, their struggle against neo-liberalism showed a zigzag development with the leadership vacillating between militancy and social dialogue, social reform and fundamental social change, and nationalism and internationalism, undermining the effectiveness of struggles against neo-liberalism. In striving to confront the neo-liberal offensive, a particular nexus between nationalism, social democracy and social corporatism emerged and secured majority leadership in the KCTU. This leadership however has been incapable of creating a wider alliance of anti-neo-liberal struggle. In the fourth the underlying reason why the KCTU can neither effectively use corporatist instruments nor charge more militant struggles against neo-liberalism is addressed. It is argued that it is largely because the KCTU failed to overcome male-dominated, formal and industrial worker-centred enterprise unionism. The concluding part suggests that for both radical socialists and nationalist social democrats, it would be extremely difficult to pursue struggles for an alternative to neo-liberalism without building up more inclusive social unionism that could integrate the increasing number of irregular workers within and outside workplaces.

THE DEMOCRATIC UNION MOVEMENT AND DELAYED NEO-LIBERALISATION IN SOUTH KOREA

The origin of the union movement in South Korea can be traced back to the period of Japanese colonisation that accelerated the capitalist transformation of Korea. A strong anti-colonial labour movement and militant unions emerged out of capitalist development with specific colonial features including indentured labour, dominance of Japanese capital over domestic capital, and surveillance and violence against workers by the implanted colonial state. Established in 1920, the Korean Labourers' Mutual Aid Association was the first labour organisation. Four years later, the Joseon General Federation of Labour was established as a nationwide labour organisation calling for class struggles against Japanese imperialism and capitalists. Marxists and socialists exercised strong influence in the early union movement by leading and supporting militant campaigns in industrial areas as well as by setting up political parties of the working class. The early union movement was capable of developing region-wide solidarity strikes and politicising labour issues to win support from a wider range of the Korean population. Although the movement suffered from the heavy suppression of the Japanese colonial authority, it continued to be one of the major vehicles of the independence movement against Japan. Militant unions re-emerged quickly after the liberation of Korea from Japan in 1945, organising the Korean National Council of Trade Unions (Jeonpyeong) in 1945 with a half-million members. However, Jeonpyeong's political struggles against US authority turned out to be an utter failure and the revived labour movement soon decomposed through the civil war. The post-war period was ruled by a strong anti-communist regime which regarded any attempt to organise unions as a threat to national security. The specific articulation of capital-labour relations in which individual capitals exercised unlimited authority at the workplaces under the auspices of the state was possible in this particular historical context. This was the social basis of successful capitalist development during the Park regime (1961–79), which tightened the state's control over collective labour through the government-established Federation of Korean Trade Unions (FKTU), emergency decrees and other super-constitutional measures. However, the control of the state over labour was by no means an absolute one as new labour activism was emerging from export industries such as the textile and garment industry where mostly young women migrants worked extremely long hours under seriously hazardous working conditions. This newly emerging labour activism took the form of individualised struggle at the beginning as seen in the desperate self-immolation protest of a young textile worker Jun Tail in 1970 but soon began to take a more collective form. Among many, women workers in Chong-gye Garment, Wonpoong Wool Textile, Bando Trading, the Dongil Textile

Company and YH Trading organised independent unions and together created a new wave of the union movement called the 'democratic union movement' by the end of the 1970s. This new union movement then penetrated into enterprises in the heavy industrial sector owned by big conglomerates (chaebols). In the early 1980s, the democratic union movement developed further in alliance with the democratisation movement, especially with the student movement (Koo 2000: 100–25). In 1987, tension built up between the growing aspiration for democracy and the military regime of Chun Doo-hwan that was increasingly utilising violent methods. In June 1987, several hundreds of thousands of people took over the streets in downtown Seoul, the capital city of Korea, and in other cities across the country and finally the military government had to promise democratic transition.

Workers not only participated in the 1987 democratisation movement but also shook the entire basis of the early capitalist development in Korea by organising a massive wave of wildcat strikes. The Great Workers' Struggle in the summer of 1987 (July–September 1987) created 1300 new democratic unions in three months through 3311 industrial disputes in which a total 1.2m workers participated (Rho 1997). Between 1986 and 1989, the number of unions increased from 2658 to 7883 and individual members from 1.036m to 1.932m (Koo 2000: 231). This led to increasing union density from 12.3 to 18.6 per cent in the same period. Democratic unions also organised a nationwide umbrella organisation, the Council of Korean Trade Unions (CKTU, Jeon-no-hyeop) in 1990. Under the leadership of the CKTU, democratic unions transformed the nature of labour relations on the shop floor by encroaching into the managerial decision-making process in enterprises. There were real gains for the workers as collective bargaining became 'a must' (Chang 2009a: 120). Wage increases in manufacturing recorded 10.4 per cent in 1987, 16.4 per cent in 1988, 20 per cent in 1989 and 16.8 per cent in 1990 while average working hours decreased from 51.9 per week in 1987 to 47.5 in 1993.

Korea's capitalist development during the decade after the Great Workers' Struggle of 1987 witnessed maturing democratic unionism, weakening state control over collective labour as well as financial market liberalisation and increasing volatility. During this period, neo-liberalisation of Korean society was only partial in nature in the sense that the restoration of the power of capital over labour remained to be achieved while the mobility of capital was greatly enhanced by relaxed state control over financial flow. Korean capital was facing increasing competitive pressure in the export market due to the changing global context of accumulation. Most of all, export-oriented industrialisation was becoming a norm among developing countries in East Asia. Thailand, Malaysia, Indonesia and more importantly China joined market competition for particularly low-end consumer goods. It was also very difficult for individual capitals to overcome this increasing competition by squeezing workers as a consequence of labour being an important socio-political force. From the late 1980s, the state was no longer as effective as before in controlling the re-emerging class struggle. Meanwhile, individual capitals, particularly the big chaebols were now able to find external funds without the mediation of the state. Individual capitals' desperate need for further investment to compensate for the eroding advantage of Korea's export drives pushed further the state to accelerate the liberalisation of financial flows. Now capital started moving beyond the early settlement of capital relations. So did labour. Therefore the early settlement of capital relations was falling into a crisis, the real implication of which was then only revealed during the Asian economic crisis. It was at this time that individual capitals began to rely heavily on private foreign loans that increased from US$31.7bn in 1990 to US$104.7bn in 1996 (Chang 2009a: 128). The first civilian government of Kim Young-sam responded to this by pursuing aggressive globalisation policies that intended to release increasing external pressure for neo-liberal reform and to satisfy internal demands for foreign loans. The relocation of productive facilities to other countries was also accelerated with foreign direct investment (FDI) outflow increasing steeply from US$591m in 1985 to US$4,740m in 1998 (UNCTAD 2002).

Although financial liberalisation coincided with global-scale neo-liberal reform, the power relations between labour and capital did not really follow the general trend. The state did attempt to overcome this emerging crisis by tightening anachronistic authoritarian control over unions and, most of all, institutionalising flexible measures that individual capitals were silently introducing (Chang 2009a: 128–30). Indeed, the state realised that 'Korea's entire future as a major centre of accumulation was critically dependent on the achievement of a substantial redistribution of income from labour to capital' (Pirie 2006: 216). However, it was during this period that labour became an important social force by establishing a nationwide union movement. The democratic union movement was consolidated by the establishment of the KCTU in 1995 that unified all major currents of the democratic union movement: the CKTU, the National Conference of Occupational Trade Unions (NCTF) and the Council of Large Companies Trade Unions (CLCTU). KCTU affiliates, with ever-growing militancy, exercised huge influence over labour relations in strategically important workplaces. Hence, ironically, a strong labour movement and a volatile financial market coexisted. The attempts of capital and the state to enhance the mobility of capital rather caused instability of the financial basis of chaebols due to growing dependency on short-term credit while attempts to remove strong unions precipitated more militant resistance from organised labour, particularly the general strike between December 1996 and March 1997. Over the four-month period, more than a million workers participated in nationwide strikes, rallies and sit-in protests, paralysing the national economy. Students, academics, civil rights and religious organisations held rallies in major cities in solidarity with the strikers. Even the largest but conservative union confederation, FKTU changed its attitude to the ruling party and organised a nationwide walkout in support of the general strike. This general strike clearly showed that the democratic labour movement established itself as a significant social and political force. Naturally, the neoliberalisation of Korea up to 1997 was essentially partial and therefore seemed not to make a great contribution to the revitalisation of Korea's capital accumulation. To complete the neo-liberal project, the state and capital needed a more dramatic turning point. Then it was the economic crisis that offered momentum. Capital accumulation based on massive credit expansion was not sustainable without restored class power of capital over labour. It burst in the form of massive liquidation of capital, triggered by a financial crisis in the East Asian region to which the Korean economy was tightly tied. It was not until the restructuring period in the aftermath of the general crisis that a new social basis of further capital accumulation emerged. The new condition of capital accumulation was based on the freer movement of capital, which went beyond the barrier of state regulation as well as organised labour. It was then more genuinely neo-liberal.

NEO-LIBERAL OFFENSIVE

Although the economic crisis involved a large-scale liquidation of capital and bankrupted many individual capitals, it worked in favour of capital's attempt to reformulate capital relations for the further accumulation of capital. It was a fundamental challenge to the labour movement. After the crisis, the newly elected government of a long-time democrat and human rights defender Kim Dae Jung 'pushed ahead with a full suite of neo-liberal reforms under the guidance of the IMF' (Shin 2010: 212). The new democratic state initiated a wholesale reform of the Korean economy with a swift financial sector reform through which unprofitable banks and non-bank financial institutions (NBFI) were merged and restructured. By 2007, about 800 troubled financial institutions exited from the market (Lim 2010: 2003) while relatively healthier ones were recapitalised by taxpayers' money and returned to the market for sale to domestic and more importantly foreign investors. This financial sector reform was accompanied by a more comprehensive and carefully designed neoliberalisation project under the principle of the rule of the market. This included three major parts: commodity and financial market liberalisation, privatisation of the public sector and irregularisation of labour.

Market liberalisation basically aimed to liberalise in-and-out flow of finance and commodities. To do so, all regulative measures that could possibly undermine the market-based flow of goods, services and finance were to be removed. Targeted were barriers against foreign borrowings of corporations, foreign exchange, purchase of public and corporate bonds by foreigners, entry of foreign insurance companies, foreign investors' ownership of the stocks of Korean firms and hostile takeovers of Korean firms by foreign investors. Also targeted by the reform were trade-related subsidies, restrictive import licensing and the import diversification programme. Financial market liberalisation was of course not a new thing to Korea as it started in the mid-1980s and accelerated in the mid-1990s. However, it was in the aftermath of the crisis that the state managed to introduce a full-scale financial market liberalisation project. Liberalisation seems to have made Korea into a good place to 'do business' particularly for international financial capital. Liberalisation did attract more investment and 'overall foreign shares in the Korean stock market increased from 14.6 per cent in 1997 to 37.3 per cent in 2006' (Kalinowski and Cho 2009: 234). Recapitalised banks and other financial institutions soon became highly profitable and began to attract 'the most buoyant foreign investments' and about 65 per cent of the stake in the entire commercial banking sector came under the control of foreign investors by 2006 (Kalinowski and Cho 2009: 233–4). This means that six out of the seven largest commercial banks are now owned by foreign capital (Lim 2010: 202). Commodity market liberalisation was not new either as Korea's trade regulation has been subjected to continuous renegotiation with countries of major export markets, such as the US. Kim Dae Jung's government showed strong determination to push this further by aggressively participating in multilateral free trade negotiation through the World Trade Organization (WTO). In the face of sluggish development of the WTO deals, the successive Roh Moo-hyun government strived to be a leading figure in bilateral free trade negotiations and succeeded in signing Free Trade Agreements (FTAs) with Chile (April 2004), Singapore (March 2006), the European Free Trade Association (September 2006) and the ASEAN (June 2007). The current Lee Myung-bak's government has been very keen on completing the FTA negotiations that the previous government initiated, particularly the US-Korea FTA while searching for new FTA opportunities with 41 countries or so.

In addition, Kim's government announced a comprehensive-scale public sector reform plan in the summer of 1998. This plan pledged to privatise 11 out of 24 large-scale state-owned enterprises (SOEs) as well as the thorough restructuring of SOEs' subsidiaries and government-invested or commissioned organisations through merger and privatisation (Republic of Korea 2000: 111–13). Kim's government and successive regimes strived to materialise the plan. Eight large-scale SOEs, including Korea Telecom, Posco and Korean Tobacco and Ginseng (KT&G) were privatised by 2002. Major public utility SOEs were also subjected to privatisation, the process of which began with dividing SOEs, such as the Korean Electric Power Corporations and the Korea District Heating Corporation, into smaller subsidiaries in preparation for sale to private investors. When full-scale privatisation was found to be unrealistic, the state introduced new management systems in SOEs that aimed to make SOEs more marketable and profitable. Although Roh's government did not pursue immediate privatisation of SOEs, it instead emphasised 'management innovation' aiming at introducing market principles into the management of public enterprises and creating profit-driven SOEs. Lee's government is pursuing a more ambitious privatisation plan focusing on encouraging market competition among SOEs as well as between them and private companies, enhancing marketability of SOEs and removing institutional barriers to private investment.

The irregularisation of labour in Korea is an integral part of the global-scale informalisation of labour, a process of labour being subsumed to the expanding circuit of capital as a more freely exchangeable/removable/disposable commodity for production and realisation of profit for capital. The current explosive growth of irregular jobs in Korea is a direct product of the consolidation of this tendency through the emerging influence of neo-liberalism that successfully mobilised the forces against the barriers to the movement of capital and to the expansion of the circuit of capital, including unions' protection of labour and state regulation of the labour market (Chang 2009b).

Indeed, this full-scale neo-liberalisation and subsequent economic recovery of South Korea did not come without cost and it was the working class in general and the poorer segment of the working class in particular who had to pay for it. The power of capital over labour has been restored to a great extent through neo-liberalisation that in turn resulted in a massive-scale transfer of wealth from labour to capital, from the poor to the rich. Clear indicators on this have been reported. The ratio of manufacturing profit to GDP started growing again after the long period of decline from the mid-1980s while the portion of earned income to total national income has been decreasing. The Gini Coefficient has been increasing from the record low 0.257 in 1992 to 0.321 in 2008. Although it is obvious that income discrepancy among the population is increasing, this does not show the entire picture of the alarming polarisation of the Korean economy. The distribution of household assets appears to be a lot worse than that of household incomes. The portion of household assets owned by top 20 per cent of the population has been continuously increasing after the economic crisis and reached about 71 per cent of total household assets in 2007 (*Hankyoreh* 22 October 2009). Lee Myung-bak, who was elected by taking advantage of the sentiment of relative deprivation of the people, accelerated pro-capital and pro-rich policies, cutting tax for the highest income earners, deregulating the property market and even refunding tax money collected from the rich by the previous government of Roh Moo-hyun (Goldner 2009: 334). It seems obvious that Korea became a good place to invest and run banks for international financial capital but not a good place to be a worker. It is the case particularly for irregular workers.

What these reforms actually intended was to allow the market to be the principal coordinating mechanism for the circulation of goods, services and finance. This was also applied to 'labour' as the state and capital made every effort to subject labour to the rule of the market and make it into purer commodities lacking protection and security. This appeared most of all in the attempts of individual capitals to introduce various irregular forms of employment and of the state to offer legal and institutional legitimacy to those forms of employment. The number of workers under various irregular forms of employment has been growing throughout the 1990s in Korea by sporadic attempts of individual employers. However, it was the crisis that made it a general trend at the national level. Through a coordinated campaign to introduce diverse non-standard forms of employment, temporary and daily contracted workers soon outnumbered those of standard-regular workers, reaching 52 per cent of total wage workers by 2001. Indirect forms of employment were also introduced, including dispatched workers and in-house subcontracted workers. It became a general practice for large-scale manufacturing firms to affiliate a number of small subcontract firms and work agencies, providing cheaper workforces to the mother companies. Also increased was non-employed (or disguised as non-employed) waged workers called 'special employment' (Teuksugoyong). This refers primarily to service workers who are legally not workers but self-employed, in spite of their labour process being supervised by management. Irregularisation hit women workers harder. In 2008, the number of male irregular workers was estimated to be about 4.156 milion, which accounted for about 47 per cent of total male employees whereas 4.424 million female irregular workers accounted for 65.5 per cent of total female workers (Kim 2008). Small- and medium-size enterprises also increasingly employ migrant workers. About half a million documented and undocumented migrant workers have contracts that are irreversibly temporary in nature. Irregular workers' average income accounts for only half of that of regular workers while they tend to work as long as irregular workers (45.2 hours per week) (Kim 2008). Korea now has the highest level of irregular workforce among the OECD member countries.

RESPONSE OF THE LABOUR MOVEMENT

The Korean labour movement, spearheaded by the militant KCTU, attempted to mobilise strong protests against all dimensions of the neo-liberal offensive.

Indeed, the union movement has been a leading figure of the anti-neo-liberal movement in Korea. The KCTU has mobilised nationwide protests to a wide range of neo-liberal policies such as FTAs, privatisation of the SOEs, market liberalisation and most of all the neo-liberal restructuring of the labour market. The KCTU has been consistently showing strong opposition to neo-liberalism and neo-liberal-driven globalisation. In the aftermath of the economic crisis and onset of neo-liberal restructuring of the Korean economy, anti-neo-liberalism appeared in a rather crude campaign to 'save the national economy' from chaebols, which were blamed for the distorted structure of the national economy, and from the IMF, which was seen as a defender of the interests of transnational financial capital and the US. Therefore the major frontline of anti-neo-liberal struggle was between Korean people and imperialist interests. In this view, neo-liberalism was presented mainly as an external force threatening 'national development'. Although this understanding of neo-liberalism remains influential even today, the KCTU's anti-neo-liberal strategy has evolved over the years and become more articulated. For example, in a letter of support to anti-WTO protest in Seattle in 1999, the KCTU defined neo-liberalism as 'an ideology of market fetishism of transnational capital blindly pursuing growth, development and efficiency at the cost of people's right to live, of women's rights and of the environment and ecosystem' (KCTU 1999). The KCTU condemned neo-liberalism as the major cause of the 'widening gap between advanced empires/core nations and developing countries/peripheral nations' (KCTU 1999). Neo-liberalism, the KCTU maintained, 'builds a world in which transnational financial capitalists earn tremendous amounts of money by speculative activities while millions of people in the world live on less than two dollars a day' (KCTU 1999).

It was not only the militant KCTU but also the conservative FKTU that recognised neo-liberalism as a threat to the union movement and workers. The FKTU, by joining 1996–7 general strike led by the KCTU, managed to recover from the legitimacy crisis it had faced after democratisation and the emergence of the independent union movement. In an attempt to revitalise itself, the FKTU began to be more involved in socio-political activism since then. However, the FKTU did not have a clear opposition to neo-liberalism until 2001 as it maintained a cooperative relation with Kim's government, which it had been supporting since the 1998 presidential election. It was then in 2001 that the FKTU began to recognise neo-liberalism as a threat to the union movement and Korean society in general. Its policy on neo-liberalism has been formed in its attempt to develop a long-term strategy for its own survival in the context of two profound challenges, namely massive scale lay-offs precipitated by neo-liberal economic restructuring in the aftermath of the crisis and the increasing influence of the more radical KCTU. The FKTU, in its manifesto for the twenty-first century, argued that 'the nature of neo-liberalism is the subordination of human to market, of all other values to market logic', the consequences of which are 'the alienation of workers, impairment of human values and environmental destruction' (FKTU 2001: 10 quoted from Yu 2005: 483). The foremost task of the labour movement is to 'build national and international anti-neo-liberal fronts with humanism as a guiding principle against neo-liberal market-first ideology and solidarity as a strategic concept' (FKTU 2001: 35–6 quoted from Yu 2005: 484).

However, in practice, anti-neo-liberalism of the FKTU was more a rhetoric than a strategy as wider alliance building against neo-liberalism has taken only a secondary importance to securing short-term economic interest for its members through negotiations with the neo-liberal state. The FKTU, rather than consistently engaging with anti-neo-liberal alliance building, often fell back into its half-century-long partnership with the government. Anti-neo-liberalism was then used merely as a leverage to push the state to provide a more privileged position for the FKTU vis-à-vis the KCTU in national policy making process. Therefore, since 2001, the FKTU has repeatedly joined the KCTU in anti-neo-liberal struggles and pulled-back from the alliance when the government promised a better deal for the FKTU. The best example of this practice was its support to the then apparently neo-liberal candidate Lee Myung-bak in 2007 presidential election after pulling-back from its long-term alliance with the KCTU against the US-Korea FTA. The Grand National Party of Lee Myung-Bak offered a policy alliance with the FKTU through which the concerns of the FKTU would be well reflected in labour policy of Lee's government. In this way, although the FKTU managed to remain as a meaningful labour organisation in national labour politics, it never became a significant ally of anti-neo-liberal struggle in South Korea. It was the KCTU that approached to the problems of neo-liberalism in a more consistent manner.

The KCTU actively participated in building national alliances against the neo-liberal restructuring of Korean society and mobilised a number of political strikes. The KCTU was, for example, a leading organisation in the 'People's Committee to Oppose Neo-liberalism and Win People's Right to Live', established in 1999. The KCTU began to include an anti-neo-liberal agenda into its annually reviewed major demands to the state and capital. In 1999, one of the three demands was that the state and capital had to stop privatisation of SOEs, give up structural adjustment and scrap all neo-liberal policies. In 2000, the KCTU leadership again vowed to stop neo-liberalism and secure the people's right to live. The KCTU's protest against market liberalisation continued. The state's attempt to introduce special economic zones in 2002 faced strong opposition from the KCTU while FTA negotiations, particularly the US-Korea FTA negotiation, were provoking nationwide protests by tens of thousands of KCTU members. The KCTU also played a major role in mobilising protest against major international summits and conferences focusing on free trade, such as the anti-Asia-Europe Meeting (ASEM) protest in October 2000 and the anti-Asia-Pacific Economic Cooperation (APEC) protest in November 2005. Furthermore, the KCTU sent hundreds of delegates to the WTO ministerial in Hong Kong and the KCTU delegation again played an important role in publicising the anti-neo-liberal campaign across Asia.

While the KCTU was desperately trying to stop further market liberalisation, KCTU affiliates also staged strong campaigns against neo-liberal restructuring at the firm level, which involved a massive wave of layoffs of union members. From Hyundai's anti-layoffs strike in 1998, through the coordinated seven-day strike of the unions of four automobile assemblers in 2000 and Daewoo Motors strike against mass layoffs and sale of the company in 2002, to the 77-day factory occupation of Ssanyong Motors unionists in 2009, strong unions under the leadership of the militant KCTU were engaging with employers attempting to introduce more flexible work arrangements, use more irregular workers, downsize production and labour force, outsource parts of production processes and undermine unions' control over labour processes. The KCTU affiliates were also in the front line of struggles against privatisation. The KCTU began to confront privatisation with its campaign against the privatisation of Korea Heavy Industry in 1999, accusing Kim's government of handing over healthy SOEs to chaebols and speculative capital at bargain prices. Anti-privatisation struggles of the KCTU developed a step further in 2002 through a coordinated strike taken by more than 100 000 workers from three major SOE unions, including the Korea Power Plant Industry Union, the Korean Railway Workers Union and the Korea Water Resources Corporation Union. In particular, the Korea Power Plant Industry Union's strike lasted for 38 days and precipitated nationwide protest against the government's plan for privatisation, contributing to widening public discussion on the impact of privatising 'the public' (Chang 2009a: 153–154).

Although the KCTU did not realise the full implication of the irregularisation of labour early enough, the KCTU is also becoming more active in defending irregular workers' rights as the size of irregular workforce has been increasing at an alarming level. The KCTU leadership started devising specific programmes to address strategies to organise irregular workers from 2000, initiating nationwide surveys on the working conditions of irregular workers, launching a fundraising project for the education of organisers and proposing 'organising the unorganised' to be one of three major strategic plans of the KCTU in 2000. The KCTU also introduced a 'strategic organising plan' in 2003, targeting the unorganised. In 2005, the KCTU unveiled a special plan to organise the unorganised and irregular workers with an ambitious training programme and a plan to raise a fund of a total US$4m. About half of the fund has been raised within three years. In 2006, the KCTU finally launched a three-year strategic organising campaign by sending out 24 specially trained organisers to industrial federations.

Having seen them all, it is clear that the KCTU opposes neo-liberalism and policies associated with neo-liberalism and strives to curb the negative impact of neo-liberalisation on the working class in Korea. However, the real impact of these struggles seems to be quite small compared with the strong rhetoric and militancy of the struggles. In spite of remarkable success in many individual cases, the KCTU failed to stop the general trend of neo-liberalisation of Korean society. More FTAs are being negotiated; more irregular forms of employment are being created; the income gap between the rich and poor is widening; and most of all the labour movement is suffering from isolation. Unions' struggles against neo-liberalism were defensive in nature and the labour movement could not propose fundamentally new strategies to overcome the changing context of the labour movement. Contrary to the image of a unified militant stance by the KCTU against neo-liberalism, the KCTU's anti-neo-liberal struggle has an extremely complicated internal dynamic largely because the anti-neo-liberal strategy has been subjected to many debates among KCTU factions that reflect diverse ideological perspectives on alternatives to neo-liberalism, ranging from socialism and social democracy to radical nationalism.

Accordingly, there are many contesting ways in which the labour movement can confront neo-liberalism. Again, and perhaps more importantly, contesting proposals from diverse perspectives, radical or reformist, have been mediated by the organisational structure and routine practices of the KCTU and its affiliates. Hence, underneath the KCTU's strong anti-neo-liberal rhetoric and the seemingly unified line of struggle, the strategy and practice of the anti-neo-liberal struggle have shown a somewhat zigzag development from the 1990s. Indeed, this contested development of the KCTU's anti-neo-liberal strategy greatly undermined the effectiveness of struggles. What were then the dynamics that prevented the KCTU from being strong and unified enough to effectively confront neo-liberalism?

NATIONALIST-SOCIAL CORPORATIST-SOCIAL DEMOCRACY NEXUS

Although labour analysts often identify the Korean labour movement, particularly the KCTU, in terms of its strong militancy, this view is based on somewhat superficial observation rather than sober analyses. 'Militant' unionism was indeed a criterion that could precisely describe the nature of Korean unionism in the past, for uncompromising struggles against the repression of the state and capital were a common characteristic of the democratic labour movement in Korea. Militancy functioned to resolve the differences at least temporarily and to unify the diverse perspectives in the democratic union movement. Although militancy continues to be one of the major characteristics of the KCTU, now it neither functions as a common strategy of all factions of the KCTU nor stops different perspectives from evolving in different directions. In many respects, 'militancy' became an empty shell, detached from the underlying value of the union movement. Whereas militancy had a value in itself before, now what is to be focused on is for what those militant struggles are charged. To understand the nature of the contemporary transformation of the Korean union movement, it is necessary to go beyond the simple dichotomy between militant and non-militant unionism.

Perhaps the single most important event in the transformation of the Korean labour movement was the formation of what can be called the 'nationalist-social corporatist-social democracy nexus' and its increasing dominance over the leadership of the KCTU. Although the central element of this peculiar combination originated from 'National Liberation' (NL), which had been a majority faction of the people's movement in the 1980s, the 'nexus' is significantly different from the NL. It had been formed over many years of competition against the diverse factions of the Korean labour movement and old ideas of the NL had been modernised by absorbing different ideas and perspectives before it emerged as a leading figure of the Korean labour movement with a much more sophisticated vision for Korean society. In terms of political vision, it aims to build a form of social democracy by modelling European social democratic regimes, such as Germany and Sweden, rather than a crude form of self-reliant society. At the same time, it is well aware of the neo-liberal-turn of those social democracies in Europe through the 'third way' strategy that they believe took a wrong turn. It strives for 'social reform' by actively engaging with the state in national politics and the policy making process and therefore takes corporatist institutions quite seriously (Gray 2008). In terms of labour relations, they tend to pursue more institutionalised and stable labour relations on the basis of mutual recognition between capital and labour, industrial bargaining and social pacts.

This nexus has been consolidated first through the debate in establishing the KCTU in 1995 through which the radical militant unionism of the CKTU has been pictured as an anachronistic strategy isolating the labour movement from the general population (Gray 2008: 488) and in doing so the radical majority of the CKTU has become a minority vis-à-vis different factions grouped together under the slogans 'the labour movement with national people' and 'struggle for social reform' – they are now generally called 'Gukminpa' (see Figure 12.1). It is important to notice the implication of putting 'national people', rather than 'people' or 'workers' in their slogan as there is significant difference in nuance between 'national people' and 'people' in Korea (national people is 'Gukmin' in Korean. This is same as 'Kuomin' in the name of the Taiwanese *Kuomintang*). The former views people most of all as a 'nation' while the latter emphasises people being members of the working class. The former emphasises 'national interest' against foreign interventions while the latter put priority on the interest of the working class against capital. The fact that social reform and the labour movement with 'national people' became the two major pillars of the first KCTU leadership of the Gukminpa meant that in spite of the leading role the CKTU played in paving the way to the establishment of the single confederation that united democratic unions, the CKTU's more class-based unionism was marginalised to a large extent. Even more significantly, although it was a 'militant strategy' that was targeted by criticism, the real question went to the radical perspective of the CKTU, which was heavily influenced by Marxist-socialists in different ways. The shifting emphasis from the working class to 'Gukmin' therefore accompanied a shift from 'revolution to reform' and from 'socialism to social democracy' (Yu 2005: 469–72). This signalled indeed a significant change in the future direction of the Korean labour movement (Yu 2005: 295–301). What featured the Korean labour movement in its struggle against neo-liberal dominance from the 1990s is that in spite of the occasional re-emergence of militancy of the KCTU, the orientation of the democratic labour movement has been greatly influenced by this nexus that has managed to become a major driving force in the Korean labour movement. Contrary to the accusations made by the Marxist-socialist faction and the nationalist-socialist faction, this nexus is flexible enough to deploy an extremely militant strategy against neo-liberalisation while pursuing reforms through building up social consensus between labour, capital and the state on the basis of a social-corporatist perspective. Therefore, militancy alone cannot capture the internal dynamics of the KCTU, nor does it address the dominant strategy of the KCTU's leadership underneath the militancy.

Another moment of the consolidation for the nationalist-social corporatist-social democracy nexus was the presidential election in 1997 where the different elements of the nexus managed to form a majority coalition in the National People's Victory 21 (Gukminseungri 21) that has later become the Democratic Labour Party (DLP). With a very controversial nationalist slogan, 'Wake Up Korea!', this coalition succeeded in consolidating its nationalist-social democracy nexus during the election campaign. The DLP was established in 2000 with whole-hearted support from the KCTU. The DLP enjoyed relative success in the general election of 2004 with nine MPs elected and attracted 13.1 per cent of the total votes. The attempt of the KCTU to combine parliamentary labour politics of the DLP with grass-roots workers' mobilising of the KCTU has strengthened the social-corporatist strategy of the KCTU. Unions began to be regarded as a mobilisation tool for parliamentary politics. Many

Ideological perspectives	Marxist-socialist			Social democratic	Nationalist-social democratic	Socialist-nationalist
Major union strategy	Mititant struggle		Social corporatism			Militant struggle
Groupings	Jwapa (the Left)				Gukminpa ('National People' faction: the Right)	
	Hyunjangpa	Jungangpa		Social democrats		
Struggle for	Socialism	Socialist values		European model	Social democracy	National self-reliance

Figure 12.1   Internal dynamics of the KCTU perspectives, major strategy and groupings

Note: Grey area shows the composition of the nexus.

general strikes were called and cancelled in accordance with the result of negotiation and struggles of the DLP within the National Assembly, and this hurt rank-and-files' trust in the leadership of the KCTU.

It was then the attitude of the KCTU leadership towards tripartite negotiation and social pacts that finally confirmed the priority the nexus gave to the social-corporatist strategy. As mentioned above, the immediate reaction of the KCTU leadership, at that time dominated by the nexus, to the emerging economic crisis of 1997 was 'saving the nation campaign'. In launching the campaign, the KCTU called for 'social dialogue' with the state and capital to discuss methods to 'save the nation'. Kim Dae Jung's administration took maximum advantage of this and responded to the request of the KCTU with a corporatist initiative, the Tripartite Commission. Overwhelmed by an urgent need for the KCTU to contribute to 'saving the nation', the KCTU leadership agreed upon a 'big deal between capital and labour' (Shin 2010: 221). This deal consisted of the legal recognition of the KCTU and its affiliates, chaebol reform and relaxation of regulation over lay-offs and irregular employment (Chang 2009a: 142). Not surprisingly, KCTU delegates rejected the agreement and the leadership responsible was soon distrusted. At the same time, the corporatist initiative was strongly rejected by KCTU members. However, the February Agreement left a long-lasting footstep in the future development of the labour movement by setting 'the rule of the game' that is based on the idea of civilised labour relations, more market based labour management, legally guaranteed labour rights, an improved social safety net and social dialogues (Chang 2009a: 142). More importantly, although the moral appeal of the radicals in the KCTU for more militant struggle rather than social dialogue worked in the immediate aftermath of the February Agreement and led to a temporary power shift from the nexus to radical socialists within the leader-ship of the KCTU, later it became clear that the nexus was firmly consolidated, embedded in the rank-and-file workers and became a formidable majority of the KCTU. The short-lived radical leadership of the KCTU, led by the former CKTU leader Dan Byeong-ho and the veteran militant unionist Lee Gap-yong from Hyundai Heavy Industry could not change the rules of the game in any significant way and the 'nexus' made a comeback and has continued to domi-nate the leadership of the KCTU ever since. Indeed, it seems the Gukminpa secured the leadership of the KCTU permanently. It was even capable of paci-fying several corruption and sexual harassment scandals in 2005 and 2007 in which some core members of the leadership were involved. The leadership had to step down after each scandal. However, the Gukminpa managed to secure leadership succession.

Although the KCTU leadership often turned to more militant tactics, for their own need to push the government for more negotiation or by pressure from minority socialists, social corporatism has become the core strategy of the KCTU. The social dialogue strategy involved occasional general strikes to threaten the state and capital to accept the unions' demands in the tripartite structure. In the end, not many of them were actually 'general' strikes, with most involving only 10 to 20 per cent of KCTU members. Many were called for and then cancelled as they are always subjected to the result of further negotiation. What is impressive is that the KCTU always comes back to the Tripartite Commission after walking out from the Commission without any meaningful gains through negotiations. The KCTU rejoined the Commission in 2005 to discuss new legislation to protect irregular workers. Then the KCTU leadership had to keep some distance from the Commission after it faced a violent protest from radical factions that criticised the social-corporatist strategy of the leadership during the KCTU conference in 2005. The KCTU again participated in the Commission to discuss the package deal called the 'Labour Relations Roadmap' to amend labour laws in 2006 and walked out again only when the reform bill turned out to be for more exploita-tion rather than protection of irregular workers (Shin 2010: 223), once again realising too late the fact that the government used social dialogue as a tacti-cal tool to obtain an agreement from unions for pre-determined policies rather than for open-ended negotiation.

Behind the seemingly united militant opposition of the KCTU to neo-liberalism, there have been emerging and consolidating divisions of ideologi-cal perspectives and strategies, which caused the zigzag development of KCTU's anti-neo-liberal struggle. In this extremely contested development of the KCTU and the Korean labour movement in general, the nationalist-social corporatist-social democracy nexus emerged as a leading figure of the move-ment. However, the sheer speed and width of neo-liberalisation over Korean society at the expense of the majority of the working population in fact did not allow much space for social corporatism to settle and the repeated failures of the KCTU to force the state and capital to sit at the negotiation table created much frustration for the members of the KCTU. Yet, this does not mean that the KCTU's rank-and-file workers are ready to choose more radical alternatives. It seems that it is unavoidable for the KCTU, at least for a while, to continually vacillate between militancy and social dialogue, social democracy within capitalism and fundamental social change, and nationalism and internationalism.

The socialist minority has been criticising the nexus for making reformist concessions. However, no matter how much they emphasise a militant strategy, it seems that the socialist minority is not capable of persuading rank and files for a more militant struggle and fundamental social change. For the radicals, perhaps the most important strategy to think about is not how to replace social corporatism with militant struggle but how to transform the militancy of the few into mass-based militancy by incorporating a large number of unorganised irregular workers. Core, big business, male, regular-workers centred militancy without much support from the vast majority of workers, particularly young and women irregular workers is unlikely to deliver the changes the radicals in the KCTU look forward to. The radical wing of the KCTU has already exhorted their resources in calling for more general strikes and they could not do much for more successful mobilisation of those strikes with their limited capacity. Both the erratic practices of the nexus and the incapability of the socialist minority are in fact two sides of the same coin – they are expressions of the dilemma of the KCTU that could not move beyond regular, core workers, enterprise union-based labour movement.

TOWARDS A MORE INCLUSIVE LABOUR MOVEMENT

Indeed, it was the irregularisation of labour that severely undermined the very basis of the Korean labour movement, which had been relying on the power of the enterprise unions of regular workers in large-scale enterprises and solidarity between enterprise unions against the authoritarian state (Yang 2007). While well organised unions were completely overwhelmed defending their heartland from repeated offensives by capital and the state redeploying authoritarian anti-union tactics (Chun 2008: 28–29), the rest of country was engulfed by small but consistent campaigns for more flexible and informal labour. As a consequence of desperate struggles to defend the stronghold of the union movement, the labour movement managed to survive. However, unions are facing a crisis of representativeness for the working class as a whole and had become a 'league of their own' in other words 'it had become a movement of regular workers' (Yang 2007). Worse still, the piecemeal introduction of irregular work arrangements, mostly through utilising dispatched labour for new job openings, imposed divisions between workers even in large-scale firms where the KCTU still exercises strong leadership. Then the greatest challenge to organising irregular workers is the attitude of regular workers towards irregular workers' unionisation (Chun 2008: 34–8). The 'democratic' regimes of Kim Dae Jung and Roh Moo-hyun, whose economic policy was deeply neo-liberal, did their best to isolate the labour movement by portraying the movement as a labour aristocracy against the poor. Indeed, without overcoming this problem, neither a social-corporatist strategy nor a militant strategy can effectively tackle the neo-liberal offensive. The catalyst of the KCTU's attempt to widen its basis was the shift from an enterprise-union-based structure to an industrial-union-based structure. However, large-scale enterprise unions whose members are mostly regular workers are still the dominant force in industrial federations. They continued to remain as 'enterprise branches' with an independent decision-making process and the right to negotiate separately. If industrial federation is regarded merely as a tool for the interest of workers in individual enterprises, the much-anticipated impact of the industrial federation as a tool for more inclusive structure of the KCTU seems far away from being realised.

Perhaps inspiration for a more inclusive union movement comes from outside of the dominant factions of the KCTU and strong large-scale enterprise unions. While the KCTU repeated the call for a general strike and cancelled the strikes for more negotiations in social-corporatist institutions, irregular workers have been waging a difficult but remarkable struggle against discrimination and exploitation (Shin 2010: 224–6). A welcoming trend is the shift of centre of more determined struggle from the large enterprise unions in the manufacturing sector to irregular workers in small- and medium-size manufacturing firms and the service industry. Major individual cases of militant struggles between 2005 and 2009 were mostly organised by irregular workers, such as workers in the Korea Train Express (KTX) Union, the Daegu Gyeongbuk Construction Workers' Union, the Pohang Construction Workers' Union and the Kyryung Electronics Union. The recent lorry drivers' strike also shows that when capital devises new methods of utilising labour in more profitable ways, there are always new forms of organising labour which often go beyond existing union boundaries. The lorry drivers' union is first of all not an official union. It is rather an 'alliance' of individual cargo transportation workers. As there is no legal employment relation, they had no choice but to organise an alliance instead of a 'proper' union. However, even this extraordinary form of workers' organisation can be very effective. The alliance form of organising among lorry drivers seemed to have made it easier for non-member lorry drivers to join actions together with the members. Second to this, the state had no legitimate method to stop the strike action of the alliance because there was no legal employment 'contractual' relation violated by the striking lorry drivers. The lorry drivers' strike showed that the irregularisation of labour has certainly edges at both ends.

Inspiration can come not only from the union movement but also from the newly emerging political activism of the unorganised critical mass. In April 2008, the new President Lee Myung-bak signed an agreement that allowed beef from the US to be imported without proper inspection for the human form of mad cow disease (CJD) in a desperate attempt to accelerate the completion of the US-Korea FTA. From 2 May, tens of thousands of people started candlelight vigils in downtown Seoul and demanded renegotiation with the US government. By 10 June, the number of participants in nationwide protests reached a million. While the conservative government was handling these protesters violently, mobilising riot police and using water cannons, etc, more demands appeared in the protests. These included reform for more participatory democracy, scrapping the plan to privatise the public sector, withdrawal of the environmentally destructive Great Canal Project, suspension of all ongoing FTA negotiations, creating a better public education system, curbing the increasing income gap between the rich and poor, more protection for rapidly increasing irregular workers and the end of corporate-driven globalisation. It was the first resistance of the critical mass against the consequences of neo-liberal reform in Korea. More interestingly, it was not the labour movement that led this protest. Unions and organised social movements joined only in the later stage of the protest, which was mostly organised spontaneously on the basis of autonomous participation. While a decade-long anti-neo-liberal struggle of the labour movement could not attract much attention from the general public, candle light protests managed to communicate with and bring a wide range of population across different generations. This struggle provoked a series of serious debates about the effectiveness of the existing social movements, especially the labour movement, in representing diverse socio-economic demands emerging from the deepening neo-liberalisation of Korean society, forcing the KCTU and the labour movement in general to rethink their strategy and urging them to build a more inclusive social movement to become once again a leading social force for democratic social transformation.

CONCLUSION

The Korean union movement and the KCTU in particular have been at the centre of anti-neo-liberal struggle for the last decade. It was a difficult time for the union movement as neo-liberalisation brought different sorts of challenges. In face of the neo-liberal offensive, many different perspectives of the labour movement, visions for the future of Korean society and alternatives to the existing form of capitalist development have contended with one another. Amid the fierce contest, the labour movement could not manage to propose either an alternative strategy or a persuasive vision of Korea's future development to the general population. It was the nationalist-social corporatist-social democracy nexus that won the battle for the leadership of the Korean labour movement. However, the nexus seems incapable of exercising leadership anywhere beyond the KCTU. The leadership of the KCTU failed to form a united front of the working class either to force the state and capital to initiate genuine social bargaining with the union or to challenge the neo-liberal capitalist development of Korea altogether for a socialist alternative. Indeed, the most important problem for the radicals and reformists alike was the KCTU's old structure in which the voices of the vast majority of the working population cannot be heard. However, this does not mean the Korean labour movement have achieved nothing from struggles against neo-liberalism. Emerging struggles of irregular workers are likely to pose a significant challenge to the continuing attempt of the state and capital to deregulate the labour market. New forms of social and political activism have also emerged out of the deepening polarisation of Korean society that appears to many as a threat to the very basis of democracy in Korea. Perhaps the effectiveness of the responses of Korean unions to neo-liberal offensive depends on the capacity of the Korean labour movement, and particularly of the KCTU to build a more inclusive social movement both by integrating irregular, women and migrant workers and by communicating with various forms of new movements emerging out of the aspiration for more participatory democracy in Korea.

ACKNOWLEDGEMENT

My research on the Korean unions' response to neo-liberal globalisation has been supported by a research project by the Gyeongsang National University in Korea on the alter-globalisation movement. This project is funded by the Korea Research Foundation (KRF-2007-411-J04602).

REFERENCES

Chang, D. (2009a), *Capitalist Development in Korea: Labour, Capital and the Myth of the Developmental State*, London: Routledge.
Chang, D. (2009b), 'Informalising labour in Asia's global factory', *Journal of Contemporary Asia*, **39**(2)), 161–19.
Chun, J. (2008), 'The contested politics of gender and irregular employment: revitalizing the

South Korean democratic labor movement', in A. Bieler, I. Lindberg and D. Pillay (eds), *Labour and the Challenges of Globalization: What Prospects for Transnational Solidarity?*, London: Pluto Press, pp. 23–44.

FKTU (2001), *21Segi Undongnoseon: him, yeondae, jeongchaek, huimang* [*Movement Strategy for the 21st Century: Power, Solidarity, Policy and Hope*], Seoul: FKTU.

Goldner, L. (2009), 'Ssanyong motor's strike in Korea ends in defeat and heavy repression', *Marxism 21*, **6**(4), 323–36.

Gray, K. (2008), 'The global uprising of labour? The Korean labour movement and neoliberal social corporatism', *Globalizations*, **5**(3), 483–99.

Kalinowski, T. and H. Cho (2009), 'The political economy of financial liberalization in South Korea: state, big business, and foreign investors', *Asian Survey*, **49**(2), 221–42.

Kim, Y. (2008), 'Bijeongyujik Gyumowa Sittae' ['The size and condition of irregular workers'], *Nodongwa Sahoe* [*Labour Society Bulletin*] accessed at www.klsi.org/magazine/magazine.htm?no=1976.

Koo, H. (2001), *Korean Workers: the cultural and politics of class formation*, Ithaca, NY: Cornell University Press.

KCTU (1999), 'Seattleui Hamseongul Seoulo' ['Bring the outcry of Seattle to Seoul'], accessed at http://nodong.org/?mid=statement&page=297&document_srl=95780.

Lim, H. (2010), 'The transformation of the developmental state and economic reform in Korea', *Journal of Contemporary Asia*, **40**(2), 188–210.

Pirie, I. (2006), 'Social injustice and economic dynamism in contemporary Korea', *Critical Asian Studies*, **38**(3), 211–43.

Republic of Korea (2000), *Jeonbugaehyeok Baekseo* [*White Book of Government Reforms*], Seoul: Republic of Korea.

Roh, J. (1997), 'Yuwolminjuhangjaengwa Nodongjadaetujaeng' ['June democratic resistance and great workers' struggle'] in Korean Association of Academic Organisations (ed), *Yuwolminjuhangjaengwa Hanguksahoesipnyeon Vol. 1* [*June Democratic Resistance and Korean Society Ten Years Afterwards, Vol. 1*], Dangdae, Seoul, pp. 183–219.

Shin, K. (2010), 'Globalisation and the working class in South Korea: contestation, fragmentation and renewal', *Journal of Contemporary Asia*, **40**(2), 211–29.

Thornton, S. (2005), 'The 'miracle' revisited: the de-radicalization of Korean political culture', *New Political Science*, **27**(2), 161–76.

United Nations Conference on Trade and Development (UNCTAD (2002), *World Investment Report 2002: Transnational Corporations and Export Competitiveness*, New York: United Nations.

Yang, G. (2007), 'The crisis and new challenges of the Korean labour movement', *Asian Labour Update*, **64**, accessed at http://www.amrc.org.hk/alu_article/labour_resurgence_under_globalization/the_crisis_and_new_challenges_of_the_korean_labour.

Yu, B. (2005), *Hangukui Nodongundong inyeom: inyeomui gwaingwa sotongui bingon* [*Ideology of the Korean Labour Movement: Excess of Ideology, Poverty of Communication*], Seoul: Korea Labor Institute.

13 Unions facing and suffering neo-liberalism in the United States

Bob Bruno

INTRODUCTION

In the 1980s, neo-liberalism washed over the American political landscape and nearly drowned the labour movement. The first sign of high water is debatable. Maybe, it was the firing of striking unionised air traffic controllers by President Ronald Reagan in 1981 that signalled the advance of an unfettered 'free market' in America. Symbolically, the strong-armed action of the nation's chief executive to punish federal employees waging an illegal strike was a watershed moment for the deteriorating relationship between capital and labour. Corporate leaders and right-wing conservative political forces interpreted Reagan's executive order as an unconditional withdrawal of state protections for worker rights. McCarten (2006: 215, 216) called the strike of Professional Air Traffic Controllers (PATCO) 'one of the most significant events in 20th century US labor history' (2006, 215) symbolising 'the declining power of the labor movement'. But as dramatic as it was in turning labour's fortunes the air traffic control firings were more a confirmation of a neo-liberal turn than the first rip in the postwar social-contract fabric. In the late 1970s, administrative deregulation had already been imposed on the trucking industry reducing incomes and eliminating union drivers. Foreign cars had driven unimpeded into American show rooms while American auto manufactures and government officials ignored the realities of the emerging global markets for durable goods. Trade policy shaped principally by cold war foreign policy concerns had invited steel imports into industrial centres of the Midwest and Northeast. Before Reagan's 'revolution' foreign competition from computer, home electronic, textile, apparel, shoe and toy-makers had already created a sizeable trade deficit.

At his inauguration, Reagan accusatorily proclaimed that government was the source of America's problems and quickly made good on a promise to unleash American capitalism, chain up the regulatory state and hallow out public service. But his was just a turbo boost to an unfolding economic and political approach that as Harvey (2005: 2) explains uses the state to 'create and preserve an institutional framework appropriate' to unregulated domestic markets and free trade. The understanding of neo-liberalism used in this chapter is similar to Harvey's and the one laid out in the introduction which separately addresses globalisation, trade policy, deregulation and diminution of the welfare state. What Reagan triumphantly heralded as a 'new day in America' was in reality the unfolding of yet another era of unchecked corporate power in America. With only minor corrections, once put in motion succeeding Democratic and Republican administrations eagerly propelled neo-liberalism forward. The harsh particulars of at least 40 years of neo-liberal public policies buttressed by anti-union corporate practices are well documented. In manufacturing and goods producing industries the national casualties of neo-liberal trade policies in terms of diminished production capacity, job loss, and reduced average pay and benefits for workers (Cormier and Targ, 2001; Ashby and Hawking 2009) are enormous. In addition as manufacturing jobs disappeared, the nation's unionisation rate tumbled steadily from a 1955 peak of 35 per cent to 16 per cent in 1990 to 12.4 per cent in 2009 (Bureau of Labour Statistics 2010a).

Along with trade policy, deregulation has likewise bludgeoned workers employed in largely domestic markets like the trucking and the airline industry (Belzer 1995; Card 1986; Hirsch 1988; Johnson 2004). By 2000, the large legacy airlines had produced a record of financial performance characterised by punishing debt and enormous unfunded pension obligations. From 1997 to 2000 the major carriers collectively lost $24.3bn despite successfully capturing $5.5bn in union labour costs cuts (General Accounting Office 2004). Accompanying the wave of private sector deregulation was a drive to starve the public sector of resources. During the Reagan Administration, a bipartisan political space was created for advocates of privatisation to attack government as a bloated, inefficient and wasteful provider of necessary services. In 1997, every state in the union had contracted out a sizeable number of services, including in many jurisdictions correctional supervision (Cyr-Racine and Jalette 2007). The unravelling of the social insurance system seemed to fulfil anti-government activist Grover Norquist's wish to 'reduce' the public sector 'to the size of where I can drag it into the bathroom and drown it in the bathtub' (National Public Radio 25 May 2001). Along with fewer work based job benefits came fewer workplace rights. Consistent with the neo-liberal drive to refashion the marketplace as a 'labour arbitrage,' administrative and judicial protections for workers were unhinged (Greider 1993). Employers had grown so emboldened that in 1979 a 'Conference Board survey on labour-management relations revealed that preventing the spread of unionism had become more important to managers than achieving stable collective bargaining' (Hale 1986: 540). One prominent 1990s study found that approximately a quarter of all workers actively campaigning to unionise their workplaces had been fired and the number of complaints against employers for anti-union behaviour had skyrocketed (Bronfenbrenner 1995).

Determining how the labour movement in the United States has responded to the imposition and carnage of neo-liberal policies implies that there is a unified union response. There is after all the America Federation of Labor-Congress of Industrial Organizations (AFL-CIO) which on national policies traditionally speaks for the organised labour movement. In 2005 a new national body, Change-to-Win was formed but has never operated as a centralised federation. In commenting on the 1980s' corporate strategy to deconstruct the labour-liberal accord, Ashby and Hawking (2009: 17, 36) offer the widely held belief that 'AFL-CIO leaders offered no resistance', adding that the Federation's president, Lane Kirkland 'had provided little leadership as major strikes were repeatedly broken, the number of workers in unions steadily declined,' and the national labour body 'failed to get pro-worker legislation passed'. Examining the AFL-CIO's behaviour over the last three decades offers important insight as to how labour did or did not challenge the neo-liberal agenda. But in addition to the Federation's response there are reactions from critically important independent and affiliated unions that contribute as much or even more to an understanding of how organised labour approached global and domestic economic restructuring. Unions in industries subjected and exposed to unregulated trade policies, deregulated national markets, as well as foreign direct investments were situated on the front lines of the neo-liberal attack. In addition, along with their private sector colleagues public employee unions have had to deal with consistent attempts to dismantle public services. Perhaps in time analyst may come to view things in more consensual terms but from my perspective there are only superficial common elements that appear to reveal the labour response.

Union positions towards neo-liberal policies vary according to the threats that each market element poses to a union's status. While public and service sector unions may express less opposition to globalisation than do the industrial unions, they do rally against deregulatory and privatisation schemes. The building unions stand acutely attentive to any attacks against prevailing minimum wage laws but have not equalled the industrial unions in their call for health care reform. The characterisation is admittedly too broad to be fully informative but it does sketch out an outline for understanding multiple labour responses to neo-liberalism. Notwithstanding the differences however, there is no evidence that the AFL-CIO or any of its affiliates viewed globalisation as an unqualified good for their members. While there is a continuum of union opposition from outright resistance to calls for a 'level playing field,' global trade was understood as mostly good for investors and company CEOs, and bad for American workers (some misplaced critiques included foreign workers) and the US economy. In brief, US labour offered a reluctant conditional support for neo-liberal policies heavily leavened with advocacy for state action to protect domestic workers and the welfare state.

In describing labour's response to neo-liberalism, it is important to note the conceptualization of the term 'welfare state' more broadly to include private social benefits. As argued by welfare state theorists (such as Hacker 2002), an inclusive approach is justified because workers typically combine employment compensation, fringe benefits, and private investments with a mix of tax supported public transfers. Therefore, assessing organised labour's response to neo-liberalism requires identifying how unions in the US resisted or accommodated a fundamental redefining of the role of the state in the economy. As Harvey (2005: 3, 11) explains that role now 'maximises the reach and frequency of market transactions' and is hostile to the 'web of social and political constraints' that once characterised post-war capitalist democracies. American neo-liberalism and its antecedents are a major cause of welfare state reductions because they trigger a 'race to the bottom, in which workers are recommodified, citizens have less social security, and capital dominates the state' (Brady *et al.* 2005: 923). The following discussion addresses labour's response to neo-liberalism described above by examining how unions have confronted large global companies and international labour markets, opposed union job threatening trade policies, and defended the (private) welfare state.

GLOBALISED (LIMITED) UNION POWER

Over the last four decades the movement of global capital has badly outpaced organised labour's intermittent efforts at international cooperation. In response, US labour has too often pursued an 'aggressive economic nationalism' that, according to Brecher *et al.* (2006: 11), replaces 'solidarity against employers with a struggle among workers over which countries can keep or lure corporate investment'. Additionally, the AFL-CIO's discredited Cold War relationship with government agencies to 'overthrow foreign governments and favor unions that cooperated with US corporations' (Brecher *et al.* 2006: 12) has complicated efforts to build genuine global partnerships. Real or imagined images of unionised Detroit autoworkers taking turns with their Big Three corporate bosses in bashing a foreign made Toyota came to symbolise the United Auto Workers (UAW) and American industrial labour's initial approach to globalisation. Throughout the 1970s and 1980s, joint UAW-auto manufacturers' opposition to government attempts to require the industry to produce fuel-efficient cars revealed how far the union's iconic-late president Walter Reuther's goal of one giant international metals union had fallen. Instead of building cross-border and international coalitions with other car builders and part suppliers, the UAW initially embraced a far-reaching form of national labour-management cooperation called 'joint-ness'. The UAW's out-of-the box response to globalisation was to partner with the very same companies that were rapidly becoming less and less American. Autoworkers, like other manufacturing-based employees were given a choice between international solidarity and in Wells's (1999: 488) term a 'new feudalism' built around workers' loyalty to their firms. Employers appealed to their own workforces for a partnership to sustain improvements in productivity and global competitiveness. According to this logic the problem was not the failed investment strategies of global firms like Ford and GM, but foreign-based automakers and their cheaply paid foreign workers. The threat of capital flight to low- wage countries and domestic job loss from imports served as a 'soft tyranny' that US workers mistakenly thought could be challenged by cooperating with their employers demands for concessions. Wells (1999: 488) has documented that an alarming number of unions joined with the UAW in entering into 'elaborate productivity alliances with management' producing a 'new industrial relations of fragmented decentralized corporate fiefdoms'.

While the auto industry experience dramatically documented the neoliberal corporate assault on the organised working class, it's very likely GE CEO Jack Welch made the most provocative and imperial expression of global restructuring. 'Ideally,' he pronounced without a hint of uncertainty, 'you would have every plant you own on a barge.' Welch did almost as much, shifting thousands of US jobs and billions of investment dollars out of the country. Under Welch's direction capital and employment mobility was accelerated; the US exported skilled, high-wage union jobs to low-wage, non-union periphery countries around the world. In 2001, the ratio of domestic GE employees to non-US workers had fallen to approximately 1.25:1 from more than 4:1 a mere decade earlier. Evading US union labour was an investment in profit taking. GE's net profits by the start of the new century had climbed north of $11bn and over 40 per cent of the company's sales occurred outside the US. But if mobile workforces generated extreme wealth for investors and owners it was responsible for astonishing levels of exploitation. Meyer (2001: 64) points out that 'each GE worker around the globe generates more in net profits per hour worked than the company pays, on average, in hourly wages and benefits – a rate of labour exploitation of more than 100 per cent'. Union workers at GE confronted this multi-national colossus by extending a near 40-year old national Coordinated Bargaining Committee (CBC) to encompass national union federations, like the IMF, from around the world. The GE-CBC international strategic campaign sought to establish programmes permitting coordinating bargaining across national boundaries to provide support for organising campaigns in every country and 'foster political power to achieve internationally recognized labour standards in all countries in which GE operates' (Meyer 2001: 62). In 2000, over 130 delegates from 20 countries attended the 'IMF-GE World Council Meetings' to construct a strategy for preventing GE from moving work to non-union countries. As employers like

GE went global, US labour remained embedded in a domestic structure that was better suited to local bargaining. The international cooperation of unions at GE was an attempt to scale up to the realities of the employer they were now confronting.

US efforts to build a coordinated international unionism were advanced in some sectors more than others. Driven by fears of global concentration in the telecommunication marketplace, in the late 1980s, the Communication Workers of America (CWA) incrementally expanded its working relationship with labour organisations in Mexico, Europe and Asia. In 1991, the union joined with the major telecommunications unions in Canada and Mexico to sign a formal agreement committing the organisations to strengthen the ability of each union to support 'joint mobilisations around strikes, and defending worker and union rights' (Borgers 1997: 110). CWA further broadened its international response to globalisation by forming the North Atlantic Alliance with communication unions in England. The alliance was organised to increase the leverage the respective unions had over trans-national corporations. Prior to the Alliance CWA incursions into international unionism were largely 'piecemeal and reactive' (Borgers 1997: 115).

While CWA's efforts lagged the global capacities and ventures of capital, it did represent a recognition that US unions could not survive strictly as national bodies operating in international markets. A number of unions also initiated actions that encouraged cross-border solidarity. In 2004 the International Brotherhood of Teamsters (IBT) led a multinational delegation of union officials to strategise on efforts to organise harbour truckers and dockworkers in several Central American countries. Coordination activities were undertaken in support of the Teamsters campaign to organise over 100 000 owner-operator truck drivers in the US who haul containers to and from seaports and intermodal rail ramps (Mongelluzzo 2006: 29). One of the US unions that have energetically approached working-class internationalism is the United Electrical Radio and Machine Workers of America (UE). The UE built an effective worker-to-worker alliance with the Mexican Frente del Trabajo (FAT). Facing similar threats from the passage of North American Free Trade Agreement (NAFTA) the neighbouring unions constructed joint organising committees, held worker exchanges, published an electronic periodical, and built worker centres. The UE/FAT alliance also generated the first formal complaint under the NAFTA side agreements on behalf of workers in both countries.

Other unions like the International Association of Machinist (IAM) and the United Steelworkers (USW) participated in 'framework agreements' and negotiated 'codes of conduct' which provided unions with the means to monitor the implementation of international labour standards. The IAM entered into an alliance agreement with the Japan Federation of Aviation Workers' Unions (KOHKUREN), the largest federation of air transport workers in Japan. Both the IAM and KOHKUREN represent workers at the same airlines, including Northwest/Delta, United, Continental and others. As helpful as codes and frameworks were to symbolically acknowledging the need for labour standards, in 2008 a possible new model of transnational unionism emerged. The largest private sector union in North America, the USW and Unite, the largest labour organisation in Britain and Ireland, merged into the 'world's first global union.' The two unions combine to represent more than three million active and retired workers from the United States, Canada, Britain and Ireland. According to the Workers United website the workers are employed in 'virtually every sector of the global economy, including manufacturing, service, mining and transportation'. The USW's venture with Unite further extended the union's global solidarity activities within the union (La Botz 2010).

Like many US-based private sector unions the USW also represents workers in Canada and over the past decade has extended its representational reach to diverse labour markets including rubber, paper, oil and chemical and healthcare workers. Extensive organising support has occurred for many years on behalf of the Mexican mineworkers union (Los Mineros), the Brazilian metalworker's, Chilean forestry workers, South African paper mill employees and rubber farm workers in Liberia. Unions in the manufacturing sector were not the only ones who saw a need to build a global capacity to react to global employers. In 2000, UNI Global Union was created to provide a voice and a platform for workers employed in the service industry. The global organisation was founded by the Service Employees International Union (SEIU) of North America. Claiming 20m workers in 900 unions (including the United Food and Commercial Workers and the CWA in the US) worldwide UNI, on its website, claims it 'fosters international solidarity and provides a voice at the international level for all its members'. UNI's focus is on signing 'global agreements' that ensure that core labour standards and collective bargaining rights are respected for workers at multinational corporations. The union's website is very explicit about its rational for being: 'The global economy is in crisis and workers are bearing a disproportionate part of the burden. The solution to the crisis must include a global employment strategy that creates sustainable well-paying employment with bargaining rights'. SEIU, as a UNI affiliate has also aggressively campaigned globally against the abuses of the private equity industry. The group called for, among other things, tighter regulations and reforms from governments to prevent future leverage-fuelled crises from undermining the global economy and engagement with unions on jobs and solutions to unstable portfolio companies. The transformation of US unions into global organisations represents one of the most difficult and necessary challenges for the labour movement. As corporations move the 'scope of decisive economic and political transactions to the international level' the balance of power between labour and capital grows ever more unequal

(Borgers 1999: 107). UNI's and the steelworkers' examples aside, Borgers (1997: 108) has observed that, 'the scale of labour's organisational response rarely matches its rhetoric'.

OPPOSITION TO TRADE POLICIES

A popular union approach to globalisation is opposition to bi-lateral and multi-lateral trade deals that exposes national union labour to products and services sourced in low-wage countries. The AFL-CIO had historically partnered with large employers to promote the export of US goods. But as the manufacturing capabilities of Japan and mostly newly developing Asian countries expanded in the 1970s and 1980s the US labour movement reconfigured itself as an opponent of free trade. While the AFL-CIO did not coordinate a united union response to multilateral trade a majority of American industrial unions were quick to raise concerns. Initially union responses were merely protectionist but by the bruising battles over NAFTA they had evolved into a more multi-pronged approach to setting new ground rules for the global economy. The USW stands out as an outstanding case of a union that in aggressively moving to protect its US workers from unfair trade practices transformed its approach from the blunt import protectionism of the 1970s into a sophisticated post-1980s demand for a level international playing field. Union actions featured a rank-and-file education programme built around a 'rapid response' communication network that allowed the union leadership to directly reach every union member with information related to legislative or regulatory action. So, according to USW records, on trade-related issues with implications for the steel industry, the programme generated an impressive rank-and-file response. In 1997 163 000 personal letters were written to members of Congress urging opposition to NAFTA. In 1998 another 170 000 notes were mailed to representatives and senators considering 'Fast Track' authority. Rapid Response Coordinators followed up their trade authority opposition action by delivering 72 212 letters to President Clinton, requesting that he stop the illegal dumping of foreign steel. Subsequent pressure on George Bush to impose restrictions on imported steel resulted in union members writing 185 000 'steel crisis' letters to members of Congress and the President (Bruno 2005). Membership activism was coupled with a federal lawsuit the union filed challenging the constitutionality of NAFTA. The court rejected the lawsuit, but it was a bold legal and political message to the 'free-traders' that the union would attack neo-liberalism from multiple fronts.

Additionally, in several trade cases brought before the US International Trade Commission (ITC) the union and domestic employers charged that foreign manufactures were violating anti-dumping and anti-subsidy duties eliminating thousands of domestic jobs. But it was the action against tyres imported from China that established the USW as a provocative defender of American manufacturing jobs. In 2009 the union did what no other US labour organisation had yet done: it unilaterally filed and won a trade petition with the ITC. To buttress their legal complaint, 60 000 individually written letters from steelworkers were delivered to Congressional leadership and the White House in less than three weeks. In a decision that was applauded by Congressional Democrats and Republicans, President Obama decided to enforce an ITC ruling in favour of the union. Solidarity actions in concert with other unions around the world and path-breaking protections against harmful trade practices, positions the USW in the forefront of US union's confronting a global corporate agenda that threatens working people.

Opposing bad trade deals was not however the exclusive practice of the USW. When NAFTA called for opening up American roadways to Mexican trucks the International Brotherhood of Teamsters took a defiant stand. The union's campaign focused on a Department of Transportation (DOT) and Federal Motor Carrier Safety Administration (FMCSA) programme that granted a limited number of Mexico-domiciled trucks access to US roadways for one year. The programme was implemented by the Bush administration to allow Mexican carriers to 'transport goods originating in Mexico to their final destinations within the United States (Richman 2009: 556).' In response the IBT contended that allowing Mexican trucks into the United States seriously threatened the safety and security of US roadways. They charged that Mexican trucks failed to meet safety requirements and that drivers were highly under regulated. At a Teamsters International Convention Teamsters' President, James Hoffa, proclaimed that the union would 'not let these time-bomb [Mexican] trucks on our highways to threaten the lives of American drivers and their families' (Press Release, 2006). Union voices were also heard expressing fears that sub-par Mexican wages would encourage US carriers to ship jobs south of the border. While the actual effects of liberalised trucking rules for both American and Mexican drivers were debated, there was no disputing that the IBT was the strongest obstacle to fully implementing the NAFTA accords.

Despite the USW and IBT cases the efforts by industrial and transportation unions to create a bulwark against trade policies that exposed US workers to unregulated foreign labour regimes characterised by oppressive working conditions and cheap labour proved mostly unsuccessful. Throughout the 1980s and 1990s domestic workers suffered significant job loss due to imported durable goods produced under international conditions favourable to global manufacturers. In 1994 organised labour mobilised a large force in Seattle against rules for admission into the World Trade Organization but had no real impact in diverting US government policy away from trade liberalisation. While labour's ability to positively impact bi-lateral trade agreements has improved under the Obama Administration, it has been less successful in breaking the bi-partisan political establishment's infatuation with domestic neo-liberal economic policies.

DEFENDING THE (PRIVATE) WELFARE STATE

While the PATCO fiasco symbolised the starting line of a neo-liberal 'race to the bottom,' industrial relations experts look at the 1979 recession as a catalyst forcing undercurrents of structural change in the labour-management social accord. The job losses piling up from the late 1970s' economic malaise were concentrated in heavily unionised 'smokestack' industries and regions. By the mid-1980s, thousands of manufacturing employees working for union firms in union strongholds were displaced. The de-industrialisation of America was accompanied by employer insistence that union workers make deep concessions. In most cases unions responded to the pressures to lower costs by 'trying to ride out the wave of concessions' (Barbash 1985: 10). From 1980 onward unions offered pay cuts, wage increase deferrals, modifications in work rules, and smaller benefit improvements in exchange for some limits on outsourcing and guarantees of job security.

Bargaining Strategies

Union bargaining now featured forms of contingent (such as bonuses, profit sharing) and two-tier compensation schemes. In the 1983–4, bargaining cycle nearly one-third of all workers covered by a major collective bargaining agreement were subjected to a wage freeze or cut (Barbash 1985). Pattern bargaining was discarded and replaced by worker compensation agreements based on firm level performance. Eventually reoccurring 'crisis' in the steel and auto industries compelled the USW and UAW in the 1990s and in 2007 respectively to negotiate creative, high-risk mechanisms to preserve employee retirement benefits. Known as 'Voluntary Employee Beneficiary Associations' (VEBA), unions would now assume the responsibility for managing a trust fund that provides health care benefits for retirees (Borzi 2009). Union proposed VEBAs were extraordinary attempts to preserve benefits for thousands of workers, but they also severed the fundamental obligation union employers had to their retired employees. What was once an employer responsibility was now a union burden. In this way, the VEBA continued a tectonic shifting of welfare responsibilities from the owning class to the working class.

In a few high profile cases union locals rebelled against their own international unions and independently waged unsuccessful fights to stop concessionary bargaining (Lynd 1982; Rachleff 1999; Ashby and Hawking 2010). In the 1990s, the UAW engaged in a costly nearly decade long series of worker struggles against Illinois based farm equipment manufacture, Caterpillar Inc. The fight ended in a terrible loss for the once formative union and some industrial relations experts suggested it was the union's willingness to adopt widespread labour-management schemes at the company that diluted its ability to stage a successful shutdown. Whether that analysis was accurate or not the vicious way that the company undercut the decades long labour agreement disproved the notion that the 1980s' corporate designed 'labour-management teams' would dissolve once adversarial (class) economic interests into common organisational goals.

Creative life-support bargaining was common within industrial labour markets but construction and public sector workers were not immune from neo-liberal attacks. In the 1970 and 1980s, leading corporate and political conservatives strategically targeted unions in the building and construction trades. Contrary to conventional wisdom the neo-liberal attack on the welfare state did not begin in the manufacturing sector. Energised and financed by the Business Roundtable, an association of industrial end-users of construction labour, the business community assumed an active and effective role in the formation of a pro-corporate public policy (Linder 1999). The Business Roundtable pressured the unionised construction industry to suppress collective bargaining settlements and to participate in a political coalition to undermine pro-labour economic and social policy. Driven by the Roundtable, large contractors worked to eliminate union control over the labour market, relax the boundaries between skilled trades, facilitate nonunion penetration in the construction industry, promote pro-business labour law reform, and enact a low-business tax and low-regulatory policy agenda. In response union trades mostly abandoned residential work to the non-union sector and in an attempt to secure and preserve work, union trades negotiated discount wages for construction done in speciality and segmented markets. Carpenters President William Sidell sounded the alarm in 1978 by declaring, 'The battle lines have been drawn and we must now decide whether we will procrastinate or launch the counter-offensive necessary to turn back the open shop threats. ... Business will not be happy until they achieve their goal to destroy the labour movement' (in Linder 1999: 352). Perhaps most importantly, with membership 'sitting on the bench' (unemployed) during recessionary periods the union trades shut the door on accepting new apprentices. Union density among construction trade workers plummeted by 2010 to barely 15 per cent (Bureau of Labor Statistics 2010a).

While neo-liberalism badly shrunk the unionised construction industry calls for smaller government eventually stunted the growth of public sector union density. Slowing membership growth did not mean initially incapacitate the unions' ability to negotiated good wages and pension benefits. But with fiscal limits established by anti-tax referendums and more public services were privatised, government unions began to look for diverse ways to block a rollback of collective bargaining rights and benefits. The American Federation of State, County and Municipal Employees (AFSCME), the nation's largest public sector union, aggressively lobbied for new regulations of public services. Public employee unions also negotiated contract language that prevented government agencies from outsourcing work without first permitting the union to offer an alternative plan for reducing costs. According to one 2002 study, 81 per cent of local government agencies that had once privatised services had brought 'back-in at least one service' (Cyr-Racine and Jalette 2007: 305). Remarkably, despite fierce attacks, middle-class pensions, the crown jewel of hard won benefits for public workers remains in place. Advocated by anti-government forces in Washington and in statehouses, the obsessive neo-liberal drive to reduce or wipe out pension benefits for bus drivers, teachers, correction officers, and a host of other professions is deeply ideological and highly energised. In response the political programme devised by AFSCME has shifted from a defensive posture to challenging the ideology that markets were inherently better in delivering services than the public sector. Public sector union strategy has not however been uniformly oppositional. The American Federation of Teachers and the National Education Association have shown an increased willingness to accommodate the insertion of business models into public school practices.

Despite the decelerated expansion of union membership in the public sector, political action has created new mechanisms for extending bargaining rights to previously non-union workers. SEIU and AFSCME used their sizeable political influence with state governments in California, Pennsylvania and Illinois to win bargaining rights for home healthcare workers (*In These Times* 21 January 2004). But travelling the political path has not been without painful setbacks. Between 2003 and 2005 thousands of state employees in Indiana, Missouri and Kentucky lost bargaining rights through executive orders issued by new incoming Republican governors. The election of anti-labour governors was repeated in 2010 and unfolded during genuinely trying times for public officials. Since the anti-tax initiatives of the late 1970s it has become harder to advocate for increased public services. Beginning in 1991 reoccurring economic crisis added enormous pressure on state, local and educational agencies to cut spending. Labour friendly governors were unlikely to punish their principal constituents so the voters in states like Wisconsin and Ohio elected leaders whose idea of 'reinventing government' included privatising services. Against the reigning anti-government ideology public as well as private sector unions were hesitant to militantly resist. Labour's once proud strike weapon had been muted by the neo-liberal demonisation of unions and canonisation of 'market-driven entrepreneurs' (Parker 2005: 625).

Strike Incapacity

Union responses to corporate shredding of collective bargaining agreements were muted by an anaemic capacity to strike. Employers took the offensive after PATCO in a number of high profile 1980s' national labour-management disputes. As strikes were crushed by a combination of employer opposition and complicit regulatory bodies, unions largely surrendered the strike as an economic tool. It was not until the 1997 IBT walkout against United Parcel Service (UPS) that for a shining if unrealised movement the hopes of a resurgent American militant labour movement were galvanised (Schiavone 2007). But despite the Teamsters campaign for full time jobs the number of major union strikes dropped that year and continued to fall across the next decade (Bureau of Labor Statistics 2010b). In retrospect what PATCO ushered in with devastating consequences was the 'passing of the bargaining initiative from labour to management' (Barbash 1985: 10). The shifting relationship was predicated on employer dismantling of collective bargaining agreements and intense corporate politicking for neo-liberal 'public policies designed to bring labor to heel' (Barbash 1985: 10). Faced with ferocious corporate political organising to strip away regulatory protections for working people, the US labour movement tried to mount a counter electoral offensive.

Union Political Action

Recognising the uneven returns from concession bargaining, labour's primary defence against management's offensive was to first actively try to limit Reagan to a one-term presidency. Reagan came to office in the wake of what commentator's called the dissipation of labour's 'bloc-like' voting behaviour at the presidential level. Democrat Jimmy Carter, for example, had attracted only 48 per cent of organised labour votes in 1980. AFL-CIO leader Lane Kirkland explained why unions had to get 'their man' in the White House in 1984 by declaring, that 'Reaganomics' was 'class warfare against the disadvantaged, the poor, and the working class' (*AFL-CIO News* 27 July 1983). In 1982, the Federation organised 'Solidarity Day' and mobilised half a million union members to rally in Washington for 'jobs and justice.' The show of political street force was the biggest seen from or since the post-WWII AFL-CIO. Union turnout in 1984 for the endorsed Democratic candidate Walter Mondale was impressive but the Minnesota Democrat won barely a majority (53 per cent) of union votes and lost convincingly (Leroy 1990). Locked out of the White House and stymied by the Democratic Party's emergent centrist leadership, union political activity floundered over the next decade. In the late 1970s a Democratic president and controlled Congress failed to enact labour law reform and the consequences were punishing. In the1980s union displacement and avoidance became realistic options for employers in several industries. Employer lockouts of their unionised workers and the use of strikebreakers, relatively rare since the 1930s, suddenly in 1980 became management's preferred choice of action (LeRoy 1995). Antiunion consultants leading decertification campaigns proliferated and the American Management Association sponsored seminars on 'preventive labour relations' (Barbash 1985: 12). The state of labour law had so badly deteriorated and radically shifted power to the employers that Weiler (1983) complained that contemporary American labour law more and more resembles and elegant tombstone for a dying institution.

The AFL-CIO did get its 'man' in 1992 when a divided labour movement coalesced around Clinton. Clinton campaigned as a traditional liberal Democrat but rising deficits and a weak economy convinced him once in office to adopt neo-liberal budget cutting measures. His policy switch came as a major disappointment to union officials but the transformation should not have been a surprise. In 1984, Clinton had helped to form and then became the first chairman of the conservative, pro-business and anti-union Democratic Leadership Council (Parker 2005). Despite labour's success at helping to put a Democrat in the White House, in 1994 with some considerable union rank-and-file help the most right-wing Congress in more than three decades was elected. Labour now found itself after having spent millions to elect a Democrat president further politically marginalised. Motivated by the shocking 1994 election of anti-union House Republicans, organised labour undertook a political education programme unprecedented in its history. Under newly elected President John Sweeny's direction political mobilisation became a priority and the AFL-CIO successfully moved to increase organised labour's presence in local, state and national politics. The increase in labour's electoral activity between the mid-1990s and 2008 also produced a discernable return of the 'labour bloc' vote. Since 1996's presidential elections no fewer than 60 per cent of AFL-CIO union members voted for the Democratic candidate (Bielski and Bruno 2010). But more than a quarter century after Reagan's inauguration and a renewed union political focus an obviously chagrined National Labor Relations Board Chairman, Wilma Liebman lamented that 'collective action and industrial democracy – the animating ideas of the law,' must 'seem foreign to many Americans' (Bielski and Bruno 2010: 19). While ineffectual electoral behaviour, limited strike activity and concessionary bargaining were the most common responses they did not fully represent union reactions to neo-liberalism. The growing vulnerability of striking workers brought on by the employer anti-union offensive stimulated a new set of union strategies that congealed under the rubric of 'alternatives to the strike' or 'corporate campaigns.' Unions initiated multidimensional non-strike pressure campaigns to rally rank-and-file workers and community groups against recalcitrant employers. The results of individual cases of coalitional-based resistance were mixed at best but at least they revealed labour's vibrant capacity to strategise around objectives. Unfortunately, little of that energy was directed at educating union members about the importance of organising and the threat of neo-liberalism.

Organising and Worker Education

Shredded labour agreements and government policies that deregulated the economy and shifted wealth from wage shares into dividends, rents and profits, should have been a catalyst for an increase in union organising. Instead from the late 1970s until at least the mid-1990s organising activities trickled to a slow drip. While prior to 1995 no reliable baseline of organising budgets existed, common wisdom held that most unions were not spending more than five per cent on recruiting new members (Fiorito and Jarley 2008). By 2004 the average organising budgets had increased substantially to a still insufficient 14.5 per cent of total union spending (Fiorito and Jarley 2008). Unquestionably unfriendly conservative governments and weak labour laws presented formidable obstructions to organising but ineffective labour leadership was also at fault. Workers could have been educated and mobilised around a political-economy analysis. The AFL-CIO created teaching curriculum more than once but more than once too few workers were provided the teaching. The Federation introduced the Organising Institute to help affiliates grow their membership but most affiliates rejected the help. Eventually by the early 1990s unions like the International Brotherhood of Electrical Workers (IBEW) and the USW embraced an appropriate educational programme that reached out to the membership.

Where American unions addressed or even made mention of neo-liberalism they offered at best a limited condemnation of 'super capitalism' (Reich 2007). But few union leaders from the AFL-CIO down conceptualised any genuine alternative to the fundamental structure of the free-market economy or the minimalist state. Government from the far-right was loudly condemned, but the need for a 'Great Society' or 'New Deal-like' return of public policy was rarely communicated. If Ronald Regan had labelled government as America's 'problem' the labour movement had not seen fit to rehabilitate Franklin Roosevelt's and Lyndon Johnson's' belief that government could be and should be the nation's solution. In fact, labour's use of the word neo-liberalism was rare until then AFL-CIO Secretary-Treasurer (now President) Richard Trumka began to analyse the problems of the American economy in the run up to the 2008 national presidential election. How the national labour movement framed a call for economic renewal is emblematic of the limitations of their regulatory free-market approach to neo-liberalism. Universal health care was broadly supported in the form of expanded Medicare coverage for all Americans by the national AFL-CIO, 39 state AFL-CIO federations, 135 Central Labour Councils, 22 international and national unions and more than 500 local unions. But few national unions (the UE, USW and the National Nurses Organizing Committee, previously California Nurses Association) called outright for the abolition of for-profit insurance companies and the adoption of a government run system. Building unions however were less enthused about any government run plans that would appear to weaken their well funded private joint employer-union insurance coverage. Some union leaders even denied the need for a public plan, recommending unionisation as the only required medicine for workers without healthcare.

Tax incentives for employers were praised as a way to create as many as 11m jobs but not by direct government employment. The auto industry needed bailing out but not a wholesale restructuring of the companies into mass transportation manufacturers. Banks and financial institutions needed reforming but not government ownership. Rules against gaming of the financial system were justified but moving towards a more progressive tax system was never mentioned. Protective trade laws, 'buy American,' and government backed loans would help bring manufacturing back to middle-America, but not a national industrial policy. Labour law reform in the form of the Employee Free Choice Act (EFCA) was desperately needed but expanding worker access to paid leave or mandating paid sick days or vacations, or reducing the standard work week was apparently not. In summary, the US response to neo-liberalism was not to advocate for socialism or something similar to European social democracy. It was not even, with a few notable exceptions, a campaign to oppose corporate globalisation or socialise the capitalist economy.

Grappling with reactive measures to preserve collective bargaining agreements left American labour unions with few resources and even less attention to the numerous tears in the once formidable New Deal fabric. As government policy reduced the percentage of people covered by unemployment insurance, shrunk welfare benefits, reduced the value of the minimum wage, privatised education and public services, prioritised monetarist policy to fight inflation and not promote job growth, stopped fighting poverty, abandoned affordable public housing, let domestic manufacturing shrivel up, allowed financial institutions to act like casinos, dramatically alleviated the corporate and upper income personal tax burden, de-regulated everything from trains to planes to telecommunications, and criminalised immigrant workers labour did not position itself as the working-class leader of a loyal grassroots opposition. In 1934, unions in America organisd a mass rebellion against FDR's weak 'first' New Deal. The result in 1936 was a stunning Roosevelt second term and a robust 'second' New Deal that institutionalised the idea that government intervention into the working of the marketplace was a virtuous tool for prosperity and essential for democracy. But while the AFL-CIO position on America's 'right turn' eventually included a critique of neo-liberalism, it has not put forth a social democratic alternative to regulated capitalism or orgnised any massive resistance.

CONCLUSION

Neo-liberalism's imprint on the American economy was authored by powerful changes to the global marketplace and dramatic upheavals in political philosophies that pushed organised labour to the precipice. Unions in America reacted by making deals to survive but they were either confused or tactical about the real goals of Reagan Republicanism and Democratic centrism. The political and economic forces at work since the late 1970s were dedicated to reordering the web of social and political constraints that influenced how wealth was distributed in America. The neo-liberal project, according to Harvey (2005: 11), was to 'disembed capital from those constraints'. Once freed from restrictive state interventions in the economy capital would be unbound and a massive transfer of wealth would take place from the working class to the capitalist class. But the neo-liberal 'restoration of class power' could not have taken place without a working class 'persuaded to vote against its material, economic, and class interests for cultural, nationalist and religious reasons' (Harvey 2005: 50). When a majority of white (but not unionised or black) working class workers voted twice for Reagan and three times more for a Bush for president they did so in an economic context missing a healthy adversarial union movement. It did not have to be this way.

Reisman and Compa (1985) made the case for a return to 'adversarial unions' as the best response to the corporate class' power grab. They pointed out that rank-and-file movements had always guarded the independence and militancy of their unions. 'Union resistance to management pressure,' they went on 'is at the heart of the employment relationship' (Riesman and Compa 1985: 30). In recommending a path forward for labour, Reisman and Compa (1985: 30) underscored and highlighted the 'inherent conflicts between labour and management'. Foreshadowing the escalating pressures of a lawless global marketplace, those divergent interests would only grow less accommodating. With every factory shuttered, public sector job sold to the lowest bidder and corporate anti-union campaign financed the 'organic adversarialism' of American labour-management relations should have spiked. In some high profile cases it did, but mostly the union leadership accepted concessions. Reisman and Compa suggested that instead of embracing a new era of labour-management relations union leaders should 'teach their members about the economic and political forces that boxed them into concessions and about the need for economic strategies and political reforms to lead them out of the box.' Reisman and Compa (1985: 36) concluded by encouraging union officers to be unapologetically and strategically adversarial because, 'they will be closer to the fundamental values and needs of their rank-and-file members and better able to represent and defend their real interests'. When John Sweeny was elected to the AFL-CIO's presidency in 1995 it seemed to many observers that labour's capacity to represent working-class people would now be fortified. Richard Trumka's election to the AFL-CIO top post in 2009 further raised expectations of labour's capacity to staunch the flow of neo-liberal policies. But at the mid-point of the Obama administration labour's agenda has been uncomfortably retrofitted into a neo-liberal mould and EFCA has disappeared from the legislative calendar. No doubt a well disciplined obstructionist Republican Party was primarily responsible for blocking any retreat from neo-liberal policies. But in a moment of self-critique, Trumka reflected upon the labour movement's inexplicable failure to fully mobilise the membership around EFCA and acknowledged that '[We] could have done a lot of things ... but we didn't, and we are where we are' (Fitch 2010). The honest assessment of the nation's top labour official raises the question whether the post-mortem on labour law reform has a broader application.

In retrospectively trying to construct a coherent thesis for understanding how American unions have responded to neo-liberalism there are at least six formative elements that limited labour's effectiveness. First, unions in the US are not structured as radical institutions ideologically critical of capitalism. Behaviourally American unions are basically conservative and reformist in their relationship with the state and the corporate class. As a result while neo-liberalism produces painful outcomes for workers, union leaders are not compelled to call for remedies that genuinely alter the power of the market-place. Second, the decentralised nature of the American labour movement makes it very difficult to mobilise labour's ranks around a unified position on any important policy or socio-economic event. The contemporary struggle over generating a strong policy position on health care reform is a classic case of a fractured US labour movement. Adding to the problem of decentralisation is the fact that US labour is not organised along industrial or sectoral lines. In any one industry there may be a dozen unions vying for worker representation and actually representing workers. Third, the component parts of neo-liberalism impacted different unions differently and at different times. Trade policy for instance was decimating the fortunes of manufacturing workers long before the financial crisis wrecked the personal balance sheets of construction workers. Likewise, outsourcing was shrinking employment in the auto industry prior to the massive waves of layoffs that hit state employees.

Fourth, neo-liberal policies first emerged in the late 1970s but they were then adopted incrementally while unions were comparatively better off than they are now. For example, Clinton's 'welfare reform' measures went into place during the economic boom of the 1990s. Additionally, the charter school movement emerged prior to the neo-liberal-caused budgetary stress imposed on American public school districts. Fifth, labour's relationship with the Democratic Party appears to explain much of how the movement reacts to neo-liberal policies. Unions in America have a dilemma. They are thoroughly dependent on a corporate aligned centrist Democratic Party, even one currently led by a moderately labour friendly president, to advance an anti-neo-liberal agenda. Unfortunately, corporate influence peddlers, free-traders and proponents of privatisation are now prevalent among the Democrats. Scholars of globalisation have found that 'class politics continues to exert pressure on welfare estates,' and that 'political parties, plausibly class actors, continue to shape welfare states in the globalisation era' (Brady *et al.* 2005: 945, 933). In other words, partisanship influences the ebb and flows of neo-liberal policies, but whenever Republicans charge organised labour with fermenting 'class war' most Democrats withdraw into a weak defensive posture. This form of political dependency produces a contradictory need for the labour movement to elect candidates largely acceptable to the corporate class in order to pass pro-worker legislation. In this way neo-liberalism is unintentionally advanced because the labour movement's need to successfully do politics and their objective interest in adopting working-class policy is internally inconsistent. Finally, in the 1980s rank-and-file union members as well as many of their leaders were ill-prepared to initially understand and then later respond to the political and corporate proponents of neo-liberal policy. Their insufficient understanding was in part caused by a deficit in workplace political and economic education. It was the exceptional union that focused on political-economy or an analysis of capitalism. While corporate America was at war with the very idea of collective bargaining, most unions were preparing their membership to live with concessions. What the membership did not receive was a larger analysis of the economic and social forces transforming the American political landscape.

But after more than two decades of neo-liberal policies have slammed America's working class with at least three major economic crises, the moment seems to be right for the labour movement to mount a unified and substantive opposition. An energetic new AFL-CIO leadership offers the possibility of a more active strategy to confront widely promoted but failed neo-liberal creeds. If observers of the future US labour movement are to look back upon this moment differently than how contemporary students are evaluating labour's pre-2007 recession performance, it will likely be the result of an extensive and analytical education of the union membership. As Crosby (n.d.), a local union president, contended, 'A movement more united politically, with a common and deeper understanding of the war of ideas and globalisation (or neo-liberalism), is better equipped to mobilise to defend workers' interests across the board'.

REFERENCES

Ashby, S. and C. Hawking (2009), *Staley: The Fight for a New American Labor Movement*, Urbana; University of Illinois Press.

Barbash, J. (1985), 'Do we really want labor on the ropes?', *Harvard Business Review* (July–August), pp. 10–20.

Belzer, M. (1995), 'Collective bargaining after deregulation: do the teamsters still count?', *Industrial and Labor Relations Review*, **48**(4), 636–55.

Borgers, F. (1999), 'Global unionism – beyond the rhetoric: the CWA North Atlantic Alliance' *Labor Studies Journal*, **24**(1), 107–22.

Borzi, P. (2009), 'Retiree Health VEBAs: a new twist on an old paradigm implications for retirees, unions and employers', Kaiser Family Foundation, accessed at www.kff.org/medicare).

Brady, D., J. Beckfield and M. Seeleib-Kasier (2005), 'Economic globalization and the welfare state in affluent democracies, 1975–2001', *American Sociological Review*, **70**(6), 921–48.

Brecher, J., T. Costello and B. Smith (2006), 'International labor solidarity: the new frontier', *New Labor Forum*, **15**(1), 9–18.

Bronfenbrenner, K. and T. Juravich (1995), 'The impact of employer opposition on union certification win rates: a private/public sector comparison', Economic Policy Institute, working paper no. 113, Washington, DC.

Bruno, R. (2009), 'Steel on strike: from 1936 to the present', in A. Brenner, B. Day and I. Ness (eds), *The Encyclopedia of Strikes in American History*, Armonk: M.E. Sharpe, pp. 360–75.

Bruno, R. (2005), 'USWA-bargained and state-oriented responses to the recurrent steel crisis', *Labor Studies Journal*, **30**(1), 67–91.

Bureau of Labor Statistics (2010a), 'Economic News Release', Washington, DC: United States Department of Labor.

Bureau of Labor Statistics (2010b), 'Work stoppages', Washington, DC: United States Department of Labor.

Card, D. (1986), 'The impact of deregulation on the employment and wages of airliner mechanics'. *Industrial and Labor Relations Review*, **39**(4), 527–38.

Cormier, D. and Targ H. (2001), 'Globalization and the North American worker', *Labor Studies Journal*, **26**(1), 42–59.

Crosby, J. (n.d.), 'Democracy, density and transformation: we need them all', accessed at www.aflcio.org/aboutus/ourfuture/upload/crosby.pdf.

Cyr-Racine, C. and P. Jalette (2007), 'What have unions got to do with reverse privatization?', *Journal of Collective Negotiations*, **31**(4), 303–18.

Fiorito, J. and P. Jarley, P. (2008), 'Union organizing and union revitalization in the United States', in *Proceedings of the 60th Labor and Employment Relations Association Series*, New Orleans, LA.

General Accounting Office (2004), 'Airline plans underfunding illustrates broader problems with the defined benefit system', testimony before the US Senate Committee on Commerce, Science and Transportation, October.

Greider, W. (1993), *Who Will Tell the People? The Betrayal of American Democracy*, New York: Simon and Schuster.

Fitch, R. (2010), 'Card check: labor's Charlie Brown moment?', *New Politics*, **12**(4), 48.

Hacker, J. (2002), *The Divided Welfare State*, New York: Cambridge University Press.

Hale, R. (1986), 'The new industrial relations in a global economy', *Labor Law Journal*, **37**(8), 539–43.

Harvey, D. (2005), *A Brief History of Neo-liberalism*, Oxford: Oxford University Press.

Hirsch, B. (1988), 'Trucking regulation, unionization, and labor earnings: 1973–85', *The Journal of Human Resources*, **23**(3), 296–319.

Hurd, R. (2006), 'Reflections on PATCO's legacy: labor's strategic challenges persist', *Employment Responsibility and Rights Journal*, **18**, 207–14.

International Brotherhood of Teamsters (2006). 'Teamster delegates stand strong against cross-border trucking', press release, 28 June.

Johnson, N. (2004), 'Airline employment, productivity, and working conditions following deregulation', *Research in Transportation Economics*, **10**(1), 79–108.

La Botz, Dan (2010), 'Unions representing workers in Canada, Mexico, and US', *Monthly Review*, 28 June.

Lerner, S. (2003), 'An immodest proposal: a new architecture for the house of labor', *New Labor Forum*, **12**(9), 30.

LeRoy, M. (1995), 'Regulating employer use of permanent striker replacements: empirical analysis of NLRA and RLA strikes, 1935–1991', *Berkeley Journal of Employment and Labor Law*, **16**, 169.

LeRoy, M. (1990), 'The 1988 elections: re-emergence of the labor bloc vote?', *Labor Studies Journal*, **15**(1), 5–32.

Liebman, W. (2010), 'The Revival of American Labor Law', Washington University Law School Access to Justice Lecture Series accessed at www.nlrb.gov/nlrb/press/releases/Access_Justice_Speech.pdf.

Linder, M. (1999), *Wars of Attrition: Vietnam, the Business Roundtable, and the Decline of Construction Unions*, Iowa City, IA: Fanpihua Press, .

Lynd, S. (1982), *Fight Against Shutdowns: Youngstown's Steel Mill Closings*, San Pedro, CA: Singlejack Books, .

McCartin, J. (2006), 'A historian's perspective on the PATCO strike, its legacy, and lessons', *Employee Responsibility and Rights Journal*, **18**, 215–22.

McEntee, G. (2006), 'The new crisis of public service employment', *Public Personnel Management*, **35**(4), 340–46.

Meyer, D. (2001), 'Building union power in the global economy: a case study of the coordinated bargaining committee of General Electric Unions (CBC)', *Labor Studies Journal*, **26**(1), 60–75.

Mongelluzzo, B. (2006), 'Teamsters go global with truck organizing campaign', *Pacific Shipper*, **80**(15), 29–39.

Parker, R. (2006), *John Kenneth Galbraith: His Life, His Politics, His Economics*, Chicago, IL: University of Chicago Press.

Rachleff, P. (1999), *Hard-Pressed in the Heartland: The Hormel Strike and the Future of the Labor Movement*, Boston, MA: South End Press.

Richman, E. (2009), 'The NAFTA Trucking provisions and the teamsters: why they need each other', *Northwestern Journal of International Law & Business*, **29**, 555–75.

Reich, R. (2007), *Supercapitalism,* New York: Alfred P. Knopf.

Reisman, B. and L. Compa (1985), 'The case for adversarial unions', *Harvard Business Review* (May–June), pp. 22–36.

Schiavone, M. (2007), 'Rank-and-file militancy and power: revisiting the Teamster struggle with the United Parcel Service ten years later', *WorkingUSA: The Journal of Labor Society*, **10**, 175–91.

Wells, D. (1999), 'Building transnational coordinative unionism', in S. Babson and H. Nunez (eds), *Confronting Change: Auto Labor and Lean Production in North America*, Detroit: Wayne State University and Benemerita Universidad Autonoma de Puebla, pp. 488–505.

14 The crisis of neo-liberalism and the American labour movement
Richard L. Trumka

INTRODUCTION

Workers in America today face the most challenging economic conditions since the Great Depression. At the same time, as a result of the financial crisis of 2008 and the Great Recession, we also have the greatest opportunity of our generation to change the economic policies that produced this crisis, to rebalance the economy, and to build an economy that works for all. To avoid the dangers and realise the opportunities of the moment, the American labour movement must build our own power by organising millions of new members and help elect worker-friendly politicians at every level of government. But this is not enough. We must also directly challenge neo-liberalism – the economic doctrine that has dominated elite thinking in the US and much of the world for the past 35 years, that has produced a generation-long stagnation of wages, rising economic insecurity and historic levels of inequality in the US and many other countries. Neo-liberalism is the ultimate cause of the 2008 financial crisis and the Great Recession from which we are still struggling to recover.

'Neo-liberalism' is a term seldom used in the US, largely because of our county's association of 'liberal' with the New Deal and the Great Society. Nevertheless, neo-liberalism is very familiar in much of the rest of the world. There is no little irony in the fact that we do not use this term in America, given that the US is among the most neo-liberal societies in the world and sponsors of much of the world's neo-liberal policies. Neo-liberalism is both a distinctive set of economic policies and an ideology that justifies those policies. The ideology of neo-liberalism holds that free markets are the most effective, efficient, and equitable means for organising economic life, and that governments are ineffective and inefficient and should be restricted to the minimal roles of national defence and protection of domestic peace and property. However, this ideological view bears little resemblance to how governments and markets actually interact in modern societies. In the wake of the financial crisis and Great Recession, we have seen quite clearly how government has intervened very actively in the economy to promote the interests of

Wall Street. The financial crisis and Great Recession demonstrate the failures of neo-liberalism and demand a new course for economic policy and a new way of thinking about the economy. Unfortunately, neo-liberalism dominates the economics profession in the United States, a profession that utterly failed to see the economic imbalances growing or the crisis unfolding. Even as I write, adherents of neo-liberalism are arguing for fiscal austerity and more government intervention in the economy to support the interests of Wall Street, in the face of massive evidence such policies will be ruinous. Because neo-liberalism is both a set of policies and a justifying ideology, I will reserve the term 'neo-liberalism' to describe the ideology of free markets and use the term 'Wall Street Agenda' to describe the distinctive set of policies that became dominant in the US and many other countries over the past 35 years.

THE GLOBAL JOBS CRISIS

Workers were not the cause of the financial crisis or the Great Recession, but workers, our families, and our communities are the real victims of the crisis, and we are paying with our jobs, our homes, and our savings. The Great Recession destroyed over eight million jobs in the US, forced over four million home foreclosures, and destroyed over US$11tn in household wealth. Unemployment is now a leading cause of both foreclosures and personal bankruptcy. Over a year since the recession officially ended, we are still mired in the most serious employment crisis since the Great Depression. Over 15m workers are unemployed, over 40 per cent of them for more than 27 weeks. Millions more are underemployed or have left the labour force altogether. Economists project that unless jobs are created faster than the last recession, we will not recover pre-recession levels of unemployment until the spring of 2021 (Schmitt and Conroy 2010). By 2009, unemployment had pushed the poverty rate among working age Americans to 12.9 per cent, the highest level recorded since before Lyndon Johnson's 'War on Poverty' in the 1960s. Globally, the International Labor Organisation (ILO) reports that the recession has destroyed 34m jobs, driving global unemployment to 212m workers, the highest number ever recorded. Moreover, over half of the world's employed workers now find themselves in various forms of 'vulnerable work': working poor, discouraged workers, involuntary part-time and the vast informal economy (Somavia 2010). The World Bank estimates the recession has forced over 60m people into absolute poverty, mostly in the developing world. The economic, social, and political implications of this level of joblessness are simply unacceptable. Governments must act with the same urgency and political will that they exhibited in saving the global banking system to put workers back to work and assure that the jobs of the future are good jobs.

THE GREAT STAGNATION AND FINANCIAL BUBBLES

There are several distinctive features of the Great Recession, in addition to the unusual severity of its impact on jobs. Namely, the Great Recession was preceded by a long period of economic stagnation, and it was the direct result of the collapse of a bubble in asset prices. As discussed below, these two distinctive features of the Great Recession are related. First, even before the financial crisis and Great Recession began, workers and their families were struggling to make a living. Although American workers are among the most productive in the world, and work longer hours than workers in any other developed country, it was becoming increasingly difficult to make a living in the richest country in the world. Workers had already suffered a generation of stagnant wages, rising economic insecurity, eroding health care and pensions, and historic levels of inequality. As wages stagnated, workers tried to compensate, first by working longer hours and more jobs. They also sent more family members into the labour force. And, finally, in response to asset inflation, workers reduced their savings and assumed more and more debt to support their families.

The American economy did not always work this way. When the middle class[1] was built in the three decades after the World War II, despite the effects of racism and sexism, the economy generated broadly-shared prosperity. During this period, real family incomes doubled, making for the most rapid improvement of living standards in history. Incomes for the poorest families increased even faster than those of the richest families, so incomes became more equally distributed. Unions grew during this period, and the power of workers helped create a more just society as the labour movement played a key role in funding and lending political support to the civil rights movement. However, beginning in the mid-1970s, the pattern of family incomes changed dramatically. First, the growth of family incomes was much slower than in the earlier period, as the rate of economic growth generally slowed decade-by-decade after the 1960s. Even more significantly, the incomes of the richest 20 per cent of families rose much faster than those of the remaining 80 per cent, with most of the increase going to our country's wealthiest families.

As a result, income inequality reversed its 50-year decline and has been rising ever since. Indeed, the share of total income of the richest 1 per cent of families rose from 8.9 per cent in 1976 to 23.5 per cent in 2007 (Atkinson *et al.* 2011). The shares of the top 0.1 per cent and 0.01 per cent of families grew even faster. As one prominent economist observed, this implies that since 1976, for every dollar of increased income, the richest 1 per cent of families claimed 58 cents (Rajan 2010). Even before the crisis, the US had become the most unequal society of any developed country, and was more unequal than at any time since the 1920s. Whereas we used to grow together as a nation, today we are growing apart – economically, socially and politically. The key to understanding what has happened to our economy and to our society, and what has happened to working people and our families, is to understand the forces behind stagnating wages and incomes and growing inequality. Economists debate whether stagnating wages and growing inequality are caused by 'skill-bias technical change' or globalisation. But as a worker and an elected leader of workers during this period, what I saw happening to my sisters and broth-ers was a dramatic shift in power away from workers and their unions and towards employers – played out in the workplace, in the courts, and in our nation's politics. The result was a rupture in the crucial relationship between productivity and wages that was so central to the growth of the middle class after World War II. From 1947 to 1973, productivity doubled, and so did the real value of average wages. (Figure 14.1). However, from 1973 to the present, although productivity continued to grow, wages stagnated. As a result, aver-age wages today are only 15 per cent higher than average wages in 1980, despite a 67 per cent increase in productivity.

But it gets worse. Working families are not only struggling with stagnating wages and the challenges that long hours pose to their family life. They are also suffering from rising insecurity and anxiety. As Hacker *et al.* (2010) have shown, the likelihood of an average worker experiencing a 50 per cent or greater loss of family income has doubled since 1980. Workers are also terri-fied about what a serious accident or sickness might mean for their family's

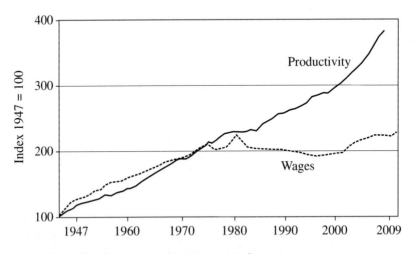

Figure 14.1   Productivity versus wage growth

Source: Economic Policy Institute analysis of Bureau of Economic Analysis and Bureau of Labor Statistics data. Wages includes benefits.

economic security, and they are anxious about their own ability to retire. The increased volatility of income and the increasing burden of risk for family health care and retirement security are aggravating the acute anxiety so many working families are feeling in a world – as Jared Bernstein puts it – where 'you are on your own'. Since the mid-1970s, the benefits of rising productivity have increasingly flowed to our wealthiest families, the owners of a majority of the shares of our public companies, and to shareholders and insiders in our corporations and capital markets. In 1980, the average CEO of major American companies earned 42 times what the average workers earned; in 2006 CEOs on average were earning over 400 times what average workers brought home. Today the average CEO earns more on the first day of the year than the average worker earns all year, and the CEO earns more before lunch on the first day than minimum wage workers earn all year. The second distinctive feature of the Great Recession was that, unlike many previous postwar recessions, it was not policy-induced. Most previous recessions were policy-induced in the sense that they resulted from the Federal Reserve's decision to raise interest rates to combat inflation in the context of an overheated economy. When inflation fell and the Fed lowered interest rates, the economy quickly recovered, powered by interest-sensitive sectors, particularly housing and consumer durables. The last two recoveries, by contrast, were different from previous recoveries. They ended with the collapse of asset bubbles – equities values in 2001 and housing values in 2008–9. The current deflation of housing values is far more serious than the deflation of equity values in 2001, and the latest data shows that after a period of stability housing prices appear to be falling once again. The result of falling housing prices is that the current recession has been, and will almost certainly continue to be, much more serious than other recent recessions. Recoveries from recessions caused by collapsing asset values, particularly when accompanied by financial crises, are much slower and more difficult to resolve by cutting interest rates. The policy tools that worked in past recessions will not work this time. Under current conditions, sustained government action is necessary until the balance sheets of business and households are repaired (Koo 2009).

CAUSES OF THE FINANCIAL CRISIS AND GREAT RECESSION

To meet the challenges posed by the financial crisis and Great Recession, we must first understand their causes. This requires us to differentiate among immediate causes; intermediate causes rooted in fundamental economic imbalances; and the ultimate underlying cause, which is the failure of a neo-liberal economic growth strategy based on stagnant wages, asset inflation, and debt-fuelled consumption. The immediate cause of this crisis was the collapse of a housing bubble in the US, which first manifested itself as a sub-prime mortgage crisis in 2007. At the time, economists and policy makers maintained that the crisis was 'well contained' and posed no serious threat to the broader capital market or the real economy. However, collapsing housing values triggered a global credit crisis in 2008, as financial assets based on housing values proved toxic, thereby freezing capital markets and undermining the solvency of under-capitalised financial firms. The failure of key financial firms like Bear Stearns, Lehman Brothers, and AIG led to a broad financial panic. Trillions of dollars of paper value in the stock market and other financial markets vanished, adding to the asset collapse that began with housing. The massive and continuing deflation of housing values, frozen capital markets, and collapsing banks, in turn, contributed to a deep and dangerous global recession that was already underway. Underlying these immediate causes, however, lay deeper intermediate causes – namely, three fundamental economic imbalances that had been developing for years: imbalances between the US and the global economy; between the financial sector and the real economy; and in bargaining power between workers and their employers.

The Imbalance Between the US and the Global Economy

Before the crisis, an unsustainable trade deficit required the US to borrow almost 5 per cent of national income to pay for things we were consuming as a nation but were no longer producing. This external imbalance had been sustained by trading partners, particularly in Asia, investing in dollar-denominated assets – US Treasury bonds and mortgage-backed securities – in order to maintain their undervalued currencies, maintain their global competitiveness, and rapidly industrialise. Ironically, our trading partners' need to reinvest in dollar-denominated assets (and not to convert them into their own currency) led them to purchase Treasury bonds and mortgage-backed securities. This flood of foreign-owned dollars into our credit markets helped lower long-term interest rates and fuels the housing bubble whose collapse precipitated the crisis. If we fail to address this global imbalance between the US and our trading partners, we will find it difficult to recover from the recession and will replicate the unsustainable growth patterns that helped produce the crisis (Palley 2009). We must produce more of the value equivalent of what we consume, or we will be forced – one way or another, sooner or later – to consume less.

To address the imbalance between the US and the global economy, we must improve US competitiveness through public investment that creates a world-class workforce and a world-class transportation, information, and communications infrastructure. A public investment-led recovery programme would bolster private investment and provide a basis for future economic growth that is stronger and more sustainable than one based on asset bubbles and high levels of debt. We must also rebuild our nation's manufacturing capacity and level the global playing field through fair trade agreements that protect fundamental worker rights and an internationally negotiated adjustment of exchange rate. Part of the solution to this global imbalance lies outside the United States. Key exporting nations like China must increase wages and domestic consumption if the global trading order is to be sustainable. At the same time, dollar-denominated capital pools that now threaten to once again ignite a new asset bubble need instead to be invested to bring billions of people without drinkable water, electric power, or access to education into the global economy as consumers. Part of the cure for these global imbalances is a global New Deal.

The Imbalance Between the Finance Sector and the Real Economy

In a well-functioning economy, finance should serve the real economy by channelling savings to productive investment and effectively managing financial risk. We were assured that financial deregulation and financial innovation would do both. But we now know that deregulation and financial innovation had the effect of diverting economic resources to the financial sector, away from productivity-enhancing investments in the real economy, and enhanced, rather than minimised, risk.

The Imbalance of Bargaining Power Between Workers and Employers

In the United States, workers' voices have been silenced in the workplace. Our legal system no longer in any meaningful way protects most workers' right to organise and bargain collectively. The erosion of worker bargaining power – for unionised as well as non-unionised workers – produced the wage stagnation that ruptured the relationship between productivity and wages that opened a chasm of economic inequality. The stagnation of wages was also responsible for the reliance of workers on debt to sustain their living standards by borrowing against the rise in asset prices – equities in the 1990s and housing after 2000 – which the crisis has shown to be clearly unsustainable. To address the imbalance in bargaining power between workers and their employers, we need a strategy centred on good jobs at good wages. Such a strategy must begin with a broad commitment to policies aimed towards full employment. Such a commitment begins with monetary and fiscal policy that sees relatively tight labour markets as a good thing – not a state of affairs to be attacked with high interest rates and fiscal contraction. But a high wage society requires more than just favourable macro-economic policies; it requires that workers have real economic and political power. Real worker bargaining power requires that the legal system once again protect workers' right to organise, and that our broader worker protections – minimum wage, the 40 hour work-week – be robustly maintained and enforced. This is why reforming our labour laws is essential, not just in terms of respect by the United States of universally recognised human rights. Protecting workers' right to organise and bargain is a necessary part of any economic strategy to assure that US consumption is based on good wages rather than bad debt. That is why the US labour movement is unified in seeking passage of the Employee Free Choice Act (EFCA). The Employee Free Choice Act would help restore workers' rights to organise and bargain collectively and help rebuild the relationship between wages and productivity that is key to restoring broadly shared prosperity and an economy that works for all. Specifically, the EFCA would streamline the process by which workers form and join unions, so employers would not be able to wear workers down through a prolonged campaign of fear, intimidation, and tension. The EFCA would establish fair rules for the conduct of representation elections to remove the current environment of fear and intimidation that is so pervasive in the process today. It would streamline the decision-making process of the National Labor Relations Board (NLRB) to limit the current endless opportunities for delay. It would protect newly formed bargaining relationships by encouraging and enhancing the ability of the parties to reach voluntary agreements, while providing a safety net in the event bargaining fails. And the EFCA would establish meaningful remedies to protect workers' rights and address the sharply escalating number of violations of the National Labor Relations Act (NLRA), which have been repeatedly documented and attributed to the remedial failings of the NLRA.

NEO-LIBERALISM AND THE WALL STREET AGENDA

Our country (and really our world) was propelled towards a global economic crisis by a set of policies and politics straight out of the age of the robber barons – the Wall Street Agenda – the intellectual revival of the economic ideas of the nineteenth century. Each of these economic imbalances is rooted in the neo-liberal ideal of the respective roles of markets and governments. So the ultimate cause of both these fundamental imbalances and the crisis were neo-liberalism and the Wall Street agenda that came to dominate economic thinking in the US and many other countries over the past 35 years. Neo-liberalism and the Wall Street Agenda are a system of economic and political power that favours capital, weakens workers and their unions, and has left America vulnerable to economic crisis and fundamentally less able to sustain a broad middle class. These policies have ruptured the crucial relationship between productivity and wages and have allowed corporate insiders to enrich themselves by undermining the wages and working conditions of all workers. For the first 30 years after World War II, the labour movement and politicians in both political parties built an economic order founded on a rough balance of power with employers. But starting in the 1970s, large corporations and their political allies used the economic crisis of the 1970s to attack the Keynesian economic policies of the earlier era.

In place of the Keynesian post-war order, American business and its political allies pursued a 'Wall Street Agenda,' seeking to radically reduce the role of government in the economy and shift bargaining power away from workers and their unions towards employers, their shareholders, and insiders in corporations and capital markets. In the process, neo-liberal trade and investment policies promoted the hollowing out of our industrial economy and the loss of millions of manufacturing jobs. Not surprisingly, employers used their increased bargaining power to keep the benefits of increasing productivity to themselves, pressure unions at the bargaining table, shift health care costs and taxes onto working families, and walk away from their responsibilities for retirement security. In the place of America's manufacturing base, the Wall Street Agenda promoted Wall Street and a string of asset bubbles as the way to get rising incomes and more consumer spending. The Wall Street Agenda reshaped the environment in which corporations compete. Corporations, in turn, respond to these policies by altering their structure and their business and competitive strategies in ways that shifted bargaining power away from workers and towards their employers. This shift in power is the source of the stagnating wages and rising insecurity of workers since the 1970s, which fed the economic imbalances that erupted in the financial crisis and Great Recession.

I think of the Wall Street Agenda is a system of power composed of six distinct, but interrelated, policy components that have fundamentally reshaped American economic life to the disadvantage of working families. Each of these components shifts bargaining power from workers to their employers and together they represent a system of economic power that explains the stagnation of wages and growing insecurity of workers that is driving social and economic inequality in the US and other countries. The six components of this system of power can be represented as a box (Figure 14.2) whose walls are pressing in on working people, compressing their standards of living and compromising our place in American society.

Small Government

It was President Clinton who first announced that 'the era of big government is over' in a State of the Union Address. However, it is the Republican Party that has advocated for budget-busting tax cuts, when in power, and balanced

Labour market flexibility

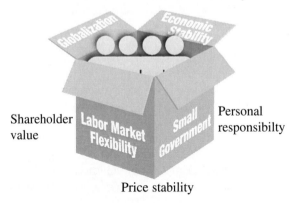

Figure 14.2   The Wall Street Agenda

budgets, when in opposition. Republicans argue that lowering taxes and reducing government's role in the economy maximises economic growth. Meanwhile, Democrats argue that reducing or eliminating the federal budget deficits lowers interest rates, stimulates private investment, and thereby maximises economic growth. In combination, these policies reduce the revenue of government and lead, in practice, to a more and more unfair tax structure. Both the lack of revenue and the unfairness of how revenue is raised reduce the role of public institutions in economic life. As the Republican strategist Grover Norquist maintained, 'My goal is to cut government in half in 25 years to get it down to the size where we can drown it in the bathtub'. The role of government in the economy has also been weakened by privatisation and deregulation of private industries, including transportation, utilities, and telecommunications. Proponents of these policies argue that they increase the effectiveness and efficiency of public services. On the contrary, they deprive citizens of needed services, reduce public sector employment, and heighten the pressure on workers' wages and benefits. Most destructively, they lead to systematic underinvestment in both physical and intellectual infrastructure – in the physical transportation and energy grids, and in our schools, colleges, and universities.

Price Stability

In the early post-World War II period, macro-economic policy involved coordinated fiscal and monetary policy to achieve full employment. Starting in the 1970s, as the Wall Street Agenda began to gain momentum, our government turned away from full employment as the objective of economic policy. The aim of fiscal policy became budget balance. Monetary policy conducted by a 'politically independent' Federal Reserve assumed the lead role in macro-economic policy and, though it was legally required to be focused on the dual goals of maximising employment and maintaining price stability, in fact the Fed used a variety of sophistries to really only pursue price stability. In this way, the congressionally-mandated objective of full employment was subor-dinated to fighting inflation. In the early post-war period (1949–75), economic growth averaged 4.6 per cent a year, but slowed decade-by-decade to an aver-age of 2.8 per cent in the subsequent 30 years (Bresser-Pereira, 2010). Slow growth produced slack labour markets that, in turn, shifted bargaining power from workers to their employers.

Globalisation

Starting around 1980, the United States aggressively pursued integration of the global economy with rapidly increasing volumes of trade, investment and migration. It pursued these broad goals through unbalanced corporate-oriented trade and investment agreements, misaligned currency policies and tax poli-cies that discriminate against domestic production. Advocates of these policies claim that elimination of trade barriers will enhance efficiency, lower the cost of living and bolster the growth of income and employment. However, by exposing American workers to direct competition with some of the most impoverished and oppressed workers in the world, corporate-oriented global-isation encourages companies to scour the world in search of the lowest wages, the lowest taxes and the lightest regulation they can find. The result has been the destruction of millions of manufacturing jobs, the weakening of the bargaining power of industrial workers and a global competitive dynamic that makes it difficult for workers in the developing world to increase their incomes.

Financialisation

The deregulation of financial markets was supposed to increase the efficiency of finance, foster increased investment and economic growth, reduce risk and promote financial stability. Instead, deregulation has fostered reckless finan-cial innovation and speculation and, by concentrating risk and heightening leverage throughout the economy, rendered the capital markets and the econ-omy unstable (as demonstrated by the financial crisis). Moreover, whereas finance should serve the real economy by channelling savings to productive investment, with deregulation finance instead became the master of the real economy, wasting savings and rendering the system vulnerable to financial crisis. Before the crisis, finance was claiming 40 per cent of total corporate profits, much of it going to the compensation of financial executives. Under cover of maximising shareholder value, CEOs and other corporate insiders enriched themselves and their capital market allies at the expense of employees and other stakeholders. Increasingly, public corporations were dominated by an alliance between insiders and the most irresponsible short term-oriented shareholders. In many cases, this narrow focus and associated abuses of corporate power destroyed the companies themselves.

Labour Market Flexibility

By weakening workers' unions and their bargaining power, and by allowing employers the maximum right to hire and fire 'at will,' we were assured that employers would be encouraged to hire more workers, lower unemployment and enhance growth. Indeed, the celebrated flexibility of US labour markets was generally regarded as the source of our rapid employment growth compared with other countries, especially in Europe. Also, allowing the real value of the minimum wage to erode under the influence of rising prices, we were told, would also encourage employers to hire younger and less skilled workers. What the crisis has revealed, however, is that labour market flexibility has allowed US employers to destroy over eight million jobs very efficiently, in contrast to other more tightly regulated labour markets. Yet it has done nothing to spur employment, which continues to languish a full year into the recovery. Behind these short term effects, the US model seems to be ineffective at fostering the combination of worker voice, continuous skill improvement and economic security that characterises high wage, innovation-driven, economies in Europe and Japan. As a result, the US lags high-wage countries such as Germany significantly in both the speed of overall recovery and, in particular, the recovery in jobs. The real effects of labour market flexibility have been stagnating wages, eroding health care and retirement benefits and other labour standards, and a loss of democracy in the workplace.

Personal Responsibility

In place of a social insurance system to provide health care and retirement security, the Wall Street Agenda has sought to shift responsibility for the security and welfare of working families onto the families themselves. Under pressure to reduce spending, governments are retreating from their role in providing health care and retirement security. Likewise, under pressure from short term-oriented capital markets, employers are retreating from their responsibility to contribute as well. As a result, the tradition of 'shared responsibility' of government, employers and workers that historically characterised the US employee benefits system has been undermined, and workers have been left to fend for themselves and their families. While close to 50 per cent of private sector workers had a real pension in 1980, less than 20 per cent do today. Employer-provided health care coverage is in long-term decline. Even in the midst of the Great Recession, fewer than half of unemployed workers receive unemployment benefits, and welfare support for impoverished families has been seriously weakened. The result of these policies is enormous unnecessary suffering and chronic insecurity. If we want to recover from the Great Recession and restore a stronger, more sustainable economy, we must correct these imbalances and turn away from the neo-liberal ideology that produced them. The labour movement – in the US and across the globe – is the most powerful potential counterweight to the economic and political power arrayed in support of neo-liberalism and the Wall Street Agenda. The labour movement must challenge neo-liberalism and the Wall Street Agenda and fight for an economy that works for all if we are to recover from the Great Recession and build a stronger, more balanced and sustainable economy.

PRESIDENT OBAMA AND A WORKING FAMILIES AGENDA FOR ECONOMIC JUSTICE

The financial crisis and the Great Recession have revealed the failure of neo-liberalism and the Wall Street Agenda. Not only did the Wall Street Agenda fail to generate a strong, balanced and globally competitive economy, but the Wall Street Agenda and neo-liberal ideology proved inherently unstable. The crisis that followed represents not just a danger to working families and the labour movement, but also an historic opportunity to change the course of economic policy. The opportunity was made more real by the election of Barack Obama, who campaigned on the theme of 'Change We Can Believe In' in 2008. Now, following serious setbacks for the President in midterm congressional elections, only decisive action will prevent us from either sliding back into policy paralysis or returning to the full-throated Wall Street Agenda. When Obama took office at the most dangerous moment of the economic crisis, he clearly recognised the complexity of the financial crisis, the Great Recession, and the imbalances that lay behind both. The first Economic Report of the President called for a new framework to 'Recover, Rebalance and Rebuild' the American economy (Goolsbee 2010). In other words, the administration recognised that this was not a normal recession and that the administration's response had to go beyond simple economic recovery. It had to also deal with the fundamental economic imbalances that produced the crisis and their underlying causes. Recognising that the crisis and the recession were global in scope, the administration assumed an essential leadership role early on with the coordination of an international fiscal policy response during the G20 Summits. In the 2009 G20 Summit, Obama (2009) supported establishing the G20 Summit as the central body to coordinate global economic policy, created a G20 'Framework for Strong, Sustainable and Balanced Growth,' and forged a commitment to 'Putting Quality Jobs at the Heart of the Recovery'. On both the domestic and global fronts, however, the administration has had difficulty translating these very high-level goals into concrete policies capable of delivering real results for working families.

With regard to recovery, the Administration at first fought hard for the nearly $800 billion American Recovery and Reinvestment Act, an aggressive fiscal policy response to an economy that was plunging into what appeared to be a second Great Depression. Shortly thereafter, the G20 agreed on an internationally-coordinated effort to increase fiscal spending by an average of 2 per cent per year through 2010. Together with the aggressive support of monetary policy by the Federal Reserve, the Recovery Act did stabilise the economy and almost certainly prevented a second Great Depression. The ARRA created or preserved more than 3m jobs and ended the haemorrhaging of private sector jobs that was underway when Obama took office. But it was not enough. The Recovery Act was premised on an underestimate of the magnitude of the recession and it was too small and too imperfectly designed to support a strong and sustained recovery. A full year into the recovery, the unemployment rate seems to be stalled near 10 per cent and the recovery seems to be weakening. Starting in late spring of 2010, the administration's economic team began saying fairly clearly that more aggressive action to create jobs and spur economic growth was necessary. But the actual steps that the administration eventually endorsed in Congress during the summer and fall of 2010 were, while directionally correct, not on a large enough scale to really alter the situation once they were enacted. With regard to economic 'rebalancing,' both domestically and internationally, the Obama administration is making serious efforts in the right direction, but it is too soon to tell whether those efforts will be sustained, or with the scale and intensity necessary to put our economy back on a healthy path.

Despite the administration's efforts to negotiate a re-balancing of exchange rates, the global imbalance of trade between the US and China, in particular, seems to remain very much in place. Ahead of the Toronto G20 meeting, the Chinese government announced new flexibility in the management of the exchange rate of the Chinese currency. Nevertheless, the exchange rate for the renminbi – which is undervalued by an estimated 40 per cent with respect to the dollar – appreciated less than 1 per cent over the summer. In response, the Obama administration has escalated pressure on China and has been increasingly aggressive in seeking multi-lateral support for pressuring China to let the renminbi rise. Yet the US trade imbalance with China, which had narrowed as a result of the global recession, has once again begun to grow. In terms of the balance between the financial sector and the real economy, Obama has spoken eloquently of the need to restore a healthy balance, and was personally involved in ensuring that the Dodd-Frank Wall Street Reform and Consumer Protection Act included key provisions such as the establishment of a Consumer Financial Protection Bureau. However, at the same time the Obama administration has continued bank bailout policies from the Bush administration. The result has been continued mass foreclosures and an unprecedented contraction of commercial lending, with serious consequences for the ability of the economy to recover. Meanwhile the financial sector has recovered pre-crisis levels of profitability, bonuses for financial executives are bigger than ever, the financial sector is more concentrated than ever, and the power of Wall Street over the real economy is undiminished. Ultimately, as a nation we will have to deal with our zombie banks and the continued imbalance in economic and political power between Wall Street and the real economy. These issues are at the heart of the dominance of neo-liberalism and the Wall Street agenda. Americans of all political persuasions share a common desire that our politics serve the public interest rather than Wall Street's interest. One of the most important challenges for Obama in the coming months will be to show the American public that he is with them and not with Wall Street.

With regard to social rebalancing, the Obama administration has fought for greater social equity throughout the economic landscape – from providing health care to tens of millions of uninsured Americans to moving aggressively to restore mine safety enforcement. However, the most fundamental fights are unresolved: the fight to restore workers' voice in our economy through restoring the right to organise; and the fight to begin to restore tax fairness by ending President Bush's tax cuts for the rich and a whole structure of tax preferences for the super rich and corporations that outsource. The right to organise and a fair tax system were the central public policies that built the American middle class after World War II. Neo-liberal politics dismantled those policies, and radical economic, social and political inequality and economic instability followed in their wake. Taking on neo-liberalism means restoring workers' rights and fair taxation for the rich. Obama has long supported the Employee Free Choice Act, as has a majority of Democrats in Congress. Like so much of the President's agenda, workers' rights have been the victim of what has effectively become a supermajority system in the Senate. In this area as in so many others, the administration will be faced in the next session of Congress with the choice of effectively abandoning its agenda or learning how to bring the fight for its agenda directly to the public.

With regard to rebuilding, Obama has been a champion of the idea that we must invest in education and infrastructure to restore our nation's competitiveness and rebuild America's manufacturing industries. Obama included spending on both education and infrastructure in the Recovery Act and moved aggressively to save the auto industry at the height of the crisis. He also appointed a special adviser in the White House to guide manufacturing policy for the administration. But in the aftermath of the passage of stimulus and health care, the President's key legislative initiatives in this areas – the energy and climate bill and a series of infrastructure bills – have faltered. As a result, although the framework of the administration's economic strategy is correct, the actually policies advanced to deliver on the framework's promise are too limited to carry the burdens assigned to them. This is partly the result of the unexpected magnitude of the crisis, as well as the determined and concerted opposition by Republicans in Congress and their 'moderate' Democratic allies. It is also, in my view, the result of a political and strategic mistake with vast consequences: the failure to bring the same level of urgency and attention to addressing the employment crisis as was mounted in response to the financial crisis.

In this mistake, we see the continuing influence of neo-liberal ideology and a resulting misplaced confidence in the ability of markets to recover their footing once the financial crisis had been stabilised. If Franklin Roosevelt's New Deal was above all characterised by imagination and vision and a focus on the plight of the public, economic policy in the era of neo-liberalism is chained by mental caution, passion about financial interests and systems, and indifference to public suffering. But the need for more robust policies is as great as ever, and it is not too late. Even though Obama is likely to face even stronger opposition from Republicans in Congress and their Democratic allies, he can reformulate and recalibrate his administration's economic strategy. To do so, however, requires the President to invite a more diverse range of economic thinking into his administration and demand an urgent and sustained focus on putting American workers back to work and changing the course of economic policy. Most of all, the success and survival of the Obama presidency rests on ignoring Washington's neo-liberal consensus, which will be in full flood after the 2010 elections, and focusing on the needs of the country for jobs and a stable housing market.

The labour movement, which did so much to elect President Obama and a Democratic majority in 2008, supports the Obama administration's economic strategy to 'Recovery, Rebalance and Rebuild' the American economy and led other governments in responding to the economic crisis. We also supported each of the important policies to serve this strategy. But we have consistently encouraged the administration to take the bolder and more imaginative steps necessary to make this strategy a success. Now is not the time to back away from the President's fundamental vision. Now is the time to assert it boldly, to stand for jobs, to stand for the public and against the Wall Street Agenda, and make it crystal clear who stands with the public and who stands with Wall

Street. Whether Obama charts a more robust economic policy, and one that holds more promise for broadly shared prosperity remains to be seen, but the position and strategy of the labour movement will largely depend on the course he chooses to pursue. Obviously, the tactics of both the Administration and the labour movement are highly contextual and change very rapidly, particularly on these hotly contested issues. But the labour movement is prepared to represent American workers at the highest levels of our country's economic policy formation, domestically and internationally.

ON THE ROLE OF THE LABOUR MOVEMENT

For the American labour movement, the economy exists to serve the needs of the people, the majority of whom earn their living by working, and the goal of economic policy is to support a strong, balanced and sustainable economy whose benefits are broadly shared. The labour movement's agenda is not simply a set of policies that happen to be different from those of the Wall Street Agenda. Our agenda stems from a different view of what kind of country we are and should be, a different view of how we should live together, a different view of what matters most in life. Our starting points are the lessons and values working families come by the hard way – the virtues of honesty and hard work and the values of solidarity, social justice and compassion. The policy objectives that spring from those values are simple. First, anyone who wants to work should have a job. Second, anyone who works should be able to support a dignified life for his or her family and enjoy quality health care. Third, workers are proud of the work we do and deserve respect for doing it. Fourth, all workers should be able to stop working at some point in their lives and still be able to enjoy a dignified and secure retirement. Fifth, every worker should be free to associate with his or her brothers and sisters at work and, if she chooses, form a union and bargain collectively.

A workers' agenda integrates the various policies necessary to make possible an economy that works for all, beginning with coordinated macroeconomic policies to assure full employment and rapid economic growth. Our agenda seeks a future of sustainable prosperity for our country by aiming to build a globally competitive economy through public investment in education, training and infrastructure, by rebuilding our manufacturing capacity, and levelling the global playing field by a negotiated adjustment of exchange rates and the adoption of a trade policies that include protection for worker rights and environmental sustainability. Our agenda recognises the important role governments play in regulating our economy, providing quality public services, providing health care and retirement security and raising taxes fairly. And to assure that the jobs of the future are good jobs, our agenda seeks to provide meaningful minimum wages, to enforce health and safety regulations and other labour standards, and to assure through the Employee Free Choice Act workers' fundamental right to join unions and bargain collectively.

THE CHALLENGE OF THE WALL STREET AGENDA AND LABOUR'S RESPONSE

In moving our country towards an economic future worthy of our people, we must fight neo-liberal ideology and the Wall Street Agenda. We can only do so if we face three great challenges. First, there is broad bipartisan elite support for the policies that make up the Wall Street Agenda. These policies seem to define economic rationality for much of our country's elite. They cannot imagine an alternative. Many politicians, policy makers and economists, particularly in the Democratic Party, show real concern for stagnating wages, rising insecurity, and growing inequality. Unfortunately, however, for too many policy intellectuals of our elite, their lack of understanding of the deep roots of these problems in the Wall Street Agenda leaves them trying to compensate futilely with minor tweaks to these policies, then wondering why working people are so angry. Thus the labour movement faces not just a battle for votes. We are in a war of ideas. This war must begin by opening up the field, because concern and compassion on the part of policy elites is not enough. We need imagination, boldness, and seriousness of purpose in the service of an economy that works for all. Such an effort must begin with a disciplined dismantling of the ideology of neo-liberalism, which exaggerates the power of free markets and undermines confidence in collective action, in the ability of people to do things together, to make the world better than we found it, to fundamentally stand together rather than fall separately. Neo-liberalism's misplaced confidence in markets and scepticism of government is founded on a basic misunderstanding of who we are – a vision of people as isolated, self-interested and calculating, not generous, not tied together by bonds of family and community.

A vast intellectual landscape has been built on this rotten foundation by neo-classical economics, which has come to dominate academic economic thinking since the mid-1970s, particularly in the US with its seeming mathematical certainty, neo-classical economics lends a false scientific authority to the neo-liberal convictions about the leading role of markets in ordering economic life. Yet the failure of economists to anticipate the financial crisis and the Great Recession has weakened the confidence of politicians and policy makers, as well as the general public, in the verities of neo-classical economics, as well as neo-liberalism more generally and the Wall Street Agenda it supports (*New York Times* 2 September 2009). It is time for new ideas built on solid foundations. Finally, the third challenge is the most important of the three. The American labour movement must grow if working people are to reassert ourselves in American life, if we are to mount an effective challenge to neo-liberalism. The labour movement represents a far smaller fraction of American workers than we have in the past. In the early post-World War II period, unions represented as many as one out of every three workers in the country. Today unions represent less than one out of every eight. As a movement, our power to bargain collectively, to elect worker-friendly politicians, and to reshape economic and social policy has been reduced. This is, as we have seen, partly the result of neo-liberalism and the Wall Street Agenda, but it is partly because our institutions became complacent. We thought the New Deal order that workers had built and fought for over generations would last forever. While the American middle class still relies upon New Deal institutions such as Social Security, the voice of workers in American society has been diminished because the percentage of workers that are organised has been falling for more than a generation.

The labour movement at every level is at work looking at new models for representing workers and breathing new life into old models. Right now, some of the largest union elections since World War II are about to begin in the airline industry. Working America, the AFL-CIO's community affiliate, just keeps growing, and now has over 3m members. The AFL-CIO continues to build on and strengthen our formal alliance with the National Day Labor Organising Network, whose hundreds of affiliated workers centres organises new immigrant workers. But if we as a movement are going to be able to meet the challenge presented by the economic failure and continued political life of neo-liberalism, we have to grow. Paradoxically, we will only grow if we show that standing together workers can fight and win, in the workplace and in the public square. Finally, the labour movement must not only grow, we must also act as one. Manufacturing workers have a visceral knowledge of the hazards of corporate globalisation. Government workers see the face of neo-liberalism in the challenge of privatisation and regressive tax cuts. Construction workers see the attacks on their pension plans and roadblocks that stand in the way of robust infrastructure investment. Information technology workers fear the threat of outsourcing. We need to see that all these issues are the result of our economy and our politics being dominated by the Wall Street Agenda and neo-liberal ideology. Only together can we take on the fight to move our economy on the road to sustainable prosperity.

The American labour movement is the most effective force for economic justice in our country's workplaces, in our communities, and in our nation's politics. Our challenge strategically is to fight for working people in the here and now, while at the same time remaining focused on the growth of our movement and the renovation of our institutions. We must be both movement and institution, source of ideas and vision, and wielder of practical power – both politically and economically. And we must never forget that, just as the Wall Street Agenda and the ideology of neo-liberalism are global in scope, working people's efforts must be likewise global. We must join with the global labour movement and our allies in every country struggling for social justice to directly challenge neo-liberalism and change the course of economic policy and the economic thinking on which it rests. We are about to go through a period when our politics and media will be filled with failed and dangerous ideas of the type Herbert Hoover espoused during the Great Depression. Budget cutting in response to 10 per cent unemployment. Foreclosure as the solution to falling housing prices. Trying to increase competitiveness by cutting wages and benefits. In this environment, some neo-liberal voices will sound relatively sane and compassionate. But the real test of public policy ideas, of politicians and of forces in civil society like labour movements, will not be whether we do no harm or whether we are well-intentioned. The real test will be whether we create good jobs and sustainable economic growth, whether we invest in our country's and our world's future, whether we add to inequality and insecurity, and whether we build a future for our children that carries the American Dream of economic security for all who contribute forward into a new century. To successfully challenge neo-liberalism, however and pursue a Working Families Agenda, requires that our leaders, activists and members understand what neo-liberalism is and what it represents in terms of our ability to grow, restore our bargaining power and build effective coalitions with our allies. Consequently the perspective on neo-liberalism sketched here has served as the basis for discussions on economic policy for union leaders in the AFL-CIO, as well as to engage the leaders of labour movements in other countries to coordinate our engagement with heads of state in G8/G20 meetings and a number of other fora. It has also served as the basis for an economic education programme in the US that has trained hundreds of union activists and thousands of union members. Together, we must build a broad social movement – in the US and globally – to build an economy that works for all and a more socially just and sustainable future for our children and future generations.

NOTE

1.   In an American peculiarity, this term is used to denote the working class.

REFERENCES

Atkinson, A., T. Piketty and E. Saez (2011), 'Top incomes in the long run of history', *Journal of Economic Literature*, **49**(1), 3–71.

Bresser-Pereira, L. (2010), 'The global financial crisis and a new capitalism?', *Journal of Post Keynesian Economics*, **32**(4), 499–534.

Hacker, J., G. Huber, P. Rehm, M. Schlesinger and R. Valletta (2010), *The Economic Security Index: A New Measure of the Economic Security of American Workers and Their Families*, New York: Rockefeller Foundation.

Goolsbee, A. (February 2010), 'Economic report of the President', February, Washington, DC.

Koo, R. (2009), *The Age of Balance Sheet Recessions: What Post-2008 US, Europe and China Can Learn From the Experience of Japan*, Tokyo: Nomura Research Institute.

Obama, B. (2009), 'G-20 leaders statement: the Pittsburgh Summit', Pittsburgh, PA.

Palley, T. (2009), *America's Exhausted Paradigm: Macroeconomic Causes of the Financial Crisis and the Great Recession*, Washington, DC: New America Foundation.

Schmitt, J. and Conroy, T. (2010), *The Urgent Need for Job Creation*, Washington, DC: Center for Economic and Policy Research.

Rajan, R. (2010), 'Fault lines: how hidden fractures still threaten the world economy', *Choice: Current Reviews for Academic Libraries*, **48**(2), 350.

Somavia, J. (2010), 'ILO Director-General addresses Brookings Institution on achieving and sustaining an employment-based recovery', Washington DC, accessed at www.ilo.org/global/about-the-ilo/press-and-media-centre/statements-and-speeches/WCMS_123573/lang–en/index.htm.

15 Interaction between labour unions and social movements in responding to neo-liberalism

Bill Fletcher Jr

INTRODUCTION

Traditional mainstream unionism tends to set itself apart from other social movements, distinguishing itself from them except under particular periods of stress. This exceptionalism has coincided with the institutionalization of labour unions as legitimate components of so-called democratic capitalist societies. Once unions had broken from the margins and were no longer seen as either explicitly revolutionary forces or organisations of the rabble, they found themselves seeking stability and a permanent role in democratic capitalist systems. Unions, in developing an institutional existence, nevertheless, constituted the core of a social movement: the labour movement. Other working class forces have existed within this larger movement and unions themselves have often existed as movement-organisations rather than solely institutions. This struggle for the identity of unions has had a direct impact on the contradictory relationship of unions to other social movements. Among, and within the unions, there have been conflicting tendencies in addressing their *raison d'être* and that of organised labour. Mainstream 'business unionism' has been at odds with that of a class struggle orientation. Those of a class struggle orientation have often, but not always, tended to see in other social movements potential allies in the struggle for social justice and social transformation. Beginning in the 1980s, new labour formations started to emerge, largely in the global South, taking an orientation to their tasks that shared a great deal in common with class struggle unionism. This orientation, which over time came to be known as social movement unionism (SMU) or, in some cases social justice unionism, tended towards a left-wing critique of capitalism but also advanced a notion of unionism that operated beyond the workplace and in conjunction with other progressive social movements. This new unionism made its appearance in the global North largely in the context of efforts at union renewal or revitalisation. It has coincided with the rise of neo-liberal globalisation and has tended to explicitly challenge it. In doing so, this new unionism has been challenged by the task of if and how to strategically relate to other progressive social movements.

This chapter examines this challenge, attempts to unpack some of the issues at stake, and suggests that a globally-oriented social justice unionism is essential in both confronting neo-liberal globalisation and ensuring union renewal. Yet in undertaking an SMU approach, the contradictory relationship between unions and other social movements is not automatically resolved so this chapter addresses this challenge from the standpoint of the union movement. The suggestions to address this focus largely upon unions adopting a thorough-going SMU that seeks strategic partnerships with other progressive social movements. This analysis is presented in the context of a crisis in neo-liberal globalisation, which goes to the very heart of the form of accumulation associated with neo-liberalism and its manifestations such as the destruction of public space (and the public sector); massive privatisation and the selling off of state assets; and the reversal of tax policies and the dramatic shift of wealth to the upper echelons of society. Neo-liberalism is a politico-economic phenomenon, and the attacks of the neo-liberal offensive over the last 30 odd years have had a demoralising impact on progressive social movements, including but not limited to the union movement. That said, the immediate crisis offers the union movement the potential for renewal to the extent to which it recognises that the terms of the so-called social contract that dominated the post-World War II era are dead and that a new popular, democratic bloc must be constructed which advances an alternative economic platform.

Workers' Organisations

Labour or trade unions constitute one organisational form that emerged in the class struggle between workers and employers. Largely based in workplaces, fundamentally, they exist to reduce competition between workers in the face of the exploitation and oppression generated by employers. They aim to bring together workers to constitute a united front against employers specifically, and against economic injustice more generally. Though they may have additional and broader objectives, as organisations their essence lies in their relationship to the economic system. Although unions have, at various times, had to confront the state, their origin is found in their relationship to capital, with public sector unions being the obvious exception. As such, there is no ideological predisposition that is necessarily associated with adhering to a labour union, nor in fact, a comprehensive world view. Thus, to the extent to which one can say that there is an objective associated with labour unionism it would be economic justice. The challenge is to define 'economic justice'. A critical feature of unions is that they are self-financing, from their members' dues even though they may obtain state funding for particular activities. This sets them apart from many other mass organisations and institutions. As Fletcher and Gapasin (2008) noted, labour unionism has been from its inception at war with itself over advocating 'exclusionist' versus 'inclusionist' paths. Exclusionist refers to narrowing the relevant constituency for purposes of representation and bargaining. Inclusionist refers to expanding the relevant constituency by incorporating all those employed in an affected industry or type of work (and in some cases, in a specific geographically-defined area).

In contrast to unions, most non-union progressive social movements have a less consistent or less institutional existence. In many cases, the organisational forms are very *ad hoc*, where individuals consciously join. For unions, it is often the case that membership, or at least representation, comes automatically with employment in a unionised workplace (as in the USA) save where a core, particularly where efforts are underway to bring it into existence, makes a conscious choice to build a union. The very nature of membership places on unions stresses and strains that other mass organisations do not experience, or at least experience to a lesser degree. In the USA, the development of worker centres – as independent organisations basing themselves among poorer and less traditionally organised workers – has been significant. In many cases, though not all, they have been reaching out to immigrant workers who often live a twilight zone existence, whether their status is legal or not. Yet these worker centres are voluntary organisations. They may or may not have an actual membership. In most cases their funding arises less from members and more from external funding sources. And, while they may claim to represent an industrial or geographic sector, membership is generally (self-) selective. Finally, worker centres may have a leadership that is self-perpetuating rather than reliant on a membership mandate. Thus, in a very fundamental way, the basic organisational culture – including funding structure – between labour unions and other progressive mass organisations and NGO clashes. The failure of both sides to appreciate their respective cultures and histories has resulted in repeated misunderstandings, not to mention complications at the level of potential alliances.

UNIONS AND THE SOCIAL CONTRACT

The notion of a social contract has almost become a cliché in the advanced capitalist societies. Originating in debates associated with philosophers of the Enlightenment, the social contract was allegedly an agreement within primitive cultures whereby an understanding was arrived at between the different classes and class fractions as to their relative role. In twentieth century capitalism, the social contract came to represent the class compromise in advanced capitalist states that followed in the wake of the 1917 Russian Revolution. Associated in many ways with the Fordist organisation of production, liberal democratic capitalism – under pressure – provided for a socio-economic safety net for a significant portion of its workers both to blunt the attractiveness of the Soviet experiment, as well as to quiet their restive working class movements (Amin 2008: xiv). This safety net was not granted out of generosity but rather out of fear on the part of capital as well as struggle on the part of workers. The social contract, however it happened to be understood in each country, was presented as a means for societal stability. This social contract, or at least the economics of it, was advanced in great relationship to the imperial presence of advanced capitalist states in the global South. The low cost of natural resources provided capital with a certain flexibility in responding to reform demands that would later be constrained, particularly after the growth of independence movements.

In many global North capitalist states, the social contract – which came to be known as the welfare state – brought with it a particular role for labour unions. Often associated or in alignment with social democratic labour parties, unions saw themselves as a component of a tripartite arrangement in each nation-state. Tripartism postulated a special arrangement between labour, capital and state, where the government as representative of the state was a supposed neutral third party. Unions, and generally their social democratic party allies, blinded themselves to the class character of the democratic capitalist state. Also central to tripartism was the notion, so critical to the official labour movement, that it had been accepted as a permanent partner by capital. In the period after WW2 and through the early 1970s, that assumption, though challenged by the radical left, seemed to many workers, scholars and political figures to have had a substantive basis to it. This changed dramatically by the mid-1970s.

NEO-LIBERAL GLOBALISATION AND THOSE LEFT BEHIND

A crisis was brewing within capitalism during the 1960s. The 1974 recession came to symbolize the shift from one era to another, but the nature of the crisis was more fundamental. As Amin (2009:4) noted:

> The second systemic crisis of capitalism began in 1971 ... Profit rates, investment levels, and growth rates all collapsed ... Capital responded to the challenge ... by a double movement of concentration and globalization. As such, capital established structures ... of financialized globalization, allowing oligopolistic groups to levy monopoly rent. The same discourse accompanied this process: the 'market' guarantees prosperity, democracy, and peace; it's the 'end of history.' Amin (2009: 4)

The social contract, which appeared a permanent part of the post-WW2 global North, began to unravel, ultimately leading to the creation of the system of neo-liberalism, and specifically, neo-liberal globalisation. In sum, neo-liberal globalisation is characterised by deregulation, flexibility, privatisation, casualisation, free trade (and global production), financialisation and hostility to labour unionism. Neo-liberalism has also reformed the employment relationship by changing the production process. It (re)introduced the core/periphery relationship in firms, whereby a relatively small number of employees were guaranteed any sort of stability and permanence, while an increasing number of workers found themselves in the category of contingent (part-time, temporary, or contract) employees. Many of these workers became part of what is known as the 'atypical workforce'. Neo-liberalism has also promoted networked production whereby items are often produced using subcontractors. These subcontractors may have a formal existence separate from the core firm, but in reality they cannot exist without the contracts provided by the core firm. The aforementioned describes the characteristics of neo-liberal globalisation and these must be understood 'as the hegemonic project of an emerging transnational historical bloc with the transnational capitalist class as its leading class fraction, supported by its allies of small subcontractors and supply firms, specialised service companies such as accountants and privileged workers' (Bieler *et al.* 2008: 7). In other words, neo-liberal globalisation is not a natural evolutionary process in the realm for it represents a strategic process of resolving a particular crisis faced by global capital. There are many implications of this conclusion, and these have ramifications for labour movements.

The first is the process of neo-liberal globalisation is one that is promoted or advanced by the activities of nation-states, and specifically, the governing blocs in nation-states. In this sense, the activities of nation-states help to set parameters for neo-liberal globalisation as much as they are conditioned by neo-liberal globalisation. For labour movements, activism at the domestic and international level, then, is not a choice but a necessity. A second revolves around the material impact of neo-liberal globalisation on working classes. Social and wealth inequality has grown massively. Such polarisation means there is increasing competition at the bottom levels of society for declining resources. This competition rests on both slowing of relative economic growth in many of the advanced capitalist countries since the late 1960s and social instability and immiseration that leads to larger numbers of people falling off of the economic wagon. This contrasts with the post-World War II period where, despite real iniquities, in the global North there was an increase in the living standards of most workers. In such a situation, the need for organisation to unite those at the bottom becomes that much more important. A third is that neo-liberal globalisation represents the overthrow of the national Keynesian model of economic development and, with it, the disintegration of the basis for the tripartite model that had been critical to the ideological construct of mainstream unionism. While nostalgia haunts the halls of many labour unions in the global North with their efforts to restore the basis for the welfare state, the rise of neo-liberal globalisation has changed the terrain forcing new thinking regarding both strategy and tactics. One example of this new thinking is what Waterman (1998: 72–3) describes as a 'new labour internationalism'. A fourth is that neo-liberalism is not introduced using the same method in each country. The 1973 Chilean coup was the advent of the neo-liberal experiment, followed by the resolution of the 1975 financial crisis in New York City, which preceded Thatcher's rise in Britain. In any case, neo-liberalism's rise has been shaped by national cultures as well as the context of the class struggle in each particular situation (see Taylor and Mathers 2002: 95).

This reshaping through neo-liberal globalisation has led to a peculiar paradox of greater global interconnections accompanied by growing segmentation of citizenship. In part the result of the competition for diminishing resources but also the questioning of overarching narratives, identity politics as well as new social movements have emerged to address these abandoned citizens. While it was at one point the case that many non-union social movements tended to look at labour as a linchpin in the construction of a progressive project, that has become less and less the case over the last few decades, particularly where unions have retreated from broader social agendas. In understanding neo-liberalism, it is critical not to think entirely of supranational developments for the struggle against neo-liberal globalisation one is primarily discussing efforts undertaken to address its domestic manifestations. Thus, the efforts that are examined here will tend to be domestic struggles.

STRUGGLE TO DEFINE LABOUR UNIONISM UNDER NEO-LIBERAL GLOBALISATION

The traditional characterisation of unionism into business versus class struggle unionism failed to dissect the nuance within each broad area and to address the evolution of unionism over the last several decades as unions have struggled to address the growing internal and external crises facing them. Camfield (2007) suggests four 'modes of union praxis' in regard of Canada but they are more broadly relevant and can be summarised as:

- 'Business unionism': A unionism that accepts the dominant power relations; focuses narrowly upon economic issues that affect union members, and sometimes within that, a segment of the workforce; tends to be class collaborationist at the broad level.
- 'Social unionism': Classically represented by the practice of the late United Auto Workers leader Walter Reuther. Tending towards broad liberal-to-progressive stands on societal issues, though this having little

to do with the internal dynamics within the union or in its relationship with employers.

- 'Mobilisation unionism': Representing a tendency to encourage grass-roots militancy, fights around social justice and the creative use of tactics and movement-building. This is also very staff-driven, a tendency towards increasing union membership at all costs (including significant compromises on collective bargaining agreements). It also may or may not pay any attention to internal democracy and the role of the member.
- 'Social movement unionism' (SMU): This term (Moody 1997) and 'social justice unionism' (Fletcher and Gaspin 2008) describe a practice that is oriented towards broad movement-building; membership control of the union; clear societal objectives focused upon social justice; the conscious effort to build strategic relationships with other progressive social movements; and a clear sense of class politics (not narrowly defined to the economic struggle in one's workplace or industry). In this sense, SMU is not distinguished from mobilisation unionism by the level of militancy, but on the basis of the role of the member; the actual objectives of unionism; and the importance of strategic relationships with other progressive social movements.

The origin of SMU in the global South has a different context to that of the global North whereby mobilisation unionism and SMU arose in order to respond to variations of a form of lethargy and decline in their respective movements. In some cases this was a clear and public break with business unionism and/or social unionism, whereas in other cases it was more a matter of evolution away from an ineffective practice. Since many of these issues will be discussed elsewhere in this handbook, suffice it to say that in the global South the rise of SMU practice tended to be in the context of anti-authoritarian struggles. Examples such as COSATU, CUT in Brazil, KCTU in South Korea and the Kilusang Mayo Uno in the Philippines represent such movements. In each case, not only did these movements introduce new and creative tactics, but they tended to ally with (and sometimes lead) broader democratic struggles. In the global North, mobilisation unionism and SMU have been introduced or are under discussion in a situation of a search for union renewal (Serdar 2009) but SMU represents a minority position within the unionism of the global North. Moreover, within the global North, the trend towards any degree of mobilisation unionism and/or SMU has tended to not prioritise *strategic relationships* with non-union progressive social movements. While there are examples of important relationships that have been constructed, they have tended to be problematic either in theory or in implementation.

Challenges in alliance-building

Some key problems inhibit or limit alliance-building generally between unions and non-union social movements. The nature of the problems that are faced on the union side are not restricted to relating to those outside of the union movement, but sometimes involve factors or forces internal to the union movement itself. Challenging neo-liberal globalisation necessitates in-depth analysis of the changes in the economic system and the balance of class forces. It also involves being pro-active. Unions are challenged by each of these, but most especially, being pro-active. US-based unions have been among the most reactive of union movements, to the point of – at least until the mid-1990s – rejecting the entire notion of planning because of a belief that a union is supposed to respond rather than initiate. The union movement, in that sense, follows along the lines of what Lenin described (critically) as 'tactics-as-process'. They are by nature spontaneous movements, which have often elevated spontaneity to the level of ideology by insisting they cannot be anything but spontaneous and reactive, particularly when they cling to a mainstream course for unionism.

Unions tend to be suspicious, then, of allies external to the union movement, and sometimes allies within the union movement. Yet coalitions with non-union social movement organisations can and do take shape. In that light, Tattersall and Reynolds (2007) identified four different coalition types in which unions normally engage (to the extent to which they engage at all) based on studies in Australia and the USA:

- *Ad hoc* coalitions: largely a reactive effort, based on *ad hoc* requests from one or another organisation. The campaign tends to be distant from members.
- Support coalitions: Dominated by the initiating group; short-term; responding, as with *ad hoc* coalitions, to political opportunities.
- Mutual coalitions: Based on shared interest; common decision-making.
- Deep coalitions: Mutual self-interest; public messages of the coalition are framed as social vision for working people; longer term strategic plan on building power; union actively engaging its own membership.

This typology helps to break with the monolithic approach to understanding the relationship of unions to non-union social movements in a coalition process. These categories, in many respects, can be used to describe how unions and non-union social movements see themselves as working together against neo-liberal globalisation, that is, when they come to agreement to do so. With this in mind, it is useful to identify some of the challenges and how unions have gone about addressing them.

FURTHER CHALLENGES

In the global South, the new unionism that emerged, associated with SMU, tended to rise in opposition to authoritarianism at the level of the state. As Serdar (2009) points out, during the process of late authoritarian industrialisation, a contradiction emerged between the state and the business classes in which there developed an opening in which the union movement could operate. In South Korea, the KCTU (one of the key 'new union movements' to emerge in the 1980s and 1990s), was an example of such a movement (Chun 2008: 24). Ironically, the transition to [neo-liberal] democratic capitalism brought with it a series of challenges that the left-oriented union movements were not entirely prepared for. Thus, in nearly all situations, neo-liberal rule resulted in an erosion of both workers' rights as well as living standards, and a disconnect developed between the unions and wider citizens. As Chun noted, militant unionism was no longer associated, in the popular mind, with anti-authoritarianism but now it was seen as socially disruptive (Chun 2008: 28).

The question is: why would this be the case? Part of the answer may lie in the nature of democratic capitalism, even in its neo-liberal variant. Labour relations of democratic capitalism provide the impression that there is the interaction between interest groups with the state playing a supposedly neutral role. The state encourages the notion that the role of the union should be restricted to the realm of the economy generally, and where possible, to the industry or enterprise. The democratic capitalist system promotes, then, the idea of the individual citizen as being the citizen-consumer divorced from their relationship to other members of their same socio-economic class or, for that matter, other groups that are under pressure, if not oppression itself. Even when the state confronts the workers, it is a 'democratic' state in which citizens have had the opportunity – or so it appears – to make free choices on political leadership. This is very different from the openly authoritarian state which was not chosen through a popular mandate and is often perceived as being arbitrary in its very essence. As Fletcher and Gapasin (2008: 95–6) argued there has been the tendency towards a neo-liberal authoritarian state but this is very different from classical one-party rule authoritarianism. Classical authoritarianism eliminates most arenas for political intervention for the populace, rather than a slow narrowing of the parameters of mainstream political discourse associated with the neo-liberal state. Neo-liberal authoritarianism shrouds the state's role, instead promoting societal segmentation and the economic advancement by any means necessary (though willing to use violence when the need is perceived). This can even be witnessed in the forms of production and the move away from generic mass production into niche markets using just-in-time production. To borrow from Thatcher, there is 'no such thing as society', for the neo-liberals, just individuals, families and markets.

The result of all of this is the wearing down, if not collapse, of notions of social unity and collective action. Thus, militant action of unions can be perceived as being disruptive as it can be presented by neo-liberal capital as undermining economic progress for individuals. This problem is accentuated when one factors in contradictions within the unions themselves. The union cannot be viewed as an instrument for true social justice if it appears to be engaging in exclusivity when it comes to workers outside of its ranks. The most obvious example of this is 'contingent' or 'atypical' worker who is employed on a part-time, temporary basis, often in the 'informal economy'. Most are women in contrast with the more heavily male workforce in the formal and regular sectors. Unions, despite declarations, have been slow to organise this sector for a host of reasons (Chun 2008: 24–35). The challenge of reaching atypical workers is not specific to any one union movement. In South Korea, as in other countries, NGOs have arisen in some sectors to reach such workers (Chun 2008: 37–38). In the USA, beginning in the 1980s, and to some extent flowing from earlier efforts, a 'worker centre' movement emerged to target workers largely ignored by the official union movement. This included, but was not limited to, immigrant workers (Fine 2006). Despite the left-wing leadership of COSATU, addressing atypical workers has been a challenge. Affiliates generally express rhetorical commitment to growth, but the actual practice is very uneven and, according to Pillay (2008: 55–6), the federation has largely not found a means for organising this sector of the working class. The notion of the 'atypical worker' represents an intriguing formulation because it can overlap with gender, a point of great significance given the historical domination of most union movements by men. With changes in the workforce, new demands emerge in the union itself for a different sort of representation, or in some cases for representation period. This can lead not only to struggles within the context of the union-as-institution, but also struggles engaged by NGOs allegedly or actually on behalf of sections of members. Some union movements have been making noteworthy, if not significant strides to reach atypical workers, an effort that responds to the actual changes brought by neo-liberal globalisation, and a step towards reaching other social forces. South Korea has witnessed the growth of women's unions to seek to fill the void brought about by the lack of organising by the official labour movement. As Chun (2008: 39–41) notes, this initiative emerges at the cross-section of economic crisis, neo-liberal restructuring and gender oppression.

In Japan, the impact of neo-liberal globalisation has included the decline of full-time work, the lengthening of the working day and the rise of atypical workers (Shuto and Urata 2008: 143–5). The official labour movement has placed a priority on the passing of legislation to protect many of these atypical workers, particularly part-timers. There has also been the increase in immigrant workers into the Japanese workforce. Until recently, mainstream

Japanese unions had not placed a priority on organising and representing them (Shuto and Urata 2008: 155). This led to the formation of a different sort of union to address this sector. Such unions came to be known as 'community unions,' and in many respects are similar to US-based worker centres (see Urano and Stewart 2007: 106–10). These community unions have tended to organise geographically, target atypical workers, address gender issues and have a variation in the number of affiliates (Urano and Stewart 2007: 108). US-based unions have been very slow to respond to the question of the atypical worker. Beginning in the 1980s an 'associate member' status was created by several unions as part of an effort to explore new approaches to organising the unorganised workers. Some unions either established worker centres or supported them to varying degrees. By the 1990s and early 2000s, there were certain experimental efforts undertaken to reach sections of the atypical workforce. Yet none of these efforts achieved any degree of scale.

The problem of unions addressing atypical workers is not, primarily, a structural problem. Instead, an overview of several national experiences seems to indicate that while there may be structural obstacles, the larger problem is political and ideological (which includes organisational culture) and these are to some extent rooted in the bases of the mainstream union movements. The formal work force, under assault by neo-liberal capital, has found itself on the defensive and in many cases uneasy about opening up to other sectors of the working class, that is, it sees the atypical worker as a potential competitor rather than a potential ally and member of the same socio-economic class. This has resulted in varied responses including tendencies by some of the more mainstream unions to experiment; a tendency towards retreating from the atypical workforce; but also a countervailing tendency towards the formation of new sorts of working class organisations outside of the realm of the official union movement.

UNIONS REACHING OUT TO THE INFORMAL ECONOMY

The ambivalence of many mainstream unions towards atypical workers helps to explain their often vacillating, if not erratic, approach towards non-union social movements, though there are other factors that are at work. Specifically, the willingness on the part of many mainstream unionists to perceive atypical workers as the 'other', that is as a semi-alien segment that may threaten the territory of the formal workforce, makes it more likely that social movements that exist outside of the official union movement will, at best, be viewed as unknown and potentially divisive forces. The informal economy is a broad reference point for that sector of the economy that exists beneath the observation of the law. It may include legal and illegal functions, but it is not mainly a reference to criminality or the lumpenproletariat. Rather, it refers to a form of activity that is unregulated. Informalisation should not, however, be seen as primarily the outgrowth or result of a collapsed economy. Instead, it represents part of the shift towards post-Fordist flexible production as one of capital's strategies to reduce costs, increase flexibility and protect (or enhance) profitability (Lindell 2008: 215). The process of de-nationalising and privatising work, in addition to the spread of subcontracting (all indicative of the neo-liberal pandemic) has resulted in the emergence of a structurally unemployed population. Survival has often necessitated operating on the fringes of the law. Many mainstream union movements have abandoned the unemployed within months of their unemployment (and ignored the structurally unemployed altogether), believing, in some cases, that there is nothing that unions can do to assist them. There are, however, a set of alternative approaches advanced by several union movements.

Lindell (2008) offers an intriguing and rarely explored examination of efforts at building alliances between official union movements and informal economy organisations in Africa. In Zambia, for instance, the Alliance of Zambian Informal Economy Associations is actually an associate member of an official union federation. In Uganda and Mozambique, organisations of informal workers are actually full members of the official union federations (Lindell 2008: 221). Ghana has a rather lengthy experience of formal and informal workers coalescing organisationally. The General Agricultural Workers Union has been organising informal workers in the rural areas for decades. A Ghana Private Road Transport Union is part of the Ghana Trade Union Congress (TUC), and represents self-employed commercial drivers and vehicle owners. It is also worth noting that the Ghana TUC committed itself both in 1996 and 2004 to the organising of informal workers, creating an umbrella alliance for informal economy worker organisations. These informal economy worker organisations can affiliate to the Ghana TUC as associate members (Lindell 2008: 221–222). In Mozambique, the main labour central, Organisacao dos Trabalhadores Mocambicanos Central Sindical (OTM-CS) committed itself to organising informal economy workers, including – in 1998 – inviting informal economy workers to organise and create their own association (Lindell 2008: 223). Lindell notes that despite these efforts, there remain serious contradictions that have emerged in the process of trying to build unity between sectors. These include matters such as conflicting interests. An example of this is the issue of secondhand clothing versus new clothing. Garment workers unions throughout Africa have found themselves in struggle with the influx of second hand clothing from the global North which, in effect, undermines the ability to establish garment industries. Informal economy workers may not perceive secondhand clothing as creating any sort of problem, particularly if it means that they can obtain such clothing for sale at very low rates. In addition to such contentious issues, there are also complex demographics. These can include gender, race, nationality and income (Lindell 2008: 226).

Perhaps underlying most of this are deeply rooted suspicions, suspicions that are enhanced by differences around policy as well as mass base. An additional factor, and one not unique to the situations explored by Lindell, is whether there can be a true coalescing of interests when there are significant differences in organisational strength and capacity. After all, most of the organisations of the informal economy workers are new and relatively weak, certainly in comparison with mainstream organised labour. In Latin America, an experiment that has received some attention has been the Argentine Workers Federation or Argentine Workers Central (CTA). This split off from the main national labour centre – the General Confederation of Labor (CGT – the Peronista-dominated labour federation) – set for itself the task of both uniting the working class and building a broad alliance against the objectives of global capitalism (Rauber 2008: 107). Fundamental to their self-conception as a federation is the notion that both employed and unemployed workers need to be represented within the federation (Rauber 2008: 108, Serdar 2009: 95–100).

FORMS OF SOLIDARITY

This chapter has attempted to situate the relationship of unions to non-union social movements in a broader context. The challenge facing these respective movements is not simply their relationship, but the question of the relationship within and between multiple movements. In order to understand the challenge of union and non-union social movement interactions, the relationship of unions to themselves, to workers outside of their ranks, and to the informal sector (which is a cross class grouping) must also be understood. There are both international/cross-border examples of unions struggling to unite with non-union social movements, as well as unions addressing their respective domestic struggles with non-union social movements. Such relationships, to a great extent, conform to the categorisation elaborated by Tattersall and Reynolds. In thinking through the responses of unions to neo-liberal globalisation (and their relationship to non-union social movements), it is important to acknowledge that unions have been attempting to address how to respond to neo-liberal globalisation across national borders for some time. There is a long history of prior forms of union internationalism. Waterman (1998: 25) offers the intriguing thesis that nineteenth-century labour internationalism was a form of what he calls 'nationalist internationalism' in that its focus was actually the establishment of national union movements and national union demands. In either case, there was a certain level of cross-border solidarity from the beginning, especially in certain key sectors, such as longshore. The extent of the political and ideological consciousness, however, was very uneven, and often Eurocentric. The Norwegian-born, US merchant seaman/union leader Andrew Furuseth is a case in point, having both a militant unionism and a strong white supremacist streak.

Unions appear to engage in pragmatic, moral and social justice solidarities. The response of many unions to the struggle against apartheid in South Africa in the 1980s, arguably, represented either a combination or overlap of moral and social justice solidarity. It was not necessarily the unions as organisations of workers that were embracing the anti-apartheid movement – though objectively that is what they were – but unions as part of a citizen or popular force were responding to the struggle for liberation. This engagement was not necessarily guided by a consistent view of social justice: the same form of solidarity was not necessarily implemented in other cases of gross injustice (Waterman 1998: 69–70). Even at the level of pragmatic, cross-border solidarity, there are significant challenges. As Crow and Albo (2005: 19) point out:

> There are ... limitations to proposals for international solidarity. Unions within each country [like Canada, Mexico, USA] remain internally fragmented ... with limited capacity to coordinate strategy within national borders ... let alone between different national union movements with distinct histories and established practices. (Crow and Albo 2005: 19)

It should be noted that none of this is to suggest that cross-border solidarity, even pragmatic solidarity, is somehow irrelevant. There are important examples of how cross-border bargaining and other forms of union solidaristic behaviour bring forward tangible results. Struggles in Europe in the early 2000s around the General Agreement on Trade and Services represent a case in point (Bieler and Schulten 2008: 241–2). A study of the British TUC and its relationship to what it terms civil alliance building paints an interesting picture of a union movement attempting to create a new framework for operations, but doing so in a manner that lacks strategic direction. Parker (2008) noted a series of TUC activities that involved significant outreach to community-based organisations and movements, initiatives that certainly differ from past activities. These included regional and youth sections' links with anti-racist community groups to counter right-wing populists; regional TUC and affiliate training courses to assist migrant agricultural workers learn English and their workplace rights; learning centres in and beyond the workplace (Parker 2008: 570). The TUC also engaged in alliances with social movement forces involved in global justice. This included the Jubilee Debt Campaign and the Make Poverty

History campaign. But Parker's analysis should not be surprising. The work carried out by the TUC with non-union social movements, while valuable at times, was nevertheless largely sporadic and not seen as central to the identity of the union movement. In that sense, again, the practice of the union movement falls into a 'tactics-as-process' approach. While the work may be well-intentioned, it runs the risk of being perceived as being opportunistic. To utilise the Tattersall and Reynolds categorisation, the TUC's work would largely fall into either the *ad hoc* or support coalition, rather than strategic engagement.

The challenge of unions relating to non-labour social movements must also be understood as reflecting a frequent union ambivalence towards government and legitimacy. As noted earlier, the issue of social partnership and tripartism is very strong in mainstream labour, particularly in Western Europe and in a different manner, in North America. The European Trades Union Confederation in many respects epitomises this challenge. Formed in 1973, it is an alliance of 66 national confederations, 14 European industry federations, and 38 Interregional Trade Union Councils (Taylor and Mathers 2002: 96). The ETUC has been accorded a place and role in the process of European integration. Yet, as Taylor and Mathers (2002: 97) note: 'The commitment of the ETUC to European integration has made it difficult to oppose its specific trajectory, even where this has had a negative impact on employment and social protection'. The manner in which the union movement locates itself politically and ideologically presents major constraints on its ability to go back and forth between its alleged social partners while at the same time engaging non-union social movements. To the extent to which the union movement accepts basic terms or directions for society as established by the national (or global) ruling elites, it is much less able to offer credible criticisms. Such a phenomenon has been witnessed in the USA, especially during the era of Democrat President Clinton. Despite intense criticism of the North American Free Trade Agreement (NAFTA) by organised labour, its leadership vacillated between forms of protectionism and critical support for neo-liberal globalisation. To some extent, proponents of critical support of neo-liberal globalisation have held to a deterministic analysis, concluding that neo-liberal globalisation was unstoppable and that the best that could be done was to fight for some reforms of that regime. The 'social clause' debate, when it came to trade agreements, reflected part of this struggle (see Munck 2002). The ambivalence of the AFL-CIO in advance of the November 1999 Seattle anti-WTO demonstrations reflected this challenge. While the AFL-CIO ultimately participated in the demonstrations, in the lead up to them there were significant concerns expressed within the top leadership of the union movement that the AFL-CIO should not be perceived to be 'anti-globalisation.'

South Africa offers an interesting case regarding the challenges of working with non-union social movements because its history of progressive social movements, a vital union movement, including but not limited to COSATU, and the history of a national liberation struggle. Added to this, however, are the complications associated with the existence of the alliance between the African National Congress, the COSATU, and the South African Communist Party (SACP). The tension that exists between many of the progressive social movements and COSATU relate largely to COSATU's relationship to the ANC-led government. On the one hand, COSATU tends to be suspicious of and keep its distance from many of the progressive social movements insofar as many of these movements (and their associated organisations) are viewed as 'anti-Alliance' (Pillay 2008: 63). On the other hand, the progressive social movements do not necessarily see COSATU as being a proponent of their interests. Desai offered a summary critique:

> The transition to democracy was underpinned by corporatism. This involved big unions, big business, and the state. Conflict was to be institutionalized. ... The [ANC's] rightward shift, however, has from time to time been challenged by ... COSATU, working within the rubric of the Alliance. However, the latter's attempts [have been] so highly ritualised, domesticated within the ANC Alliance and otherwise institutionalised that [it] shows little inclination to act outside and against the [ANC's] major policy decisions ... Crucially, COSATU sees its alliance with the ANC as the bulwark against job losses by tempering the worst excesses of neoliberalism. (Desai 2003: 23)

Notwithstanding both COSATU's suspicion and Desai's critique, the sources of conflict are multilayered. For instance, the SMU associated with the South African unions – and most especially COSATU – emerged in the struggle against apartheid capitalism. In other words, it was taking place against an authoritarian regime in the context of a national liberation struggle. In the post-apartheid period, many of the leaders of the union movement – and members for that matter – viewed the tactics from the anti-apartheid period utilised by the union movement of the time as no longer being appropriate in addressing today's challenges in confronting neo-liberal regimes (Lier and Stokke 2006: 809). Studies of COSATU affiliate, South African Municipal Workers Union (SAMWU), help to underline the extent to which this is multilayered. SAMWU is a left-led union, but one that has been highly critical of the tripartite Alliance. It has been inclined towards building ties with non-union social movements. Nevertheless, there have been challenges. Efforts to forge a coalition with the Western Cape Anti-Eviction Campaign met with limited success. One study pointed out that different membership systems and decision-making structures posed a barrier to collaboration. As a result, few SAMWU members – even those residing in areas where the Anti-Eviction Campaign was active – were active in it. Further, different attitudes towards the ANC government and towards municipal authorities and services led to conflicting demands and suspicion between the partners (Lethbridge 2009: 105). SAMWU has also worked with the Cape Town Anti-Privatisation Forum. The same sorts of challenges have emerged. SAMWU was not always capable of mobilising its mass base behind the activities of the Forum (Lier and Stokke 2006: 815). In addition, SAMWU and the social movements associated with the Forum found themselves contesting the veracity of claims regarding actual membership and base. This is a recurring theme in contradictions that have emerged in different national settings between unions and non-union social movements.

An additional challenge is that many SAMWU members have overlapping memberships and affiliations with the ANC (and its various components) and the SACP (Lier and Stokke 2006: 819). The significance of this cannot be overstated. Among other things, it means that whereas many non-union social movements may look forward to a head-on collision with the government, there will tend to be ambivalence in SAMWU, at least at the tactical level. In fact, in the Secretariat Report to SAMWU's 2003 Congress there was mention made of a lack of appeal for militant and political unionism among the members and the attractiveness of legal centres and service organisations as alternative ways of protecting jobs and benefits (Barchiesi 2007: 64). The significance of this report may go beyond the multiple affiliations of SAMWU members and may point to the often conservatising impact of labour/management relations in capitalist societies. The challenge facing COSATU, and even its particularly militant affiliate SAMWU, with the complicated relationship to the government is not unique to South Africa. Argentina's CTA found itself facing a similar problematic after years of conducting a very militant struggle against the pro-neo-liberal Menem government. With the election of reformer Kirchner, however, CTA entered into a relationship of 'critical support' for the new administration. Criticism began to emerge within and of CTA precisely because it altered its tactical approach to incorporate both struggle and the building of relationships with political authorities. For segments of CTA's base, this was unacceptable (Serdar 2009: 209, 215, 231).

CONCLUSION

The challenge of building a strategic relationship between labour unions and non-union social movements is not one dimensional. While there are different specificities depending on national conditions, it appears that there are several recurring themes. Using Tattersall and Reynold's construct, while there are examples of unions engaging in each of the four sorts of coalitions, there is a strong tendency towards *ad hoc* and support coalitions. Such coalitions demand far less commitment on the part of the components and do not necessarily challenge the culture of the respective organisations. The culture of unions, as opposed to non-union social movements, remains a matter of great significance. As noted in the example of SAMWU, from their respective cultures arise different assumptions regarding one's own organisation, but also other organisations, including potential allies. The fact of a fairly reliable membership, for instance, compared with fluctuating memberships or, in the case of some NGOs, a non-specific membership, can lead to a situation where efforts at coalescing are fragile at best. Another critically important challenge to these relationships can be found in the interaction between unions and governments specifically, and the larger question of electoral politics more generally. The case of South Africa is most pointed due to the structural rela-tionship that COSATU has and has had with the ruling party (ANC), though similar observations could be made of the relationship of organised labour in the USA to the Democratic Party. Union concerns, albeit quite legitimate, to have access and political influence in government can often put them at odds with non-union progressive social movements for several reasons. Progressive social movements may or may not have an electoral component. Insofar as such movements are not institutionalised via permanent mass organisations with a critical mass (at the level of membership), they may tend to see them-selves as single issue efforts and/or oppositional formations. They may have neither hope for access to government leaders or they may wish to have no such relationship (particularly if led by anarchist influenced forces). This disconnect between unions and non-union social movements can lead to tension on matters of tactics even if they share similar world views. The situ-ation facing informal economy organisations in Africa pointed to another arena of tension, specifically, that of objectives. In that case, informal econ-omy organisations may have had different objectives compared with labour unions. Thus, while the intent may exist for unity of action, conflicting objec-tives can get in the way.

Despite these challenges, there are examples of successful tactical and strategic efforts. Time and space do not permit examination but it is worth adding that of the Stamford Organizing Project that the AFL-CIO initiated in the mid-1990s in the state of Connecticut. This was an example of one of the most advanced attempts at building a strategic alliance between labour unions and non-union community-based organisations (Clawson 2003: 110–24). In this initiative, the union movement saw itself as positioning unions as one means for economic justice and economic advancement, not just for the members and potential members of the unions, but for the larger working class community. This effort won significant numbers of adherents, but unfortu-nately was not replicated more broadly on the national level due to contradic-tions within the parent bodies. Indeed, the Stamford Organizing Project, along with other attempts at what were called 'geographic organising projects' came to an end due to the fact that the national parent unions were not interested in moving organising campaigns in areas that they deemed to be non-strategic for their respective unions. The fact that these geographic organising efforts were creating local alliances was largely irrelevant to the parent unions.

Much of this discussion raises a question as to whether there is a form of unionism that is best suited to the building of strategic alliances to confront neo-liberal globalisation. The answer is both yes and no. One thing that is clear is that militancy alone is insufficient. As Camfield (2007: 296) noted 'greater militancy, member involvement and willingness to expand the repertoire of methods of action ... are not enough for unions faced with hostile employers and governments'. Yet it appears that there exists a partial answer in an appeal to SMU insofar as this form of unionism *tends* to uphold the need for strategic relationships with non-union progressive social movements. Nevertheless, one must be cautious about the simple adoption of an approach. Even in cases where union movements have adopted a SMU approach, such as many of the unions within COSATU, the relationship with non-union progressive social movements has been tenuous. Argentina's CTA may be one of the union formations that have taken significant steps to address these contradictions insofar as they positioned themselves to be leading a strategic bloc which opposes neo-liberal capital. This is to be distinguished from the anti-authoritarian efforts mentioned earlier. The alliances against classical authoritarianism are not identical to those that confront neo-liberal capital (or the neo-liberal authoritarian state), having emerged in a different period with a different alignment of forces. As such, the expectation that alliances from yesteryear can survive into the neo-liberal age – whether one is conducting struggle in the global South or global North – is misplaced. The construction of popular democratic blocs that can confront neo-liberal capital will, therefore, necessitate the identification of different social forces and the development of different coalitional forms, some of which are being experimented with today, ranging from the efforts in Africa to build unity between unions from the formal economy to informal economy organisations, to initiatives such as the Stamford Organizing Project.

ACKNOWLEDGEMENT

Thanks to Todd Dickey and Roy Bannis for providing research assistance material for this chapter and to Gregor Gall for help in editing.

REFERENCES

Amin, S. (2008), 'Foreword: rebuilding the unity of the 'labour front', in A. Bieler, I. Lindberg and D. Pillay (eds), *Labour and the Challenges of Globalization: What Prospects for Transnational Solidarity?*, London: Pluto Press, pp. xiv–xxii.

Amin, S. (2009), 'Seize the crisis!' *Monthly Review*, **61**(7), 1–16.

Barchiesi, F. (2007), 'Privatization and the historical trajectory of 'social movement unionism': A case study of municipal workers in Johannesburg, South Africa', *International Labor and Working-Class History*, **7**(1), 50–69.

Bieler, A. and Schulten, T. (2008), 'European integration: a strategic level for trade union resistance to neoliberal restructuring and for the promotion of political alternatives?', in A. Bieler, I. Lindberg and D. Pillay (eds), *Labour and the Challenges of Globalization: What Prospects for Transnational Solidarity?*, London: Pluto Press, pp. 231–47.

Bieler, A., I. Lindberg and D. Pillay (2008), 'The future of the global working class: an introduction', in Bieler, A. I. Lindberg and D. Pillay (eds), *Labour and the Challenges of Globalization: What Prospects for Transnational Solidarity?*, London: Pluto Press, pp. 1–22.

Camfield, D. (2007), 'Renewal in Canadian public sector unions: neo-liberalism and union praxis', *Relations industrielles/Industrial Relations*, **62**(2), 284–7.

Chun, J. (2008), 'The contested politics of gender and irregular employment: revitalizing the South Korean democratic labor movement', in A. Bieler, I. Lindberg and D. Pillay (eds), *Labour and the Challenges of Globalization: What Prospects for Transnational Solidarity?*, London: Pluto Press, pp. 23–44.

Clawson, D. (2003), *The Next Upsurge: Labor and the New Social Movements*, Ithaca, NY: Cornell University Press.

Crow, D. and Albo, G. (2005), 'Neo-liberalism, NAFTA, and the state of the North American labour movements', *Just Labour*, **6**(7), 12–22.

Desai, A. (2003), 'Neoliberalism and resistance in South Africa', *Monthly Review*, **54**(8), 16–28.

Urano, E. and Stewart, P. (2007), 'Including the excluded workers? The challenges of Japan's Kanagawa City Union', *WorkingUSA*, **10**(1), 106–10.

Fine, J. (2006), *Worker Centers: Organizing Communities at the Edge of the Dream*, Ithaca, NY: Cornell University Press.

Fletcher, B. and F. Gapasin (2008), *Solidarity Divided: The crisis in Organized Labor and a New Pat to Social Justice*, Berkeley, CA: University of California Press.

Lethbridge, J. (2009), 'Trade unions, civil society organizations and health reforms', *Capital and Class*, **97**, 101–29.

Lier, D. and K. Stokke (2006), 'Maximum working class unity? Challenges to local social movement unionism in Cape Town', *Antipode*, **38**(4), 802–24.

Lindell, I. (2008). 'Building alliances between formal and informal workers: experiences from Africa', in A. Bieler, I. Lindberg and D. Pillay (eds), *Labour and the Challenges of Globalization: What Prospects for Transnational Solidarity?*, London: Pluto Press, pp. 217–30.

Moody, K. (1997), *Workers in a Lean World: Unions in the International Economy*, London: Verso

Parker, J. (2008), 'The Trades Union Congress and civil alliance building: towards social movement unionism?', *Employee Relations*, **30**(5), 562–83.

Munck, R. (2002), *Globalisation and Labour: The New 'Great Transformation'*, New York: Zed Books.

Pillay, D. (2008), 'Globalization and the informalization of labour: the case of South Africa', in A. Bieler, I. Lindberg and D. Pillay, D. (eds), *Labour and the Challenges of Globalization: What Prospects for Transnational Solidarity?*, London: Pluto Press, pp. 45–64.

Rauber, I. (2008), 'The globalization of capital and its impact on the world of formal and informal work: challenges for and responses from Argentine unions', in A. Bieler, I. Lindberg and Pillay, D. (eds), *Labour and the Challenges of Globalization: What Prospects for Transnational Solidarity?*, London: Pluto Press, pp. 98–114.

Serdar, A. (2009), *Limits to the Revitalization of Labor: Social Movement Unionism in Argentina*, Ph.D. thesis, Binghamton University-State University of New York.

Shuto, W. and M. Urata (2008), 'The impact of globalization on trade unions: the situation in Japan', in A. Bieler, I. Lindberg and D. Pillay (eds), *Labour and the Challenges of Globalization: What prospects for transnational solidarity?*, London: Pluto Press, pp. 139–60.

Tattersall, A. and D. Reynolds (2007), 'The shifting power of labor-community coalitions: Identifying common elements of powerful coalitions in Australia and the US', *WorkingUSA: The Journal of Labor and Society*, **10**(1), 77–102.

Taylor, G. and Mathers, A. (2002), 'Social partner or social movement? European integration and trade union renewal in Europe', *Labor Studies*, **27**(1), 93–108.

Waterman, P. (1998), *Globalization, Social Movements and the New Internationalisms*, London: Mansell.

16 Unions, globalisation and internationalism: results and prospects
Ronaldo Munck

INTRODUCTION

Unions and the workers they represent have always been part of a transnational system of labour relations. Capital has always been mobile and the capital/wage-labour relation has never been hermetically contained within national boundaries. However, until quite recently, the dominant system of industrial relations had been confined, almost exclusively within a national frame. In the 1970s, a 'new' international division of labour emerged as the ex-colonial countries began to industrialise and the multinational corporations became central players in the neo-colonial global system. This period saw a major flourishing of transnational labour activity and the hope, soon dashed, that union internationalism could act as a 'countervailing power' to that of the multinationals. Later, in the 1990s, the era of globalisation began, characterised by the hegemony of neo-liberal economics, the victory of the West in the Cold War and the rise of international institutions such as the World Trade Organization. The international union movement was unified during this phase and clearly recognised the major challenges posed by globalisation to a 'business as usual' approach. Today, with the unravelling of the neo-liberal consensus and its whole global development model in 2008, a new period of crisis and uncertainty opens up. Will a greater internationalism be part of this repertoire and will it be the turn of labour to be truly globalised?

This chapter will explore the shifting relationship between unions, globalisation and internationalism through a structural historical approach, that is to say unions are seen to operate within a historically specific system of production with its particular social relations of production. In economic terms, unions by and large reflect the structures of capitalist production, organising workers in trades or branches of industry as they have developed. When unions move beyond the workplace they may take up political positions within/against the capitalist state on behalf of their members. But unions are also part of society and may make alliances with other social groups or movements. This economic/political/social triad clearly takes different configurations across countries and across time of course. So, a structural analysis needs to be dynamic and foreground the historical context. Union developments in the 1990s need to be set in the context of 1970s moves towards internationalism and, indeed we have much to learn from the first wave of labour internationalism in the 1870s.

Sometimes it is assumed that labour internationalism will emerge with that of capital (Nash 1998 and others) as though capital's global reach automatically generates labour internationalism. Internationalism should rather be seen as a political project that needs to be constructed. Nor is it a timeless political project reaching back seamlessly to the formation of the First International in 1864. Labour internationalism does not trump all other forms of union activity at the local, national and regional levels. Internationalism has sometimes been deployed against workers who struggle in a very localised or parochial manner and, particularly, against those in the colonial and neo-colonial world who embrace the banners of national liberation. So, while this chapter examines the structural and historical development of unions in a transnational context it does not take for granted an internationalist compass.

THE NEW INTERNATIONAL DIVISION OF LABOUR (1973–88)

> The development of the new international division of labour ... contains the possibility of international solidarity between workers. (Fröbel *et al.* 1981: 35)

The post-World War II period was marked by the 'long boom' in the West and the consolidation of a post-colonial relationship with the South. For some, the unequal exchange between the industrialised and non-industrialised worlds meant we needed to forgo the 'delusions of internationalism' (Emmanuel 1970). Emmanuel (1970: 18) expressed the clear view that the level of differentiation within the global working class was such that the objective basis for internationalism had disappeared: 'National disintegration has been made possible in the big industrial countries at the cost of international disintegration of the proletariat'. So, in the North workers were deemed to be co-opted by the welfare state while in the South workers would be super-exploited. Thus there could be no 'objective' basis for labour internationalism. However, in the 1970s the Western capitalist model itself entered into crisis and, in a parallel process, the once colonial world began to industrialise, thus creating a 'new' working class.

The so-called 'oil crisis' of 1973 was simply a highlight of a whole period of capitalist disarray. The generalised revolt of 1968 had shown that the social relations of neo-capitalism were neither secure nor immutable. The declaration in 1971 that the US dollar would no longer be convertible against gold signalled the beginning of the end for US hegemony. This was further marked in 1975 by the Vietnamese defeat of the most powerful military machine the world had ever known. Workers in the West were in open revolt, not least in the 'hot autumn' of 1969 in Italy but also more widely across the capitalist world. The rate of profit was being threatened by workers' militancy. The sociological wisdom that workers in the West had been pacified through consumerism and welfarism was abruptly overthrown. By the late 1970s and early 1980s capital had prepared its counter-offensive with first Thatcherism in the UK and then Reaganism in the US taking class war to the workers and their unions. This neo-liberal offensive – based on financial liberalisation, driving back the state sector and cutting back labour rights – laid the basis for a new phase of global capitalist accumulation in the 1990s that we have come to know as globalisation.

In the majority world of the global South the 1970s saw the emergence of a new international division of labour (NIDL) replacing the old colonial model in which it had been relegated to the production of raw materials for the West's industrialisation. The NIDL fundamentally restructured the relation of production in the South and led to the emergence of a substantial manufacturing sector oriented towards the world market. These new 'world market factories' – based largely on female labour – were but one symptom of a world-historic shift of basic manufacturing to the South. The NIDL led to a wave of relocations of electronics and textile plants from the North to the 'newly industrialising countries' (NICS). When Northern unions complained about the super-exploitation of workers in the South they were often accused (in the South) of simply being engaged in national protectionism behind a façade of international solidarity. The role of the Southern state was crucial in driving this process of industrialisation, contrary to the later myths of neo-liberalism. As the golden age of the postwar boom became tarnished in the North, the South went through a dynamic period of growth which resulted in a massive process of proletarianisation and the emergence of a 'new' working class (see Silver 2003 for a full analysis of this period).

Looking back on the 1970s the main defining characteristic of the era was undoubtedly the rise of the multi- or trans-national corporations (MNC or TNC). This phase is characterised by the internationalisation of the cycle of productive capital. Whereas in previous phases it was the cycle of commodity-capital (trade) and then finance-capital that was internationalised in the era of classic imperialism, now production itself was internationalised. The MNCs or TNCs became the 'bearers' or agents of these new international relations of production, much as the nineteenth century trusts and cartels had been for an earlier era. Through their competitive advantage the MNCs came to dominate the global production of goods and services. Whether this advantage is put down to technological innovation, superior management techniques, or simple oligopoly tactics the MNC's became dominant global players in the 1970s/ 1980s (see Dunning 2000). Possibly the globalisation of production has been exaggerated as some sceptics argue (Hirst and Thompson 1996 and others) and it is quite clear that the MNC were not as 'footloose and fancy free' as some saw them back then but, still, they have undoubtedly changed the world of labour and acted as a powerful focus for labour activity.

The question arising for the unions then was about how they would respond to this new transnational employer configuration. A leading strategist of the era was Charles Levinson – General Secretary of the International Federation of Chemical, Energy and General Worker's Unions – who argued that 'in terms of international action to develop a new countervailing union response to the multi-national companies, the most important thing is that there exist bargaining relations with these undertakings' (Levinson 1972: 106). This was a quite logical scaling-up of traditional national wage bargaining mechanisms to the trans-national scale. While there were various preliminary levels of transnational negotiation unions could engage in, the best bet in the long term was to seek integrated negotiations across the multinational around common demands. A fierce attack was launched on this thesis by academics Northrop and Rowan who claimed to have examined all the evidence of transnational actions cited and found them non-existent (Northrop and Rowan 1978: 331). Be that as it may (and there were plenty of examples of cross-national plant union co-operation) Levinson had hit a raw nerve. At a Kodak executives retreat in 1973 one speaker admitted that 'today our biggest fear is the international union movement move against the multinational corporation' (cited in Munck 1998: 56).

Arguing directly against the Levinson thesis, but from a left perspective, Olle and Schoeller (1974) posited that the internationalisation of capital though the MNC did not in fact provide new and unique 'objective' conditions for labour internationalism. They argued against Levinson's rationale of find-ing an economic basis for solidarity given that a union based 'economistic' internationalism can only reproduce the competition between national capi-tals. From this angle, international union politics look like a form of national protectionism. The only progressive option, for Olle and Schoeller (1994: 71) was to move 'in the direction of a politicisation of union activity combining the struggle for … [better wages]…with the perspective of developing the power of the proletariat'. Other writers pointed to the fundamental asymmetry between capital and labour who were not really fighting on the same terrain and thus there was no reason for labour to follow capital's lead. Ramsay (1999: 203), one of the protagonists of this debate, was to write much later of the one-sidedness of this 'left pessimist' view which seemed to suffer from 'a shifting combination of structural determinist and political voluntarist reason-ing'. Today most would accept that the fate of international unionism is a contradictory and contingent affair.

One of the main mechanisms deployed by labour during the 1980s were the so-called Codes of Conduct designed to 'put manners' on the MNCs. This was a voluntary form of regulation which was aimed at setting standards of behaviour by the company in regards to its employees and suppliers. As Fairbrother and Hammer (2005: 410) note: 'Some of these codes include a focus on labour rights, the implications of corporate practice for the environment and related practices'. An obvious issue then arises as to how these Codes of Conduct might be monitored let alone enforced. In some cases unions promoted these codes and sought 'buy-in' from companies, in other, the MNC themselves adopted these codes as an early form of CSR (Corporate Social Responsibility). One limitation is that the majority of these codes are concerned with health and safety issues whereas only a minority mention freedom of association. What is probably most significant about these first generation Codes of Conduct from our perspective is that they often led to the multi-stakeholder codes know as International Framework Agreements (IFAs) which were to play an important role in the 1990s (see below).

Prime movers in the internationalisation of labour in this period were the International Trade Secretariats (ITS) whose origin went back to the 1880s. These included the International Transport Workers' Federation (ITF), the International Metalworkers Federation (IMF) and the International Federation of Chemical, Energy, Mine and General Workers Union (ICEM). During this phase a number of ITS responded to the growing power of the multinational through the formation of World Company Councils designed to coordinate and strengthen inter-union co-operation within a given company. This was at the heart of Levinson's campaign to create 'countervailing power' on behalf of labour to confront the growing power of capital. By the late 1970s this campaign had petered out but, as Stevis and Boswell (2008: 65) note, 'the longer-term impact was an opening of the practical horisons of these sectoral organisations which had been largely inactive'. Thus, the first wave of labour recomposition in the face of a fundamental restructuring of capital through the multinationals failed (for political, practical and ideological reasons but also, maybe, because it was simply too early) but it did set in motion a reactivation of labour's internationalist instincts and placed the ITS in a position to play a leading role in the next phase.

In relation to the South, the dominant form of international solidarity was undoubtedly 'political' and set firmly within the development co-operation discourse. Partly as a response to the scant purchase of the economistic collective bargaining perspective some unions then turned towards active engagement with global development issues. This work built on the unprecedented international campaign of solidarity with the emerging independent black unions in South Africa from the late 1970s onwards. According to one study of this campaign 'the resultant picture of trade-union internationalism ... is incoherent, inconsistent, muddied and almost definitely unheroic; nonetheless although trade-union internationalism may have been distanced from its working class base, it could never be entirely disconnected' (Southall 1994: 167). The moral and material aid provided by the international labour movement to its counterparts in South Africa was of crucial importance in the struggle against apartheid. Overall, though, the international unions were engaged in development co-operation along the lines of the famous 1981 Brandt Report (Report of the International Commission on International Development Issues) which was essentially about pacifying the South on behalf of Northern social democracy.

In the South itself, the NIDL had fostered a massive process of industrialisation and had generated a 'new' working class. During this period mass independent unions were formed in Brazil, South Africa and South Korea which began to articulate workers' power in a quite radical way. In the auto industry in particular a new militancy came into being which had considerable transnational impact, particularly across the South. The strikes they engaged in, under highly authoritarian regimes, mobilised wide sectors of the population. A new form of community or social movement unionism was born which in a later period would find echoes in the North. As one analyst put it for Brazil: 'the identification of the population with the metalworkers' cause, transform[ed] the city into a broad supportive network, in which the struggle gained multiple and varied spaces of solidarity' (Kowarick 1985: 85). A new model of unionism was developing going beyond the US imposed tradition of 'business unionism' and the indigenous 'political unionism' traditions to embrace a more holistic social understanding of labour and the role of its unions. In the long term this model would be influential internationally not least through the impact of the Workers' Party.

In any retrospective consideration of the 1970s and1980s undoubtedly the main characteristic of the era has to be the Cold War as an ideological and material divide running through the international union movement. The union movement was deeply divided between the 'Free World' ICFTU (International Confederation of Free Unions), the Soviet backed WFTU (World Federation of Unions) and the much smaller WCL (World Confederation of Labour) affiliated ideologically to western Christian Democracy (see Myconas 2005 for this history). In Western Europe, where social democracy was the hegemonic force in many ways, transnational labour activity (for example in the auto industry) was often hampered by these divisions and the fierce anti-communism of the era. As one leader of an International Trade Secretariat put it, 'the early 1990s were difficult because some Western European unions were determined to crush all old Eastern European unions and/or to 'finger' anyone from West or East who was suspected of being a communist' (interview). In Latin America, where many unions were aligned with nationalist and anti-imperialist forces, the conflict with Western unions was even sharper. In this region the US AFL-CIO (American Federation of Labor-Congress of Industrial Organisations) acted as a virtual labour arm of the US State Department and the CIA. The term 'union imperialism' (see Thompson and Larson 1978) was hardly exaggerated as a description of this phase of labour history.

From a present-day perspective, the 1970s and 1980s would probably be viewed as a transitional period. Capitalism at a global level began to hit structural contradictions which would finally unravel in the crisis of 2008–9. However, as the class struggle intensified capitalism prepared for the great leap forward under neo-liberal globalisation. Workers and their unions in the North began an incipient process of transnational organisation. While not resulting in the transnational collective bargaining many hoped for, it did begin to break down it nation-statist attitudes. The global South was beginning to play a more important role with many new labour initiatives being pioneered in this world zone. While we might question the dualism of counterposing 'objective' condition and subjective responses by labour to them, undoubtedly this phase of global history did set the terrain for a hugely expanded global labour force and for greater interactions between its national and sectoral fractions. It all set the basis for capital to take a great leap forward to overcome its inherent contradictions and to strengthen its position in relation to an increasingly uncooperative Western working class and a South in open revolt.

THE RISE AND FALL OF GLOBALISATION (1989–2007)

> A new way of life spread over the planet with a claim to universality unparalleled since the age when Christianity started out on its career, only this time the movement was on a purely material level … The true implication, if economic liberalism can now be taken on at a glance. Nothing less than a self-regulating market on a world scale could ensure the functioning of this stupendous mechanism. (Polanyi 2001: 136, 145)

A qualitative transformation in the nature of global capitalism was discernable in the 1990s. The multinational corporations became increasingly disconnected from the 'real economy' and turned truly global. The transport and communications revolution gestating throughout the 1970s and 1980s now greatly speeded up trade and all economic transactions. Of course, the abrupt removal of the alternative economic model of state socialism and the exhaustion of the national economic development model in the South cleared the way for the one true economic model of neo-liberal globalisation to become the new common sense of the epoch.

While capitalism in the so-called Golden Era of the post World War II period was primarily national, now the transnationalisation of economic, political and social relations ushered in a new era. What Karl Polanyi had foreseen at the start of this period was that unregulated market mechanisms would inevitably lead to the world becoming 'one world market'. What its neo-liberal turn in the late 1980s allowed for was precisely this outcome. Capitalism entered into a period of great dynamism, the 'animal spirits' of the financial markets were given free rein and the much vaunted gains of workers in the West were under severe threat. For Castells (1997: 354), in a major treatise on the new global economy, the effect on labour was quite clear: 'Torn by internationalisation of finance and production, unable to adapt to networking of firms and individualisation of work, and challenged by the engendering of employment, the labour movement fades away as a major source of social cohesion and workers' representation'. While these challenges were and are undoubtedly real I will now present an analysis that shows how the labour movement was able to reinvent itself and, indeed, use adversity as a spur to revitalisation.

In the Post-Cold War period, the previous ideological divisions of the international union movement began to lose their logic. By 2006, the time was ripe for the formation of the International Union Confederation (ITUC) from the old ICFTU and WCL. The ITUC brings together national centres in 156 countries which, in turn, are composed of sectoral unions with a claimed membership of 168m workers across the world. Ending more than 100 years of political division this was, undoubtedly, a significant development in the union response to globalisation. Of course there was still a shadowy Communist era organisation with some affiliates. Above all, the approximately 150m strong All-China Federation of Unions (ACFTU) remained outside the camp. At a regional level the process of unification proceeded apace, albeit with some ups and downs in terms of jockeying for position with head office. As Traub-Merz and Eckl (2007: 3) put it, despite the US labour movement heading in the opposite direction the new trend was one of 'overcoming fragmentation and regaining negotiating clout through organisational strength'.

This period also saw the dramatic rise of the Global Union Federations (GUFs) as the old ITSs became known after 2002. The old title of 'trade secretariat' was no longer accurate as the dividing line between different employment categories had become blurred. In a wide-ranging survey of ITS/GUF activities, Bendt (2003: 34) has argued that these bodies 'are the most significant direct opponents of the TNCS when it comes to interventions' which follow 'logically' from the globalisation of corporate activities. He does admit though that binding collective agreement in the traditional union sense remain the exception even today. This conclusion is supported by the findings of the

European Foundation for the Improvement of Living and Working Conditions (2009: 21) in 2009 which found that while 'a small but growing number of MNCs have negotiated transnational framework agreements ... these do not address wages or working time, widely regarded as the core issues of sector and company-level bargaining within countries'. Nevertheless there is a measurable increase, at least in Europe, since 2000 in the number of agreements signed with transnational union bodies, mainly against MNCs operating in producer-driven supply chains.

Between the ITUC and the GUFs there was a fairly explicit division of labour. According to its own statements the ITUC 'focuses on policy matters and on the defence of union rights and represents the interests of working people to global organisations' (ITUC website). The GUFs, on the other hand, represent workers in the different economic sectors (from education to manufacturing, from public services to mining) and they are mainly concerned with the introduction of minimum social standards in multinational corporations. We thus see a broad distinction between a 'political' wing (ITUC) and an 'economic' one (GUFs) which is quite traditional and, arguably, not adequate to the era of globalisation. There is a broader critique as articulated by Asbjørn Wahl, namely that while 'it is good that there is co-ordination between the ITUC and the industrial federations' still 'the biggest problem is that they both are very far from their members' (interview). Also they are very policy-oriented and not turned towards co-ordinating actions and activities. They produce a lot of (rather moderate) documents and statements, but they do not seem to be very eager to mobilise industrial actions or initiate solidarity movements. So still, the gap between words and actions seems highest at the international level. The high level needs of diplomacy and the lingering attachment to the tripartite model of labour, employers and the state long after it has ceased to deliver, go a long way to accounting for the disjuncture with quite radical sounding analysis and quite traditional forms of action or inaction.

The tendency towards amalgamation or at least the formation of strategic partnerships has also been evident at the level of national unions. Increasingly unions are establishing bilateral relations with sister organisations in other countries to confront common problems. In the shipping industry the Dutch and British maritime sector unions merged in 2009 into Nautilus which had already submitted a common pay claim two years previously. Instead of the much touted 'race to the bottom' in terms of labour standards this co-operation led to a leveling upwards of pay and conditions. Perhaps the most dramatic merger was that of the biggest union in the UK and Ireland, Unite with 1.4m workers and the largest private sector union is the US and Canada, the United Steelworkers with 850 000 members. The new organisation is known as Workers Uniting which covers a range of sectors including manufacturing, services, mining and transport. It will undoubtedly be a spur to more effective coordination of transnational collective bargaining and for political campaigning.

The International Framework Agreements (IFAs) were undoubtedly the major vehicle for transnational labour activity during this period (but see Gallin 2008 for a critical union perspective). The IFAs, which have their origins in the 1980s, aim at securing core labour rights across the global supply chain of the multinationals. These basic rights include the prohibition of forced and child labour, non-discrimination in employment, minimum standards for wages and working time as well as freedom of association. The MNC is obliged to inform its suppliers of the IFA and in some cases this is made mandatory. Early on, 'socially responsible' firms such as Danone were one of the few promoters of IFAs but since 2000 they have become more widespread. Within the European Union there are known to be 70 IFAs in force and the signs are that their number will increase. This points towards the emergence of a transnational regime for labour rights though not necessarily for collective bargaining as such. However, rather than focus on how Levinson's transnational collective bargaining has not materialised we might, more usefully stress with Hammer (2005: 525) that 'one of the most important innovations of IFAs is that they allow unions a grip on the global supply chains, hereby extending (core) labour rights beyond national frontiers'.

There are, of course, major sectoral differentiations in terms of the modalities and effectiveness of transnational union activity. The global competition at the heart of neo-liberal globalisation severely weakened the organising capacity of unions. So, unions have responded to outsourcing, for example, through the establishment of international union links. In some sectors such as transportation there was a long history of international solidarity to build on. Thus, in the shipping sector the International Transport Workers' Federation (ITF) now acts effectively on behalf of its members across the globe setting wages and effectively campaigning against the so-called 'flags of convenience' (see Lane 2000). In the air transport sector representation at a transnational level is not so strong but, nevertheless unions have contested the restructuring/flexibility agenda of the employers (see Blyton *et al.* 2004). In the motor industry, a key locus in the 1980s attempts to create cross-plant union networks, there was a flourishing of company level World Employee Committees; which allowed workers to share information between themselves and with management across borders. But as Anner *et al.* (2006: 15) remark, 'the links between unionists in different firms are not, however, strong enough to take wages out of competition industry-wide'. However uneven and differentiated the process of internationalisation has been, unionists since 2000 have increasingly begun to challenge unfettered capitalist control over the labour market. We can see that in particular branches of industry (such as docks, as covered in Turnbull 2007) or areas of the world (such as North America, covered in French 2004) but also in the flourishing of broader accounts of the international labour revival since 2000 (see for example Waddington 1999, Jose 2002 and Bronfenbrenner 2007) which describe a plethora of initiatives by unions at international level at both official and grassroots levels.

There is little doubt that in the early 2000s international labour activity found considerable resonance and reached levels only dreamt of in the 1970s. Transnational communication and networking had become easier and many of the political obstacles had been overcome. But this need for internationalism had also, arguably, changed. As Asbjorn Wahl puts it, 'after 30 years of neo-liberal deregulation, international co-ordination is much more of a must' (interview). On a whole range of issues now even the seemingly most localised struggle needs to adopt a global optic. Indeed, we could argue that there is a new local-global terrain which does not necessarily 'pass through' its national level. Local struggles may turn to transnational repertoires of actions directly. Fairbrother and Hammer (2005: 418) have referred to the recent emergence of 'a multi-faced form of unionism', with different levels working to achieve recognition and an impact on international sectors and regions'. We could also think of this more complex unionism as a multi-level response to globalisation which has impacted on workers at local, national and regional levels as well as at the transnational level.

It is, of course, highly debatable whether the international union movement has entirely overcome the structural and political impediments to full international labour solidarity. For Moody (1997: 247), 'official international labor at almost all levels appears inadequate to the changes taking place in the internationalising economy and workplaces across the world'. With the ITSs at one remove from the workplace their solidarity campaigns may appear remote to the shop floor activists. With most national unions still committed to an outdated concept of 'partnership' international solidarity is reduced to ritual. The only alternative for Moody (1997: 290) – picking up on debates in the global South during the 1980s – would be a global social movement unionism which would maximise working class power by embracing 'the diversity of the working class in order to overcome its fragmentation'. Above all this perspective recognises the social role of labour and the unions for too long confined to their economic and political roles. It would certainly be a challenge, though, to take this perspective which played a role in combating authoritarian regimes in the South by constructing a community unionism and 'scaling it up' to the global scale.

In retrospect globalisaton probably opened as many doors for labour as it closed. Neo-liberalism as a dominant capital accumulation strategy of course represented a class offensive against workers and their representative organisations. Overall, labour recovered a considerable amount of its organisational capacity during this phase. By the end of this period the inherent contradictions of capitalism had re-emerged with a vengeance with the great bubble of financial speculation that drove its final phase. The capitalist crisis began to unravel in 2007 but it reached a critical point in September 2008 as a number of major 'name' banks failed. There was simply no trust left in the basic financial intermediation mechanism which underpins the capitalist system. Governments across the world were forced to engage in an unprecedented bailout of the banks and emergency stimulus packages. It was clear to all that the 'new economic model' that had pulled the world out of stagnation and inflation of the 1970s, was no longer functional. The architecture of the global financial system was now openly in question. But will the workers of the world and their representative bodies such as the unions be able to articulate a viable and credible alternative economic system?

As capitalism's 'credit crunch' turned into a global recession in 2008 (see Wade 2009 and Peck *et al.* 2009 for a critical overview) the union movement was at first taken aback, as were many sectors in society. The spectre of the 1930s recession was uppermost in many people's minds. By early 2009 there was at least a clearer analysis and credible alternative being presented by the global unions even if this was not translated into practice due to the lack of social power to impose it. Their statement to the London G20 Summit in April 2009 started from the premise that there could be no return to 'business as usual' and went on to argue that 'The crisis must mark the end of an ideology of unfettered financial markets, where self-regulation has been exposed as a fraud and greed has overridden rational judgment to the detriment of the real economy' (Global Unions London Declaration 2009). Nothing less than a redrawing of the governance of the global economy to foreground social (and environmental) issues would suffice. However, the means proposed to implement this alternative programme – a revival of the postwar tripartite structures involving government, capital and labour – seemed somewhat of an anachronism given the collapse of this model in the 1990s and its inherent limitations to the afferent North where this corporatist model had some purchase.

BACK TO THE FUTURE? (2008–)

In 1863, the 'working men of England' addressed their French counterparts. The following year, the First International was formed launching the formal history of proletarian internationalism one might say. During this period union internationalism was at the very core of socialist internationalism. The craft workers and artisans of the period were the main bearers of internationalism as an ideology and practice. This was a largely West European milieu with London at the heart of many initiatives. It was an internationalism which did not preclude solidarity with the nationalism of oppressed peoples such as the Irish and the Poles. Emigration was a natural form of labour mobility and xenophobia was relatively rare among workers. It can probably be best characterised as a pre-national phase (van der Linden 2003) although from 1870 to the turn of the century we saw a decline of this old internationalism as national incorporation of the working class proceeded apace.

The working class was not born in large factories and it was not its industrial proletariat as such which pioneered labour internationalism. Rather, it was the 'journeymen' (after the French word *journée* meaning day) defined as a craft worker who has served an apprenticeship under a master craftsman, who has not become an employer or master craftsman. These travelling journeymen played the key role in the development of internationalism. As a result of their continuous migration patterns they developed a clear understanding of the emergent capitalist system. Thus, as Callensen (2002: 3) points out, this experience of the contradictions between work and capital meant that 'Marx and Engels were able to formulate the international experience of workers into a coherent theory recognisable to these groups'. This was such a problem that many ruling groups sought to limit transnational migration. This process had peaked by 1870 and henceforth a more institutional path prevailed with the creation of Britain's Trades Union Congress in 1868 followed by most European countries which had union peak organisations by the end of the century. Likewise the International Trade Secretariats began to flourish after 1890 with 17 being created by the end of the nineteenth century. Labour was now becoming a mass movement and the level of organisation required created, perhaps inevitably, a permanent bureaucracy. While the labour movement came of age and increased steadily in influence age to 1914, spontaneous internationalism was now in the past.

So, if labour internationalism first became a significant factor in the pre-national phase what are its prospects today in what we might call a 'post-national' phase of global history? Looking towards the future of unions at a time when they are in deep crisis can we posit a 'Back to the future' type of strategy with internationalism as its core philosophy of action? Hyman (2002: 10) has argued persuasively that 'Unions in the twenty-first century confront old dilemmas, but in new forms'. Some of the main characteristics of unions in the past according to Hyman were that they were built mainly on pre-existing solidarities and a collective identity pre-dating capitalism (today, unions would thus need to construct a collective identity, it is not pre-given and it is not pre-capitalist of course). As they moved from opposition movements to acceptance there was always a tension between their broad social transformation aims and their representation of relatively advantaged sectors (this dilemma is still with us with unions being accused of representing a 'labour aristocracy' compared to the working poor of the majority world); most were based on standard full-time employment relationships where industrial 'muscle' resided (this is still largely the case although many unions accept the need to organise wider layers of the working classes); they were seen to represent a popular majority even while they might exclude women and insecure labour categories (this is probably not the case today as most unions are seen as unrepresentative and remote from popular majorities); and while unions proclaimed internationalism they were embedded in national societies and their effectiveness derived from this (things are arguably different now and all unions need an international optic and strategy if they are to be effective) (Hyman 2002: 7–8).

In mapping out alternative union strategies to overcome the difficult period of the 1980s and 1990s a body of literature on union revitalisation has emerged (see Frege and Kelly 2004). While improved external conditions do not lead automatically to revitalisation they do create the conditions for this to happen. Unions usually react with a considerable time lag to a crisis. It is thus not surprising that it took a decade at least before unions began to respond decisively to the deleterious effects of neo-liberalism in their structures and mission. Frege and Kelly list a number of clear modalities through which unions have begun the urgent task of revitalisation. These include union organising directed at union membership recovery; expanding the bargaining agenda to enhance union effectiveness; political action to increase union political power; union restructuring through mergers and closer links between confederations; coalition-building through closer links with civil society; and, finally, reconstructing forms of international union action (Frege and Kelly 2004: 33–5). What this agenda for union revitalisation adds up to is a strategy not dissimilar to that pursued by social movement unionism in the South during the 1980s. This can be seen as an impact of globalisation as is also the foregrounding of international work no longer seen as a nostalgic add-on or window dressing.

Across the board, unions which in the past were quite traditional or even conservative are adapting innovative union strategies. Thus the Teamsters Union in the United States has in the mid-1990s shifted from epitome of business unionism to a quasi social unionism orientation (see Teamsters 2010). The Dutch union federation FNV (Federatie Nederlandse Vakbewegin – Dutch Labour Movement Federation) has launched a very explicit and nuanced call for union renewal given the 'crisis in the union movement' (Kloosterboer 2007). There is a new emphasis on strategic research (see Juravich 2007) and a renewal of a very 'old' commitment to workers education (see Croucher and Cotton 2009). Unions are responding to declining union density through concerted membership drives into 'non-traditional' sectors. Above all, as the Dutch unions put it, 'Increasingly unions are aware of the importance of international unionism in an environment of globalisation of capital, not just out of solidarity with workers in other countries, but also as a strategic necessity' (Kloosterboer 2007: 51). I would call this the 'mainstreaming' of international labour solidarity and would argue it is a major step forwards.

My basic argument here, as developed previously (Munck 2002) is that we are now, indeed, dealing with a new form of internationalism. The era of globalisation has created a novel and complex terrain for labour internationalism, where local, regional and global levels interact and where community, consumption and production levels are all present. There is now a growing literature focused on the spatial dimension of labour struggles (see McGrath *et al.* 2010, Waterman and Wills 2001, Webster *et al.* 2008) and we can no longer afford to ignore the complex interplay of the spatial dimension of labour activity, not least when dealing with the international, once seen as separate domain from the national or local, higher or lower in terms of hierarchy according to one's political stance. Likewise we now see a labour inspired analysis of the 1980s and 1990s consumer boycott campaigns which argues for a return to more traditional forms of labour struggle rather than collapsing all energy into high visibility consumer based campaigns (see Frank 2003; Seidman 2008). Unions are developing new strategies to bridge the gap between an abstract 'global standards' and a parochial localism. Globalisation has undermined the national union strategy of eliminating labour costs as a factor in competition. While the obstacles to international labour solidarity are huge, not least in terms of the resources required, we should recognise the potential now evident. As Brecher *et al.* (2006: 17) put it

> Unions have tried, with varying success, to utilise international solidarity in particular struggles. Building a global labour movement next requires something further: proactive approaches designed to make international communication and cooperation part of the daily practice of the labour moment at local, national and international levels. (Brecher *et al.* 2006: 17)

There are, of course, many analysts who reject as hopelessly optimistic this relatively positive analysis of the current prospects for international labour. Thus, for example, Stuart Hodkinson carries out a detailed study of the ICFTU from 1996 to 2002 and concludes that the ICFTUs new symbolic orientation to alliance building and membership mobilisation is a largely strategic manoeuvre to cope with its weakened status within both the international corridors of power and the radical contours of the 'global justice movement' (Hodkinson 2005: 37). No doubt some official labour strategists did feel squeezed on the one side by globalisation from above and on the other side by globalisation form below, but we cannot discount a genuine shift. For his part, Waterman (1986) lists the key attributes of the 'new labour internationalism' – it must occur at grassroots level, surpass bureaucratic models of organisation, move beyond verbal declarations, move beyond an aid model, be based on the expressed needs of ordinary working people, overcome financial dependency and so on – and then, not surprisingly finds the official union work around internationalism wanting.

The critique of actually existing labour transnational practices could be ascribed to the perennial critique of reformism within the labour movement. Of course bureaucratisation is a problem for unions in the sense of routinisation. Certainly, union leaders often do not lead and seem more concerned with maintaining their respectability with the state. But we have to recognise the step change represented by John Sweeney of the AFL-CIO standing up in Davos in 2001 to declare a 'new morning dawning' and declaring that 'This movement for a new internationalism is building from the bottom up, not the top down. ... Its forum is the public square, not the boardroom' (AFL-CIO: 2001). The opening up of labour leaders to the new social movements at least since Seattle 1999 is but one symptom of this new mood. Perhaps, as Dan Gallin puts it the North/South development divide and other major issues of the day 'can only be solved if the [labour] movement becomes desperate enough to seriously democratise and radicalise' (interview). However uneven, partial and hesitant this process has been it does seem to have begun and it has confounded the left critics.

The future of labour internationalism does not hinge around whether as labour analysts we are optimists or pessimists. What is important is to recognise the major shifts that have occurred over the last 20 years as labour has rebuilt at least some of its structures that had been decimated by neo-liberalism. If labour is now catching up with capital's long campaign of internationalisation (known as globalisation) then it may now be the turn of labour to become globalised. I would agree here with Peter Evans for whom 'New orientations on the part of national unions, like the concatenation of diverse organisational forms, are still incipient in terms of their ability to counter the offensive from global capital and its political allies. Nonetheless, the gradual accretion of experience and institution building and the continual emergence of innovative new cases point towards an ascendant arc of transnational labour mobilization' (Evans 2010: 367).

CONCLUSION

In conclusion I will address three seemingly simple questions, namely: who are the subjects of union activity? What are the main issues for unions today? And finally, how can these best be addressed? The post-globalisation working class is very different from the post-World War II working class. It is certainly more fragmented and the 'norm' of full time, permanent employment is now the exception overall. The labour force is more feminised and informalisation and flexibilisation has destroyed all vestiges of stability. The massive entry of the Chinese and Indian working masses into the global labour force has entirely altered the old North/South divide. While it is as yet unclear what role these two labour movements will play (but see Bowles and Harriss 2010) they have clearly altered the terms of reference of the question 'Who is the working class?' Within the West there has been a serious decomposition of labour as the welfare state withered and the national bargaining frame was undermined by globalisation. Unions are now turning their sights to 'non-traditional' recruits and broadening their vision from the economic to the political and the social domains of labour activity.

The overarching task now ahead of the international labour movement is the (re)regulation of global capital after a period of unrestrained activity. This may take place at the global governance level where the ITUC is pressing, along with others, for financial (re)regulation after the 2008–9 crash. It is also happening at the enterprise level with the International Framework Agreements as we saw above. These will only be a positive development for global union cooperation if, as Stevis and Boswell (2008: 132) argued, 'agreements do not segment workers along corporate lines and strengthen rather than weaken global union organisation'. They must be judged on whether they contribute to the recomposition of labour faced with the fragmentation caused by neo-liberal globalisation. A long-term task is the construction of a global social movement unionism which unites workers at the place of production with the wider community. These tasks are necessarily multi-scalar and therein lies the main challenge ahead. As Tattersall (2007: 17) puts it, 'Multiscalar campaigning is the great challenge for global alliances, stretching from the local to the global, takes resources, and meaningful local engagement requires meaningful local action which can be a challenge'.

For Haworth and Hughes (2002: 79): 'Internationalization of collective bargaining was to be the antidote to the internationalization of capital. This has not happened'. Levinson's vision in the 1970s of unions as a countervailing power is probably misplaced today anyway due to the profound informalisation of labour which took place under neo-liberal globalisation. Only a more broadly based labour – as against union – movement is adequate to the tasks posed by globalisation. Workers find it increasingly difficult 'to improve their living and working condition solely through local organising drives and efforts that target the national state' (Anner 2006: 85). That task can only be achieved by 'going global' based on an understanding of the accumulation of capital on a global scale. There is a wide range of social movement contesting the global rule of capital. The global working classes will be a key component of that 'movement of movements' articulating a multi-scalar strategy unifying the much expanded, if fragmented, global labour force produced by globalisation.

REFERENCES

AFL-CIO (2001), 'Remarks by AFL-CIO President John J. Sweeney, World Economic Forum, Davos, Switzerland', accessed at www.aflcio.org/pub/speech2001/sp0128.htm.

Anner, M. (2006), 'The paradox of labour transnationalism: trade union campaigns for labour standards in international agreements', in C. Phelan (ed), *The Future of Organised Labour: Global Perspectives*, Berne: Peter Lang, pp. 63–90.

Anner, M., I. Greer, M. Hauptmeier, N. Lillie and N. Wineherler (2006), 'The industrial determinants of transnational solidarity: global interunion politics in three sectors', *European Journal of Industrial Relations*, **12**(1), 7–27.

Bendt, H. (2003), *Worldwide Solidarity – the activities of the global unions in the era of globalization*, Bonn, Germany: Friedrich Ebert Stiftung.

Blyton, P., M. Martinez Lucio, J. McGurk and P. Turnbull (2004), 'Globalisation and trade union strategy: evidence from the international civil aviation industry', in R. Munck (ed.), *Labour and Globalisation: Results and Prospects,* Liverpool: Liverpool University Press, pp. 227–44.

Bowles, P. and J. Harriss (eds), (2010), 'Special issue on globalization(s) and labour in China and India', *Global Labour Journal*, accessed at www.digitalcommons.mcmaster.ca/globallabour.

Brecher, J., T. Costello and B. Smith (2006), 'International labor solidarity: the new frontier' *New Labor Forum*, **15**(1), 9–18.

Bronfenbrenner, K. (ed) (2007), *Global Unions: Challenging Transitional Capital Through Cross-Border Campaigns*, New York: Cornell University Press.

Callesen, G. (2002), 'Aspects of internationalism at the turn of the 19th/20th century', Labour Movement Library and Archives, Copenhagen.

Castells, M. (1997), *The Information Age, Vol II: The Power of Identity*, Oxford: Blackwell.

Croucher, R., and E. Cotton (2009), *Global Unions, Global Business: Global Union Federations and International Business*, London: Middlesex University Press.

Dunning, J. (2000), 'The new geography of foreign direct investment' in N. Woods (ed), *The Political Economy of Globalisation*, Houndmills: Macmillan, pp. 20–53.

Emmanuel, A. (1970), 'The delusions of internationalism', *Monthly Review*, **XXII**, 2.

European Foundation for the Improvement of living and Working Condition (EFILWC) (2009), *Multinational Companies and Collective Bargaining*, Dublin: EFILWC.

Evans, P. (2010), 'Is it labour's turn to globalise? Twenty first century opportunities and strategic responses', *Global Labour Journal*, **1**(3), 352–79.

Fairbrother, P. and N. Hammer (2005), 'Global unions: past efforts and future prospects', *Relations Industrielle /Industrial Relations* **60**(3), 405–31.

Frank, D. (2003), 'Where are the workers in consumer-worker alliances? Class dynamics and the history of consumer-labor campaigns', *Politics and Society*, **31**(3), 363–79.

French, J. (2004), 'Labour and NAFTA: nationalist reflexes and transnational imperatives in North America, 1991–1995', in R. Munck (ed.), *Labour and Globalisation: Results and Prospects,* Liverpool: Liverpool University Press, pp. 149–68.

Frege, C. and J. Kelly (eds) (2004), *Varieties of Unionism: Strategies for Union Revitalization in a Globalizing Economy*, Oxford: Oxford University Press.

Froebel, F., J. Heinrichs and O. Krey (1981), *The New International Division of Labour*, Cambridge: Cambridge University Press.

Gallin, D. (2008), 'International framework agreements: a reassessment', in K. Papadakis (ed.), *Cross-Border Social Dialogue and Agreements: An Emerging Global International Relations Framework*, Geneva: ILO, pp. 15–42.

Global Unions London Declaration (2009), accessed at www.ituc-csi.org/IMG/pdf/No_16_ _G20_London_Declaration_FINAL.pdf.

Hammer, N. (2005), 'International framework agreements: global industrial relations between rights and bargaining', *Transfer*, **11**(4), 511–30.

Haworth, H. and S. Hughes (2002), 'Internationalisation, industrial relations theory and international relations', in J. Harrod and R. O'Brien (eds), *Global Unions? Theory and Strategies of Organized Labour in the Global Political Economy*, London: Routledge, pp. 64–80.

Hirst, P. and G. Thompson (1996*), Globalisation in Question*, Cambridge: Polity Press.

Hodkinson, S. (2005), 'Is there a new trade union internationalism? The International Confederation of Free Trade Unions Response to Globalization, 1996–2002', *Labour, Capital and Society*, **38**(1), 37–65.

Hyman, R. (2002), 'The future of unions', *Just Labour*, **1**, 7–15.

Hyman, R. (2005), 'The international labour movement on the threshold of two centuries. agitation, organisation, bureaucracy, diplomacy', *Labor History*, **42**(2), 137–54.

Jose, A. (ed.) (2002), *Organised Labour in the 21st Century*, GENEVA: International Institute for Labour Studies.

Juravich, T. (2007), 'Beating global capital: a framework and method for union strategic corporate research and campaigns', in K. Bronfenbrenner (ed.), *Global Unions: Challenging Transnational Capital Through Cross-border Campaigns*, Ithaca, NY: ILR Press, pp. 16–39.

Kloosterboer, D. (2007), *Innovative Trade Union Strategies*, Utrecht: Netherlands: FNV.

Kowarick, L. (1985), 'The pathways to encounter: reflections on the social struggle in São Paulo', in D. Slater (ed.), *New Social Movements and the State in Latin America*, Amsterdam, Netherlands: CEDLA, pp. 73–93.

Lane, T. (2001), *The Global Seafarers' Labour Market: Problems and Solutions*, Seafarers International Research Centre, Cardiff: Cardiff University.

Levinson, C. (1972), *International Trade Unionism*, London: Allen and Unwin.

Moody, K. (1997), *Workers in a Lean World. Unions in the International Economy*, London: Verso.

McGrath, S., A. Herod and A. Rainnie (eds) (2010), *Handbook of Employment and Space. Working Space*, Cheltenham, UK and Northampton, MA, USA: Edward Elgar.

Munck, R. (1998), *The New International Labour Studies*, London: Zed Books.

Munck, R. (2002), *Globalisaton and Labour: The New 'Great Transformation'*, London: Zed Books.

Myconas, G. (2006), *The Globalizations of Organized Labour: 1945– 2004*, London: Palgrave Macmillan.

Nash, B. (ed.) (1998), 'Globalizing solidarity: praxis and the international labor movement' *Journal or World Systems Research*, **4**(1), 1–3.

Northrup, H. (1978), 'Why multinational bargaining neither exists nor is desirable', *Labor Law Journal*, June, 330–42.

Olle, W. and W. Scholler (1984), 'World market competition and restrictions upon international trade union policies', *Capital and Class*, **2**, 56–75.

Peck, J., N. Theodore and N. Brenner (2009), 'Postneoliberalism and its malcontents', *Antipode*, **41**(1), 94–116.

Polanyi, K. (2001), *The Great Transformation. The Political and Economic Origins of our Times*, Boston, MA: Beacon Press.

Ramsay, H. (1999), 'In search of international union theory' in J. Waddington (ed.), *Globalization and Patterns of Labour Resistance*, London: Mansell, pp. 192–220.

Seidman, G. (2007), *Beyond the Boycott: Labor Rights, Human Rights and Transnational Activism*, Cambridge: Cambridge University Press.

Silver, B. (2003), *Forces of Labour: Worker's Movements and Globalisation Since 1870*, Cambridge: Cambridge University Press.

Southall, R. (1994), 'The development and delivery of 'northern' worker solidarity in South African trade unions in the 1970s and 1980s', *Journal of Commonwealth and Comparative Politics*, **32**(2), 166–99.

Stevis, D. and T. Boswell (2008), G*lobalizaton and Labour. Democratizing Global Governance*, Lanham: Rowland and Littlefield Publishers.

Tatersall, A. (2007), 'Labor-community coalitions, global union alliances, and the potential of SEIU's global partnership' in K. Bronfenbrenner (ed.), *Global Unions: Challenging Transitional Capital Through Cross-Border Campaigns*, New York: Cornell University Press, pp. 155–73.

Teamsters (2010), International Brotherhood of Teamsters, *Global Solidarity*, accessed at www.teamster.org/content/teamster-partners-around-world.

Thompson, D. and R. Larson (1978), *Where Were You, Brother? An Account of Trade Union Imperialism,* London: War on Want.

Traub-Merz, R. and J. Eckl (2007), 'International trade union movement: mergers and contradictions', Friedrich Ebert Stiftung briefing paper, no 1.
Turnbull, P. (2007), 'Dockers versus the directives: battling port policy on the European waterfront', in K. Bronfenbrenner (ed), *Global Unions Challenges Transitional Capital Through Cross-Border Campaigns*, New York: Cornell University Press, pp. 117–36.
van der Linden, M. (2003), *Transnational Labour History, Explorations*, Aldershot: Ashgate.
Wade, R. (2009), 'From global imbalances to global reorganisations', *Cambridge Journal of Economics*, **33**(4), 539–62.
Waddington, J. (ed.) (1999), *Globalisation and Patterns of Labour Resistance*, London: Mansell.
Waterman, P. (ed.) (1986), *For a New Labour Internationalism*, The Hague: ILERI, The Hague.
Waterman, P., and J. Wills (eds) (2001), *Place, Space and the New Labour Internationalisms*, Oxford: Blackwell.
Webster, E., R. Lambert and A. Bezuidenhout 2008), *Grounding Globalisation: Labour in the Age of Insecurity*, Oxford: Blackwell.

17 A future for the labour movement?

Lowell Turner

INTRODUCTION

By any measure, prospects for labour unions in the current era do not look good. In a context of neo-liberal globalisation, unions in many countries have been beaten down by 30 years of pressure from employers and states. When the economic logic of neo-liberalism collapsed in the crisis that began with financial meltdown in the US in 2007–8, weakened influence dampened the voice of unions in contemporary debates aimed at policy reform. On the other hand, the crisis has opened up an historic opportunity for proponents of sweeping reform. In this chapter, I suggest that prospects for unions are closely linked to broader long-term battles for sustainable society, and can be best understood in the tension and interplay between relative union weakness and the opportunities afforded by deep economic crisis.

Wolfgang Streeck (2009), who once explained German economic success with a virtuous circle that included strong worker representation, high wages, and up-market manufacturing, now builds on Karl Polanyi to show how markets over the past 30 years have increasingly escaped from social regulation. The result, he argues, is an incrementally growing disorganisation that has finally added up to neo-liberal transformation, even in Germany. Capitalism has come back to trump apparently stable institutions of coordination and regulation. After picking apart the cross-national institutional analysis of the varieties of capitalism literature for its emphasis on equilibrium, Streeck concludes the book as follows:

> Every new generation seems to have to devise its own answers to the puzzles posed by the fundamental tension between the inherent dynamism of capitalism and the need for stability in human affairs. Nobody knows how long the interplay between market expansion and social reconstruction can continue, and one may well be pessimistic and see the time coming when society will run out of answers. But then, it is true that humans specialize in the unexpected; that people have achieved the most astonishing things; and that there always is a fighting chance. (Streeck 2009: 268)

Since the beginnings of industrialisation, unions have been among the key actors pushing to contain markets. If markets are once again to be regulated in the interests of society, unions surely have a central role to play in battles for transformation. There will only be a 'fighting chance' if revitalised unions rise to the challenge.[1]

Unions, however, cannot do this on their own. Key findings presented in this volume point towards the urgency of participation in broad campaigns for social reform. Dibben and Wood, for example, foresee a return to bitter struggles of the past. But this time around, the decline of regular employment has made unions just one among many social actors fighting for reform. Fletcher calls for unions to play their part in a broad democratic force confronting neo-liberal capitalism. Munck views social movement unionism as a potentially key component in an international 'movement of movements' for the re-regulation of global capitalism. For popular mobilisations aimed at building power, Kelly emphasises the importance of ideas and agenda-setting. Fletcher pinpoints 'globally-oriented social justice unionism' as the core principle, and identifies major internal reforms necessary to reorient union strategies toward a global movement for social justice.

Can unions make the internal, ideological, and strategic changes necessary to participate in the heroic battles these authors see as essential if global capitalism is to be fundamentally reformed? Although seeds of change may be widely present in contemporary unions, the challenges are immense and the forces defending free-market capitalism are powerful. I share the belief that the future offers hope for unions – beyond remaining strongholds in places such as Scandinavia – only as workplace-based actors joining in broad social and political campaigns called forth by the failures of neo-liberal economic governance.

CYCLES OF CRISIS, RESISTANCE AND REFORM

Things look grim at this moment in history because we find ourselves in a period of prolonged economic crisis and because alternatives to neo-liberal governance have so far been suppressed. The crisis has demonstrated the fundamentally unsustainable nature of free-market capitalism, yet no coherent, politically viable policy framework for true reform has taken hold. In debates at national and global levels between advocates of expansionary and contractionary economy policy, austerity all too often wins out. Still, I think it is too soon to declare victory for neo-liberalism in the wake of ongoing economic crisis. A review of the two most recent periods of economic governance in the global North – and by extension the global economy – give perspective to contemporary battles confronting unions and their social and political allies.[2]

Two recent, overlapping historic failures in the US have opened the door for contemporary battles for economic and political transformation. First, the

Bush/Cheney presidency morphed into failure, one so obvious that approval ratings dropped in 2006 close to 30 per cent and stayed there for the final two years of a largely unsuccessful eight-year reign. And second, by 2008 economic crisis had shattered the credibility of 'laissez-faire' policy dominance. Together, these failures challenged the legitimacy of an ideology that had governed for 30 years, an appealing but flawed world view variously referred to as free-market capitalism, market fundamentalism, laissez-faire, global liberalisation, YOYO economics ('you're on your own'), and for the purposes of this book, neo-liberalism.[3] Politically brilliant in its simplicity, the ideology called for government to get out of the way so that entrepreneurs could make markets work their magic. Multinational corporations led the call to cut taxes and stifling regulation, to let liberty serve as the key to prosperity.

Politically compelling in its appeal to voter interest in lower taxes and 'liberty,' the ideology took hold in Britain under Margaret Thatcher beginning in 1979 and in the US after the election of Ronald Reagan in 1980. An attack on unions was a central component of the ideology's implementation. Apparently validated by the collapse of the Soviet Union a decade later, free-market capitalism spread by way of globalisation, to dominate American and global economy policy through the administrations of Reagan, Bush I, Clinton and Bush II. While relations of social partnership and the institutions of 'coordinated market economies' may have softened the impact for unions and social policy in some European countries, economic integration increasingly favoured 'liberal Europe' over 'social Europe.' Economies grew but so did inequality. The flawed one-dimensional logic of market fundamentalism came finally to fruition in the twin collapses of the Bush/Cheney government and the US financial system in 2007–8.

As the ground shifted, a charismatic leader emerged with a vision of a better society, one governed not by markets, greed and war but by common effort and equal opportunity. He seemed a thoughtful, intelligent leader capable of seeing the world in its complexity and grappling with extraordinary challenges and innovative solutions. Young people flocked to a campaign for change. Unions in the US campaigned as never before for his election and for a Democratic Congress. People around the world, including social democrats and unionists, cheered. The election of Barack Obama in November of 2008 punctuated expectations of social transformation: collective responsibility to balance individual liberty, social solidarity to counter corporate greed, re-regulation to curb the excesses of an economic and financial system run amok.

No one thought it would be easy, but still many Obama supporters, including the unions at the heart of his campaign, underestimated the enemy. In the wake of demoralising defeat, opposition mobilised with accelerating intensity through Obama's first two years in office. Resistance to change came from three directions: from a populist, anti-government, anti-Obama, right-wing social movement; from powerful vested interests, especially in finance, health insurance, and energy; and from a deflated Republican party that in the absence of alternatives gained traction as a pure-and-simple opposition to almost everything of substance that Democrats in Congress and the White House proposed.

History's lesson is that fundamental change takes time, even in the worst of crises. Roosevelt and allies had to slug it out for years to get major reforms in place: from expansionary economic policy to breakthrough legislation such as Social Security and the National Labour Relations Act – both passed only in Roosevelt's third year in office. The Reagan administration waged major battles against unions and their political allies to replace Keynesian policy and its social contract with monetary austerity, setting in motion long-term, step-by-step deregulation. There is no reason to expect battles to be any less prolonged or intense in the turbulent present.

Although gradual change is endemic to market societies, so are cycles of crisis, resistance and reform. Even in the most stable periods of market expansion or democratic regulation, the tension between markets and democracy is forever unresolved. While gradual change can accumulate into fundamental change, transformation is more likely to accelerate in times of crisis. Since the most recent economic crisis, especially in the US and Europe, is widely regarded as the most serious since the Great Depression that began in 1929, it makes sense to go back at least that far for perspective on modern history's cycles and the battles that unions and other progressive social actors now face.

FROM MANAGED MARKETS TO CAPITALISM UNCHAINED

The collapse of a 1920s market-led bubble economy, beginning with the stock market crash of 1929 in the US, led to worldwide economic crisis and far-reaching struggles for political, economic and social transformation. Outcomes ranged from the destruction of democratic institutions in Nazi Germany to social democracy in Sweden and a New Deal in the US (see Luebbert 1991). The defeat of fascism in the Second World War opened the door in West Germany for that country's first stable democratic institutions, and for the beginnings of a peaceful process of European economic integration. Society-wide mobilisation for war in the US accelerated the legitimacy of New Deal economic and social policy. For most of three decades after the war, democratically managed capitalism yielded steady economic growth and social stability, a period now often referred to by historians and political economists in Europe, Japan and the US as the 'Golden Years' (Hobsbawm 1996).

If we cut through all the details and complexity – as we must to understand fundamental forces at work – I believe the postwar period of successfully managed capitalism was undone first in the US by two things: racism and the war in Vietnam. Racism in a backlash against the accomplishments of the civil rights movement – itself not a campaign for transformation but for inclusion – that drove southern whites out of the New Deal coalition and into a more natural home in the Republican party. And a Vietnam War that undermined the legitimacy of 'big government' while generating inflation that laid the groundwork for the economic crises of the 1970s. Prolonged 'stagflation' (high unemployment combined with rising inflation) in turn challenged the credibility of Keynesian economic policy and opened the door for Thatcher in Britain and Reagan in the US, whose central accomplishment was to replace a managed market economy with an increasingly deregulated capitalism.

It is thus commonplace to identify the two most recent periods of political economy in the global North: a 'managed capitalism' that can be marked off roughly between the Second World War and the economic crises of the 1970s; and a 'free-market capitalism' that took hold with the election of Thatcher and Reagan and appeared to end in financial collapse and the election of Barack Obama in 2008. The first period relied on proactive government intervention to guide economic growth; the second viewed government as the problem and for three decades promoted policies of deregulation, privatisation and ever freer markets, both at home and abroad. In the first period, one could argue that to a significant extent society governed a market economy. In the second period, a market economy increasingly governed us all.

Because the US remained the dominant market economy through both periods, the global economy (or the 'West' before the end of the Cold War in 1990), operated within similar policy frameworks. In Western Europe, for example, the two periods ran parallel to developments in the US, although with significant differences of timing and substance. The shift to the second cycle came in stages: the election of Margaret Thatcher in Britain in 1979, the policy 'U-turn' of French President Francois Mitterrand, a socialist, in 1983, and the decision of 12 countries to deepen economic integration with the passage of the Single European Act in 1986 (Hainsworth 1988; Sbragia 1992).

The substantive differences are more significant. While Thatcher moved quickly to deregulate and to weaken the opposition of unions and the Labour Party, the rest of Western Europe moved more slowly. Governments, unions, business federations, social-democratic and even conservative parties continued to play important roles, in different ways across a range of countries, in managing the economy. Comprehensive social policies and institutions of market coordination persisted in spite of increasing economic competition, gradual deregulation and global liberalisation (Hall and Soskice 2001). It became commonplace in Europe to warn of excessive 'marketisation' (also referred to as 'Americanisation'), yet persistent differences would prove important when the economic crisis of 2007–8, made in America, spread throughout the global economy (*New York Times* 11 January 2008; Beck and Scherrer 2010).

SOCIAL MOVEMENTS AND POPULAR MOBILISATION

Each of the two distinct periods of political economy since 1945 was preceded by social movement upheaval. In each case, transformation was driven by both economic crisis and social mobilisation: in the 1930s and 1940s the Great Depression, social upheaval and mobilisation for war; and for the 'Golden Years' the social movements of the late 1960s/early 1970s and the economic crises that began in 1973. In the 1930s in the US, economic collapse, mass unemployment and foreclosures drove social unrest, including demonstrations, mass migration, factory occupations, and union organising campaigns. Crisis and mobilisation undercut the legitimacy of existing policies and institutions, opening space for breakthroughs such as Social Security, expanded unemployment insurance, massive public spending on infrastructure and job creation, and the National Labour Relations Act. A broad shift towards government intervention in the economy accelerated during the war, laying the foundation for a regulated postwar market economy. The story has many details but the key point here is that the historic transformation to a democratically managed market economy – in the face of intense opposition from powerful vested interests that opposed both regulation and social policy – was possible in the US only because of the protest movements of the 1930s and social mobilisation for war in the 1940s.

Major problems and inequities notwithstanding, for three decades a managed market economy produced real wage gains and rising living standards for large shares of the population in the US, Western Europe and Japan. But just as they fought against regulation and social policy in the first place, powerful business interests and conservative politicians strained against limitations imposed by state- and labour-led regulation. While more expansive social policies took root in Western Europe, Medicare, health and safety, civil rights and equal opportunity legislation prevailed in the 1960s in the US only against militant opposition. When political configurations in the US changed in the wake of social upheaval and economic crisis, when southern whites became Republicans and a so-called 'silent majority' reacted against the social upheaval of the late 1960s and early 1970s, forces advocating freer markets broke through political constraints. In the US, the election of Ronald Reagan in 1980 signalled the beginning of three decades of deregulation, including attacks on social policies and labour unions, and a corresponding 30 years of average wage stagnation and rising inequality in the US (Mishel *et al.* 2009: 18–38; Reich 2010).

BREAKTHROUGHS, BACKLASH, AND DECLINE OF THE US LABOUR MOVEMENT

This was not what social activists of the 1960s intended. To put it bluntly, the social movements of that era produced both social breakthroughs and political failure. As Daniel Cohn-Bendit – famous as 'Danny the Red' for his leadership in the uprisings of May 1968 in Paris, and more recently a leading member of the Green Party delegation in the European Parliament – has summed up the accomplishments: 'socially we won, politically we lost,' in both Europe and the US.[4]

While critics are quick to look back on the failures of social movements of the 1960s–1970s, successes were many. In the US, civil rights, women's, and environmental movements generated pressure for breakthroughs in social and workplace legislation as well as fundamental changes in cultural norms and individual possibilities. The gay rights movement brought growing numbers of men and women out of the closet and into society. While all of these groups confronted enduring opposition – from 'culture wars' and homophobia to red-baiting and climate crisis denial – the place in society and in the labour movement of women, racial and ethnic minorities, gays and lesbians is very different today than it was 40 years ago. Offering great promise for the future both then and now, long-term changes that began with social protest in the 1960s are reflected in the increasingly tolerant attitudes of much of today's younger generation throughout the global North (see Keeter 2008 and others).

On the other hand, in the US a backlash against those movements of protest gave us Richard Nixon, Ronald Reagan, and a long-term policy shift from managed to laissez-faire capitalism. Conservative reaction played on the fears of 'middle America' and helped to mobilise an enduring right-wing populist base, rooted to a large extent among white evangelical Christians, and including a small but not insignificant working class presence. Conservative political dominance, combined with the break-up of the New Deal coalition, union decline, and the stigmatising of 'tax-and-spend liberalism,' underpinned three decades of deregulation, wage stagnation, and growing inequality.

I believe that in the 1960s, unions in the US missed an historic opportunity for revitalisation by way of engagement in the vibrant social movements of that era (Turner 2003). The purge of communists, socialists, and other activists in the 1950s had stripped unions of the 'bridge builders' that had promoted coalition building. The AFL-CIO had long since sold its foreign policy to the State Department, adopting a vigorous anti-communism at home and abroad. George Meany, the federation's president, and many other top labour leaders viewed the social movements of the 1960s as threats to the established order and in some cases communist-led (although in the US this was a patently false claim). The AFL-CIO supported the war in Vietnam almost to the bitter end, even as most Americans turned against this ill-fated, imperialist venture. White male union leaders – and, it must be said, many of their members – responded defensively to the civil rights and women's movements. The emerging environmental movement, sometimes rightly so, was viewed as a threat to good union jobs in construction, logging, manufacturing, and other industries. A conservative-bred 'generation gap' diminished the credibility of the labour movement in the eyes of an activist generation.

While many European unions, in Italy, France, Germany, Britain and elsewhere, found new strength in contagious social movement activism, often in wildcat strikes that pushed unions into greater inclusivity and militancy, unions in the US stood aside. The extraordinary movie, *At the River I Stand*, documenting the power gained from a blending of labour and civil rights activism in a 1968 sanitation workers strike in Memphis, Tennessee, shows the potential – and the missed opportunity – for a broader social movement engagement in the US. The historic failure of the US labour movement to ride the social movement wave of the 1960s deprived unions of a revitalisation that could have placed them in much better stead when the employer offensive accelerated in the 1980s.

As traditional go-it-alone union strategies wilted in the face of state and employer opposition, more inclusive, activist approaches gained credibility (Clawson 2003; Hurd 1998; Moody 1997; Turner, Katz and Hurd 2001). The election of John Sweeney as AFL-CIO president in 1995 marked the rising influence of organisers and coalition builders. Ironically, European unions have in some cases learned strategies of grassroots organising from their counterparts in the US, where labour was clobbered earlier and thus gained 'advantages of backwardness' in developing new approaches (Gall 2003; Turner 2009). Although union decline persisted in a context of global liberalisation, a result in part of the halting commitment of many union leaders to strategic reorientation, the notion that the best hope for a stronger future for labour unions lay in common effort with other social actors and movements came sharply into focus (Fletcher and Gaspasin 2008; Getman 2010).

THE CRISIS OF NEO-LIBERALISM AND THE BATTLE FOR TRANSFORMATION

When market fundamentalism crashed in the US financial collapse of 2007–8, the government stepped in, beginning in the final year of the Bush administration, to pick up the pieces and redirect policy, to bail out and re-regulate the market economy. As always when major change is on the agenda, the battle over the direction of institutional and policy reform sharpened quickly. As resurgent Democrats pushed for fundamental reform – in campaigns to expand health care, regulate the financial sector, rebuild infrastructure, promote a job-creating shift to a clean energy economy – right-wing populists fought to defend a different conception of America. The tide shifted back and forth from the election of Obama in 2008 to the town hall meetings of 2009, from the passage of health care bills in the House and Senate in late 2009 to the victory in early 2010 of Republican Scott Brown in a Massachusetts election to replace Ted Kennedy in the US Senate, from the passage of (watered down) financial regulation in July of 2010 to the collapse of energy policy reform later that same month. Along the way, while unions fought for health care, financial regulation and job creation, labour's top priority, the Employee Free Choice Act, withered under a massive assault led by the US Chamber of Commerce. The resurgence of neo-liberalism, driven by populist anti-government rage and billionaire funding, was confirmed in the midterm elections of November, 2010. Republicans swept to victory in the House of Representatives, pledging to cut government spending, extend tax cuts for the wealthy, and attack the diminished power of 'Big Labor.' Progressive forces, in disarray, sought to lay the groundwork for renewed counter-mobilisation with a sharpening focus on the long-term, massive upward redistribution of wealth in the US.

As in the 1930s and 1970s, the battle for a new political settlement promised to stretch out not for months but for years. In retrospect, the US story line in the 1930s and 1940s appears the most direct: social movements led by workers and unions pushed policy to the left, towards New Deal dominance and a moderate managed capitalism in the early postwar decades. In the 1960s and 1970s, the story is more complex. Progressive social movements engendered reaction. While some unions, especially at the local level, supported or collaborated with the social movements, many unions, including the leadership of the AFL-CIO, stood aside. A right-wing movement, crushed in the electoral defeat of Barry Goldwater in 1964, re-emerged in the 1970s and 1980s to topple the established order and its social contract in favour of a new era of laissez-faire capitalism. Then in 2008, an Obama campaign driven by a social mobilisation of the young, African Americans, labour, and a resurgent progressive left pushed for far-reaching change: for a more active government role in managing markets, reducing inequality, and revitalising the American economy through public investment and a shift to clean energy.

The Obama victory and first steps towards reform – the recovery act, health-care campaign, financial regulation, and energy policy – confronted a surprisingly rapid counter-mobilisation. In the wake of an overwhelming Democratic victory in 2008, made possible by the active engagement of the unions and to a significant extent embodying labour's hopes, the opposition to reform quickly gathered steam. The backlash that began in 2009 showed an eerie similarity to the backlash against the civil rights and other social movements in the 1960s and 1970s. Capital, led by finance, health insurance and energy companies, rode (and financed) 'Tea Party' momentum and its own massive lobbying efforts to rail against 'big government' re-regulation and reform (Herbert 2009). The neo-liberal corpse roared back to life. The US in 2010 settled in for a long period of conflict over the shape of a new policy era.

UNIONS AND THE CRISIS IN EUROPE

Made in America, the financial crisis spread quickly to Europe and other parts of the world, where banks had 'spread the risk' by investing heavily in mortgage-backed securities and other complex instruments of speculation. Compared to the US, the social impact in much of Europe was cushioned by more expansive social policies, and by union-backed programmes such as short-time working in Germany. Nonetheless, the crisis threw millions of workers out of work, in a context already marked by a decade-long expansion of contingent work and gradually rising inequality.

As economic crisis spread to Europe in 2008, unions and their allies denounced the failed logic of neo-liberalism and demanded fundamental reform. A window opened to promote the values and policies of social Europe, including expansionary fiscal and monetary policy, financial re-regulation, and inclusive employment policies (Clark *et al.* 2006; Watt and Botsch 2010). In spite of many years in which employers, in the name of competitiveness, had railed against excessive regulation, workplace rigidities, strong unions and high wages, none of these played any role as causes for the Great Recession (Watt 2009). On the contrary, the crisis that began in the US was caused by precisely the opposite: 30 years of deregulation and wage stagnation (Reich 2010).

The crisis, however, arrived in a period of weakened influence for unions, social-democratic, and socialist parties across Europe. The window of opportunity for major worker- and union-friendly policy reform closed quickly with the collapse of the Greek economy and the eurozone crisis of 2010. Debt crises and German domestic politics strengthened the hand of European policy makers favouring austerity – even as Obama and others called for more government spending at meetings of the G20.[5] As the tide shifted back towards neo-liberalism, Europe, as in the US, faced a protracted struggle over the contours of future economic and social policy. Workers and unions across Europe, in Greece, Spain, France, Ireland and elsewhere, joined general strikes and massive demonstrations in protest against attacks on labour and social standards. Defensive in orientation, labour-led mobilisations also represented the longer-term battle for a social Europe and a regulated, labour-friendly global economy.

Facing contrasting but parallel circumstances in different countries and sectors, unions struggled for united responses to the crisis, within and across national boundaries. European economic integration, set within a broader framework of neo-liberal globalisation, ensured that both conflicts and solutions would include significant transnational dimensions. These ongoing, crisis-driven battles for reform provide the context in which to understand future prospects for unions in the global North.

SOCIAL COALITION BUILDING: LABOUR AND THE ENVIRONMENT

At such a pivotal moment in history, the notion that unions could go it along, relying on labour market strength and their own bargaining capacity, diminished in credibility. Without the support of social and political allies, unions have little chance to influence the course of events in the protracted struggles ahead. The urgency for labour to engage in broader social movements for reform is a common thread that runs through the chapters of this book.

What are unions fighting for, aside from the immediate interests of current membership? In day-to-day battles the answer is not always clear, as immediate campaigns centre on defensive efforts to protect past gains. The mobilisation of workers across Europe to defend pension standards, for example, is both inspiring and important. But if the context remains neo-liberal economic governance at both national and global levels such campaigns are clearly not enough. The idea that we can return to a Keynesian past is a vision-free approach to the problems of the future. There must be alternatives to an unjust, unstable neo-liberal future in which unions and other social actors fight rearguard battles to preserve elements of protection (see Clark *et al.* 2006; Watt and Botsch 2010).

The wastebaskets are full of blueprints and I won't offer one here. Outcomes will be shaped in struggle. For unions, the question is what kind of broad vision can frame the common efforts of social movements for reform, what kind of society do unions want to help build, what framework can offer a basis for broad mobilisation? A sustainable society must bring markets under control in ways that nurture inclusive social justice, equal opportunity, diminished inequality, broad social tolerance, and preservation of the environment. The good news is that much of today's younger generation – in spite of a less apparent class consciousness – embodies such values (see Keeter 2008).[6]

Union leaders can whine about individualistic young workers – or women or immigrants or vegetarians – who don't want to join unions, or they can look for common values and interests. They can learn to speak the language of the young and other potential allies. To do this, unions have to move beyond traditional concerns to build alliances with community organisations, immigrant rights and ethnic groups, faith-based organisations, youth groups, advocates of same-sex marriage, and more. While transnational and national movements are essential, coalition work must to a large extent build on vibrant local and urban campaigns: what Dean and Reynolds (2010) call 'regional power-building' (see also Milkman 2006; Turner and Cornfield 2007; Lerner 2007). Especially important in this regard is the 'greening' of the labour movement. A deepening engagement in climate crisis and clean energy issues must surely be a key component of labour's participation in social movement alliances of the future. If properly framed, the transformation to a clean-energy economy can also help revitalise manufacturing, stimulate job creation, and provide fertile ground for future union growth and popular mobilisation (Renner, Sweeney and Kubit 2008; Sweeney 2009).

Although governing red-green alliances have not often turned out the way labour has hoped, unions in Europe have made considerable advances in common workplace- and society-based efforts aimed at environmental concerns.[7] In Spain, for example, CCOO calls anti-austerity general strikes but also works closely with SustainLabour, to educate unions on environmental issues and climate-change action. In 2004, the German DGB launched a ground-breaking coalition effort to retrofit commercial and residential buildings, a successful programme that has grown yearly and provides a model for unions in other countries (such as the US Emerald Cities project described below). The British TUC has developed a 'Green Workplaces' initiative that includes training for 'green reps' and the building of workplace/community links. Cross-national collaboration is promoted at meetings such as the 2009 German-British Trade Union Forum that focused on environmental industries and green jobs (Doelfs 2009). Across Europe, internal union debates as well as growing external alliances address sustainability issues, from industrial policy and green workplaces to organising the growing workforces in clean-energy industries (Broughton 2010).

In the US, in spite of diverging interests on particular issues and a history of conflict, unions and environmental groups have expanded common efforts over the past decade – in political and economic development campaigns from national to local levels (*cf.* Mayer 2009; Obach 2004; Rose 2000). Central to the development of common interests has been a shift away from 'pure and simple' versions of environmentalism and unionism to a focus on environmental justice. A redefinition of interests has opened the door to broad alliances for comprehensive policy reform (Jones 2008).

A watershed moment occurred at the 'Battle of Seattle' demonstrations in 1999, when 30 000 unionists joined 20 000 environmentalists and other allies to protest the neo-liberal global governance of the World Trade Organization (see Hawken 2000). Leaders of participating organisations – such as David

Foster and Leo Gerard of the Steelworkers and Carl Pope of the Sierra Club – went on to build alliances that would develop specific campaigns and help reshape a vision and set of policy proposals for a sustainable society. Founded in 2003, with roots in the Seattle mobilisation and the Alliance for Sustainable Jobs and the Environment, the Apollo Alliance brought together labour, environmental and other groups to exert growing influence on the development of energy policy, at national, state, and metropolitan levels (*New York Times* 6 June 2003; Rogers 2005). Although a comprehensive set of job-creating, clean-energy policies has so far been blocked by conservative opposition in Congress, the Obama administration – under pressure from labour and environmental groups – arguably did more to promote green jobs and clean energy in its first two years than all previous administrations combined.

A promising example is a project called 'Emerald Cities' (Grabelsky and Thompson 2010). Driven by a working group with participants from building trades unions, construction firms, environmental and minority organisations, with support from the Obama administration, Emerald Cities developed plans to retrofit millions of residential and commercial buildings across the country. Since buildings are responsible for 30–40 per cent of total carbon emissions in the US, the effort brought together a variety of social interests: environmental, job creation, skills training in minority communities, and a revitalisation of the construction industry and its unions. As of fall 2010, negotiations among stakeholders were underway in ten pilot cities: Atlanta, Providence, New York City, Cleveland, Milwaukee, Seattle, Portland, San Francisco, Oakland and Los Angeles.

While political paralysis, driven by an unholy alliance of fossil fuel interests and right-wing populism, stalled national-level reform, blue-green efforts at state and especially metropolitan levels continued to develop, promoting specific projects as well as a germinal vision for the future in industries such as construction, transportation, and power generation. Coalition campaigns including unions, environmental groups, and a broad range of allies offer great potential in future battles – local, national and global – for the social justice unionism that can help drive a 'movement of movements' towards a globally sustainable society (see Silverman 2006; Waterman 1999; Smith and Johnston 2002; Lillie 2006; Anner *et al.* 2006).

ALTERNATIVE SCENARIOS

When all is said and done, this is the choice facing unions in today's global economy: to get aboard broad local, national and global movements for comprehensive reform in a period of protracted economic crisis, or to confine efforts to defensive battles against overwhelming opposition. Defensive battles, such as the massive protests led by European unions in 2010 against the social cutbacks in austerity budgets, are essential and can help build broader coalitions for reform. But if efforts go no further than heroic battles to defend past gains, the opportunity for transformative movements will be missed and neo-liberal governance will remain dominant.

Coalition campaigns, whether proactive or defensive, can build relationships among organisations and individual 'bridge builders,' within and beyond the labour movement (Brecher and Costello 1990; Clawson 2003; Moody 1997; Tattersall 2010). Environmental justice is cited above as an example, but the same dynamics are true for campaigns advocating the rights of immigrants, people of colour, women, low-wage and contingent workers, gays, and other oppressed minorities – and majorities. Issues such as community-based economic development, rising inequality, public education, and clean energy provide rallying points for labour and its allies to push forward efforts for broader economic and social transformation. There is no necessary contradiction between defence and offence, between particular and general interests, as long as goals are broad and the vision is comprehensive.

The current crisis has shown neo-liberalism to be inherently unstable, thereby opening an historic opportunity for transformative reform. A sustainable society requires a far greater measure of economic, social and environmental justice. The best prospects for labour movement revitalisation thus lie in active participation in local, national and global movements for broad social change. And without the active engagement of unions, such movements will lack the popular base necessary to build power.

In the US, the battle appears likely to play itself out as a choice between sustainable society and 'Tea Party America'. Resurgent right-wing populism is compelling to many for its vision of individual liberty and small government. As much as the left loves to ridicule the transparent idiocy of much Tea Party rhetoric (health-care reform 'death panels,' Obama as a foreign-born Muslim socialist, 'drill baby drill'), these people are not all idiots. At the grass roots – and there is a strong grassroots element – people know they have been victims of big government as well as big business. The contradiction is that small government essentially hands economic and political power over to big business – which is why Tea Party groups are funded by 'populist' billionaires. Small government can only reinforce the dominant neo-liberal policies that generate stagnant incomes, rising inequality, and a vast concentration of wealth. The Tea Party – and its past and future incarnations – is dangerous for the populist base it provides for continuing neo-liberal dominance. The same is true for the anti-immigrant populism so prevalent in contemporary European elections, with echoes inside the various labour movements.

The alternative vision, a sustainable society based on strong labour, environmental and social standards, is less clearly articulated. The forces behind it, including a potentially revitalised labour movement, are in disarray. Yet social movements – and 'movements of movements' – come in unpredictable upsurges. This is just as true on the left as it is on the populist right. Although neo-liberal policy dominance has proven resilient in the crisis, extrapolation into the future is always a shaky enterprise. So much depends on what unions and their allies do.

NOTES

1. For the record, I do not agree with Streeck about the extent of liberalisation in Germany: this is still by and large a 'coordinated market economy.' The point here is Streeck's well-founded emphasis on capitalism as a dynamic force exerting constant pressure on institutions of regulation, and the ongoing dialectic between market expansion and social containment (Polanyi 1944).
2. The focus here is on the global North, and especially the United States, for two reasons. First, because states and multinational corporations of the rich countries have dominated the global economy and are responsible for the spread of neo-liberalism; and second, because that is the part of the world where my own expertise lies. I leave it to other experts, including authors of the many fine chapters in this book, to analyse the roles and prospects of unions in the global South. Given the essential nature of ongoing efforts to build transnational union collaboration, long-term prospects for unions throughout the world are closely linked.
3. While my preference would be to banish all words beginning with 'neo'– after all, who but academics and political activists has any idea what such words mean? – 'neo-liberalism' is a convenient signpost and is well-defined in the introductory chapter of this book. To break the monotony, I use terms such as 'free-market capitalism' and 'market fundamentalism' more or less interchangeably.
4. Daniel Cohn-Bendit, from a talk at Cornell University, 11 November 2005.
5. For contrasting views of the causes of the eurozone crisis from within the financial industry, see Soros (2010) and *The Economist* (8 July 2010). Where Soros sees at the core a financial crisis, the free-market-oriented analysis of *The Economist* emphasises fiscal crisis and advocates austerity. For an earlier, pre-crisis but perceptive analysis of the expansion of global finance and its consequences, see Glyn (2006).
6. My sense is growing social tolerance accompanies a strong environmental consciousness among young Europeans as well.
7. Thanks to Lara Skinner of Cornell University's Global Labour Institute for her input on labour-environmental coalitions in Europe.

REFERENCES

Anner, M., I. Greer, M. Hauptmeier, N. Lillie and N. Wineherler (2006), 'The industrial determinants of transnational solidarity: global interunion politics in three sectors', *European Journal of Industrial Relations*, **12**(1), 7–27.

Beck, S. and C. Scherrer (2010), 'The German economic model emerges reinforced from the crisis', Global Labour column 29, August 16, accessed at http://column.global-labour-university.org/.

Brecher, J. and T. Costello (1990), *Building Bridges: The Emerging Grassroots Coalition of Labor and Community*, New York: Monthly Review Press.

Broughton, A. (2010), 'Final report on the main findings of the Expert Workshop on Industrial Relations and Sustainability', Institute for Employment Studies, European Foundation for the Improvement of Living and Working Conditions.

Clark, D., N. Kinnock, M. Leahy, K. Livingstone, J. Monks and S. Twigg (2006), 'A democratic left vision for Europe', in A. Detlev, S. Haseler and H. Meyer (eds), *Social Europe: A Continent's Answer to Market Fundamentalism*, London: European Research Forum at London Metropolitan University, pp. 11–24.

Clawson, D. (2003), *The Next Upsurge: Labor and the New Social Movements*, Ithaca: ILR Press/Cornell University Press.

Doelfs, G. (2009), 'Green technology – good jobs?', *Magazin Mitbestimmung*, English online, 9/2009.

Fletcher, B. and F. Gapasin (2008), *Solidarity Divided: The Crisis in Organized Labor and a New Path to Social Justice*, Berkeley, CA: University of California Press.

Gall, G. (2003) (ed), *Union Organising*, London: Routledge.

Getman, J. (2010), *Restoring the Power of Unions: It Takes a Movement*, New Haven: Yale University Press.

Glyn, A. (2006), *Capitalism Unleashed: Finance, Globalization and Welfare*, Oxford: Oxford University Press.

Grabelsky, J. and P. Thompson (2010), 'Emerald cities in the age of Obama: a new social compact between labor and community', *Perspectives on Work* (winter), 15–18.

Hainsworth, P. (1988), 'The re-election of Francois Mitterrand', *Parliamentary Affairs*, **41**, 536–47.

Hall, P. and D. Soskice (2001) (eds), *Varieties of Capitalism: The Institutional Foundations of Competitive Advantage*, Oxford: Oxford University Press.

Hawken, P. (2000), 'On the streets of Seattle', *The Amicus Journal (OnEarth)* (Spring), 29–51.

Herbert, B. (2009),'Chutzpah on steroids', *New York Times*, 14 July.

Hobsbawm, E. (1996), *The Age of Extremes: A History of the World, 1914–1991*, New York: Vintage Books, New York.

Hurd, R. (1998), 'Contesting the dinosaur image: the labor movement's search for a future', *Labor Studies Journal*, **22**(4), 5–30.

Jones, V. (2008), *The Green-Collar Economy*, New York: HarperOne.

Keeter, S. (2008), 'The aging of the boomers and the rise of the millennials', in R. Teixeira (ed.), *Red, Blue and Purple America: The Future of Election Demographics*, Washington, DC: Brookings, pp. 225–57.

Lerner, S. (2007), 'Global unions: a solution to labor's worldwide decline', *New Labor Forum*, **16**(1), 23–37.

Lillie, N. (2006), *A Global Union for Global Workers*: *Collective Bargaining and Regulatory Politics in Maritime Shipping*, New York: Routledge.

Luebbert, G. (1991), *Liberalism, Fascism or Social Democracy*, Oxford: Oxford University Press.

Mayer, B. (2009), *Blue-Green Coalitions: Fighting for Safe Workplaces and Healthy Communities*, Ithaca, NY: ILR Press/Cornell University Press.

Milkman, R. (2006), *L.A. Story: Immigrant Workers and the Future of the US Labor Movement*, New York: Russell Sage Foundation,

Mishel, L., J. Bernstein and H. Shierholz (2009) (eds), *The State of Working America, 2008–2009*, Ithaca, NY, ILR Press/Cornell University Press.

Moody, K. (1997), *Workers in a Lean World. Unions in the International Economy*, London: Verso.

Obach, B. (2004), *Labor and the Environmental Movement: The Quest for Common Ground*, Cambridge, MA: MIT Press.

Polanyi, K. (1944), *The Great Transformation. The Political and Economic Origins of our Time*, New York: Farrar and Rinehart.

Reich, R. (2010), *Aftershock: The Next Economy and America's Future*, New York: Alfred A. Knopf.

Renner, M., S. Sweeney and J. Kubit (2008), 'Green jobs: working for the people and the environment', Worldwatch report 177, Washington, DC: Worldwatch Institute.

Rogers, J. (2005), 'An Industrial policy that works', *Challenge*, **48**(68), 6–16.

Rose, F. (2000), *Coalitions Across the Class Divide: Lessons from the Labor, Peace and Environmental Movements*, Ithaca, NY: Cornell University Press.

Sbragia, A. (1992) (ed), *Euro-Politics: Institutions and Policymaking in the 'New' European Community*, Washington, DC: Brookings Institution.

Silverman, V. (2006), 'Green unions in a grey world: labor environmentalism and international institutions', *Organizations and Environment*, **19**(2), 191–213.

Smith, J. and H. Johnston (eds) (2002), *Globalization and Resistance: Transnational Dimensions of Social Movements*, Lanham, MD: Rowman and Littlefield.

Soros, G. (2010), 'The crisis and the euro'm *New York Review of Books,* 19 August.

Streeck, W. (2009), *Re-Forming Capitalism: Institutional Change in the German Political Economy*, Oxford: Oxford University Press.

Sweeney, S. (2009), 'More than green jobs: time for a new climate policy for labor', *New Labor Forum*, **18**(3), 53–59.

Tattersall, A. (2009), *Power in Coalition – Strategies for Strong Unions and Social Change*, Crows Nest, NSW: Allen and Unwin.

Turner, L. (2003), 'Reviving the labor movement: a comparative perspective', in D. Cornfield and H. McCammon (eds), *Labor Revitalization: Global Perspectives and New Initiatives*, JAI series Research in the Sociology of Work, Amsterdam, Netherlands: JAI Press, 23–57.

Turner, L. (2009), 'Institutions and activism: crisis and opportunity for a German labor movement in decline', *Industrial and Labor Relations Review*, **62**(3), 294–312.

Turner, L., H. Katz and R. Hurd (eds) (2001), *Rekindling the Movement: Labor's Quest for Relevance in the 21st Century*, Ithaca, NY: ILR Press/Cornell University Press.

Turner, L. and D. Cornfield (2007) (eds), *Labor in the New Urban Battlegrounds: Local Solidarity in a Global Economy*, Ithaca, NY: ILR Press/Cornell University Press.

Waterman, P. (1999), *Globalization, Social Movements, and the New Internationalisms,* London: Mansell.

Watt, A. (2009), 'Six things that didn't cause the crisis – but really ought to have', *Social Europe Journal,* 24 September.

Watt, A. and Botsch, A. (eds) (2010), *After the Crisis: Towards a Sustainable Growth Model*, Brussels: European Trade Union Institute.

Index

accommodatory responses
Argentina 49–50
Australia 64
Britain 87–98
administrative functions, Chinese unions
114–15
Advisory, Conciliation and Arbitration
Services, Britain 84
Africa
informal economy organisations
281–2
social movement unionism 37–8
African National Congress (ANC) 5,
285–6, 287
Agenda 2010, Germany 151
agenda control 16–17
Albo, G. 283
All-China Federation of Unions
(ACFTU) 105, 298
expanding functions 114–15
recruitment drive 115–16
resource dependence 113–14
service provision 118–19
structural constraints 111–13
All-India Trade Union Congress
(AITUC) 167, 174, 178, 182,
183
All-Union Central Council of Unions
(VTsSPS), Russia 192
alliance building, challenges of 277
'Alliance for Jobs', Germany 155–6
Amalgamated Engineering and Electrical
Union (AEEU), Britain 90, 99
Amalgamated Engineering Union
(AEU), Britain 88, 89, 90
American Federation of
Labour–Congress of Industrial
Organisations (AFL–CIO) 1, 230,
235, 245, 246, 284, 317–18
Cold War alliances 231, 297
Organising Institute 242
'Solidarity Day' 240
Stamford Organizing Project 287–8
worker education 242–4

American Federation of State, County
and Municipal Employees
(AFSCME) 239
American Federation of Teachers 239
American Recovery and Reinvestment
Act (ARRA) 262, 264
Amicus, Britain 92, 93, 97
Amin, S. 273
anti-apartheid movement 283, 285, 296
Apollo Alliance 323
arbitration system, Australia 63, 65, 66,
67, 68, 69, 75, 77
Argentina
informal economy organisations 282
neo-liberal reforms 52–5
Peronism, state and union structure
45–7
revitalisation of unionism 55–8
union opposition to military regime
47–9
union reactions to structural
adjustments 49–52
Asian economic crisis 210, 211
'Assembly of Social Partnership', Russia
194
Australia
constrained neo-liberalism under
Accord 67–70
revisionist neo-liberalism under Rudd
74–7
Stalinist neo-liberalism under
Howard 70–74
unions before neo-liberalism 64–7
Australia Reconstructed report 69–70
Australian Council of Trade Unions
(ACTU) 67–8, 69, 71, 72, 73–4,
76, 77
Australian Workplace Agreements
(AWAs) 71, 72, 73, 75
authoritarianism, opposition to 278, 285,
288
auto manufacturing industry
Germany 145, 152, 157–8, 161